Romain Rolland

Romain Rolland

R.A. Francis

BERG

Oxford • New York

First published in 1999 by
Berg
Editorial offices:
150 Cowley Road, Oxford, OX4 1JJ, UK
70 Washington Square South, New York, NY 10012, USA

Berg is the imprint of Oxford International Publishers Ltd.

Library of Congress Cataloging-in-Publication Data

A catalogue record for this book is available from the Library of Congress.

British Library Cataloguing-in-Publication Data

A catalogue record for this book is available from the British Library.

ISBN 1 85973 270 4 (Cloth)

Typeset by JS Typesetting, Wellingborough, Northants.
Printed in the United Kingdom by WBC Book Manufacturers, Bridgend,
Mid Glamorgan.

Contents

Acknowledgements

My first debt of gratitude is to the late Marie Romain Rolland, custodian of her husband's archives until her death in 1985. Along with many young researchers. I profited greatly from her encouragement and her generosity in making unpublished papers available to me. In recent years the Archives Romain Rolland have been housed in the Manuscripts Department of the Bibliothèque Nationale in Paris, and I owe much to Marie-Laure Prévost and her colleagues, who met my constant requests for documents with patience, courtesy and efficiency. The unpublished documents quoted in this study are reproduced with the kind permission of the trustees of the Fonds Romain Rolland. As with all students of Romain Rolland, I am indebted to the work of Bernard Duchatelet and all those who have produced editions of some of Rolland's many *inédits*.

I am grateful to the British Academy and the University of Nottingham, whose financial assistance enabled me to work on the Archives Romain Rolland in Paris, and I have benefited from the encouragement of my Nottingham colleagues, Nick Hewitt, Diana Knight and Rosemary Chapman. Thanks are also due to the Inter-Library Loan section of the University of Nottingham Library, which made a major contribution to the scope of my bibliography, and to the University of Nottingham Research Committee and School of Modern Languages, who provided a subvention to facilitate the publication of this book.

I am grateful, as ever, for the constant support of my family, especially my wife, Judith, and her mother, Teresa Sadler, for her labours as typist. My work on Romain Rolland as a young research student would have been impossible without the support of George Oxley, and especially of my late father, Nehemiah Francis, to whose memory this book is dedicated.

List of Abbreviations

AE:	*L'Ame enchantée.*
AL:	*Textes politiques, sociaux et philosophiques, ed. J. Albertini.*
B:	*Beethoven. Les grandes époques créatrices.*
BAARR:	*Bulletin de l'Association des Amis de Romain Rolland.*
C1, etc.:	*Cahiers Romain Rolland 1, etc.*
CB:	*Colas Breugnon.*
CG:	*Comment empêcher la guerre?*
CL:	*Clerambault.*
CR:	*Compagnons de route.*
EL:	*L'Esprit libre.*
H:	*Haendel.*
HO:	*Histoire de l'opéra avant Lully et Scarlatti.*
I:	*Inde.*
IS:	*Correspondance intégrale. Panaït Istrati – Romain Rolland.*
JAM:	*Le Jeu de l'amour et de la mort.*
JC:	*Jean-Christophe.*
JCCB:	*De Jean-Christophe à Colas Breugnon.*
JG:	*Journal des années de guerre.*
JJR:	*Les Pages immortelles de Jean-Jacques Rousseau.*
LB:	*Romain Rolland – Lucien et Viviane Bouillé. Correspondance.*
LE:	*Les Léonides.*
LI:	*Liluli.*
LU:	*Romain Rolland et Lugné-Poe. Correspondance.*
M:	*Mémoires.*
MG:	*Mahatma Gandhi.*
MAF:	*Musiciens d'autrefois.*
MAJ:	*Musiciens d'aujourd'hui.*
P:	*Péguy.*
PF:	*Pâques-Fleuries.*
PR:	*Par la Révolution, la paix.*
QC:	*Quinze ans de combat.*
R:	*Robespierre.*
SD:	*Au Seuil de la dernière porte.*

TF:	*Les Tragédies de la foi.*
TP:	*Le Théâtre du peuple.*
TR:	*Le Triomphe de la raison.*
TRD:	*Le Théâtre de la Révolution: Danton.*
TRL:	*Le Théâtre de la Révolution: Les Loups.*
TRQ:	*Le Théâtre de la Révolution: Le Quatorze Juillet.*
VB:	*Vie de Beethoven.*
VI:	*Le Voyage intérieur.*
VMA:	*Vie de Michel-Ange.*
VR:	*Vie de Ramakrishna.*
VT:	*Vie de Tolstoy.*
VV:	*Vie de Vivekananda.*

Introduction

With echoes of imperial grandeur and Old French epic, the very name of Romain Rolland suggests heroism, and to many contemporaries he was indeed a heroic figure. To others, he was, in the words of a wartime wit, 'le moins romain des Rolands furieux'. Controversy raged over him during his life; even today there is no consensus on his career. His historic importance is accepted, especially in the First World War context, but his literary status is contested, and the range of his achievement makes judgement difficult.

Rolland first attracted controversy as an innovative dramatist on the fringe of the Dreyfus affair. In *Jean-Christophe*, his attack on the Paris cultural world made enemies who took their revenge during his courageous anti-war stance in 1914, which put him at odds with most of his compatriots. These battles are now largely a matter of history; his views on the First World War seem more balanced and moderate today than they did in 1914. Yet his reputation in France never altogether recovered from the wartime onslaught, and the problem was compounded by his inter-war evolution towards communism, which is far more likely to arouse strong feelings today than his stance in 1914. His reaction in 1939 was different again, and his movement towards Catholicism in his last years confirms his capacity to disconcert friend and foe alike.

Rolland wrote prolifically over a wide range, any account of him must do justice to his diversity, and my concern will be to trace the inter-relationship of his political, literary, academic and musical work, without over-privileging any one aspect. It is particularly needful not to over-stress his political writings, which by their controversial nature have attracted most attention. They are important, but should be understood in the context of other texts, especially his volumes on the Vedantists, Beethoven and Péguy, which have their admirers but have not been drawn into the overall framework of Rolland studies as much as they deserve.

Rolland was an assiduous letter-writer and diarist, and any assessment must take account of this side of him, while recognizing that the texts involved, reactions of a moment with a particular audience in mind, should not be read in the same way as works destined for publication. Massive efforts have been made to publish some of these texts, chiefly by his indefatigable widow, Marie Romain Rolland, who fought for his reputation with a generosity for which many researchers, including myself, have cause to be grateful. She allowed liberal but controlled access to her husband's papers, and since her death in 1985, when they passed to the Bibliothèque Nationale, even wider access has been possible. Under the terms of his will, his diaries and more intimate correspondence cannot be made public until early next century, which means that the present study cannot be a definitive biography, although it does claim to make advances over previous biographies. Its main focus is the published works, and it is structured around a study of individual texts. The sheer wealth of the correspondence makes it easy to forget that Rolland's essential message lies in the published writings; the proper use of his more personal texts is to illuminate and supplement. The aim in this study will be to trace the themes of Rolland's thought as they evolve across the whole spectrum of his works. I shall not seek to impose neat intellectual patterns where they are inappropriate; Rolland would be the first to admit that any attempt to define the unity of his career should not be based on a search for rigorous intellectual coherence. The unity is, however, there; it is sound and firm when taken on its own terms, and my concern will be to make it perceptible.

–1–

Origins

Romain Rolland was born on 29 January 1866 in Clamecy, a small Nivernais inland port. He left the area at fourteen, and only later learned to love its rolling countryside and waterways, but his accounts of his childhood express his deep roots in this landscape and a strong sense of family continuity. The Rollands and Courots were well established locally, modestly well-off small-town notaries with a strong sense of professional rectitude and little ambition. Intellectual vitality is evident in both lines; Rolland's father's grandfather Jean-Baptiste Boniard was a revolutionary in 1789 and a prolific diarist, and his mother's father, Edme Courot, owned a library which the young Rolland loved to explore. Both are recalled in *Le Voyage intérieur*, an autobiographical text in which he reacts against the rather fleshless internationalist image with which the war years saddled him. His family and environment made him, and all were profoundly French.

Rolland was his parents' firstborn, loved and cherished, but his childhood was not altogether happy. His father was 'de nature trop différente de sa mère' (*VI*:51),[1] cheery and extrovert where his mother was intense and severe. His easygoing republican anticlericalism clashed with the Courots' Jansenist leanings, and family unity was strained when the boy was five, on holiday in Arcachon, where a younger sister died suddenly of a mis-diagnosed throat infection. The bereaved mother was deeply affected. Her religious faith, though strong, did not preclude intense feelings of revolt which left her 'étrangère et hostile à ce monde provincial d'égoïsme riant' in which her husband was still at ease (*VI*:86). She became highly possessive towards her son, whose own health had been undermined in babyhood, supposedly after a nurse left him in the cold. Though inheriting some of his father's iron constitution, he contracted a bronchial weakness which left him a martyr to respiratory infections. The yearning to breathe freely is a constant presence in his work.[2] Gaunt, thin and sensitive to cold, he spent most of his seventy-nine years obsessed with the prospect of imminent death, which he counteracted with an image of individual life as merely a manifestation of universal, cosmic life from which the individual comes and to which he returns, like a river flowing into an ocean.

Rolland's close relationship with his over-protective mother lasted all her life and made relationships with other women difficult; some critics have hinted at a related latent homosexuality.[3] His father was largely excluded from this bond, but he shared it with a second sister, born after the death of the first and given the same name, Madeleine. Nowhere does Rolland celebrate her in writing in the way he celebrates his elders, but they were always close, and she was a staunch supporter. A distinguished Anglicist who never married, she served as his housekeeper and interpreter, and merits an honourable place in the pantheon of exceptional women overshadowed by great men to whom they were too close.

Rolland's childhood was pervaded with a sense of entrapment. His gloomy old house, with a canal beneath its walls, became a prison for a child with few playmates. He had a childhood sweetheart, Sélina de Montille, whose Mauritian origins gave her an exotic touch often found in the women he loved, but his only reference in his autobiographies to other children is to rivals for top place in class with whom relations were correct rather than close (*M*:21). Of school he writes little and coolly. He absorbed the traditional academic culture based on Latin and the seventeenth-century classics, but shows scant sign of being inspired by it. Religion had little more to offer; he attended mass, but it was not from the church of Clamecy that his personal faith developed. From an early age, however, he yearned to escape from the confines of his material self: 'le petit prisonnier, d'instinct aveugle et encore assoupi, tâtait dans l'air les chemins invisibles d'évasion' (*VI*:21). Evoking this period in *Le Voyage intérieur*, he cites the canal boats, clouds and the sound of bells as images of the escape to which he aspired. To these should be added holiday travel, which he always loved, and his exploration of his grand-father's library. The books he found there, not on the school syllabus, focused a dream life which, he claims, was intense from the age of six or seven (*VI*:114); by his early teens he was writing stories in the style of Jules Verne and a Cornelian tragedy, all flavoured with Chateaubriand. Rolland did not preserve them, but they show that his urge to write came early.

The need to escape was intensified by his educational situation. When he reached fourteen, his mother decided that her clever but sickly son should study in Paris, and being reluctant to let him board, she dragooned the whole family into moving there. This was hard on Rolland's father, who had to abandon his practice and take modest employment in a bank. Money was tight, especially after the bankruptcy of a relative who had to be helped,[4] and the boy felt under pressure. He knew what his parents were sacrificing, and he felt the whole of the family's future on his weak shoulders. His task was to pass the fiercely competitive entrance examinations for the *grandes écoles*; the plan was for him to study mathematics in the Polytechnique, but after a change of *lycée* he turned his attention to literature and aimed at the Ecole Normale Supérieure. This change, very much his own decision, was appropriate to his talents; his diary, which he began to keep at sixteen, describes it as a step away from childhood passivity towards controlling his destiny (*M*:22). Yet academic study was not ideal for him. Though better at it than most, he chafed under the bit. He was torn between the need to respond to his family's investment in him and incoherent aspirations which he knew pointed elsewhere. Though reluctant to defy his family, his need for total honesty, undoubtedly encouraged by his mother's high standards, drew him into striking displays of intransigence. His disconcerting blend of sensitivity to the views of others with uncompromising adherence to his own stayed with him all his life.

Rolland did not adapt easily to Paris. The onset of puberty coincided with a school atmosphere which he found repulsive, partly because of the sheer pace of a world where he was no longer automatically top of the class, but essentially because of the undermining of his fragile religious certainties:

> Dieu était mort. – A vrai dire, en province, lorsque je croyais croire, je ne l'avais jamais vu vivant. Quand je le priais de mon mieux, il n'était jamais là. Mais je me disais que sans doute il était dans la chambre à côté. – Quelques mois à Paris firent bâiller toutes les portes. Derrière, il n'y avait rien [. . .] Et comme, sans m'en douter, l'essence de mon être était – fut toujours – religieuse, fille de Dieu, – *c'était moi qu'on tuait.* (*VI*:93)

The Paris of Taine, Zola and Bourget was dominated by 'un positivisme matérialiste, plat et gras' (*M*:21), which never tempted him, but it weakened his attachment to the world, and he was at times close to suicide. His reaction was to brave his mother's distress and abandon religious practice: 'Ce fut mon acte le plus religieux'(*VI*:94). This hard decision freed him from pretence and opened the way to a faith of his own.

Rolland had always had a tendency to mysticism. His childhood was punctuated by moments of intense experience when he briefly lost the sense of his limited existence and felt invigorating contact with something beyond. The first such experience he describes, no doubt transformed by hindsight, took place on Arcachon beach the day before his sister died, when she consoled him after a game which had gone wrong:

> J'ai reconnu en elle la Révélation, dont elle avait été la frêle messagère, – le sens divin de la chaste étreinte qui m'a uni à elle, en ce suprême instant de son passage terrestre: – la Compassion humaine. (*VI*:26)

This traumatic episode may be seen as his initial step towards a personal faith in which human love is central. Equally significant are the 'trois éclairs' of his teens, described, again in highly schematized form, in a chapter of *Le Voyage intérieur*. The first, during a visit to Voltaire's estate at Ferney, apparently in 1882, was the revelation of nature, for which he claimed no conscious feeling before. The view of distant mountains overwhelmed him with a force evoked in a violent sexual imagery in which his acceptance of the feminine role encourages speculation about his sexual orientation:

> L'esprit, vierge violée qui s'ouvre sur l'étreinte, sentit se ruer en lui la mâle ivresse de la nature. Et, pour la première fois, il conçut [. . .] Dans cette même seconde, où je vis nue la Nature et où je la 'connus', je l'aimai dans mon passé, car je l'y reconnus. Je sus que j'étais à elle, depuis mes premiers jours, et que j'enfanterais. . . (*VI*:31)

The imagery recurs in a note of 1889, describing a similar experience in the Swiss mountains:

> J'étais possédé par la nature, comme une femme violée. Il fut un moment où mon âme m'a quitté pour se fondre dans la masse lumineuse du Breithorn. . . Oui, si extravagant que cela puisse paraître, pendant quelques minutes, *j'ai été* le Breithorn. . . (*M*:23)[5]

Here, nature becomes a life spirit, intimately associated with the process of creation. Mountain scenery remained a powerful source of inspiration, and Switzerland a favourite holiday destination.

The second 'éclair', provoked by Spinoza, led to a philosophical definition of this life spirit. Rolland was studying philosophy at the Lycée Louis-le-Grand, but not greatly inspired by it. He was fascinated by the pre-Socratic Greeks, but the Cartesian rationalism which dominated his course did not inspire him, and he admits that what he gained on the winter afternoon when the 'éclair' came to him was not an accurate understanding of Spinoza's thought. It was rather that Spinoza triggered a process in his own mind, and the trigger was the juxtaposition of the terms 'êtres réels' and 'choses fixes et éternelles'. Eternity, he decides, is no fleshless abstraction, but a real 'Substance' embracing all that has existence. The result is liberating:

Voilà donc [. . .] la réponse à l'énigme du Sphinx qui m'étreint depuis l'enfance, – à l'antinomie accablante entre l'immensité de mon être intérieur et le cachot de mon individu, qui m'humilie et qui m'étouffe! . . . '*Nature naturante*', et '*nature naturée*'. . . C'est la même – '*Tout ce qui est, est en Dieu!*' Et moi aussi, je suis en Dieu! [. . .] Je m'évade au gouffre de la *Substance*, dans le soleil blanc de l'Etre. (*VI*:36)

Images of imprisonment, suffocation and liberation blend in this pantheist revelation that he, along with all that exists, is part of God as universal Being – 'l'Etre' is one of his most frequent terms for the divinity – and his inner life escapes the confines of individuality to merge in 'l'Océan de l'Etre' (*VI*:37). This basic idea coloured his thought for his whole career.

The third 'éclair', more briefly evoked, involves a similar sense of liberation, this time experienced while trapped in a train broken down in a tunnel. Instead of feeling imprisoned or panic-stricken, he feels detached from himself as his soul escapes into the light and air:

Protée aux mille formes, je glisse entre les doigts, je m'échappe au travers des planches et des ferrailles tordues, et des chairs écrasées, et des voûtes de pierre. Je suis ici et là, partout, et je suis tout. . . (*VI*:44)

Again he experiences liberating unity with universal Being; what is new is the serenity it imparts. This capacity to free himself from a distressing situation and function calmly on the level of the universal relates to his disconcerting ability to combine uncompromising views with extreme breadth of vision. Rolland named this experience 'l'éclair tolstoyen' after a similar episode in *War and Peace*.

These 'éclairs' were of course exceptional; of more everyday help was music. He had been aware of it since early childhood; his mother was a music lover and he took piano lessons, but only in his late teens did he break free from the conventional tastes of his milieu. Beethoven, Berlioz and Wagner brought him a revelation which coincided with his rejection of conventional faith, and music became 'mon vrai culte religieux' (*VI*:95). It helped to save his relationship with his mother; through music they could communicate despite their disagreement on religion. It also offered him communication with powerful creators who built him 'un monde plus beau que la terre immonde' (*M*:26). It is no coincidence that Beethoven and Wagner, composers of heroic character, were his idols; though gentler composers like Mozart seemed closer to his own soul, he drew encouragement from the strength and will-power of these masters. It was a performance of Beethoven's Seventh Symphony which gave him the courage to abandon mathematics for literature.

Rolland wanted to be a composer. Disappointment at his family's opposition to this had much to do with his unenthusiasm for any other career; he regarded literature as a poor substitute for the musical career he might have had. Lack of formal musical tuition did not help. He played the piano at near professional level, but with expression rather than with brilliance; he was no virtuoso by temperament. Musical imagery abounds in his writings, and musical techniques influenced how he thought about his art. This emerges in many ways, but especially through the influence of the one music teacher who made a lasting impression on him. On holiday in 1888, he met an eccentric Breton aristocrat, the Marquis de Breuilpont, who took to him and gave him lessons in musical interpretation from which he absorbed

> le premier [principe] de tous, le plus essentiel, celui qui seul permet d'entrer au cœur des grandes œuvres musicales: la loi de l'*unité intérieure*, qui domine chacune de ces grandes constructions. Chacune d'elles est menée, d'un bout à l'autre, [. . .] par une idée centrale [. . .] qu'il s'agit de découvrir, car tout le reste de l'œuvre lui est subordonnée. (*M*:152–3)

This notion of unity offered the key to the musical forms of the great classical composers. The quest for a central structuring idea dominates his studies of Beethoven at the end of his life, and it informs his own artistic practice.

Two literary enthusiasms of the same period stayed with him, neither drawn from the academic syllabus. In Shakespeare and Tolstoy he found a profound understanding of the human soul which made them love the characters they created. Having discovered Shakespeare in his grandfather's library, Rolland responded to his 'don d'universelle sympathie, d'humanité pénétrante, qui fait qu'on *vit* les âmes des autres comme son âme propre' (*CR*:69); he concluded that the English dramatist was more truthful and natural than Corneille, whose heroic but narrower vision he had previously admired (*CR*:61). Rolland's earliest preserved writing is a meditation on *Hamlet*, written in 1886. It combines enthusiastic commentary on a favourite work with a first formulation of a central problem of his career, that of the balance to be established between dream and action. Beset, like Hamlet, by a rich inner life and the temptation to lose himself in dreams, the young Rolland was tormented by strict imperatives imposed by his family's faith in him, and concludes that in the final triumph of Fortinbras, 'Shakespeare remet à l'homme d'action la succession de l'homme de pensée, et tous ses droits et ses pouvoirs, que l'homme de pensée inactive n'a jamais pu ni su exercer' (*M*:31). Much of Rolland's later career is governed by the desire to avoid Hamlet's paralyzing surrender to inaction.

Just as Shakespeare weaned him off Corneille, Tolstoy offered a more acceptable version of the realist novel than the French tradition could. All Rolland saw in Stendhal, Flaubert and Maupassant was clinical analysis, but in Tolstoy he found a genuine creator, breathing life into a huge cast of characters with whom he could identify; 'Il les pénètre, non du dehors, mais du dedans, parce qu'il se fait eux, parce qu'ils sont lui' (*CR*:224). Surveying vast historical movements as if from a great height, Tolstoy nevertheless entered into the souls of each and every one of his characters. The result, in *War and Peace*, was a world which combined a truthful realist vision with a sense of epic grandeur. It is easy to see how Rolland's Spinozism harmonized with Tolstoy's vision of masses of disparate individuals united in a historical process, and Rolland recognized Tolstoy's contribution to the inspiration of *Jean-Christophe*. Yet he was reluctant to admit to influences, and found plenty in Tolstoy to disconcert him, especially the diatribe against art in *What then must we do?* which appeared in 1886. Having only just discovered *War and Peace*, Rolland was disturbed by the great man's doctrine of manual labour and renunciation of artistic egoism. He wrote to Tolstoy, to seek enlightenment and defend his own conception of art:

> J'ai cru comprendre que si vous condamnez l'Art, c'est parce que vous y voyez un désir égoïste de jouissances raffinées [. . .] Mais n'y a-t-il pas autre chose, Monsieur, autre chose, qui pour certains est le Tout? C'est justement l'oubli de la personnalité, la mort de l'Individu fondu dans la Sensation qu'il finit par ne plus sentir, quand elle atteint la complexité infinie à laquelle est arrivée par exemple la Musique. [. . .] C'est là ne plus être, c'est l'absorption dans l'Un, l'extase, l'hypnotisme de l'ouïe et de la vue, ou de tout l'esprit, si je puis dire. (*C24*:19–20)

The Wagnerian and the Spinozan join forces in this conception of art as an aid to ecstasy, abolishing the sense of selfhood which separates the individual from oceanic Being. Rolland hoped to persuade Tolstoy that this was as legitimate a way of renouncing egoism as manual labour. Tolstoy replied at considerable length. What he said, a reaffirmation that art should be a self-sacrificial vocation showing solidarity with the masses, was of little immediate importance to Rolland's thought. It appealed to him less now than it did in 1902, when he published the letter in the *Cahiers de la Quinzaine*, or in the 1930s at the height of his involvement with communism (*CR*:219ff). What mattered was that Tolstoy answered at all, that he troubled to reply so fully and generously to Rolland's brash appeal. It was a splendid example of the artist accepting his responsibilities, and it was not lost on the older Rolland, who himself became an unusually forthcoming correspondent.

By the time of this correspondence, in 1887, Rolland was in his first year at the Ecole Normale. The route there had been painful, as he succeeded only on his third attempt, after failures which he attributed to enthusiasm for authors not on the syllabus, Shakespeare and Hugo respectively. Yet the Spartan, cloistered atmosphere of the Ecole came as a liberation, as he found himself among intellectual peers with whom friendships were possible. He had formed no lasting bonds with earlier schoolfellows; a passing friendship at Louis-le-Grand with his fellow-Wagnerite Claudel was forgotten for many years, and even in his first days in the Ecole his manifest distaste for japes and initiation rites suggests that sociability was not his strong point. Yet his intense manner and strong views commanded respect, and two intimate friendships developed.

'Le premier ami vrai de ma vie' was André Suarès. A Jew from Marseille, he was very different from the Nordic Rolland, but they shared a passionate artistic sensitivity, their tastes overlapped, and Rolland's friendships thrived on difference. Suarès was not easy company; Rolland had difficulty in moderating his excessive likes and dislikes, his sharp tongue and an egocentrism which made enemies. In fighting anti-Semitic attempts to have him expelled, Rolland was drawn into the world of polarized cliques which he later denounced in *Jean-Christophe* as typical of French intellectual life:

> Mon amitié avec Suarès finit par m'isoler, volontairement, des autres. Et ce fut un mal: car, personnellement, quand j'étais entré à l'Ecole, je ne comptais pas un seul ennemi [. . .] Cette sympathie générale, qui m'était offerte, aurait pu m'aider à surmonter certains défauts de ma nature, qui m'ont rendu la vie plus difficile. (*M*:41–2)

What should have been a period of broadening contacts became one of partisan conflict, of closing rather than opening doors. Already Rolland was 'l'un contre tous', the nonconformist struggling for justice against the herd instinct. If Suarès appealed to Rolland the dreamer, Georges Mille had more to offer the man of action. This friendship too thrived on difference, but at first the differences seemed too great. Mille appeared cold and calculating, a careerist with a first-class mind who 'prétendait jouer les Julien Sorel' (*M*:45), and at the outset they were merely sparring partners. Their reserve was overcome only in the face of illness, which brought Mille to an early death in his second year. In these extreme circumstances, the two achieved an intimacy which might otherwise have eluded them, leaving Rolland to meditate on the union of souls in death and to mourn the disappearance of a man who, he felt, would have been an ideal guide in the world of action.

Mille flippantly described Rolland as 'le Bouddhâ musical d'une mysticité révolutionnaire' (*C4*:18), which highlights his cult of music and gives a hint of his political sympathies. The allusion to Buddha is intriguing in the light of his later interest in the East; Buddhism was not the Eastern faith which appealed to him most, but he did take extensive notes on it.[6] Of the 'mysticité' there is no doubt, for it was now that he formulated his pantheism in the *Credo quia Verum*. The genesis of this text can be followed through long, feverish diary notes for which Rolland, rereading them years later, could muster only 'une pitié irritée' (*M*:53). Even then, he did not see his *Credo* as a first step in his career:

> Le temps n'est pas venu pour moi d'écrire des œuvres d'art; la vie me manque encore, et je n'aurais ni intelligence, ni probité artistique, si j'essayais de peindre, sans avoir regardé la réalité multiple [. . .] et sans avoir encore en ma possession un instrument assez fin, une main assez souple, pour les saisir nettement et les fixer avec précision. (*C4*:353–4)

This suggests that he saw his career more in terms of Tolstoyan realism than philosophy and felt unprepared for it, though he did work in 1888 on two fictional projects, *Amour d'enfants*, a love story stimulated by a holiday reunion with Sélina de Montille, and a study of a musician called *Artistes*.[7] The value of the *Credo* was that, by ordering his religious thoughts, it freed him from mystical obsessions and helped him progress to other things.

It springs from a process related to Cartesian doubt, but more intuitive than rational. 'L'Intuition', he is convinced, 'peut être une méthode scientifique, non moins rigoureuse, mais bien autrement féconde que nos pauvres ressources, la sèche Déduction [. . .] et la lente Induction' (*C4*:361). He arrives at two basic axioms: that the only reality is sensation and the only certainty 'l'Etre en soi et par soi, dont Spinoza a eu l'intuition'. Combining these, Rolland reformulates the Cogito as 'Je sens, donc IL EST' (*C4*:357–8). Each individual is the consciousness of a sensation, all sensations are united in God, therefore God is in each individual:

> Au fond de la conscience du moi, dans mon étroite poitrine, sommeille le Moi divin, le *Je* absolu. *Je* seul existe. *Je* suis Romain Rolland, et en chacune de ses sensations. Mais *Je* le déborde, *Je* suis en dehors de lui, *Je* suis tous ceux qui l'entourent, l'univers des âmes et des corps. (*C4*:362)

All souls commune in God, but all have their separate existence, so communication between individuals is problematic. So too is individual liberty: 'Il n'est de liberté qu'en l'Etre absolu. Dans le fait qu'il est tout et que les Lois sont le rythme de son souffle. Il marie en lui Liberté et Nécessité' (*C4*:366). Here, Rolland makes his first attempt to solve the problem of destiny which haunted him all his life. The only way the individual can be free is to accept destiny, be himself and, for the thinking man, raise himself to the divine level and appreciate his role in life in the same way as one views a single note, which may be a dissonance, in a musical work:

> Seul m'intéresse l'ensemble du morceau. Une dissonance prise à part peut blesser l'oreille; elle l'amuse, entendue à sa place, dans la suite du morceau. Je suis cette dissonance [. . .] Mais écoutons la mélodie entière, dont ma dissonance est un anneau! (*C4*:367)

This vision of life as a musical work in which discords contribute to a harmonic whole became one of Rolland's most characteristic images. In a saying of Heraclitus, which Rolland frequently quoted, the most beautiful harmonies are woven from dissonances.

The tragedy is that the individual's vision is through his individual eyes rather than those of God: 'Tout être est à la fois une âme individuelle, et un rôle de la Divine Tragédie. Mais chacun ne sent bien, d'ordinaire, comme âme que la sienne' (*C4*:370). Individual life is therefore an illusion, for which Rolland already uses the Indian term Mâyâ (*C4*:365). We cannot, however, escape this illusion, except fleetingly, and we should live our role to the full, cultivating irony, which brings us 'le soleil de la sérénité, ce calme hautain des beaux dieux grecs' by teaching us that life is no more than a role. This by itself, however, is egoism. Rolland does not reject self-love, since to love oneself is to love one manifestation of God, but love should strive for higher things (*C4*:373). It is rightly concentrated on those close to us, and its essence is sacrifice, which Rolland associates with Tolstoy and Alyosha in *The Brothers Karamazov*. Religion orients us towards the eternal, art breaks barriers between individuals, morality teaches sacrifice and science leads us to live by the laws of nature. As for death, it is omnipresent, the fulfilment of life in that it represents ecstatic union with the universal as expressed in the *Liebestod* of Wagner's Isolde, although Rolland rejects Wagner's term 'Unbewusst' – 'sans conscience' (*C4*:377), for he does not welcome the annihilation of individuality. This is perhaps why he is not tempted by the Buddhist Nirvana. The *Credo* ends with a hymn to love, in which he takes issue with Maupassant, who bewails the unbreakable barriers between individuals; the fraternal love of Tolstoy and Dostoevsky, he claims, can overcome these barriers.

Despite a certain pretentiousness, this work expresses many of the concepts shaping Rolland's thought, liberty, destiny, love, sacrifice and death as union with all; his later reaction against it is more a matter of tone than content. It did not, however, help him to define his own role, and decisions had to be taken about his studies. Rolland was a conscientious student, but not over-conscientious. He did not want to teach, and as his student days progressed he felt out of harmony with his fellow-students, most of whom had only modest ambitions. Yet he had to study something, the options were philosophy, literature or history, and history won. This was not a soft option, for the work involved was notorious, but to study philosophy he would have had to bend to the 'spiritualisme papelard' of Ollé-Laprune, which he disliked, and in literature his tutor would have been Brunetière, whose opinionated rhetoric smacked of charlatanism (*M*:52). In history, the teaching was in the hands of three men he respected, Paul Guiraud, a historian of antiquity, the innovative geographer Vidal de la Blache and above all Gabriel Monod, Michelet's disciple and biographer, an upright Protestant with whom he remained friendly for many years. Rolland later recognized his debt to his historical training. He found it irksome, but the respect it instilled for factual precision complemented his mysticism, and in the project he formed of writing a history of the French wars of religion, he sought to combine both sides of his mind,

> mes besoins de rigoureuse recherche des faits, et d'intuitionnisme qui fait revivre – qui revit l'âme – les âmes mortes, du passé. J'envisageais une histoire d'une espèce peu ordinaire, conçue sous le signe du mysticisme réaliste, selon Tolstoy, de *Guerre et Paix*. (*M*:55)

The period he had chosen was one of passion, faith and striking personalities acting a tragedy of conflicting roles of the type evoked in the *Credo quia Verum*. Rolland aimed to embrace this turbulent picture by espousing the souls of each personality in turn:

> La seule voie pour bien comprendre et pour bien peindre les personnages de l'histoire: s'incarner en eux. Et on ne le peut, sans les aimer. Le réalisme sans la sympathie est une flamme sans feu [. . .] Je serai Catherine et Coligny, un homme du peuple, un parlementaire, un curé de campagne, un réître, etc. Et quand j'aurai vécu toutes ces vies, je les fondrai en un ensemble 'symphonique'. (*M*:55–6)

The project never went beyond a few academic exercises, but it is characteristic of Rolland in its desire to break barriers between souls in a realism suffused by love and its quest to transcend conflicts in a unity described as symphonic. Many of Rolland's later writings are based on the technique of entering into the mind of some great individual. His approach was frankly intuitive, and his teachers criticized him for taking texts as a basis for a psychological approach rather than rigorous analysis (*M*:60), but Rolland felt that textual analysis alone offered insufficient access to souls. As evidence, he cited his own experience as a diarist:

> Je défie de pénétrer mon être vrai quiconque voudrait le reconstruire d'après mes seules notes classées et cataloguées [. . .] Quand je fais le compte de tout ce que je n'ai pas inscrit et de ce que j'ai inscrit, je me convaincs de l'insuffisance du procédé historique qui refait la vie avec la traîtrise des mots écrits. (*M*:58)

Only a Tolstoyan realist could supply the crucial intuitive leap beyond the written word.

Rolland was already a voluminous diarist. It was a habit he maintained all his life, initially no doubt as a means of self-expression for a lonely adolescent, but increasingly as a way of developing literary skills. His original student diaries he destroyed in 1912 after transcribing them and making a few cuts, which means that the document published in the *Cahiers Romain Rolland* is to some extent an arranged image, but in essence it is a remarkable testimony of a student's life. It reveals an intense, serious-minded youth, striving to clarify his thoughts and impressing his peers with his idealism. His intensity sometimes caused him problems, as his innate shyness did battle with strongly-held views:

> Ma timidité profonde, je ne l'ai jamais portée dans l'action; une fois engagée dans une discussion, j'ai toujours été ferme, brave, souvent téméraire, violent; j'ai trop de foi pour être timide, quand on touche à mes convictions [. . .] Dans nos discussions, tout de suite je devenais pâle; mes lèvres, mes mains tremblaient; les larmes me montaient aux yeux; et en même temps que ma pensée arrivait à une très grande lucidité que je ne lui soupçonnais pas, elle

arrivait aussi à des violences d'expression, dont j'étais affligé plus tard. (*C4*:165)

This helps to explain why Rolland always avoided public performance or debate; nervous tension locked him into uncompromising stances and he could not trust his self-control. Another passage shows how hard he found it to combine self-assertion with the need to live with others:

> Ma sensibilité est assez fine pour vivre intimement leur vie; mais ma person-nalité est trop forte et trop à part des autres [. . .] pour que je puisse jouer une scène de la pièce des autres, prendre part à une conversation que je ne dirige pas [. . .] – C'est pourquoi tout en m'estimant pour mon caractère droit, tout en me sachant gré du bien que je pourrai faire, les autres se méprendront souvent sur mon compte et taxeront de dédain ou d'orgueil ce qui ne sera que le désir d'être moi-même et de vivre librement. (*C4*:249)

This is interesting on several grounds. Not only does it reveal the urge to preserve his freedom which played so marked a part in his life, it also hints that his stance of 'l'un contre tous' does not spring from aloofness from his fellow beings, but from an insistence on serving them in his own way. His diaries show that his declared interest in people is perfectly genuine. Sympathetic studies of his friends rub shoulders with witty observation of the mannerisms of his teachers, and the combination of a strong satirical element with formal portraiture anticipates his later techniques as a novelist. His diaries reveal a would-be Tolstoyan realist cutting his teeth.

They also simply express spontaneous interest in the world around him. As a boarding student, his movements were curtailed and he could hardly be a man about town, but he enjoyed outings to theatres, concerts and, more surprisingly, the occasional public ceremony. One such was the reception of Leconte de Lisle in the Académie Française by Dumas *fils*, of which Rolland gives a sharply humorous account (*C4*:54–8). He admired neither writer, and was amused at how their dislike of each other emerged through the ceremonial proprieties. The shrewd corner-cutting whereby he obtained tickets for the occasion reveals that he was neither naïve nor devoid of cunning. Celebrity scalp-hunting was another pastime; as a student in a prestigious institution he was not backward in seeking contact with the great, both to express admiration and to argue. As well as his letter to Tolstoy, he wrote to Edmond de Goncourt to support him against the hostile reception of *Germinie Lacerteux*, and, in his first public foray against nationalism, to Saint-Saëns to complain of his opposition to the performance of Wagner in Paris. He arranged to meet César Franck, and after writing to Renan, rather brashly, to ask if he was right to detect stoicism in his philosophical dramas, he was rewarded by an invitation to visit the great man. In their conversation, Renan developed his philosophy of history and expressed confidence that progress would triumph whatever the setbacks (*C4*:19–27). Rolland was charmed, but not entirely seduced; Renan's unsympathetic reaction to weaker souls who might be hurt by being deprived of religion struck a jarring note, a token of a philosophical detachment to which Rolland never aspired. Yet Rolland often returned to Renan's image of the uneven progress of history as 'la route en lacets qui monte', and Renan's smiling scepticism, for all its limitations, appealed to Rolland in moments when he sought, in the terms of the *Credo quia Verum*, to see the world through God's eyes. Renan is quoted there as the exemplar of Rolland's concept of irony.

The bulk of Rolland's diary observations are on artistic matters: theatres, concerts and the newly-discovered world of painting. Affairs of state play a relatively minor role; the intrigues of the Third Republic were too much part of all he detested in Paris for him to take much interest in day-to-day politics. He was, however, a convinced republican, like his father, who had supported the republic during the Second Empire when it was controversial to do so. He admired Gambetta and Ferry (*C4*:163), in student intrigues he tended to oppose the monarchists and Bonapartists, and when the republic seemed threatened by the Boulanger crisis he was among its defenders, avoiding street demonstrations other than as an observer, but involving himself with petitions and subscriptions, and railing at the cowardice of less committed fellow-students (*C4*:214). This concern was matched by the constant fear of war with Germany. *Normaliens* had to do military drill, he knew he risked conscription if war broke out, and the knowledge did little to assuage his sense of imminent death. His political views were simple; he supported his nation insofar as it embodied an ideal, but no further:

> Je n'aime pas spécialement la France, parce que je n'aime aucune nation. Il n'y a qu'une patrie: l'Amour, et les autres sont le fruit de l'orgueil et de la haine. – Mais la France seule, en Europe, incarne la République; et la pensée de la République morte me serre la gorge. (*C4*:300)

On the content of French republicanism he says little. Socialism barely touched him; in a moment of irritation he could declare that: 'J'ai honte quand la femme de journée, chez ma mère, me voit assis à ma table et lisant. J'ai honte, quand je rencontre un ouvrier, qui rentre, le soir, écrasé, d'une journée de gros travail' (*M*:52), but this remains an isolated outburst.

Rolland emerged from the Ecole Normale triumphant, having obtained his *agrégation*, but triumph gave him no joy. It left him with a hatred of the system, a sense of having wasted his time on meaningless forced labour and a profound reluctance to honour his commitment to work within the academic system. He had no plans beyond a sense of literary vocation with no clear notion of what he wanted to write. The loss of his musical career still rankled. The way ahead lay in a vacant post in the French School of Archaeology in Rome. He had no ambition to go there, the post came his way only after the failure of a more fancied candidate, and his acceptance was unenthusiastic. Yet it proved one of the most positive moves of his life.

Notes

1. References to Rolland's works published in volumes follow quotations in the texts; for abbreviations of titles, see the table at the beginning of the work. Other published works, unpublished documents and secondary sources are identified in footnotes.
2. See Barrère (1966), pp.37–75.
3. See especially Starr (1971), p 146ff.
4. See Vermorel (1993), p.49.
5. Serge Duret (1992, p.82) thinks this passage is in fact the source of the account in *Le Voyage intérieur* of the Ferney 'éclair', which does not appear to be mentioned anywhere in Rolland's notes. In all passages from Rolland's diaries transcribed by the author in later texts, it should, however, be realized that he habitually made slight textual modifications. They are not totally accurate reflections of what he originally wrote.
6. See Duret (1992), p.53.
7. See Duchatelet (1975), p.82ff.

–2–

Rome

Rolland's task in Rome was a study of Cardinal Salviati, a sixteenth-century papal nuncio, and he researched conscientiously in the Vatican archives, but he found it sufficient to work in the mornings and treat the rest of the day as his own. In unusually good health and free of examination worries, for two years he was happy. Rome also freed him, temporarily, from his family, although his mother had resisted his departure. She made him promise to write home daily, and the resultant correspondence bears testimony not only to Rome, but also to his struggle to be his own man in face of her constant worries. It expresses conflict, but also the fledgling writer practising his skills to a sympathetic audience. He knew he was entertaining her as well as thinking aloud, and their resultant easy-going tone places these letters among his most appealing personal documents. Being away from Paris was also liberating. Rolland set off with no positive enthusiasm for Rome, but the simple fact of being abroad freed him from the indignation that Paris inspired. He saw the same faults, but in Rome he could laugh at things which in Paris offended him. He approached Rome like an enthusiastic tourist, elated by the novelty, relishing the good and tolerating the bad, knowing he was living through a short episode which would come to an end.

The aspect of Italy that he was most disposed to admire was Renaissance art. Ancient Rome reminded him too much of school; ruins and archaeology had little charm for a budding author looking for human contact and life, but the Renaissance offered a satisfying warmth:

> L'art antique [. . .] est très beau; mais moi, je ne puis pas me contenter de la beauté pure; il ne me suffit pas d'admirer; j'ai impérieusement besoin d'aimer. C'est pour cela que j'aime tant l'art individuel de la Renaissance, tout imprégné de la personnalité des artistes ou de leurs modèles. (*C*6:77–8)

He had already discovered the artists of the Florentine Quattrocento, who mirrored his religious sensibilities, and the prospect of visiting Florence excited him more than Rome itself. Gradually, however, his tastes changed, and by the end of his stay his favourites were Michelangelo, with heroic qualities akin to Beethoven's, and Raphael, who shared with Mozart 'la grâce – non pas alanguie, efféminée, parfumée – mais virile, robuste et saine' (*C6*:146). He developed a knowledge of Italian art which stood him in good stead in his early career, when he taught and wrote on the subject.

Equally important was the countryside around Rome. He had always responded to the frozen phallic energy of mountains, but in the Roman Campagna the hills became a distant backdrop to a plain where the quality of light and the intermingling of earth and sky gave an impression of serenity and harmony:

> Cette musique de la lumière et des lignes n'a, depuis, cessé de chanter, même au fond de mes jours les plus sombres [. . .] Et je lui dois, dans le voyage d'une vie tourmentée, d'avoir toujours pu sauver et préserver '*l'art du grand calme*'. (*M*:79–80)

A similar calm came from the Greeks, whom he discovered at the temples of Paestum. He arrived there on a gloomy February day, which he evokes with a careful notation of visual effects typical of his Roman correspondence:

> Le temps était gris; les montagnes à-demi voilées; il tombait des gouttes de pluie; la grande plaine déserte, la mer blanchâtre à quelques centaines de mètres, le ciel couvert, tout devait disposer à la mélancolie. Je me sentais au contraire tout joyeux à la vue de ces temples [. . .] Les éléments en sont si simples, que notre langue d'analyse n'en peut, en les détaillant, que montrer l'absolue pureté de goût, sans qu'on puisse imaginer la puissance qui s'impose avec tant de naturel ces règles de bon sens [. . .] Ce qui me ravit ici, c'est cette force toute franche, cette grâce virile, cette fleur d'héroïsme. (*C6*: 188–9)

The 'grâce virile' of the Greeks echoes what Rolland found in Raphael, a disciplined simplicity combining strength and elegance, in which passion is mastered and grief blends into joy. Beethoven's 'Durch Leiden Freude' is not far away.

Roman society offered more field for observation. After his cloistered student years, his pianistic skills opened the door to an active social life in the French community and, later, fashionable salons. He played in public more than at any time in his life, struggling to preserve his independence in face of constant invitations, and his letters are full of entertaining portraits of the salons where he played. He had little in common with his fellow students at the Palazzo Farnese, but he enjoyed the company of Laura Minghetti, a sparkling society hostess, a few open-minded theological students and priests, even Hébert, director of the Villa Medicis, an execrable violinist whom Rolland tried to avoid accompanying but who complimented him by trying to relaunch his musical career. He took only a distant interest in Italian politics, but like Laura Minghetti he reacted against the Piedmontese who had annexed the Papal States, failed to live up to Risorgimento ideals and vandalized old Rome with speculative building. He even expresses nostalgia for 'un pape moyen âge, qui déclarât la guerre aux Savoyards' (*C8*:151).

Most important to him were two women, one young, one old. The young woman was Sofia Guerrieri-Gonzaga, sixteen-year-old daughter of an aristocratic family, for whom Rolland experienced his first serious passion. She showed no interest in his undeclared love, and he needed all the serenity he could muster to control his wounded feelings, expressed in his first sustained fictional attempt, a love story called *Mai romain*, which survives only as a sketch. The older woman, one of the most important influences of his life, was Malwida von Meysenbug. A German aristocrat with Huguenot forebears, she had known Wagner and many of the 1848 revolutionaries, especially Mazzini and Herzen, whose daughter she had brought up. Olga Herzen had married Monod, who introduced Rolland to Malwida, and through Malwida he met Sofia. Malwida had conquered serenity after a difficult life, and Rolland, struggling to achieve it himself, was drawn to her on that account, as well as for the link she offered with heroes of an earlier generation. The intensely idealistic Malwida rediscovered her own lost heroes in the young Rolland, and he spent many evenings playing her Bach, Beethoven and Wagner. Their intimacy may seem surprising in view of their age disparity, but Rolland's platonic friendships with women were always more successful than his loves. There were clouds in the relationship; Rolland's Catholic mother feared her Protestant influence, and they disagreed on politics. Both were internationalists, but Rolland was sufficiently French and Malwida sufficiently German to clash over some of the diplomatic conflicts of the period. Malwida embodied the strengths and weaknesses of what Rolland called 'la vieille Allemagne' (*VI*:149), and he admits that she inspired Modesta in *Jean-Christophe*, the blind girl who perceives only what she wants to perceive. Yet their ideas harmonized in many areas, and what mattered most was her affectionate confidence in Rolland at a formative period: 'L'ami qui vous comprend, vous crée. En ce sens, j'ai été créé par Malwida' (*VI*:154–5).

Malwida was Rolland's first supporter in his literary career, which had reached a crucial moment of definition. It came in March 1890, when, as he watched sunset from the Janiculum, he experienced another 'éclair', a moment from which he dated the beginning of his artistic self-awareness and, specifically, the conception of *Jean-Christophe*. The experience is evoked in *Le Voyage intérieur*, in an account which, though shaped by hindsight, bears eloquent testimony to how he viewed his art:

> Je vis de loin mon temps, mon pays, mes préjugés, moi-même. Je fus libre, pour la première fois... Une seconde avant, – et derrière, vingt-quatre années de vie, – j'étais esclave du temps, asservi à son rythme, entraîné par son flot, respirant sa pensée. Lors même que je condamnais, je l'aspirais, je l'expirais, je vivais d'elle. Et je mourais par elle. – Suis-je mort? . . . Je ressuscite! Et j'ai franchi le couvercle du tombeau, cette 'fin de siècle'. . . Je sors du temps. . .

The detachment inspired by Rome frees him even from those negative aspects of his environment which he had internalized, and the result is a vision functioning simultaneously on two levels:

> J'appris à dégager mon esprit de mon cœur. A partir de cet instant, ils ont suivi des routes parallèles; et même quand ils s'associent, ils restent indépendants. A partir de cet instant, le plan de ma vision fut, demeura toujours *'au-dessus de la mêlée'*.

Separation of mind and heart was crucial to artistic creation because it made control possible:

> Le mot magique inscrit en ce soir de mars Romain [. . .] fut le mot souverain: l'Ordre. La suprême liberté de l'esprit affranchi, qui 'sereine' l'anarchie chaotique du cœur.

With a mind capable of serenity, 'je fis de mes passions mêmes les servantes de mon art: je les laissais jeter leur premier feu; et je les attachais ensuite à ma charrue'. He could live passion to the full, but his mind could harness it to creative purpose, and the result was 'l'harmonie des cordes de la lyre' (*VI*:133–5), that Heraclitean harmony woven from dissonances expressed in the *Credo quia Verum*.

It is unlikely that Rolland saw all this in precisely these terms at the time, but it is in keeping with his previous evolution. Detachment from present troubles was the essence of the 'éclair tolstoyen', and the *Credo quia Verum*'s emphasis on playing an individual role to the full while aspiring to see through the eyes of God anticipates the simultaneous functioning on two levels of awareness. This dual vision is central to

Rolland's creativity; his choice of the fateful phrase 'au-dessus de la mêlée' shows that he recognized its centrality, and he needed it in the summer of 1890 as he strove to reconcile his passion for Sofia with the serenity of Malwida and the Campagna.

Another form of dual vision can be seen in his description of the variety of moods in a favourite Roman work, Michelangelo's *Moses*:

Je ne l'ai pas trouvé aussi irrité que d'habitude. Hier, il était triste plutôt, et concentré dans sa propre pensée. Mais bien certainement, une âme sommeille en lui; car à peine deux badauds bruyants sont-ils venus interrompre sa méditation, que sur ses traits a reparu la méprisante fureur que je lui connaissais; et après leur départ, il est retombé dans sa hautaine mélancolie. – La vérité, c'est qu'il y a en lui deux hommes; le haut du visage est celui d'un penseur solitaire qui souffre de la solitude de son génie: et le bas, la mâchoire, la lèvre inférieure gonflée de mépris, dit l'homme d'action qui écrase le monde de sa force méprisante. Suivant la disposition d'esprit, on est plus ou moins frappé de l'une ou de l'autre expression du visage [. . .] Tristesse et colère se fondent en une puissante sérénité. Oui, il y a même de la sérénité dans *Moïse*. (*C6*:329)

This passage, for all its playful mood, illustrates how dissonant passions blend into serenity, but also present is another kind of lofty vision, 'le mépris', the indignant gaze cast by the great man on the petty beings at his feet. Scorn, for Rolland, became a useful defence reaction, though it needed to be used with care. In his early plays it is associated with proud withdrawal from action, and it subsists in different form in satirical texts such as *La Foire sur la place*.

It is too simple to describe the Janiculum 'éclair' as the starting point of *Jean-Christophe*;[1] it is better seen as the birth of the vision which produced it rather than that of a precise project. Yet it was followed by a period of germinating ideas, most of which point to the novel as Rolland's chosen genre. The mood is set by a text written in the same month as the 'éclair', developing ideas from the *Credo quia Verum*.[2] Contemporary art, he claims, is marked by a 'maladie de l'analyse', an intellectual refinement dooming it to decadence. It should be replaced by a new art revealing the pantheist God present in all men:

C'est là notre mission: donner à l'Homme, enfin libre, l'incomparable joie – non d'être Dieu (*il l'est*) – mais de se sentir Dieu, de jouir de la Vie pleine, toute d'amour. – Il le peut, s'il le veut. Il le voudra, s'il sait qu'il peut.

This mission, of particular importance in an age when 'les peuples sont appelés à boire à [la] source sacrée [de l'Art]', is realized through love and sacrifice and an analysis of souls working from within rather than without. In this, this text harks back to Rolland's projected history of the wars of religion, and it anticipates *Orsino* and *Jean-Christophe* in the importance attached to 'la Vie'. The interest in art for the people looks forward to his theatrical ventures and his socialism.

Rolland toyed with several fictional projects in 1890. Apart from *Mai romain*, there was a plan based on the character of Georges Mille[3] and a return to his earlier sketch, *Artistes*, in which the central figure acquires elements of Beethoven and Michelangelo, men of genius passing scornful judgment on the world.[4] Rolland was unsure of how to pursue this vein, which at one point he condemned as 'malsain et faux',[5] but the idea of basing a novel on a Beethoven figure is clearly a step towards *Jean-Christophe*. More interesting is his projected musical novel:

> La matière du roman musical doit être le Sentiment, et de préférence le Sentiment dans ses formes les plus générales, les plus humaines, avec toute l'intensité dont il est capable. Il ne doit pas en faire ce qu'on nomme aujourd'hui 'l'analyse psychologique', [. . .] mais les faire revivre sous le revêtement de telle ou telle apparence, qui n'est là vraiment que pour *porter* ce sentiment [. . .] Toutes les parties du roman musical doivent être issues du même sentiment général et puissant. Comme une Symphonie est bâtie sur quelques notes exprimant un sentiment, qui se développe en tous sens, grandit, triomphe ou succombe, dans la suite du morceau, – un roman musical doit être la libre floraison d'un sentiment qui en soit l'âme et l'essence. (*C1*:26)

This is a striking synthesis of much that has gone before, his rejection of analytic realism, his notion of the symphony evolving from a central idea, the pantheistic sense that characters of a novel should incarnate something more than themselves, above all the sense of a missed musical vocation. The programme was too idealistic to be realized; it is both more and less than a blueprint for *Jean-Christophe*. Yet one cannot but be struck by the anticipation of the name of Christophe, the God-bearer, in the notion of a character carrying a sentiment.

Rolland's first completed works, however, took a different direction after a crisis of confidence during his visit to Paris in the summer of 1890, a sad reminder of the world waiting for him on his return. Its most immediate expression was a brief article on Mozart, showing the artist transforming private grief into creation,[6] but it also gave rise to two plays, *Orsino* and *Empédocle*. As often, he thrived on working on simultaneous projects of contrasting character. Of the two, the unfinished *Empédocle* just has priority. Rolland had been drawn to the pre-Socratics in his schooldays; the Empedoclean vision of a world governed by an alternation of love and hatred accorded well with his pantheistic ideas, and was supported by his study of history and Renan's vision of 'la route en lacets'. In this fragment, which like many of Rolland's early plays remains unpublished, Empédocle, the demigod miracle-worker, is enthroned by the people in place of the tyrant Hiéron, converses with the inhabitants of the decadent world around him and hands power back to Hiéron before immolating himself in the crater of Etna. Rolland later described him as an 'héros sage, qui a le mépris des hommes, mais qui les aime et qui les aide' (*M*:109); as with many of Rolland's figures, his problem is how to serve a mediocre humanity which lacks his loftiness of vision. Empédocle is marked by scorn, but his suicide, the first of many in Rolland's early plays, combines scorn with serenity, for in death he relinquishes his human role and reassumes his divinity, a true pantheist hero. The play has echoes of Wagner's *Tristan*, Renan's philosophical dramas and the closing scene of *Hamlet*, with Hiéron as Fortinbras.

Orsino, by contrast, is action incarnate, an outburst of vitality embodying everything Rolland would like to be, rather than his hesitations and weaknesses. The name is Shakespearian, and Rolland later admitted an affinity with Nietzsche, whom at that date he had not read, but more important is the Renaissance itself, whose vitality and passion inspired many of Rolland's early plays. Orsino is a *condottiere* fighting for petty Italian princelings whom he scorns and does not hesitate to betray. He dreams of founding an empire, shows respect only for the artist Lionardo and dies poisoned by a woman he has wronged, but leading his troops into battle and denying the reality of death. Where Empédocle conquers death by submerging his individuality in the divine spirit, Orsino defies it by asserting his individuality to the last; the tension between individualism and collectivism which pervaded his later work can already be glimpsed. This was the first work that Rolland completed to something like his own satisfaction, but he worried about his hero's defiance of morality. He explains to his scrupulous mother: 'On ne doit pas [juger Orsino] avec les règles de la morale ordinaire. Il est tellement supérieur à tous, que la libre et violente expression de sa personnalité est belle et bonne, quelque mal qu'elle puisse faire' (*C8*:352–3). In a decadent age, even amoral vitality is beneficial. Yet in 1902, when he showed *Orsino* to its inspirer, Sofia, he declared he would never write such a work again: 'La force pour la force, je n'en veux plus' (*C10*:48).

A contemporary note suggests that Rolland had symphonic form in mind in the work's construction:

Poser, dans chacun des premiers actes, un thème de passion, qui se développe librement. Au dernier acte, opposer entre eux et superposer les thèmes. Construire, avec un robuste contrepoint, complexe et plein, où se mêlent, sans qu'aucun perde sa forte caractéristique, les motifs d'êtres qui composent l'Etre total de la symphonie. (*M*:109)

After a first act of exposition, the second, centred on Orsino, is entitled 'la Libre Action', in the third his beloved, Cathérine, embodies 'la Libre Passion', and in the final act, 'La Mort', both meet in a tragic clash. By making his characters incarnate sentiments, Rolland fulfils an aim of the 'roman musical'; their conflict recalls sonata form's contrasting themes. The mature Rolland mocked this over-ambitious work; rather than Nietzsche's laughing lion, it reminded him of the roaring of Shakespeare's Bottom (*M*:106). Yet for all his irony, he kept his affection for it.

These works, complete early in 1891, convinced Rolland that he could and should write. His family were sceptical, but he convinced Malwida, who pleaded his case with Monod. Rolland's undertaking to work for ten years in the academic profession, the price he had to pay for his Ecole Normale training, was an obstacle to his ambition, and Monod, with his strict sense of duty, was anxious to keep Rolland within the system. Yet he was impressed enough by *Orsino* to seek a compromise, and arranged for the play to be read by Mounet-Sully, of the Comédie Française, who had been Rolland's theatrical hero in his student days.

Rolland spent his last months in Rome on another Renaissance drama, *Les Baglioni*, portraying a Perugian family torn apart by rivalries catalyzed by a bastard akin to Edmund in *King Lear*. More ambitious even than *Orsino*, its elaborate stage effects involving fires, battles and massacres suggest Wagner as well as Shakespeare. Rolland himself points to the analogy of Greek tragedy:

J'ai été saisi [. . .] plus par le caractère Eschylien des événements que par le caractère shakespearien des personnages. Je l'ai conçu comme une tragédie de haine, de destruction, de néant. Ce n'est pas le seul crime d'un Jago, c'est la fatalité toute entière où s'engouffre la race des Baglioni, semblable au monde qui se détruit de ses propres mains.

In Empedoclean terms, the play portrays a swing towards the cycle of hatred; destiny rules, and the mood is more pessimistic than in *Orsino*: 'Pas un n'a la force d'Orsino qui triomphe de la fatalité; les uns la subissent aveuglément, les autres avec conscience; tous obéissent au destin qui les tire'.[7] The one glimmer of hope is voiced by Atalanta, survivor of an older generation, whose warning that hatred will end only if the spirit of vengeance is overcome anticipates Rolland's 1918 text on Empedocles, but as her nephews massacre each other, that hope seems remote. The play's gloomy mood reflects Rolland's depression at his impending departure from Rome, but it was admired by Mounet-Sully, whose tastes, like Rolland's, were for the heroic and the passionate.

On his way back, Rolland had one last treat when Malwida took him to Bayreuth to introduce him to the Wagner family. Rolland's reactions were mixed: he enjoyed the music, but did not feel that the operas worked well on stage, and he was put off by the sycophancy and commercialization of the Wagnerian mini-court. For the first time, Rolland sensed a split in the German character between a noble idealistic past and a crass materialistic present. After his two-year Roman dream, this was his first step back towards the painful realities of modern Europe.

Notes

1. See Duchatelet (1975), p.113ff.
2. Quoted in Duchatelet (1975), p.128ff.
3. See Duchatelet (1975), p.139ff.
4. See Duchatelet (1975), p.167ff.
5. Diary, May 1890, quoted by Duchatelet (1975), p.171.
6. Published in *MAF*:273–94; see Duret (1992), p.129ff.
7. Letter to Malwida von Meysenbug, May 1891, partially quoted in Duret (1992), p.168.

–3–

Early Struggles

Back in Paris, Rolland faced career decisions. There was no prospect of living by writing, but he refused to teach, or even study for a doctorate. In later life he mellowed, and advised young writers in his situation to earn their living by other means to safeguard their liberty (*M*:115), but he could not see this in 1891. He obtained a year's leave from the academic profession on grounds of ill-health, during which he hoped either to find a congenial post or conquer literary fame, but a quest for posts in libraries and museums proved unfruitful, and the Comédie Française rejected his plays. He was not to know that Mounet, mistrusted by his colleagues, was a dangerous advocate. As a result, his first winter back was frustrating, worsened by his sense of isolation in a world governed by a 'lourd, grossier et sanglant pessimisme' (*C1*:59). The threat of war was ever-present, the literary world was still dominated by the Zolas, Bourgets and Maupassants, and those reacting against them were little better. He did not share Suarès's taste for the Symbolists, Maeterlinck proved a mere 'Sardou symboliste',[1] and the Rosicrucian salon of the Sâr Péladan disgusted him:

> Je sais bien que c'est une réaction naturelle contre le matérialisme environnant; mais je ne l'estime pas plus sain [. . .] L'idéalisme n'est beau que chez de fortes âmes qui ont vécu, qui ont goûté le pain de la vie, de la souffrance et de la joie humaine. Mais dans ces cœurs faibles et troublés, ce n'est que rêves malsains [. . .] Je veux être idéaliste, matérialiste, spiritualiste, sensualiste, panthéiste, sceptique, chrétien, païen; et je veux être moi en étant tout cela. (*C1*:66)

This places a characteristic emphasis on health; he rejects lifeless idealism, preferring the symphonic approach of a strong temperament able to embrace both idealism and materialism. The one promising new name was Ibsen, currently being introduced to Paris at the Théâtre de l'Œuvre. Rolland saw something of himself in this 'homme du Nord qui a eu le malheur de voir le midi' (*C1*:48), and responded to Ibsen's denunciation of social hypocrisy, but he mistrusted art which argued a thesis, and found no consolation in Ibsen's bleak vision. He wrote to Ibsen, but had only a polite reply.

In the winter of 1891–2, Rolland started two more plays. For lack of inspiration among the moderns he turned to the grace and serenity of Sophoclean tragedy, which he tried to recapture in *Niobé*, his only verse work. The story is familiar; Niobe offends Apollo by boasting of her children's beauty and is punished by seeing them struck dead, while her brother Atreus is pursued by the Furies for his murder of Thyestes's children. There are echoes of *Orsino* in the defiant pride of Tantalus's children, a personal nostalgia for Southern beauty and a consoling pantheist touch in the conclusion when Hermes tells Niobe that her children, freed from their tragic destiny, sleep in nature, their souls blended with the immortal soul. This too was rejected by the Comédie Française; later plans to revise it for Eleonora Duse came to nothing.

The other play of this period, *Caligula*, is a drama of scorn akin to *Timon of Athens*. In a decadent Rome, three men stand out but fail to master the situation. Caligula himself, embittered by his childhood, aspires to immortality, but seeks it only through evil deeds; he embodies the Empedoclean reign of hatred. Messala cultivates ironic detachment but makes no attempt to change the world; his sole achievement is dignified serenity in suicide. Crates, a sculptor hired to immortalize Caligula in a statue, has a robuster ideal of humanity, but Hamlet-like procrastination ruins his plan to assassinate the emperor. Fortinbras awaits in the person of Corbulon, a general winning victories against the Eastern barbarians whom Rolland expected soon to overrun the Europe of his own day, but Corbulon is far away, and Caligula succumbs to a conspiracy of freed slaves with the idiot Claudius as its figurehead; the only victor is corruption. *Caligula* is a pessimistic work whose keynote is the failure to act; Messala, though later described by Rolland as 'mon préféré d'alors' (*M*:210), shows the inadequacy of Renanesque irony, and in Crates the author castigates his incapacity as artist to impose himself on the world. The subject of this play was 'terrible à supporter pour un cerveau déjà un peu fou, comme le mien' (*C1*:74); he never attempted to have it performed.

Caligula is not even mentioned in a May 1892 document entitled 'Préface à mon Théâtre'. He takes as his first principle 'l'art pour l'art', not a Parnassian cult of empty form, but an art free of the socio-moral concerns of Tolstoy or Ibsen, dedicated to 'l'expression du fond impériss-able de l'Etre'. His second principle is 'l'art du peuple'; the rise of the people is 'la Force mystérieuse qui mène notre siècle', and the theatre should serve it. The genres envisaged reflect Rolland's twin concerns with dream and action. A theatre of action appeals to the whole nation through subjects such as Saint Louis, Joan of Arc and the Revolution, and should aim, like *Orsino*, to inspire. A theatre of dream should follow *Empédocle* in an ironic play of ideas, or *Niobé* in its Olympian serenity, but this is a remote ideal, 'l'art d'après les Révolutions qui remplirent notre siècle'. Realist drama and Ibsen's sermons have their place, but they are not for Rolland; art should not just imitate reality, but extend man within the limits of the possible. He concludes with a pantheistic declaration: '"Dieu a créé l'homme", dit-on. Mais l'homme le lui rend bien! Il est loin d'avoir fini de créer Dieu!' (*M*:140–4). In this document, Rolland sets himself an agenda, much of which he went on to realize; he resists mediocrity, corruption and death, and seeks to stimulate the heroic faculties through which man fulfils his divinity. The plan is ambitious and quixotic; to succeed, he would need a dramatic revolution which proved far from easy.

This was written shortly after Rolland met Clotilde Bréal, whom he married in October 1892. The courtship was rapid and the approach to the marriage stormy and fraught with misgivings; he knew he would be difficult to live with, his mother, upset that there would be no religious ceremony, came close to refusing to attend, and there was the problem of Claudine Funck-Brentano, who had formed unrequited feelings for him. She had the support of Malwida, who disliked Clotilde, and Rolland was made to feel he had treated her badly. Clotilde was a music lover, highly intelligent and in emotional disarray after the death of her mother and her music teacher, César Franck. Rolland felt he had found a woman who could share his ideals, but he knew her roots were in the Paris he despised, and on the eve of the wedding he made the amazing request that Suarès should join them on the honeymoon so that they could mould her character together:

> Elle est de notre temps (ce qu'il a fait de mieux). Il s'agit de l'y enlever, car nous n'en sommes pas, nous. Je sais ce que les six premiers mois d'amour ou d'amitié peuvent sur une jeune âme, pour la transformer; mais ce qu'elle est après, elle le reste presque toujours [. . .] Il faut qu'elle sache de qui elle est la femme, de qui elle est l'amie, – et tout ce qu'elle peut et *doit*, pour sa propre grandeur.[2]

This suggests that Rolland sensed from the start the disharmony which undermined their marriage. Suarès, unsurprisingly, declined the invitation.

Rolland met Clotilde through the Monods. Her father was the philologist Michel Bréal, Renan's friend, highly placed in the university world which Rolland so mistrusted, and as such there was potential tension between them. Rolland speaks with affection of his kind broad-mindedness, but at times he sensed a threat to his independence. The family was Jewish, which worried Rolland's family more than Rolland himself, who had already battled against anti-Semitism on Suarès's behalf; Sofia, too, had a Jewish mother. Yet it did create a barrier between himself and his wife's milieu, and irritation at his in-laws, predictable enough in a thin-skinned young husband, led him at times to the verge of anti-Semitism. The focus of his irritation was young Léon Blum, who moved in the Paris literary world with an ease which repelled Rolland. Blum married Clotilde's cousin in 1895; Rolland resisted family attempts to impose Blum's friendship upon him, and Clotilde, ominously, sided with her family.

Bréal agreed to the marriage on condition that Rolland worked for his doctorate. Rolland grumbled, but he found a congenial subject, and the couple spent their first year in Rome, researching the origins of opera. Rolland amassed an immense amount of material on neglected seventeenth-century music, Clotilde was his loyal assistant and the honeymoon was happy; the return to Paris in 1893 was less euphoric, but he was awarded his doctorate in June 1895. He gives an amusing description of his examination; none of the jury understood him and they were struck by his dogmatic approach (*M*:222), but his work was genuinely original and it began to make him a name.

A thesis on music history was a novelty, but Rolland felt it could contribute to historiography in general because of the immediate access music gives to the soul of its creator: 'Quelques pages d'un grand musicien apprennent plus sur son âme que ses biographies ou ses lettres' (*HO*:9). By this power, music reveals the intimate spirit of an age, and Rolland's study of it was always closely linked with biography of musicians. Opera was relevant to Rolland's theatrical ambitions, for it unleashes vitality in a way that appealed to the creator of *Orsino*, to whom morality in art was secondary to dynamism:

> Ce sont de terribles puissances [que les maîtres du drame lyrique] ont entre les mains; en elles-mêmes elles ne sont ni bonnes, ni mauvaises; à vrai dire, elles sont bonnes toujours, puisque ce sont des forces pour l'action, mauvaises seulement par l'usage qu'on en fait. (*HO*:13)

In studying early opera, Rolland raises questions about the relationship of art and action, and also about what his own art could achieve in decadent times.

Rolland performed a real service to music history by rehabilitating many forgotten musicians. Alessandro Scarlatti, then one of the earliest recognized opera composers, was for Rolland merely the decadent end of a cyclic evolution whose beginnings were in the Vecchi madrigal. Opera found its form among the Florentine aristocracy and reached its peak in Monteverdi, the Wagner of his day, whose vivid expression of passion created a truly popular theatre; Rolland was one of the first modern scholars to rediscover this forgotten master. After Monteverdi, wealthy aristocratic patrons drove the form into decadence, although Carissimi and Provenzale were still popular composers in the best sense. As opera declined in Italy it spread through Europe, but only the Italians could balance dream and action; German music theatre, too inclined to dream, privileged music over words, while the French, too inclined to action, privileged words over music. This somewhat naïve typology of national styles raises the issue of whether cosmopolitan art is desirable. Lully, the authoritarian Florentine stifling the development of a specifically French style, exemplifies what Rolland considers the wrong kind of order, based on suppression rather than harmonization of conflicting elements.[3] Seeing history in terms of cyclic historical process was not original; it was common in a generation dominated by the hated Taine. Yet it harmonizes with his vision of the Empedoclean cycle of love and hate, and is given point by his sense of living in a decadent age. His views on what a popular artist might be in such an age are pertinent to his own aspirations:

> Il y a deux sortes d'artistes populaires: les uns, mêlés à la vie de leur siècle, sont le reflet de ses caprices, et donnent des jours qui passent un écho harmonieux et éclatant; ce sont les génies d'occasion. Les autres, plongeant leurs racines dans la bonne terre de la patrie, prêtent une voix aux puissances magiques qui dorment dans son sein. Ceux-là sont les vrais génies, les apparitions mystérieuses de l'esprit de la race. Aux époques de grandeur, quand la nation est arrivée à la mûre moisson de ses forces, cet esprit s'épanouit [. . .] Aux époques de décadence, il n'en va plus de même. C'est à force de volonté, de recueillement et de profondeur, que le génie parvient à retrouver [. . .] les veines fécondes où toute la vie de la terre s'est réfugiée. (*HO*:155–6)

The true popular artist is not the amuser, but the one who incarnates the profound soul of the people. At high times of a nation's history he may play a public role, but in decadent ages he withdraws into himself and keeps the flame alive until times improve. Schütz, the composer of the Thirty Years' War, is such an artist; this was how Rolland saw himself in the coming decade of obscurity.

Decadence is analysed further in Rolland's secondary thesis, a study of Italian painting, less original in its material but vigorously argued. The phenomenon seems to him inherent in the Renaissance itself. Led by the Florentines, Italian painting tended to observe nature filtered through the intellect:

> Tant que cette intelligence est neuve encore, elle se contente de surveiller les sensations, et de se former à leur école; mais lorsqu'elle est remplie d'idées apprises, elle déforme et tyrannise ce qu'elle observe [. . .] L'idéalisme italien prête aux objets un charme ou un accent, qui leur appartient moins qu'à l'esprit où ils se mirent. (*C9*:139–40)

While the movement is young, intelligence structures genuine sentiment and great art results, but once it passes its peak, the intellect loses touch with nature, fostering an idealism remote from reality and an obsession with past models, particularly dangerous when the model is the genius of Michelangelo which lesser mortals cannot understand. This accompanies a moral weakening, and the result is the empty formalism of Del Sarto and the corrupt sensuality of Correggio. The reforms of the Carraccis failed, but Italy inspired the rest of Europe, where her faults were corrected by Poussin, Rubens, Rembrandt and Velasquez. In this one glimpses again Rolland's concern with the causes of contemporary decadence: weariness, weakness of character, fleshless idealism and excess analysis. A tone of moral indignation emerges as the author castigates even Michelangelo, Leonardo and Raphael, whose very virtues contribute to decline. Rolland's minor thesis is a thinly veiled polemic, related to his two plays of decadence, *Caligula* and *Le Siège de Mantoue*.

This latter play was conceived on honeymoon in Rome, but not written until 1894. It is set in a besieged Italian city, about to fall to German barbarians but wallowing in pleasures and party politics as if there were no tomorrow. Unlike *Caligula*, it presents a few characters rising above the corruption. The draper Claudio organizes civic resistance despite aristocratic intrigues against him. The painter Olivier, modelled on Raphael, and Ariane, daughter of a treacherous Marquis, are a Romeo and Juliet destroyed by political intrigue. The sickly Persée foreshadows Olivier Jeannin, and the organist-priest Pier-Maria brings balm with his music and words of pantheist consolation, preaching resignation to the rhythms of history. His words are echoed, as the curtain falls on a scene of *Götterdämmerung*-like destruction, by an Empedoclean chorus:

> La haine fait ton œuvre et balaye la boue,
> Tu te sers du néant, pour tuer le néant.
> Dieu, fais que je sois fort, pour le combat suprême,
> Que je ne haïsse point même ce qui me tue,
> Et que, pareil aux fleuves qui courent vers la mer,
> Je répande ma vie, afin d'alimenter
> La tienne, Eternité. (*M*:212)

The lives lost will return to the ocean of Being, and the destruction of the old world will release a new cycle of love, prefigured in Olivier and Ariane, the only lovers in Rolland's early plays who live and die together in harmony. The play reflects the happiest period of Rolland's marriage; it remained a favourite of his.

While finishing his theses, Rolland accepted part-time work in an attempt to earn independence from his wife's dowry. He taught art history in Paris *lycées*, and for a year gave a course on civic morality in an unprestigious suburban school. The latter, from which he was saved by nomination to the Ecole Normale Supérieure on completion of his doctorate, was one of the least agreeable experiences of his life. He did not believe in what he was teaching; civic morality was the state educational system's way of claiming moral respectability in the battle against religious education, and in later years Rolland expressed respect for the ideals behind it (*M*:241), but he found them hard to apply. Writing to Malwida, he raises two objections:

> J'ai peu d'intérêt et même un certain éloignement pour les questions morales, *prises en elles-mêmes*, indépendamment d'une foi (religieuse ou métaphysique) qui les soutienne. Devoir, Bien et Conscience, me semblent sans la foi, des noix vides, de vagues fumées [. . .] C'est la foi que je voudrais enseigner, la foi dans les héros, et dans la Divinité. Mais mes programmes de cours sont tout laïques [. . .] En revanche, j'y enseigne la supériorité du gouvernement de la République, l'excellence de l'armée, du capital, etc., – enfin tout ce qu'il faut pour persuader à un mouton qu'il est né pour être mangé. (*C1*:123)

First, he considered faith more important than morality and could not envisage one without the other. This reflects the fact that, during 1894, he was going through a pro-Catholic phase. A reaction against materialism and symbolist idealism, it was given focus by the atmosphere of his family and professional circles:

> Même chez les grands Juifs et les grands protestants, à qui la Troisième République avait confié presque exclusivement la réorganisation de l'enseignement et le gouvernement de l'intelligence, avait cours une dépréciation railleuse de la foi catholique, dont ces honnêtes gens ne mesuraient point le caractère – ou l'effet – insultant. (*M*:230)

Rolland is almost certainly thinking of Monod and Bréal; in face of their possibly unwitting persecution of Catholicism, Rolland swung back to the faith he esteemed in his mother. While preaching civic virtue in Auteuil, he worked on a play about Saint Louis.

His Catholicism was soon replaced by socialism. The key to this change is in his second objection to Malwida, that civic morality was an instrument of social conformism designed to keep the masses obedient. A note of 1895, anticipating many of his future themes, claims that the whole of contemporary morality is in transformation, and the forms of society with it:

> Sur presque tous les points, – famille, patrie, Etat, – une morale nouvelle surgissait: – l'autorité des parents ébranlée par les droits des enfants, l'émancipation de la femme, conquise par elle contre l'homme, la charité, vertu inefficace, supplantée par la justice et l'obligation sociale, la guerre convaincue de crime, la patrie discutée, ramenée au rôle d'étape vers un idéal d'association humaine, plus vaste et plus haut. (*M*:243)

As, in the year of the Panama scandal, he taught establishment platitudes to streetwise urchins who knew that neither he nor they believed them, Rolland began to think critically about society and welcome the possibility of revolution. This did not make him an activist. He was resistant to party discipline, was no great reader of socialist texts and resented being regimented by socialists such as Lucien Herr, the authoritarian Ecole Normale librarian, with whom he quarrelled after refusing to be bullied into signing a petition whose contents he agreed with (*M*:286). What appealed to him in socialism was a force and faith that might regenerate a decadent world, and he conceived his socialist role in religious terms:

> L'action politique ne saurait être mon fait; je m'y associerai, quand il sera nécessaire, sans m'affubler d'une tâche que je porterais mal. Mon rôle, tel que je le conçois, sera d'abord de faire rentrer le divin dans la révolution sociale, qui s'en est dépouillée, dans les années de découragement qui ont suivi 1848. (*M*:253–4)

Rolland's pantheism could accommodate socialism as one means of releasing the divine in man, but he knew that this was not how contemporary socialists saw themselves, and this discouraged close integration in the movement. The religious dimension to his socialism does, however, demonstrate that behind his apparently capricious evolution lies a profound consistency. He hoped to serve socialism by creating inspiring art, but there was to be no socialist *Saint-Louis*. Before the Dreyfus case, his one attempt to treat contemporary subjects was the unfinished *Les Vaincus*, which did not satisfy him. His short-term expedient with his Auteuil pupils was to read them *Les Misérables*; this apparently had some effect, and it taught him that practical example had more impact than theoretical instruction, a lesson from which he profited in the *Vies des hommes illustres*.

Once appointed to the Ecole Normale, his life outwardly stabilized. He was busy preparing lectures on art and music history, subjects which he loved despite his distaste for teaching. As well as his plays, there was the slow evolution of what became *Jean-Christophe*, parts of which date to 1896. His social life was not active; he and Clotilde enjoyed travelling, visiting Provence, Italy, Germany, England and of course Switzerland, but he felt no urge to develop a wide social circle in Paris. He had contacts in the university and found supporters among his students, notably the Tharaud brothers and Louis Gillet, the latter filling the gap left by Suarès, whose difficult character combined with Clotilde's dislike had caused them to drift apart. Otherwise, Rolland chose not to cultivate acquaintances he did not respect; the salon circles which amused him in Rome lost their appeal in Paris.

Clotilde, who lacked Rolland's faith, would have preferred a more active social life. She had been willing to make sacrifices to help her husband establish himself, but only in the hope of a successful career, and once Rolland had completed his theses it was clear that their aspirations were different. He did not wish to shine in the university, and failure at the Comédie Française led him not, as one might expect, to approach less prestigious theatres, but to stop trying to seek performance. *Saint-Louis* was published in the *Revue de Paris*, to which Clotilde submitted it without his knowledge (*LU*:31), but he did not like that journal and resented the support of Jules Lemaître, who understood him so little that he thought the sympathetic character in the play was the unbeliever Manfred (*M*:273). Rolland resented supporters who failed to understand him, and in May 1896 his notes reflect a sense that his creative development required him to restrict his contact with the surrounding world:

> Le rôle vrai du génie est de créer un monde, de toutes pièces, organiquement constitué, selon ses lois intérieures. Pour cela, il doit y vivre tout entier, il lui faut croire absolument que ce monde intérieur est le seul vrai. Or, ce ne lui sera plus possible, s'il ne s'y bloque hermétiquement, s'il se mêle et s'il se fond dans l'être des autres hommes [. . .] Mais si, parmi ces 'autres' qui l'entourent, il en est qu'il aime et dont il soit aimé, malheur à lui! Car, à moins de les entraîner despotiquement dans sa foi, [. . .] c'est sa foi qui, chaque jour, s'émiette entre leurs doigts. (*M*:257–8)

This uncompromising attitude was related to the emergence that year of the characters of Christophe and Aert, but its price was domestic disharmony, reflected in all five plays between *Saint-Louis* and *Les Vaincus*.

The ending of *Saint-Louis* recalls *Orsino*, with the hero leading his troops into battle in defiance of impending death, but more is at stake here than individual self-assertion. Louis is a man of faith, who overcomes his weak body and galvanizes all of France into action behind him. This play presents a French people capable of the heights of self-sacrifice in the name of a faith, in this instance the Christianity of the Crusades, but other faiths have the same effect, and *Saint-Louis* prefigures *Le Quatorze Juillet* in its ambitious attempt to represent a people in action, using complex crowd scenes and devices such as taking a child – Bérengère in this play, Julie in the later play – as a voice of popular fervour.

The main conflict is not the king's battle against his weakness, or even against the pagans, but rather against the unbelievers around him, such as Manfred, an enemy agent whose ironic verve goes some way to excuse Lemaître, and Gaultier de Salisbury, a violent baron whose sole faith is superstitious fear of damnation. The battleground is the vacillating souls of Thibault and Rosalie de Brèves. Rolland put much of himself into Thibault, another forerunner of Olivier Jeannin; Brèves was his father's home village, and Thibault expresses a nostalgia for home rare in Rolland's work before *Colas Breugnon*:

> O Morvan, collines bleues, rivières transparentes, saules de pâle argent, comme un ruisseau léger; voûtes profondes des forêts; auguste bourdonnement des cloches de Vézelay, qui dresse sur son roc, au-dessus de la plaine, sa sainte cathédrale aux deux puissantes tours; chant lointain qui me vient de mon doux Nivernais! (*TF*:77)

Thibault's situation is a projection of Rolland's; his bored wife succumbs to Gaultier who engineers Thibault's death, then she makes public penance, devoting the rest of her life to serving the king. The play ends with a paradoxical vision of 'le vaincu vainqueur' which often recurs in Rolland's work; Louis's army is shattered, but instead of retreating he thrusts on to Jerusalem and dies poised to attack it, snatching spiritual victory from the jaws of material defeat.

In the fragment *Savonarole*, dating from early 1896, the hero is another physically weak man of faith, but at an earlier stage of evolution, fighting against his own weakness before committing himself to action. He is a rebel against a society which recalls *Le Siège de Mantoue*; Rolland toyed with making Luther or Zwingli his hero, but in Savonarola he focuses his attack on the Florentine Renaissance. Uneasy about the moral implications of ill-directed vitality, Rolland reacted against the mood of *Orsino*. A reading of the repellant memoirs of Aretino led him to castigate his previous cult of the *condottiere*: 'Dans mon ardeur d'enfant à adorer l'Uebermensch [. . .], j'ai vu de l'héroïsme où il n'y en avait pas trace' (*C1*:168). Among the work's characters are Botticelli, an intelligent if effete representative of Florentine society, and Maria Strozzi, a former sweetheart of the hero despatched by the authorities to undermine him, but inspired by him to devote herself to charitable works; like Rosalie de Brèves, she is a projection of Rolland's wish to impart his faith to his wife.[4] The closing scene is another Wagnerian immolation by fire; the flames from Savonarola's stake threaten to engulf Florence.

Jeanne de Piennes, also written in 1896, and *Aert*, written a year later, were both highly regarded by their creator. Eschewing ambitious stage effects, they return with profit to the disciplines of traditional French theatre, and their central characters, close to Rolland's heart, are isolated youths trying to sustain their ideals in a corrupt world. Of *Jeanne de Piennes* Rolland wrote: 'J'ai une tendresse particulière pour cette pièce, parce qu'elle est plus pure moralement que les autres, et parce qu'il n'y a rien là pour l'effet' (*C22*:50). Its setting is the court of Henri II, it shares some characters with *La Princesse de Clèves*,[5] and both heroines have the same uncompromising integrity in love. Jeanne is secretly engaged to François de Montmorency, whose father, the Connétable, wants him to marry the king's illegitimate daughter. Jeanne fights to keep her lover, confessing to the Connétable that she has slept with him, but the Connétable suppresses the information to prevent its use by political rivals. Jeanne stands trial, François betrays her and she retires to her estates to devote herself to charity, her friend Robertet commenting on 'l'énorme puissance du royaume de France unie pour écraser une pauvre petite fille'. As in *Savonarole*, Rolland's interest lies in the corruption of a Renaissance society uncomfortably like his own, and his sympathies are with the heroine who fails to communicate her faith. Despite the reversal of roles, the analogy with Rolland's domestic situation is clear.

In *Aert*, the hero is heir to an ousted Dutch dynasty, held captive by a usurping Stadhouder who rules with Spanish support. Though surrounded by people professing to cherish his interests, young Aert is in fact victim of a systematic attempt to corrupt him and neutralize him as a nationalist figurehead. He makes contact with a group of rebels, but is betrayed by his cynical friend Dirck and by Lia, the Stadhouder's daughter; the revolt is suppressed, and Aert leaps from his window to die with his supporters. This clash between an idealistic youth and a corrupt environment is made more poignant by the genuine affection Aert inspires. The analogies between Lia and Clotilde hardly need emphasis; more interesting, perhaps, is the maternal style of her affection. She is married, older than Aert, and in the scene between them which takes the whole second act she plays mother to him in a way which points to the influence of Rolland's own over-protective mother.

What is new in this play is its political focus. It reflects a visit to Germany in 1896 which crystallized Rolland's vision of that nation, divided between an idealistic past and a materialistic present. He admired the old Germany of Beethoven and Goethe, but prolonged contact with modern Germany focused his attention on 1870 and its consequences. French defeat and decadence seemed to be related, and he formed a more nuanced attitude to nationalist warfare than the visceral fear which had dominated his reactions so far. He writes to Malwida: 'Je ne crois pas [. . .] que la guerre soit le plus grand des maux. Une paix jouisseuse et matérialiste est bien plus funeste à l'humanité, qu'une guerre rendue nécessaire par de nobles raisons' (*C1*:185). *Aert*, like *Saint-Louis*, suggests that a just war sustained by faith would be preferable to wallowing in spiritless quiescence. Lia, Dirck, the Stadhouder and Trojanus, the kind of peace-at-any-price intellectual with whom Rolland never identified, believe Holland would be better at peace even under foreign domination, a view which to Aert is just as corrupting as the sexual temptations put in his way. The outcome is again 'le vaincu vainqueur'; Aert's ideals conquer at the cost of his death.

It is misleading, however, to view this play as a 'drame de la Revanche'.[6] It is certainly no blanket approval of war; writing to Clotilde's brother Auguste, he asserts his hatred of 'la guerre comme on la fait aujourd'hui, la guerre marchande, la guerre d'intérêts, de spéculations financières, d'affaires commerciales et politiques' (*C17*:56). War is acceptable only in defence of ideals and as a prelude to a juster peace, not as an aid to commerce. This idea, anticipating his attitude in 1916, would have been more fully treated had Rolland fulfilled his original aim of writing a trilogy in which Aert would escape, lead a revolt and ultimately conquer peace, but the project was curtailed for the sake of writing a performable play. Under family pressure, Rolland compromised and modified his text: 'J'ai cédé [. . .] au douloureux désir de me voir enfin représenté sur une scène' (*M*:279). The work was performed in May 1898, with modest success, at the Théâtre de l'Œuvre, for which Rolland had little esteem, but once the ice was broken he formed a cordial relationship with its director, Lugné-Poë. With the actress who played Aert, Cora Laparcerie, he formed the kind of affectionate friendship possible only when complete dissimilarity of temperament precludes anything more intimate.

Last in this series of plays was the unfinished *Les Vaincus*, sketched late in 1897, the bitterest reflection yet of Rolland's marital disharmony, which makes the major departure of portraying a present-day social conflict. Its inspiration is the assassination of Sadi Carnot, transferred to the context of an industrial dispute. Georges Berthier, a teacher, sympathizes with a group of striking workers, but is restrained by a distaste for violence and the bourgeois prejudices of his wife. As with his creator, his tongue runs away with him in debate; this costs him his job, and a chance remark of his inspires an Italian worker to murder the factory owner. Unwillingly implicated in violence, Berthier is joined in suicide by his wife's sister, with whom he is timidly in love, and the play ends cataclysmically as the strikers march into government gunfire. No sympathy is expressed for the dead couple by the strikers; Berthier's sole supporter is the enigmatic Boehmer, who takes the long historical view, concludes that the world never changes and refuses to join the strikers. It is not clear whether he is inspired by defeatism or a Pier-Maria-like serenity.

Berthier's suicide lacks the triumphant assertion of Aert's, and the modern setting makes the situation all the more oppressive. As the author contemplates social upheaval, Hamlet-like hesitations obscure the way forward; men like Berthier who strive for justice above party cannot act effectively, and if they attempt action they cannot master it. He is the most autobiographical character in Rolland's early dramas, but he embodies only Rolland's doubts. Rolland aimed to offer his public vitality and heroism, not weakness and impotence, and *Les Vaincus* is not the kind of play he wanted to write, but in 1921, when revolutionary action was again problematic, he considered it relevant enough to publish it.

Rolland's aims in these plays are summarized in this 1896 note:

Ce qui importe, c'est l'énergie de l'âme, la grandeur, l'héroïsme [. . .] On estimera que j'ai flotté parmi les opinions diverses, sans savoir me décider. Cependant, mon objet n'a jamais varié: faire surgir de toutes les formes de la foi et du doute le feu caché, l'éternité que chacun porte en soi, quoi qu'il pense et qu'il croie, s'il veut seulement être un homme. (*VI*:245)

Contemporaries indeed found it hard to understand this man who considered the psychological force of faith more important than its precise form, who sympathized with Catholics and socialists without identifying with either, who could strive both to animate partisan vitality and to rise above it to a serene vision of vast cyclic processes. As soon as the Dreyfus affair began to bring him into the public eye, he found himself misunderstood. Yet the above quotation indicates a strong substratum of consistency; faith needed to be revived, and his mission was to stimulate it in whatever form.

Notes

1. Letter to Malwida von Meysenbug, 27 November 1891.
2. Letter to A. Suarès, 26 October 1892.
3. Rolland took a kinder view of Lully in his later article in *Musiciens d'autrefois*.
4. See Duret (1992), p.238.
5. Rolland had reread that work recently, though with little enthusiasm; see letter to Malwida von Meysenbug, 12 March 1895.
6. See Robichez (1961), p.41.

Heroes (I): Plays and Biographies

Politics were not Rolland's main concern in the 1890s. His socialism was more a faith than a programme, and it would be hard to pin him down to a set of policies more precise than distaste for materialism, hatred of war, distrust of modern Germany and a desire for France to behave honourably. This left him ill-prepared for the Dreyfus affair, but well equipped to keep his head in it.

Rolland's thoughts first turned seriously to Dreyfus in November 1896, when at a dinner party Monod voiced fears that the case for Dreyfus was being suppressed, and spoke of massacres in Armenia. Both crimes appalled Rolland, but he noted that French politicians were making more of the former than of the latter, greater crime. This suggested that political convenience more than moral indignation was at work, and his in-laws confirmed this by uncritically supporting their fellow Jew. Rolland's own family were patriots reluctant to believe in a state machination against an innocent man (*M*:287), he himself found the evidence unclear, and he saw strengths and weaknesses on both sides. Writing in December 1897, he tartly observes that 'je n'ai pas vu un Juif qui ne fût convaincu de l'innocence de Dreyfus, et pas un catholique qui ne le fût de son crime' (*C1*:216). Sympathy for the underdog and hatred of injustice inclined him towards Dreyfus, but in February 1898 he could still declare to his dogmatic friend Suarès that 'la défense nationale est le premier devoir de la France', that Jewish money threatens it, and that of the two possible correctives, socialism and Catholicism, the latter, more rooted in French history, stands more chance of success (*LU*:73–4). This is a fleeting outburst, but it contrasts sharply with his return to the Dreyfusard camp after Zola's condemnation, which inspired *Les Loups* in the following month.

The first draft was finished in a week, and Rolland frightened himself with it (*M*:290). It transposes the affair to the 1793 siege of Mainz, where the Dreyfus figure is D'Oyron, a suspect aristocrat in the Revolutionary army. He is implicated in a royalist plot, but Teulier, a scientist turned soldier who corresponds to Colonel Picquart, considers the evidence has been falsified by a fellow officer, the *sans-culotte* Verrat. Quesnel, the commander, finds it inexpedient to favour D'Oyron, who is executed and Teulier is sent before the Committee of Public Safety. The Dreyfusard implications are obvious, but no sooner was the draft complete than Rolland revised it to make the situation less clear. Originally, Verrat's crime was actually to forge a letter – this at a time before the Henry forgery became known – but in the final version he merely suppresses evidence that the forger is D'Oyron's estranged *émigré* brother, which diminishes Verrat's guilt without confirming D'Oyron's innocence. Neither D'Oyron nor Teulier are particularly attractive characters, and Quesnel has some excuse for rejecting Teulier's case. The play thus loses its partisan character; Teulier's scruples are pitted against genuine patriots willing to sacrifice life and reputation for their country. Quesnel's closing word is: 'Que mon nom soit flétri, mais que la patrie soit sauvée!' (*TRL*:94)

Les Loups reveals a Rolland already 'au-dessus de la mêlée', seeking to set partisan conflict in a broader context in which the responsibility lies with 'l'implacable Destin [. . .] qui est le vrai coupable de tous les crimes de l'humanité' (*C1*:231). Though basically siding with Teulier, he recognizes that Quesnel is doing his duty, and wants to celebrate what is positive on both sides, 'porter à la génération future l'écho de la vie tumultueuse qui nous emporte' (*M*:291). He celebrates vitality wherever he finds it, and perhaps the vitality unleashed by Dreyfus indicates that France is not as moribund as he had thought. He writes to Auguste Bréal: 'Ma pièce est faite pour l'unique gloire de la patrie française, grande même quand elle se déchire' (*LU*:120).

Rolland's hesitation over Dreyfus has caused eyebrows to be raised, not least his own (*M*:284–6), but his attitude is consistent with the *Credo quia Verum*'s desire to break down barriers rather than strengthen them, also with the detached vision of the Janiculum 'éclair'. His natural timidity enters into it, as does the influence of his in-laws, pressing him either to be silent or say things he did not want to say. A further key may lie in an 1896 letter to Malwida, explaining why he does not attack a pet aversion, Sarah Bernhardt:

> Toute cette odieuse clique m'écraserait dès les premiers pas, et ma vie serait barrée. Je dois attendre à être un peu fort déjà, et d'avoir un public. Mais je ronge mon frein. Que de choses j'amasse dans mon cœur, et qui en sortiront un jour, si je vis! (*C1*:190)

Rolland was far from naïve, and capable of calculated career moves; his correspondence with Lugné-Poë shows him well able to operate in the rough-and-tumble of theatre intrigue. He knew that an unknown could be stifled, he sensed the need to restrain his attacks until he was established, and Dreyfus came too soon for him. His caution is shown by his use of a pseudonym, Saint-Just, for the first performance, to avoid compromising *Les Loups* if *Aert*, performed only a fortnight before, had proved a failure.

The first performance, on 18 May 1898, created a stir. Word had spread, Picquart was present and the audience was noisily partisan. Rolland, however, felt misunderstood. The public did not respond to his wish for even-handedness; like many a prophet of moderation, he found himself isolated in no-man's-land. In retrospect he claims serene detachment – 'Je frétillais d'aise, dans ce vacarme, comme un poisson dans l'eau' (*M*:294) – but at the time he told Malwida of his disgust at discovering that 'il y a quelque chose de pire que d'être haï pour ce qu'on est; c'est d'être loué pour ce qu'on n'est pas' (*C1*:232). Afterwards he feared that, like Georges Berthier, he might lose his teaching post, but all that happened was that he had difficulty publishing the play, which he refused to give to Jewish publishers (*C1*:233). In the end it appeared in a small publishing house run by Gillet's friend, Charles Péguy.

Rolland's work was beginning to become known. His theatrical contacts broadened; through Suarès he met Maurice Pottecher, organizer of a pioneering village theatre in the Vosges, who introduced him to Lucien Besnard, editor of the *Revue d'art dramatique*, where he joined a team of writers trying to create a theatre for the people. At the same time he began to take more of an interest in politics. He attended parliamentary debates, and was impressed by the sheer theatre of the orators of the far left, 'le seul parti qui parût vivant' (*M*:296), battling against a hostile assembly. Millerand, Guesde and Jaurès fascinated him, and left their mark on the dramatic cycle which grew from *Les Loups*.

The Revolution had struck Rolland as a possible subject as early as 1892; like the age of Saint Louis, it revealed the French people fighting for a faith, and the historical documents were better. He did not believe that historical theatre needed to be slavishly faithful to fact, and his plays take many liberties, but he undertook extensive research to make the atmosphere authentic. He used the actual words of some of the figures he put on stage, finding that the declamatory tone of the age blended well with his own style. He felt he gained strength by rooting his art in the soil of his country, but at the same time he stressed the cosmic significance of events. He aimed to write a series of twelve plays, presenting the period as a historical cycle analogous with the Empedoclean alternation of love and hatred. In seeking to give full value to individual roles while situating them in a wider process, Rolland always favoured large cyclic constructions, and this is how he explains his project to Gillet:

> Croyez-vous que ce soit la Liberté ou la Révolution que je chante? – Non, mais une Tempête de l'humanité; je ne sers pas un parti; je vis, et je vois et je chante la Vie. La Vie et la Mort. La Force éternelle. Mon héros n'est pas Danton, ni Robespierre, ni le peuple, ni l'élite: il est la Vie. Ce peuple transfiguré par l'espoir de la résurrection, ce peuple adolescent et virginal des premiers jours de la Révolution, vous les verrez peu à peu s'avilir, s'ensanglanter, se domestiquer, et s'endormir. Vous verrez les héros libres peu à peu enchaînés par les liens de leur fatalité [. . .] Et vous aurez surtout l'impression d'un grand orage qui se forme dans un ciel tranquille et lourdement endormi [. . .], et qui après avoir couvert le monde de ruines, disparaît dans le ciel purifié et attendri. (*C2*:192–3)

Rolland's Revolution is a force of nature driven by destiny, a cosmic process evoked in celestial imagery anticipating the ending of *Les Léonides*, written thirty years later. It swings from peace through conflict and crisis to peace recovered, and the effect, since it enhances life, is beneficial.

Of the twelve plays only eight were written, and only four at this period. After *Les Loups*, *Le Triomphe de la raison* and *Danton* were performed in 1899, the former produced by Lugné-Poë, the latter at the Cercle des Escholiers, after a private performance at the Ecole Normale with Gillet in the title role. *Danton* was later staged for the benefit of a group of strikers, with an oration from Jaurès, whom Rolland saw as the modern Danton. *Le Quatorze Juillet* was presented by Firmin Gémier in 1902. With complex crowd scenes and musical elements inspired by composers of the period, these plays were ruinously expensive to perform; Rolland's refusal to let Gémier seek sponsors did not help. Though grateful to his interpreters, Rolland felt that they did not understand his blend of realism and heroism:

> C'était toute une esthétique du jeu et de la déclamation à substituer à celle des pattes sans ailes de l'école d'Antoine et à celle des ailes sans pattes du romantisme à la Mounet-Sully. Je n'avais ni la vocation, ni les dons naturels, ni le temps pour l'entreprendre. (*VI*:252)

His plays achieved only modest success. *Le Quatorze Juillet* collapsed unexpectedly after early signs of a good run, and the disappointment turned Rolland away from the theatre for years.

The first three plays are set during the Terror, when the Revolution was threatened by foreign war, internecine conflict and the decline of the revolutionary people. Apart from some noble roles, the vast majority of characters are committed Revolutionaries, and their genuine sacrificial fervour gives these plays a sustained heroic character. The tragedy springs from conflicting notions of Revolutionary ideals. In *Les Loups*, we have seen, the conflict is between Teulier's devotion to truth and the patriotism leading Quesnel and Verrat to sin against truth, and *Le Triomphe de la raison* similarly confronts purists with a popular movement as it begins to degenerate.

This ironically titled play explores conflicting concepts of the ideal of reason. It portrays a group of Girondins, tempted by military alliance with enemies of the Revolution, who choose instead to surrender to the Jacobins, confident that they have saved their faith and that their defeat will favour the triumph of their cause. Most idealistic among them is Adam Lux, who reveres Charlotte Corday for trying to bring peace by striking down hatred incarnate in Marat, but the Jacobin Haubourdin shows him that Marat, too, loved the people and that Charlotte Corday did evil by trying to do good. Like Berthier in *Les Vaincus*, Lux feels tainted by an assassination with which he is associated by proxy; to maintain his purity and spare anyone else responsibility for the crime of killing him, he commits suicide. During the war, Rolland's adversaries used Lux's claim that 'la victoire est mauvaise [. . . et] la défaite est bonne' (*TR*:69) to brand Rolland as a defeatist, and Rolland had to distance himself from a character who undoubtedly did reflect something of his mood at the time of writing. It is the Girondin leaders, however, Hugot and Faber, who express the play's main dilemma. Like Empédocle, they seek to work for the good of an unworthy people, and they await the guillotine amid frenzied celebrations of the cult of reason in a desecrated church. Gone are the early Revolutionary days when force and reason were united in popular action. Yet they too serve reason, and die identifying it with a destiny they have helped to form: 'O Raison, Raison, notre Dieu et notre création! Que ces hommes t'outragent: ils t'obéiront. Tu es la Loi. Tu es la reine de l'univers [. . .] Triomphe dans leurs orgies! Triomphe dans notre mort!' In a familiar paradox, physical defeat entails moral victory: 'J'ai devancé la victoire; mais je vaincrai!' (*TR*:80–1)

Danton portrays the power struggle between Danton and Robespierre. Their conflict is less ideological than personal; it echoes the struggle between Jaurès and Guesde, in which, though he admired Jaurès, Rolland felt that the Guesdistes held the moral high ground (*M*:301). Danton, full of a vitality that Rolland envied, has withdrawn from action because he is sickened with bloodshed, feeling it necessary that either he or Robespierre sacrifice their ambitions. Seeking to rise above partisan rivalries, he works with men Robespierre mistrusts, and his debauchery and venality bring suspicion upon him. Hamlet-like, he postpones action to protect himself, confident that his oratory can always save the day, but his stage-managed trial silences him.

Robespierre is a complex character. Rolland's researches led him to conclude that he was no ogre, but a man of vision and humanity trying, like Danton, to stop the Terror. Moreover he was a man of faith, a believer in the God of Rousseau opposed by Voltaireans like Vadier; in him the Revolution lost its chance of creating a truly new order. Rolland shared Robespierre's physical frailty and distaste for working with people he did not respect, and his letters to Malwida suggest that he sided more with Robespierre than Danton, though he probably exaggerated in reaction to Malwida's uneasiness about the way he was evolving (*C1*:245–6). Surrounded by traitors, Robespierre regards virtue as the key to national survival and accepts the distasteful task of extirpating vice. He grudgingly recognizes Danton's merits and is slow to move against him, yet when pressed to do so, his reluctance seems hypocritical; as the cynic Vadier understands, he needs to be fed virtuous-sounding arguments before following his desires. Yet his love of virtue is more humane than that of Saint-Just, who perceives vice even in his own nature and frightens Robespierre by his determination to root it out.

Both sides are humanized by their domestic life; Danton's supporter Desmoulins has his young wife Lucile, and Robespierre draws chaste consolation from his landlady and her daughter. Robespierre tries to save his schoolfriend Desmoulins, but events are no respecter of persons. Desmoulins, aware that his oratory has speeded Hébert's fall, is frightened by the way events are running out of control, but Saint-Just, like Hugot and Faber, sees himself as part of a historical process and is prepared to further it even at the cost of his life. His closing words: 'Les peuples meurent, pour que Dieu vive' (*TRD*:119), are not necessarily the essence of Rolland's thought, and like Lux's words they were later used against him, but they express the cosmic significance of the Revolution, and they accord with Rolland's pantheist notion of a divinity realizing itself through historical processes.

The fourth play, *Le Quatorze Juillet*, representing an earlier stage of the Revolution, joyfully celebrates a popular movement achieving an improbable victory by capturing a fortress whose defenders no longer believe in their task. Written in 1901, the darkest year of Rolland's life, he later saw it as 'un défi de la foi contre le désespoir'.[1] The play is an ambitious fresco, taking considerable historical liberties by assembling a cast of figures not all of whom were involved on the day. As well as

Desmoulins, the orator of the hour, there are roles for Marat, the paranoid but generous lover of the people, Hoche, the ideal Revolutionary soldier, Hulin, the strong man slow to be roused, Robespierre declaiming the Declaration of the Rights of Man and the actress La Contat, who loves the trappings of the old regime but is swept away by enthusiasm. Among the Bastille's defenders, Vintimille has ironic panache, but cannot hide his complete lack of faith. More important than any individual are the people of Paris discovering their force. Their fictional representatives, the sentry on the barricade and little Julie who, with Hoche, is the first to enter the Bastille, are as important as the leaders known to history. Ominous hints of the future appear in the frenzied massacre of the garrison, but they are palliated by the self-sacrificial willingness of the perpetrators to accept responsibility, and the play ends with a popular festivity in which Rolland hoped the audience would participate. Even this was merely the first step in a wider ambition: 'rallumer l'héroïsme et la foi de la nation aux flammes de l'épopée républicaine, afin que l'œuvre interrompue en 1794 soit reprise et achevée par un peuple plus mur et plus conscient de ses destinées' (*TRQ*:3). A religious dimension is hinted at in the palm branches waved in the closing scenes.[2] Their symbolism anticipates the opening play, written years later under the title of *Pâques-Fleuries*.

This of all his plays best reflects Rolland's interest in popular theatre, but by 1902 it was clear that little would come of the *Revue d'art dramatique*'s endeavours, which had failed to attract state support. In 1903, to defend the *Revue* and inform future generations of its efforts, Rolland collected some of his articles in a volume called *Le Théâtre du peuple*, his first significant polemic work. For Rolland, popular theatre should cater for a different set of needs from those covered by bourgeois theatre, and he begins with a sweeping rejection of the existing repertoire. Not content with attacking boulevard theatre and the bogus heroism of Rostand's *Cyrano de Bergerac*, he rejects most of French classical theatre and even his own favourites, the Greeks, Shakespeare and Wagner. Works which suited bourgeois intellectuals like himself risked infecting the working class with precisely the weaknesses that he was trying to throw off. Better models were offered by the dramatic thoughts of Rousseau, Diderot, Michelet and the French Revolutionaries, and Rolland praises Pottecher and a few recent ventures in the Paris suburbs. He addresses the organizational problems of popular theatre, such as ticket prices and the most appropriate type of building, and reflects on what type of play might be performed. Melodrama, plays inspiring thought on social issues, works based on popular legend and his own favourite, the historical epic, all come under consideration. The aim of popular theatre should be to promote joy, force and intelligence, but it should not do the people's job for it by specifying what to think or do; its task is to inspire. This is particularly important with moral issues, for preaching morality is not the task of the theatre:

> Au lieu de bonté, donnez-nous seulement plus de raison, plus de bonheur et plus d'énergie; la bonté, nous nous en chargeons. Le monde est plus sot que méchant, et méchant surtout par sottise. La grande tâche est de faire entrer plus d'air, plus de clarté, plus d'ordre dans le chaos de l'âme. Mais c'est assez de la mettre en état de penser et d'agir; ne pensons pas, n'agissons pas pour elle [. . .] De la santé. La morale n'est qu'une hygiène de l'esprit et du cœur. (*TP*:116–17)

Though much of what Rolland says in this volume is dictated by its specific circumstances, this statement points to wider issues. His rejection of prescriptive morality in favour of force and health is familiar; what is new is the idea that morality is the imposition of order on inner chaos and the emphasis placed on reason and artistic discipline. In later years this became central to Rolland's view of how art could contribute to action.

Rolland was readier than many of the *Revue d'art dramatique* team to accept the socialist implications of popular theatre. As he wrote in 1903 to Alphonse Séché, the journal's new editor: 'Je crois à la nécessité d'une révolution dramatique, qui renouvelle entièrement les pensées et la forme même du théâtre français. Cette révolution ne peut s'accomplir que par la révolution, ou l'évolution socialiste' (*C13*:24). In *Le Théâtre du peuple* he avoids mentioning socialism, to prevent the project from looking too partisan, but he clearly intends popular theatre to awaken and direct class consciousness. The present working class, he observes, can be divided into the less poor, whom the bourgeoisie absorbs, and the most poor, who are too abject to respond to popular theatre; Rolland's aim was to weld them together again:

> Non pas que nous cherchions à dresser haineusement une classe contre l'autre, mais que, tout au contraire, pour réaliser la plus riche harmonie des forces de la nation, nous voulons que chacune des classes qui la constituent, – et surtout celle où les énergies sont restées les plus saines et les plus neuves, – garde la saveur intacte de son individualité. (*TP*:106–7)

Working-class consciousness should be stimulated, not for class warfare, but to realize Rolland's ideal of harmony. The France he wanted was not one in which any particular element imposed its personality upon others; all should contribute in their own way, tapping the best sources of energy in a dormant nation. Such a France, however, does not yet exist. In his closing words, he asserts: 'Vous voulez un art du peuple? Commencez par avoir un peuple' (*TP*:169).

Two brief texts should be read alongside *Le Théâtre du peuple*. In 'Le Poison idéaliste', published in the *Revue d'art dramatique* in 1900, he attacks the false idealism of the 1890s, the neo-mysticism which had been an understandable reaction against positivism, but which now was an obstacle to reason, realism and national vitality; Wagner's seductions and Rostand's neo-Cornelian verbiage risked trapping France in a dream world. The only response is to separate true and false idealism and trust reality:

> Il faut voir la vie comme elle est et la dire comme elle est. Idéalistes, réalistes, tous ont le même devoir: prendre pour base l'observation réelle, les faits réels, les sentiments réels. Que, sur cette base, ils élèvent ensuite à leur gré une maison bourgeoise ou un palais poétique, une comédie réaliste ou un drame héroïque, c'est leur affaire. Mais d'abord, que l'œuvre ait les pieds bien appuyés au sol! (*CR*:19)

In his support he quotes 'le plus grand peintre idéaliste', Leonardo da Vinci: 'Trasmutarsi nella propria mente di natura' (*CR*:20–1); all ideals are meaningless unless firmly based on nature. More than in *Le Théâtre du peuple*, Rolland's catholicity of taste emerges from this document; there is more than one way of creating truthful art. His emphasis on reason and reality anticipates his move to the novel, away from the stylized world of theatre.

The second of these texts is a diary note of 1898, quoted in his *Mémoires*:

> 1e. – Ne jamais faire partie d'un groupe, d'une association politique. Toute association d'hommes corrompt les idées, pour lesquelles elle s'est assemblée, – les fait dévier de leur vrai sens. Je suis et je veux demeurer libre. Et si je fais la guerre, en marge d'un camp, je le ferai, seul responsable de moi seul. 2e. – Règle morale: – n'être jamais passif en rien, – même dans l'acceptation. Se soumettre, peut-être, – n'être pas soumis. – Se sacrifier, – ne pas se résigner. (*M*:316)

The second of these maxims holds few surprises; its main interest, perhaps, lies in the way it anticipates his later understanding of Gandhism. The first seems hard to conciliate with his socialism, but it does underline his resistance to party discipline; if he served a cause, it was freely and in his own way. This maxim is the key to his tactics for the next three decades; the only way he could operate was by maintaining independence in a partisan world. He achieved it at the cost of his marriage.

Clotilde remained attached to her social world, and in 1899, attempting to buy the success she wanted, Rolland abandoned the Revolution to write two plays in contemporary taste, set in the French seventeenth century, never his favourite period. *La Montespan* takes liberties with history to portray Louis XIV's fading mistress trying to retain influence through desperate measures and finally killing herself with poison prepared for the king; *Les Trois Amoureuses*, lighter in tone, portrays the rivalry of three women for the love of the Prince de Condé. Rolland became ashamed of these plays, dismissing them as 'les plus faibles œuvres que j'aie écrites' (*M*:307). This does not entirely reflect his view at the time; *Les Trois Amoureuses* was offered, unsuccessfully, to the Comédie Française, both works were published, and he thought there were good things in *La Montespan*. Their stagecraft is as competent as anything he wrote at that period. Yet apart from the main character of *La Montespan*, a striking personality rising above a mediocre age, they do little to further Rolland's ideals.

The Bréals disapproved of Rolland's Revolutionary theatre. In the euphoria of his completion of *Danton*, he was reproached by his father-in-law for his interest in a dangerous theme and his general lack of success (*M*:303),[3] and on 30 December 1900, the day after Jaurès's presentation of the play, Rolland agreed to Clotilde's request for a divorce.[4] There is no evidence of misconduct on either side, but it was Rolland who took the formal step of moving out of the family home. In Clotilde's milieu, divorce was more acceptable than it was to Rolland with his Catholic upbringing, but he felt it his duty to release her although he still loved her. A year later, he stated his views to Gillet with characteristic distaste for false situations:

> Je recommencerais, étant donné les circonstances et les caractères. – Mais le divorce en soi est une chose abominable, et je le condamne avec autant de sévérité que le chrétien le plus intransigeant. Du moment qu'il existe la pensée, la possibilité si lointaine, si problématique possible, du divorce, le mariage n'existe plus [. . .] Je comprends mieux l'union libre, la libre amitié amoureuse. (*C2*:171)

This idealistic view of marriage combined with a willingness to consider alternatives already suggests *L'Ame enchantée*. Rolland was deeply wounded by the sordid legal processes, the pent-up bitterness released in his wife (*C2*:140), the sense that her family was turning mutual friends against him, and above all her remarriage, two years later, to the pianist Alfred Cortot. He was left with a sense of failure: 'Triste effet de ma force et de ma tendresse, de n'avoir pu réussir à sauver l'âme à qui je me suis le plus attaché', he wrote to Gillet (*C2*:130), and he uses the same phrase, 'sauver l'âme', to Malwida (*C1*:296). For a man of faith, his inability to save even his wife from social corruption was a particularly bitter pill.

The material effects of divorce were equally shattering, since during their marriage he had lived mainly off Clotilde's money. Thrown on his own resources, he moved to a cramped upstairs apartment on the Boulevard du Montparnasse and became less choosy in the work he undertook. Journalism, lecturing and commissioned books took him away from the works he really wanted to write, to which he often devoted only an hour or two a day. His health suffered; late in 1901 his chest troubles returned and nearly killed him. His doctors were baffled; cardiac illness was suspected, but years later old tubercular lesions were discovered, which confirmed Rolland's own suspicions. There was probably a psychosomatic element to it.

Rolland points out, however, that the illness did not strike until he was over the worst of his grief,[5] and after the suffering came signs of renewal. As he wrote to Malwida in his New Year letter of 1902:

Tout cet orage m'a ravagé et renouvelé. Je sens qu'il m'a débarrassé des parties mortes de mon âme. Pauvre, je me sens plus riche. Attaché à des besognes, je me sens plus libre. Je n'ai plus de ménagements à garder, plus de compromissions mondaines, plus de fièvre de réussir. (*C1*:304)

At last his independence was secure, he could allow himself the luxury of not trying to buy success, and the way was clear for him to voice his criticisms of society. He also felt he had learned a lesson and acquired a new mellowness: 'Puisque la vie humaine est une bien petite chose, [. . .] il faut être indulgent pour elle, et laisser le pessimisme à ceux qui ont des exigences, aux riches, aux enfants gâtés'.[6] His university work, though time-consuming, genuinely interested him, and though he did not realize it at the time, his first major commission after his divorce, an article for the *Revue de Paris* on a cycle of the Beethoven symphonies in Mainz, was a revivifying experience with far-reaching effects. Consolations of a different kind came from reading; he discovered Diderot, and took a growing interest in Goethe.

At Morschach, in Switzerland, in August 1901, Rolland experienced a new 'éclair' which, we shall see, stimulated his work on *Jean-Christophe*. It was part of a 'retour à la vie'[7] which led him in the same month to visit Sofia Guerrieri, herself holidaying in Switzerland after a family crisis. Unlike the meeting of Christophe and Grazia in *Jean-Christophe* which reflects it, this was no chance event, but set up by Malwida, who hoped they would marry. This was not to be; their meeting was not altogether easy, Sofia already knew her future husband and Rolland barely seems to have known what he wanted of her. Sofia, however, had achieved an ironic serenity in face of her own problems, and she communicated it to Rolland. As he put it defiantly to Clotilde: 'Le hasard a voulu, par bonheur, que je me sois trouvé [. . .] en présence d'amis très malheureux, beaucoup plus malheureux que moi, et dont l'intelligente bonté, la compassion, le calme et la résignation souriante, m'ont fait honte et m'ont relevé'.[8] When he met Sofia again in 1902, he claims, they came close to considering marriage, but he declined to propose because, with his slender prospects, he had little to offer a woman of her rank.[9] It is hard to believe that a man so recently wounded was ready for a new love. Instead, they embarked on a long correspondence, which continued throughout her marriage to Pietro Bertolini. Rolland cast her as the successor to Malwida, who died in 1903, a safely remote recipient of his intimate thoughts, an island of ultramontane calm in a troubled world.

Meanwhile his reputation was growing. His plays had had little success, but he was about to begin a remarkable partnership with Péguy. Their relationship was not intimate, and never altogether free of the wariness to be expected between an author and publisher whose interests did not wholly coincide. Yet Rolland was less mercenary than most authors and Péguy was no ordinary publisher. Like Rolland, he was too independent to make common cause with the socialists, and he insisted, in the wake of Dreyfus, that political action should be moral in character. In 1900 he founded the *Cahiers de la Quinzaine*, whose contributors could be as outspoken as they liked within the context of an 'œuvre d'assainissement public' (*CR*:17). Rolland was not involved in their foundation, as he suggests he was in his study of Péguy (*Pi*:79), but he did try to fuse the *Cahiers* with the *Revue d'art dramatique*, failing because few of the *Revue* team shared his willingness to operate on the fringes of the literary world (*C22*:36–41). What made the *Cahiers* valuable was the chance they gave Rolland to state his whole thought without commercial compromise. They also gave him an audience:

> [Péguy] a trouvé à sa Revue 1,500 abonnés; et le plus remarquable, c'est que ce sont tous des isolés, des indépendants, vivant presque tous en province [. . .], ayant la foi socialiste, mais aussi un peu de cette intransigence morale qui ne peut supporter que son idéal se déforme en s'accommodant aux exigences de la politique. C'est donc une élite, moins intellectuelle que morale, et une avant-garde de la Société en marche vers des formes nouvelles de la civilisation. Il y a plaisir à être ainsi en relations avec ces humbles et libres individualistes, où brûle ce qu'il y a de plus pur dans la conscience française. (*C1*:305–6)

No doubt this is idealized; in many respects he is describing his own perfect public. Yet the very fact that he could believe in it was encouraging; it suggested there was a kernel of support from which could grow his longed-for national revival. Communicating with this public became the focus of Rolland's ambitions, and though Péguy was not his only publisher during the coming decade, it was to him that he gave his most valued work.

The discovery of this public helps to explain his abandonment of the stage. The failure of *Le Quatorze Juillet* suggested that the theatre was not ready for him, and it made sense to opt for direct communication with *Cahiers* subscribers through his long-planned novel. He did, however, write one more play, late in 1901, on the Boer War. Like most Europeans, Rolland supported the Boers, but he carefully pointed out that *Le Temps viendra* was not specifically anti-British: 'Ce drame met en cause, non un peuple européen, mais l'Europe' (*TF*:199). His correspondence shows little sustained indignation over the war; in principle he was against colonialism, but he had relations in the colonial army, recognized their heroism and even quotes 'l'épopée africaine' as a possible topic for national drama in *Le Théâtre du peuple* (*TP*:138). Chabran in *Jean-Christophe* is a sympathetic portrayal of a retired officer of the African army. Rolland wrote on colonial conflict because the issues raised were of wider significance:

> Je voudrais représenter des hommes capables de voir le mal, d'en avoir horreur, de désirer y mettre fin, – et entraînés malgré tout par une fatalité d'instincts, d'habitudes, de croyances héréditaires, qui les fait s'enfoncer à chaque pas davantage dans le crime. Le grand tragique des actions humaines me paraît être qu'elles sont le plus souvent accomplies contre la volonté des hommes, par un Destin irrésistible qui les mène à la ruine. (*C1*:301)

As in *Les Baglioni*, the vision is of man helpless in the grip of destiny.

The central figure is Clifford, a British field marshal occupying a captured town. He has lost all taste for war, but can do little to humanize it in face of business interests, journalistic blood lust and brutal subordinates poised to replace him if he falters. Nor can he fight hatred; British and Boers alike assume that God is with them and stimulate their fanaticism by quoting the Bible. Clifford, shot dead by the six-year-old son of a Boer woman he has befriended, falls victim to this fanaticism and his death triggers more repression, but hope is offered by the boy's mother, who, like Berthier and Lux, kills herself to break the cycle of hatred, and the soldier Owen, who in a gesture inspired by Tolstoy's portrayal of the Doukhobors, refuses to fight and is taken to be shot quoting the Biblical passage which gives the work its title:

> Le temps viendra, quand tous les hommes sauront la vérité, quand ils fondront les piques pour des faux, les sabres pour les herses, et quand le lion s'étendra près de l'agneau. (*TF*:287)

As a play in a modern setting, *Le Temps viendra* is more effective than *Les Vaincus*, anticipating Rolland's stance in 1914. Again, the tragedy lies in the individual's failure to resist a historical process. The world is caught in a cycle of hatred, to which even good men cannot avoid contributing, but Rolland's vision is bleaker than in his Revolutionary dramas in that the cause inspiring the action, bogus nationalism supported by bastardized religion, is less noble. Like *Le Siège de Mantoue*, the work ends hinting at a new cycle of love, but the hope is remote. This is one of Rolland's bleakest works, whose portrayal of men doing harm as they try to do good reflects its author's personal crisis. Instead of moral victory through physical defeat, its theme is moral defeat after physical victory, and it is not surprising that Rolland did not wish to continue in this vein. It met with indifference, so much so that Rolland later thought of recycling its title for the volume which became *Au-dessus de la mêlée*. Rolland took no sudden decision to abandon the theatre, however. In 1902 he was working on an eighteenth-century version of the Tristan story (*C10*:75), and in 1903 he complains of having to abandon a play in which a wife stands by her unloved husband during a crisis, because of a debased treatment of the theme by the boulevard dramatist Coolus (*C10*:146–7). These are the distant ancestors of *Le Jeu de l'amour et de la mort*.

Rolland's university career now moved centre stage. He taught at the Ecole des Hautes Etudes Sociales, and when after the 1903 reorganization of the Ecole Normale his post there was transferred to the Sorbonne, he concentrated more on his main interest, music history, at the cost of chores such as conducting examinations. His life became that of a busy lecturer, researching courses and publications during term and spending his summers on his novel, usually in quiet Swiss hotels. He was overworked, often ill and jealous of his privacy; his door was closed except to coded knocks known only to close friends, and his social life was minimal. Gradually, however, financial independence came. By 1908 he could think about reducing his commitments, and those he accepted he enjoyed more. After receiving the 1905 Prix Femina for *Jean-Christophe*, he took leave in the winter of 1906–7, travelling in Italy and Spain. A further sabbatical was spoiled in October 1910, when he was knocked down by a car and spent some months convalescing; his injuries included a broken arm which permanently weakened him. In the summer of 1911 he thought of resigning from the university, but instead took another year's leave on health grounds, again spending much of it in Italy. The final break was delayed until 1912, when he completed *Jean-Christophe*. Having come to realize that it was doing him a service by preventing him from being a recluse,[10] he was slow to abandon the university, especially at a time when it was subject to nationalist attack from Péguy among others (*CII*:112). It had fed his literary career more than he liked to admit.

At first he was still prepared to work on art history. He wrote commissioned studies of Millet and Michelangelo, and was induced to write for the *Revue de Paris* on the Salons of 1901 and 1903. In music history he continued his work on early opera, moving forward into the seventeenth and eighteenth centuries. His findings are published in *Musiciens d'autrefois* and *Voyage musical au pays du passé*; a further volume, *Musiciens d'aujourd'hui*, includes writings on recent composers, and he devoted a substantial study to Handel. These works continue to explore the place of music in the general study of history, and a keynote essay, 'De la place de la musique dans l'histoire générale' (*MAF*:1–17), compares the cyclic processes of history with those governing artistic evolution. The two differ in that one can achieve a perfection in art which is never possible in the constant uphill struggle of social history; Gregorian chant and Palestrina are unsurpassable in their kind. Nor do the cycles necessarily correspond; music, revealing a nation's inner rather than outer strength, may flourish in periods of apparent decline. Yet they reflect each other, and Rolland seeks to illuminate the character of an era by studying individual musicians. Detailed musical analysis concerns him little; his main interest is in composers' lives and writings. His preferred subjects are musicians with heroic qualities; the history of opera, whose exponents had to impose their will both on the heterogenous elements of their art and the public world of the theatre, provides many such cases, notably Lully, Handel, Rameau and Gluck.

In modern music, Rolland praises neglected young composers such as Hugo Wolf and Lorenzo Perosi, but his main concern is the relationship of French and German music. Though he wrote admiringly of Wagner and Richard Strauss, he came to see in them the triumphalism of the Kaiser's Germany as well as the inner strength of old Germany, with Strauss's *Salome* a disturbing watershed. Conversely, he stressed the renewal of French music since 1870, expressed in improved educational and orchestral standards and the works of Franck, D'Indy and Debussy. These he discussed in a brochure commissioned by Strauss, with whom he was on cordial terms, for publication in Germany (*MAJ*:201-78), and in an article on the 1905 Strasbourg music festival, in which the French made their presence felt despite heavy-handed German organization. Rolland stayed in Strasbourg with Albert Schweitzer, and he took an interest in the situation of Alsace as it sought to form its own personality between two rival nations. Rather than being a pawn in Franco-German conflict, he felt Alsace should be 'un petit état indépendant, un des états d'une grande Lotharingie, dont la Suisse serait le libre prolongement'.[11]

Rolland made no exaggerated claims for this revival. *Musiciens d'aujourd'hui* was closely followed by *La Foire sur la place*, in which, he admits, he attacked many of the musicians praised in the brochure. 'Les œuvres,' he explains, '– à part deux ou trois, – valent moins que l'effort' (*MAJ*:210). Debussy presented a special problem; his refined salon art embodied an aspect of the French genius for which Rolland did not greatly care, his preference being for 'l'action héroïque, l'ivresse de la raison, le rire, la passion de la lumière, la France de Rabelais, de Molière, de Diderot, et, en musique, dirons-nous – (faute de mieux), – la France de Berlioz et de Bizet' (*MAJ*:206). He was keen for Germans to appreciate French art; his correspondence shows him struggling to persuade Strauss of the real merits of *Pelléas et Mélisande* and to wean him off his view that the second-rate Charpentier was typical of French music. In this, Rolland set his personal taste aside. In *Jean-Christophe* his approach was more combative; to appreciate the complexity of Rolland's vision, ever capable of functioning on two levels at once, one must be aware of the detached academic alongside the pugnacious novelist.

Rolland's predilection was for biography, and in these years he wrote lives of Millet, Beethoven, Michelangelo, Handel and Tolstoy. The study of Millet, for an English publisher and appearing only in translation, dates from late in 1901, in the depths of Rolland's divorce crisis, and he was not inspired; he told Sofia to ignore the bulk of the text, a sketchy evocation of the paintings for an uninformed public, and read only the biographical part (*C10*:95). Millet did appeal, however, as an artist of independent integrity, a provincial struggling in Paris[12] and a man of faith, not the socialist that some claimed, but a Christian in an un-Christian age, finding austere joy in accepted suffering and Tolstoyan love of the peasantry. His faith was not Rolland's, but his stoicism appealed to Rolland as he tried to come to terms with his own suffering.

Suffering was, however, but a first step which the hero must transcend. Such was the achievement of Beethoven, and of Rolland under his influence. The cycle of the symphonies in Mainz was a turning point in the revival after his divorce, and he reworked his *Revue de Paris* article into a *Vie de Beethoven* for the *Cahiers*, first of a series of planned *Vies des hommes illustres* aimed at bringing encouragement to Péguy's isolated readers. Of all his works this is the most closely modelled on the *Cahiers*'s ideals, and its preface is a manifesto. It begins by denouncing the 'matérialisme sans grandeur' of contemporary Europe; for those who reject it, life is a solitary struggle against mediocrity, and to support them Rolland aims to 'grouper autour d'eux les Amis héroïques, les grandes âmes qui souffrirent pour le bien' (*VB*:13-14). Heroism is not dead; as contemporary examples Rolland cites Picquart and the Boers. They may not have triumphed, but the essence of heroism is not conquest; it is being 'grands par le cœur':

> Où le caractère n'est pas grand, il n'y a pas de grand homme, il n'y a même pas de grand artiste, ni de grand homme d'action; il n'y a que des idoles creuses pour le vile multitude [. . .] Peu nous importe le succès. Il s'agit d'être grand, et non de le paraître. (*VB*:15–16)

Again, Rolland develops his paradox; material defeat implies spiritual triumph, and vice versa. Suffering is therefore the lot of the hero, to be accepted with virile lucidity.

Beethoven's life was full of suffering. His childhood was difficult, he was deaf, misunderstood and never rich, and his great capacity for love met with little return. Yet he remained a fighter, a Revolutionary, a lover of justice and moral purity who in his Ninth Symphony triumphantly conquered joy:

> Un malheureux, pauvre, infirme, solitaire, la douleur faite homme, à qui le monde refuse la joie, crée la Joie lui-même pour le donner au monde. Il la forge avec sa misère, comme il l'a dit en une fière parole, où se résume sa vie, et qui est la devise de toute âme héroïque:
> 'La Joie par la Souffrance'
> *Durch Leiden Freude*. (*VB*:101–2)

The echoes of Isaiah in this passage confer a Christ-like redemptory status on Beethoven. This does not mean that suffering should be masochistically courted. It is rather a cathartic recognition that suffering is part of the fight for integrity; by accepting this fact, the hero is sustained by faith and will and achieves inner triumph. Such was Rolland's own experience as he emerged from crisis, and his portrayal of Beethoven is focused on how his subject achieved it. The work is short, the music is not discussed in detail and even the biographical material is thin, scrupulously documented but selected to highlight a theme. Rolland admitted his portrayal was 'fardé' (*C10*:277), and he can be accused of veiling the distinction between Beethoven's aesthetic conquest of joy and his much less complete conquest of joy in his personal life. The *Vie de Beethoven* is essentially lyrical testimony to what Beethoven meant to Rolland, not a definitive biography. Yet as such it was most successful. By portraying a heroic life it confirmed Rolland in the way *Jean-Christophe* was taking, it contains some memorable prose, and above all it found an audience; though there was little publicity, it rapidly went through several editions. It saved the *Cahiers* from bankruptcy, and was Rolland's first significant success.

As future subjects, Rolland considered Millet, Hoche, Garibaldi, Thomas Paine, Michelangelo, Mazzini, Schiller and Vauban,[13] but most fell by the wayside, either because Rolland was refused access to documents in private hands or because he discovered that his subjects did not meet his ideal of heroism, but he did work long on Mazzini, whom he chose for his second *Vie*. Mazzini had been Malwida's friend, and Rolland admired his purity of character, as well as his idealistic nationalism which contrasted with the triumphant nationalisms of the present generation, but after being diverted to Michelangelo, Rolland lost sympathy with him:

> Je l'admire toujours autant, je le regarde comme un prophète, un martyr, un homme de Dieu. Mais Dieu a pris presque toute la place; il n'en reste plus pour l'homme. Cela manque d'air, cela manque de joie de vivre. (*C10*:353)

Mazzini's 'religion de la douleur et du sacrifice m'a paru [. . .] inhumaine, si elle est autre chose qu'*une étape* nécessaire de *la marche en combattant, vers la joie*'.[14] Suffering was valueless if it did not lead to joy, and the *Vie de Mazzini* remained unwritten.

Michelangelo superseded Mazzini for the most mundane of reasons, a publisher's commission. The result, the 1905 *Michel-Ange*, is primarily biographical, but with more study of the works than Rolland usually included in his biographies. Rolland set little store by this 'petit livre de vulgarisation pour les écoles' (*C10*:253), preferring his lyrical reworking of it in the *Vie de Michel-Ange*, published by Péguy in the following year. This was more substantial than the *Vie de Beethoven* and much more problematic. Superficially, Michelangelo was an ideal companion to Beethoven; Rolland had always seen them as analogous, and works like the Sistine Chapel and *Moses* emanated a towering force and idealism. Rolland's celebration of these works in the earlier volume, dropped from the *Cahiers* version, is enough to ensure that that volume is still worth independent study; its vision of the artist welding together disparate elements of his personality by force of will anticipates ideas developed in the *Beethoven* of later years. Yet the more Rolland studied Michelangelo, the more he faced the problem he had avoided with Beethoven; the life did not correspond to the art. Michelangelo the man proved a rather unheroic vacillator, prone to panic fears, who left projects uncompleted and was both servile and disloyal towards his masters. Like Beethoven, he was a loving soul who failed to inspire love; Rolland skirts round his homosexuality, but celebrates his platonic friendship with Victoria Colonna, which recalls his own with Sofia. Unlike Beethoven, Michelangelo could not transmute suffering into joy: 'Beethoven fut triste par la faute du monde; il était gai de nature, il aspirait à la joie. Michel-Ange avait en lui la tristesse' (*VMA*:21). Where Beethoven was a 'vaincu vainqueur', Michelangelo was a 'vainqueur vaincu', with many qualities of a fighter but lacking the will to win: 'Contradiction poignante entre un génie héroïque et une volonté qui ne l'était pas, entre des passions impérieuses et une volonté qui ne voulait pas!' (*VMA*:8) Rolland found him a painful and disturbing subject, but as Duret suggests, this study had a cathartic effect as he grappled with his own difficulty in reconciling dream and action.[15]

In his preface, Rolland makes Michelangelo representative of all he admired and disliked about Christianity:

> Refuge de ceux qui ne réussissent point à vivre ici-bas! Foi qui n'est rien souvent qu'un manque de foi dans la vie, un manque de foi dans l'avenir, un manque de foi en soi-même, un manque de courage et un manque de joie! . . . Nous savons sur combien de défaites est bâtie votre douloureuse victoire! . . .
>
> Et c'est pour cela que je vous aime, chrétiens, car je vous plains. Je vous plains et j'admire votre mélancolie. Vous attristez le monde, mais vous l'embellissez [. . .] Louée soit la joie, et louée la douleur! L'une et l'autre sont sœurs, et toutes deux sont saintes. Elles forgent le monde et gonflent les grandes âmes. (*VMA*:10)

This analysis seems to spring from a debate with Clotilde in 1901, in which he objects to 'cette ridicule étiquette de *Pascalisme* épris de la souffrance, de ce christianisme, dont vous m'affublez';[16] he refused to let her regard him as a Christian, and he certainly did not accept that he was obsessed with suffering. Christianity inspires an acceptance and resignation which are heroic only to a degree; its negative side is a failure to achieve joy and a non-acceptance of life which falls short of the full heroic ideal, reformulated in this work as 'voir le monde tel qu'il est – et de l'aimer' (*VMA*:9).

The painful spectacle of Michelangelo presented the biographer with a further problem:

> Je me demande si, en voulant donner à ceux qui souffrent des compagnons de douleur qui les soutiennent, je n'ai pas fait qu'ajouter la douleur de ceux-ci à la douleur de ceux-là. Aurais-je donc dû plutôt, comme tant d'autres, ne montrer des héros que l'héroïsme et jeter un voile sur l'abîme de tristesse qui est en eux? (*VMA*:209)

The answer is a resounding no; truth must out, and to the true hero it is bracing. Yet for the unheroic, truth is hard to bear: 'Je ne prétends point que le commun des hommes puissent vivre sur ces sommets' (*VMA*:209). This problem intensified for Rolland over the years, as his social mission made it ever more necessary to state unpalatable truths. In the short term, it explains his reluctance to write more biographies; though he never abandoned the genre, no more of his original list were written. A more profound implication is that Rolland's work, at this stage, is essentially elitist. Though eager to work for all humanity, and disgusted with the Parisian elite, his true audience remains an elite of another kind, the ideal readership of the *Cahiers*; he knew he was not writing for a mass audience.

Rolland's study of Handel appeared in 1910 and arises directly from lecture notes. He enjoyed working on Handel so much that his first draft was too long for his publisher and he had to rewrite it, redeploying his unused material in a series of articles later incorporated in an expanded edition. Rolland did not attach this work to the *Vies des hommes illustres*, but his enthusiasm survived intensive research better than it did with Michelangelo. Handel's work expresses a robust moral purity which Rolland also finds in Gluck and Beethoven. A man of the theatre even in religious oratorio, Handel struggled to conquer the musical world of his day, and his work has a cosmopolitanism which appealed to Rolland the internationalist, as well as a popular outdoor character akin to *Le Quatorze Juillet*. The biography does not, however, attempt lyrical highlighting of heroic themes, as do the *Vies*; it is a sober account supported by a wealth of detail on the musical world of the day. One of Rolland's concerns is the relationship between an artist and his environment; to those who do not know the latter, the great artist may appear more original than he is, and in his study of Handel's works, Rolland aims to show how his subject assimilated his cultural environment. In this respect, Handel is a symphonist in Rolland's personal sense, a creator of harmony from dissonance. In a projected volume, abandoned when he left the university, Rolland hoped to argue a similar thesis about Mozart.

Rolland took a particular interest in the accusations of plagiarism levelled at Handel, showing how themes Handel borrows from other composers, and from his own early works, are given fuller realization under the pen of the master musician (*H*:215–58). This Rolland sees as a legitimate process, and he reflects on the precise expressive sense of Handel's works, which he insists cannot be reduced to cold formalism. Rolland saw music as an expressive language, and his musical studies always seek the expressed content rather than dwelling on mechanisms. In this context, the adaptation of themes from one purpose to another is of central importance, and his studies of Handel's plagiarisms are a first attempt at a technique he later applied to Beethoven. The most satisfying of his academic writings, *Haendel* deserves a more important place among Rolland's works than it is usually given.

The *Vie de Tolstoy*, written during Rolland's convalescence after his road accident, was another commission, this time from the *Revue de Paris*, following Tolstoy's death. It is normally counted among the *Vies*, but Rolland did not give it to Péguy because the *Cahiers* had published a study of Tolstoy by Suarès (*C22*:294) and he did not wish to highlight the differences between Suarès's work and his own. As a biography, it is limited by the documentary material available in 1910, but Rolland shows a deep knowledge of Tolstoy's writings, and airs several of his own problems as an artist. Once again, he celebrates *War and Peace*'s realism suffused by love, but his comments on that work mainly aim to reveal the 'unité cachée' of its large-scale construction:

> Il faut s'élever au-dessus et embrasser du regard l'horizon libre, le cercle des bois et des champs; alors on percevra l'esprit homérique de l'œuvre, le calme des lois éternelles, le rythme imposant du souffle du destin, le sentiment de l'ensemble auquel tous les détails sont liés. (*VT*:62)

With its stress on overall shape and breadth of vision, this is how Rolland hoped *Jean-Christophe* would be read.

By 1910, however, Tolstoy is more than the sympathetic realist of 1886; he is the painfully sincere believer struggling, like Rolland in the 1890s, to live by a faith which pits him against family and class. The basic tenets of Tolstoy's unorthodox Christianity, rejecting the divinity of Christ but holding to a mystic faith in reason, were in Rolland's view wholly admirable, as was his concern for the peasantry and peace; though no socialist, Tolstoy was clearly a revolutionary. Tolstoy's attack on art, which had so disturbed the young Rolland, took a little more explaining. The diatribes against Shakespeare, Beethoven and Wagner he presents either as a misunderstanding or indirect homage to their creative power, but when the target is the art of a false elite, the author of *La Foire sur la place* concurs, insisting that Tolstoy's attack is in the name of a higher ideal of religious art, 'l'art vivant, l'art humain, celui qui unit les hommes'(*VT*:123). Tolstoy did not always succeed in living by his ideals: 'La fusion n'était point parfaite entre ses natures diverses: sa vérité d'artiste et sa vérité de croyant' (*VT*:154). He resists systematization, and cannot be annexed to any single party. He was caught, like Rolland writing Michelangelo's life, in 'un magnifique combat entre les deux plus hautes puissances de son âme: la Vérité et l'Amour' (*VT*:198); the sincerity which led him to voice hard truths conflicted with his love for his fellow men, particularly those closest to him. It was only later that Rolland learned of Tolstoy's family drama from his heirs, but he knew enough already to sense painful analogies with his own marriage, and was sympathetic to his subject's faltering attempts to solve his dilemma: 'Il était faible. Il était homme. Et c'est pour cela que nous l'aimons' (*VT*:188).

It is significant that, of all Rolland's biographical projects, only studies of artists were completed; no soldier or political figure inspired him enough to continue. With many projects competing for his time, Rolland stayed with subjects close to his own endeavours, whose struggles could help him fulfil his own ideals. Despite the labour involved, biography satisfied a need for Rolland. He had always seen it as his task to foster human unity by entering into the souls of others; in this, his biographies are the successors of his projected history of the religious wars. The need for heroic mentors to celebrate was equally important to a writer who sensed his weakness and isolation. He always loved to write studies of great men; some of his most important late works take that form. Yet the *Vie de Beethoven* could not be easily duplicated. The deeper his studies, the harder it was to maintain the clear, over-simplified structure of that work and the heroic image he wished to project. Rolland was eager to treat a heroic life at full length and in its full complexity, but to do so he needed the freedom of a work of imagination. This is the importance of *Jean-Christophe*.

Notes

1. See *Mémoires* 4, feuille 19. This unpublished continuation of the *Mémoires* is in the Archives Romain Rolland.
2. See Duret (1992), p.289.
3. See the account of the incident in Arcos (1950), pp.37–8.
4. See *Mémoires* 4, feuille 3.
5. See *Mémoires* 4, feuille 13.
6. See *Mémoires* 4, feuille 17.
7. See *Mémoires* 4, feuille 10.
8. Letter to Clotilde Bréal, 9 September 1901.
9. See *Mémoires* 4, feuille 24.
10. See letter to Louise Cruppi, 6 June 1911, quoted in Starr (1971), p.143.
11. See *Mémoires* 4, feuille 40.
12. Duchatelet (1969, pp.541-83) has shown how Christophe's arrival in Paris in *La Foire sur la place* reflects Millet's first impressions of Paris.
13. See Wilson (1939), p.132.
14. Quoted by Wilson (1939), p.218.
15. See Duret (1992), p.366.
16. Letter to Clotilde Bréal, 9 September 1901.

–5–

Heroes (II): *Jean-Christophe*

Rolland claims to have begun the definitive draft of *Jean-Christophe* on 20 March 1903 (*JC*:xii). This was in fact the date of an important planning document[1] anticipating the final shape of a work which already had a long prehistory. Its roots lie in Rolland's student efforts to write an artist's life; the Janiculum 'éclair' and his notion of the musical novel gave him an idea of its direction, but when he set seriously to work he seems to have had no conscious aim to apply the principles of 1890.[2] The first passages were drafted after visiting Germany in 1896, at a time of marital distress, but in the false dawn of his theatrical career he prioritized his plays until after his divorce.

Most obviously the work is a study of a modern Beethoven, but other musicians give elements to Christophe, notably Hugo Wolf, whom Rolland discovered in 1903. Rolland's aim in 1896 was to explore the process of creation: 'L'originalité de ce livre serait d'être le premier parmi les romans à prendre pour héros des génies, non pas dans des actions indifférentes à leur génie, mais dans leur plein accomplissement'.[3] Genius, neglected by earlier novels, offered a new field for psychological study, penetrating areas of the soul where the divinity is to be found. Rolland also sought to embody the tension between dream and action in the Beethoven character and a figure based on Mazzini, later dropped. Over time, the Beethoven figure acquired a further role as focalizer of the modern world. The novel offered more scope for contemporary subjects than the stage, and through a figure surveying his contemporaries from a viewpoint blending scorn and serenity, Rolland could voice both his long-fermenting satirical vision and his ideal of symphonic unity.

Rolland had always seen the artist as a divine voice whose mission was to break barriers between individuals. This was confirmed by the Morschach 'éclair' of August 1901, when he wrote this dedication of his embryonic novel:

> A tout ce qui est mortel j'offre ce livre mortel, dont la voix cherche à dire: 'Frères, rapprochons-nous, oublions ce qui nous sépare, ne songeons qu'à la

misère commune où nous sommes confondus! Il n'y a pas d'ennemis, il n'y a pas de méchants, il n'y a que des misérables: et le seul bonheur durable est de nous comprendre mutuellement pour nous aimer'. (*JC*:xii)

This reflects his new mellowness after his divorce, and it marks an important shift of emphasis. Not content with studying genius, *Jean-Christophe* will be about 'l'humble vie héroïque',[4] common men and women, the modest sufferers of the *Vie de Beethoven* who are the nation's backbone. Rolland came to sense, relatively late, that he had written the 'tragédie d'une génération humaine' (*JC*:xviii). He had not set out with that intent, but with hindsight he saw his work as a testimony to all that was heroic in the years between 1870 and 1914 (*JC*:xvi).

Another strand in the work's genesis is autobiography. Already in 1897 Rolland described it as 'l'histoire de mon âme transposée en un plus grand que moi';[5] after his divorce this element became more important, and many elements of his life can be traced in both Christophe and Olivier Jeannin. The temptation is to identify Rolland with Olivier, but in his *Mémoires* he suggests something more complex:

Qui a bien voulu lire ces Mémoires aura peut-être gardé le souvenir du Jean-Christophe avant la lettre, avec ses passions, sa foi, son orgueil et ses injustices, qu'était le jeune pensionnaire de Rome, à son retour à Paris. L'Olivier, lui, remontait plus loin, à l'enfance dans la petite ville de province, et aux premières années de Paris. Mais [. . .] je me déchargeais, en l'un et en l'autre de mes gémeaux, d'une partie de ce qui m'oppressait; et en retour, je recevais leur empreinte. Christophe me communiquait son assurance, son allégresse, et renouvelait mon sang. Olivier, offert par moi, au lieu de moi, en sacrifice, me léguait son Au-delà de toutes le barrières entre les hommes, et son 'Au-dessus de la Mêlée'.[6]

Olivier is Rolland the child, Christophe the intransigent youth of the 1890s. Olivier embodies aspects of himself above which he sought to rise, Christophe the creator-hero he wished to become, and indeed felt himself becoming, for in 1910 he could write: 'Christophe m'a plus communiqué de sa personnalité, que je n'ai donné de ma personnalité à Christophe'.[7] Both became ideal imaginary companions;[8] his letters refer to Christophe as if to a living person, an unruly younger brother capable of transmitting a satirical message which Rolland in his own voice might not attempt. Rolland denied that the work was a *roman à clef*, but admitted it was based on experience:

> S'il vise souvent des événements et des individus réels, il ne renferme pas un
> seul portrait – ni du passé, ni du présent. Mais tous les êtres mis en scène sont
> naturellement nourris d'une quantité d'expériences et de souvenirs de la vie,
> fondus et transformés dans le travail de création. Il n'en est pas moins advenu
> que nombre de notoires contemporains se sont reconnus dans mes satires, et
> qu'ils m'ont voué une haine implacable, dont les effets se manifestèrent en
> 1914. (*JC*:xviii)

This 1931 disavowal affects injured innocence in face of wartime attacks,
and shows the artist properly conscious of his role as synthesizer. Yet it
admits that parallels between fiction and reality could be traced, and the
work contains several recognizable portraits.

Though *Jean-Christophe* is not a musical novel in the strict 1890 sense,
music is ever-present. Musical works, real and imaginary, are alluded to,
though rarely in technical detail, and musicality may be found in the
lyricism pervading the novel. Rolland seeks to transmit the emotional
impact of scenes he describes, and mood is often more important than
detail; his style is sensitive to rhythm, metaphors recur like leitmotifs
and particular attention is paid to aural effects such as flowing water,
bells and the buzzing of insects. This is noticeable at key moments such
as Christophe's walk with Gottfried in *L'Aube* (*JC*:90ff), or the *foehn* in
Le Buisson ardent, which Rolland singled out as one of the 'développe-
ments et crescendo symphoniques et rythmiques' which constituted the
work's 'procédés symphoniques' (*C2*:263). The pathetic fallacy of this
passage (*JC*:1419), in which a storm accompanies Christophe's rebirth,
is in a tradition of prose writing stemming from Chateaubriand and as
such has no need of musical interpretation, but it is revealing that the
author himself feels that the technique is musical.

Another type of musicality is evoked in a letter to Gillet denying that
his work is a novel in the usual sense:

> Ce n'est pas des aventures ou des psychologies que je cherche à créer, c'est
> une sorte de grand massif montagneux d'âmes, isolées et différentes des autres,
> avec leur floraison, leurs torrents, et leur atmosphère spéciale. (*C2*:158–9)

Apart from the obvious point that plot matters less than character, this
implies that the interest lies in the interplay and development of souls. In
attributing a mood, or 'atmosphère', to each character, it strongly recalls
the musical novel of 1890 which aims to 'faire revivre [un sentiment]
sous le revêtement de telle ou telle apparence' (*C1*:26). This aspect of
the work is seen in the author's weakness for symbolic names. These

were not consciously planned; in 1901 he even dismissed the device as 'enfantin'.[9] Yet his hero is called Krafft (strength), after being Schmerz (pain) in early drafts; Christophe recalls the God-bearer St Christopher, and Rolland later thought of Jean as an allusion to John the Baptist, the precursor (*VI*:259). Christophe's uncle, another God-bearer disseminating calm, is Gottfried (God's peace). His serene French friend, first named after Raphael, becomes Olivier, wise counsellor of that epic hero whose name resembles the author's. His Italian beloved is Grazia, a name with strong religious overtones. In this, characters appear as incarnations of sentiments, which are contrasted and interwoven as in a symphonic development.

More problematic is the question of whether the work's ten volumes can be related to the four movements of a symphony. The attempt has been made, most notably by Gillet,[10] but the results rarely satisfy because Rolland himself gave no clue to which volume represents which movement. Yet the symphonic model of related but contrasting self-contained elements moving towards resolution is undoubtedly helpful. The symphony as Breuilpont saw it is the working out over time of a unifying idea, and the process reflects the portrayal of an artist's life evolving from grief to joy, from conflict to serenity. Artistic creation is itself a process, and Rolland's vision of the creative act in a richly imagistic passage of *La Nouvelle Journée* stresses the dynamic model of a work arising from hidden depths to be shaped, over time, by reason and will. It first emerges in the form of 'une torpeur vague et puissante, l'obscure joie de la grappe pleine, de l'épi gonflé, de la femme enceinte qui couve son fruit mûr'. Gradually 'le rythme qui la mène' defines itself, then 'la volonté paraît [. . .] L'esprit reconnaît les lois du rythme qui l'entraîne; il dompte les forces déréglées, et leur fixe la voie et le but où il va. La symphonie de la raison et de l'instinct s'organise'. The work is given structure, every aspect of the artist's being contributes to its realization and:

> La cathédrale s'achève.
> 'Et Dieu contemple son œuvre. Et il voit qu'*elle n'est pas bonne encore*'.
> L'œil du maître embrasse l'ensemble de sa création; sa main parfait l'harmonie.
> (*JC*:1565–6)

This vision of creativity, a quest for perfection evolving from the interaction of subconscious urges and conscious control, stayed with Rolland all his life. It pervades his volumes on Beethoven and his comments on *Jean-Christophe* in 'Le Périple', where he alludes to the interaction of 'l'ascétisme', self-discipline, with 'le feu' of subterranean inspiration. Again, there is nothing exclusively symphonic about this; the cathedral image, another of Rolland's favourites, just as effectively symbolizes a harmonious though diverse art form evolving over time. What matters is that Rolland found his way to the notion through music rather than any other route. It was the symphonic analogy which focused his attention on art as a dynamically evolving structure:

> Mon état d'esprit est toujours celui d'un musicien, non d'un peintre. Je conçois d'abord comme une nébuleuse l'impression musicale de l'ensemble de l'oeuvre, puis les motifs principaux, et surtout le ou les rythmes, non pas tant de la phrase isolée que la suite des volumes dans l'ensemble, des chapitres dans le volume, et des alinéas dans le chapitre.[11]

For Rolland, creation is a matter of transforming the moving processes of inspiration into a structure which reflects them. The following survey, while highlighting the work's autobiographical elements, will attempt to recapture the trajectory of this movement.

'Jamais ouvrage ne fut aussi totalement organisé dans la pensée que *Jean-Christophe*, avant que les premiers mots fussent jetés sur le papier' (*JC*:xiii). The most cursory reading of Bernard Duchatelet's study of its genesis shows that this is an overstatement; major changes took place during composition. Yet the broad lines were in place by 1903, and the volumes follow a pattern recalling Dante's *Divina Commedia*, which provided epigraphs for several sections. The work portrays a descent followed by an ascent, and its volumes fall into three groups. *L'Aube*, *Le Matin* and *L'Adolescent* portray Christophe's childhood, his emergence into the world of suffering and the birth of his genius. The transitional *La Révolte* presents his German environment in a pattern which anticipates the second group of volumes, *Jean-Christophe à Paris*, in which *La Foire sur la place* is a satirical portrayal of the Paris Inferno, through which Christophe descends alone until he meets his Virgil in Olivier (*JC*:958), whose childhood is presented in *Antoinette* and who guides him, in the Purgatorio of *Dans la maison*, through the more redeemable parts of France. The third cycle, *La Fin du voyage*, falls into two halves. *Les Amies* and the first part of *Le Buisson ardent* portray Christophe's attempts to rise through love and political action. Mirroring *La Révolte*, they mark the transition to the spiritual crisis of the second part of *Le Buisson ardent* and the Paradiso of *La Nouvelle Journée*, where he achieves serenity through Grazia as Beatrice (*JC*:1555). The symmetry of this descending and ascending trajectory is reinforced by the parallelism of two violent clashes with authority, at the end of *La Révolte* and halfway through *Le Buisson ardent*, which mark the beginning and end of Christophe's life in Paris. The pivot of the work is *Antoinette*, which, at the nadir of his career, prepares for his future rise.

Jean-Christophe is the original 'roman fleuve', and the river is the Rhine which dominates *L'Aube*. Its sound fills Christophe's ears as it would have filled those of young Beethoven in Bonn, and it recalls the canal beside Rolland's Clamecy home. It also symbolizes the flow of individual life into the ocean of universal life; as such it is Christophe's point of contact with the God within him, especially in the scene where he is consoled by the sound of the river bearing a vision of his future (*JC*:67–9). The analogy with the prelude to Wagner's *Ring* is inescapable. *L'Aube* functions as a symphonic prelude in which themes later developed appear in embryonic form, and its juxtaposition of the artist's joys and sufferings recalls the contrasting themes of sonata form.

Suffering is the lot of the individual separated from universal life and confined in a limited role. None suffer more than the child, who cannot differentiate its causes:

> L'homme qui souffre peut diminuer son mal, en sachant d'où il vient; il l'enferme par la pensée en un morceau de son corps, qui peut être guéri [. . .] L'enfant n'a pas cette ressource trompeuse. Sa première rencontre avec la douleur est plus tragique et plus vraie. (*JC*:10)

Christophe's suffering springs from a difficult family background based on Beethoven's, but some details come from Rolland's experience, notably the fear of death enhanced by the premature demise of a sibling (*JC*:52). Christophe reacts against suffering by revolting against his social superiors and his father's bullying; this anticipates the satirical elements of later volumes.

On the other hand, Christophe has a rich inner life and enjoys moments of contact with the universal. Limitless suffering has its counterpart in an equally limitless embryonic creativity, 'la force qui est en lui et qui s'amasse énorme, inconsciente, l'océan bouillonnant qui gronde dans l'étroite prison de ce petit corps d'enfant' (*JC*:11). *L'Aube* shows this being moulded into a vocation, culminating in two musical experiences, Christophe's traumatic concert before the court as a child prodigy and his encounter with folk music through Gottfried, who condemns the falsity of his early efforts. The juxtaposition of these episodes reveals a tension between art's ideal function as expression of the soul and its abuse by a shallow elite. The volume ends with Beethoven's music pointing the boy towards the heroic passage through suffering to joy.

The representation of childhood in *L'Aube* has always been admired. Rolland judged *Le Matin* less good, but its portrayal of two loves framed by two deaths gives it a perceptible structure. It opens with the death of Christophe's grandfather, which the boy watches just as Rolland had recently witnessed his own grandfather's death. This leads Christophe to revolt against God (*JC*:130), but Gottfried tries to persuade him to accept his destiny, and when at the end of the volume his father dies, his attitude has modified. The struggle continues: 'Il vit que la vie était une bataille sans trève et sans merci, où qui veut être un homme digne du nom d'homme doit lutter constamment' (*JC*:221). Yet he no longer revolts against God; he accepts life and concentrates on becoming a man. This is an important refinement of his heroism, and the problem it raises, of how far a man should accept his destiny, points to one of the novel's pervasive ambivalences.

The relationships with Otto and Minna draw on Rolland's life as much as Beethoven's. Otto recalls Suarès, and for the Minna episode Rolland pillages his first fictional efforts, *Amour d'enfants* and *Mai romain*, based on his early loves. These episodes mark a change from *L'Aube*, whose theme, the griefs and joys of genius, was essentially heroic. Now, as Rolland treats adolescent excesses which are not confined to geniuses, a tone of ironic detachment appears; a rather obtrusive omniscient narrator makes comments to show what fools his characters are making of them-selves. The resulting oscillation between internal and external focalization, with the author identifying and ceasing to identify with Christophe by turns, is a device put to various uses as the work progresses.

L'Adolescent was originally intended to take Christophe to his depar-ture for Paris, but fails to reach that stage.[12] As Rolland worked on it in 1904, he was uneasily aware that his project was expanding, and the autobiographical intimacy of some passages left him doubting whether they could appear in his lifetime. Rolland had vivid memories of adol-escence, and in its incoherent fermentation Christophe knows moments of contact with his inner God, recalling the young Rolland's 'éclairs' (*JC*:263), but the main impression is of rising sexual urges and revolt focused on the puritanical Euler family with whom he lodges. The medi-ocre piety of Leonhard Euler inspires a revulsion against conventional religion which echoes Rolland's loss of faith, and the plain daughter Rosa's unrequited love for Christophe recalls Claudine Funck-Brentano. With these first targets of Christophe's revolt, Rolland develops narrative techniques which feature throughout his satirical volumes, notably the counterbalancing of Christophe's outbursts with narratorial passages pointing out his injustice. The following is the sequel to Christophe's attack on Amalia Euler:

> Sans doute, ces pauvres gens étaient à peu près tels qu'il les voyait. Mais ce n'était pas leur faute: c'était celle de la vie ingrate, qui avait fait leurs figures, leurs manières et leurs pensées ingrates. Ils avaient subi les déformations [. . .] de la mauvaise chance, constamment répétée, de la petite misère qui s'épand goutte à goutte, du premier jour au dernier. . . Grande tristesse! car sous ces enveloppes rugueuses, que de trésors en réserve, de droiture, de bonté, de silencieux héroïsme! (*JC*:342–3)

Here, the narrator dissociates himself from Christophe; as an artist, Rolland functions on two levels, playing a combative role while at the same time rising to a more mellow Tolstoyan vision. This passage makes the point that heroism is not confined to the genius; it is also in the Eulers' humdrum lives, and Gottfried helps Christophe to recognize it by redefining the hero as 'celui qui fait ce qu'il peut' (*JC*:371).

L'Adolescent is structured around two affairs with women of contrasting character which set the tone for most of Christophe's love life. The affair with Sabine, the Eulers' tenant, remains unconsummated due to her early death. Her name alludes to the hills around Rome; her calm irony and the Italianate beauty of her 'jeune figure florentine' (*JC*:273) recall Sofia. As with Antoinette and Grazia, their love culminates in a moment of wordless communion, as they stand separated only by a bedroom door which neither can bring themselves to open (*JC*:297). This love is more positively portrayed than the affair with the shopgirl Ada, whose physical energy contrasts with the languid Sabine. Like his other consummated loves, with Françoise Oudon and Anna Braun, this is a threat as much as an inspiration. True, in their first night of love he is in contact with 'la force de l'Etre, obscure et dévorante' (*JC*:326); Rolland thought of naming this volume after Dionysos, god of ecstasy, and the analogy between the religious and erotic 'éclair' is undeniable. Yet Ada, sensing a superiority in Christophe which escapes her, seeks to drag him down and deceives him with his brother, just as Clotilde conspired against Rolland with Léon Blum. In the ensuing crisis, Christophe follows his father into the crudest Dionysiac activity, drunkenness, but the volume concludes with his rescue by Gottfried.

In narrative terms, *La Révolte* develops Christophe's conflict with Germany and points him towards France, but it evolved into something Rolland had not foreseen. It took a long time to write; 1904 had been a year of euphoria, but in 1905, deep in his painful research into Michelangelo, he found writing difficult as his subject grew and the emphasis shifted to social portrayal.[13] Rolland had chosen a German setting because he needed a musician-hero to focalize a vision of France, not because he had strong views on Germany, and the prospect of attacking German targets left him uneasy. He was eager that the volume's three *Cahiers* should appear in rapid succession, to avoid giving an unbalanced picture.

La Révolte's Germany anticipates the France of *Jean-Christophe à Paris*; the first part projects a satirical view, the second a contrasting interlude featuring Antoinette and the third a more positive vision. This recalls a symphonic scherzo and trio; the grotesque tone of the two first parts suggests a scherzo of the sinister Mahlerian type. *Sables mouvants*, the first section, shows Christophe full of creative euphoria, rejecting his early work and with it, with sweeping injustice, the whole German tradition. His basic target is 'le mensonge allemand' (*JC*:385), and his revolt in the name of sincerity reflects 'Le Poison idéaliste'. The decadent Jewish review to which he contributes recalls the *Revue blanche*, and the Mannheim family is modelled on the Bréals.

The second part, *L'Enlisement*, continues the battle between Christophe and his town, but its main function is to reveal France as an escape route. The revelation comes from another contrasting pair of women, the actress Corinne and the governess Antoinette, representing 'la France séduisante et superficielle' and 'la France qui travaille et qui se tait'.[14] In this they anticipate the two faces of France revealed in *La Foire sur la place* and *Dans la maison*, but the analogy is unkind to Corinne, an affectionate portrait of Cora Laparcerie. Her exuberant frivolity is a tonic, but her presence swamps that of the morally superior Antoinette, whose dismissal on Christophe's account contrasts with the holiday mood of his escapade with Corinne. Their encounter is brief, a single evening in the theatre and a glance through the window of a departing train,[15] but their latent attraction has consequences later.

In *La Délivrance*, Christophe discovers the better side of Germany, but only after a false start in his visit to Hassler, the great composer in decline. Hassler is substantially based on Richard Strauss, but Rolland strenuously denied that this was a portrait of a musician he knew and esteemed; Hugo Wolf's meeting with Wagner also contributes to the picture. Yet he conceded that Hassler might represent 'le Straussisme' (*C16*:117); Duchatelet concludes that Hassler is what Rolland feared the composer of *Salome* might become.[16] Christophe finds better representatives of German idealism in Schulz and Modesta, both based on Malwida von Meysenbug. Schulz, the provincial academic, is the first person to respond to Christophe's music. Their meeting is an improbable alliance of age and youth such as Rolland experienced with Malwida, but it overtaxes Schulz's shattered respiratory organs and he dies; as Anna Braun will discover, art burns as well as warms. Modesta, the blind girl reconciled to life by Gottfried at the cost of closing her mind to everything inconvenient, embodies the ambivalence of German idealism:

> Il vit la grandeur de l'idéalisme allemand, qu'il avait tant de fois haï, parce qu'il est chez les âmes médiocres une source d'hypocrite niaiserie. Il vit la beauté de cette foi qui se crée un monde au milieu du monde, et différent du monde, comme un ilôt de l'océan. – Mais il ne pouvait supporter cette foi pour lui-même. (*JC*:593–94)

This judgement coincides with the redefinition of heroism in the *Vie de Michel-Ange* as 'voir le monde tel qu'il est – et de l'aimer'; truth must be respected, however much it hurts.

The novel resumes its course with the attack on a soldier which forces Christophe into exile, leaving his mother in a painful scene based on Rolland's departure for Rome in 1889. The soldiers reflect post-1870 Germany, a theme which has so far appeared only fleetingly, in the person of Christophe's businessman uncle Theodore. This curious gap raises chronological problems. Allusions in the Paris volumes fix the date at approximately the time of writing, which means that the German episodes are post-1870, but Christophe's Germany is still Beethoven's world of small courts and dukedoms. Musically it is contemporary, with its quarrels between supporters of Wagner and Brahms, but politically it is a vacuum. Something similar occurs after the Paris episodes; Christophe's subsequent life occupies a good twenty years which in no way relate to historical time, but can hardly be described as the future since in many ways they reflect the present. The Paris episodes should be seen as being in the world of the present, with what precedes and follows best regarded as mythical.

In *La Foire sur la place*, Rolland at last launched his attack on Paris, parts of which had been drafted years before, but with some trepidation. He saw, as his audience could not, how it would be complemented in future volumes, and he again feared that the rhythm of publication would mislead. He had to respect the dimensions of the *Cahiers*; *La Foire* needed two, *Antoinette*, which he wanted to publish at the same time, made a third, and the commercial difficulties provoked fraught exchanges with Péguy's team. Moreover, when they appeared in 1908 he was beginning to make a name, and he feared that he stood to lose all he had gained. In the event there was little polemic; Rolland sensed a conspiracy of silence among critics who hoped to bury the work or feared being identified among its targets if they attacked it. In the first part, he concentrates on the musical and literary world, attacking talentless creators, ignorant critics and the all-pervading cliquishness and corruption. In the second, his targets embrace salon and political life where the faults are similar, with, in the political world, a blend of dilettantism and fanaticism which makes a mockery of the French capacity for faith. The prevailing tone is of death, culminating in Christophe's vision of the city's monuments as 'un géant mort, dont les membres immenses couvraient la plaine' (*JC*:768). Christophe's mentors are Sylvain Kohn, the German Jew who thinks he represents France, Théophile Goujart, the music critic with no understanding of music and Achille Roussin, the salon socialist.

In castigating his homeland in *La Révolte*, Christophe is in effect chastizing himself, but in Paris his reaction is that of an outsider. His personal development is thus less at issue, which reduces the psychological interest; for much of the volume polemic takes over from narrative. Rolland gives his focalizer his head, and when he speaks as omniscient narrator, it is often to extend the attack, rather than to soften it as in the example from *L'Adolescent* quoted above. When, for instance, in discussing the mediocrity of critics, the narrator intervenes to talk of 'un mouvement de réaction contre la veulerie anarchique du jour' of which Christophe is unaware, it is not to correct Christophe, but to support him by saying how ineffective this movement is (*JC*:722). After this intervention, the attack continues and it is hard to say whether the focalizer is Christophe or the narrator; Rolland's claim that Christophe's vision is distinct from his own does not always carry conviction. As to the identity of his targets, Rolland avoids naming names. Some are identified, such as *Pelléas et Mélisande*, *Cyrano de Bergerac* and the worthy but dull Schola Cantorum, and Lucien Lévy-Cœur is recognizably Blum, but generally Rolland prefers the composite picture, uniting a series of traits from various sources in a single figure or list. This does not, of course, prevent details from being recognizable.

In the second part of the volume, the narrative revives as Christophe competes with Lévy-Cœur for Colette Stevens, and the intrigues surrounding his work, inspired in part by the Paris performance of *Salome*, culminate in the concert where he insults his audience by playing a popular song. This apparently ruins his Parisian career, but in fact he is at a turning point, for his art and personality are beginning to impose themselves: 'Il ne savait pas [. . .] qu'à cette heure même, où il se croyait isolé pour toujours, il était plus riche d'amour que les plus heureux du monde'

(*JC*:781). Present at that concert are his future supporters, Grazia, the Jeannins and the publisher Hecht, and his beneficial influence reaches representatives of the hidden France he will soon discover, the 'petite grisette' who loves music and Sidonie, the servant who nurses him through his illness. Both, significantly, are of the lower orders.

Christophe's illness, following another moment of eye contact with Antoinette, is his personal nadir, but its influence is beneficial: 'elle l'avait dépouillé de ce qu'il y avait de plus grossier dans son être'. Through Sidonie he discovers 'les souffrances silencieuses des humbles âmes' (*JC*:816–17), and in Michelet's study of Joan of Arc he learns the value of a 'bonté' which he has failed to achieve:

> 'J'ai péché. Je n'ai pas été bon. J'ai manqué de bienveillance. J'ai été trop sévère. – Pardon. Ne croyez pas que je sois votre ennemi, vous que je combats! je voudrais vous faire du bien, à vous aussi. . .' (*JC*:21)

There are signs that Rolland felt this passage was too sentimental (*C22*:250), but it is an important pivotal moment, when Christophe's attitude is transformed from revolt to benevolent love. It recalls Rolland's mellowing after Morschach, at the nadir of his own fortunes. Christophe has developed the vision of the Janiculum 'éclair', in which combativity coexists with the ability to rise above combat, and he is ready to meet Olivier Jeannin.

Olivier's story, *Antoinette*, was written in 1906 in Oxford, whose sleepy atmosphere reminded Rolland of Clamecy.[17] It is dedicated to his mother, whose devoted nurturing of her son is celebrated in this intensely auto-biographical volume. The Jeannin's prehistory, the health and financial problems, the move to Paris, the loss of faith and the struggle to pass examinations are all drawn from Rolland's life. What is fictional is the harrowing story of decline: financial ruin and his parents' death leave Olivier to be brought up by a self-sacrificing elder sister, whose brief life recalls Rolland's own first sister. The pattern of decline reflects the earlier volumes, but Antoinette will not know the rise which Christophe enjoys; after realizing that she loves him, she falls ill at the same time as he and dies, secure only in the knowledge that Olivier is on the right path and in the faith, expressed in one of Beethoven's Scottish songs, that 'I will come again' (*JC*:920). This faith in resurrection is no hollow gesture; her death is the turning point of the whole novel, for she is still present in those she leaves behind:

Il semblait qu'Antoinette, en mourant, eût soufflé une partie de son âme à son frère. Il le croyait. Sans avoir la foi, comme elle, il se persuadait obscurément que sa sœur n'était pas tout à fait morte, qu'elle vivait en lui, ainsi qu'elle l'avait promis. Une croyance de Bretagne veut que les jeunes morts ne soient pas morts: ils continuent de flotter aux lieux où ils vécurent, jusqu'à ce qu'ils aient accompli la durée normale de leur existence. – Ainsi, Antoinette continuait de grandir auprès d'Olivier. (*JC*:922)

Antoinette survives as a developmental force which pervades the friendship of Christophe and Olivier: 'Dès lors, l'âme d'Antoinette les enveloppa tous deux [. . .] Son amour était le lien où leurs cœurs s'unissaient' (*JC*:940). The death which prevails in the Paris 'foire' has been conquered, and Antoinette cements the friendship which sets the work on a rising path.

Dans la maison, like *La Révolte*, is not prominent in Rolland's 1903 plan. Though essential to the diptych of modern France, its late addition suggests that Rolland did not originally intend such a detailed survey. For this portrayal of the hidden France, Rolland must reshape his focalizer, which he does by adding Olivier's vision, both through his own eyes and as an influence on Christophe. The narrative interest, which Rolland confessed was weak (*JC*:1599), lies in the development of their friendship, the duel with Lévy-Cœur, the threat of war and the death of Christophe's mother. Rolland's portrait of Olivier, weak, shy, a touch effeminate, reacting violently when roused and lacking the ability to impose himself, but lucid, affectionate and with an inward calm, reflects aspects of himself. Such men are 'les compagnes idéales des génies' (*JC*:944), and it is interesting to speculate what light this throws on Rolland's interest in writing the lives of great men. Through Olivier, Christophe discovers the national renewal which, in a variation of the paradox of 'le vaincu vainqueur', springs from the defeat of 1870 (*JC*:988). Olivier reveals France's refined artistry, idealism, individualism and deep reserves of faith, and in communicating his lucidity to Christophe he acquires some of his friend's strength.

This France is shown in action in the apartment house where the friends live. Its residents represent the best aspects of French life, but are locked in their own little worlds, separated by ideological differences. Their separateness is presented through a series of portraits, then Christophe's influence is seen bringing them together, forging a new French unity of the symphonic type, in which individual elements keep their identity. It is confirmed by a threat of war with Germany, when even Christophe thinks of returning home to fight, but the threat passes and he returns only briefly, to see his dying mother. As he surveys his life at this moment, the Rhine shows him the meaning of his friendship with Olivier:

> Il coulait entre eux, non pour les séparer, mais afin de les unir; ils se mariaient en lui. Et Christophe prit conscience, pour la première fois, de son destin, qui était de charrier, comme une artère, dans les peuples ennemis, toutes les forces de vie de l'une et l'autre rives. (*JC*:1077)

The Rhine, like the Christophe-Olivier couple, symbolizes Franco-German unity, the canalizing of all that is vital in Europe. Death does not quench this vitality, and the volume closes with Christophe reaffirming the presence within him of all his beloved departed; he himself is the river in which the lives of the dead flow on:

> 'Nous sommes un seul être, vivants et morts; où je suis, vous êtes avec moi, Maintenant, je te porte en moi, ô mère, qui m'as porté. Vous tous, Gottfried, Schulz, Sabine, Antoinette, vous êtes tous en moi. Vous êtes ma richesse. Nous ferons route ensemble. Je serai votre voix'. (*JC*:1085)

This apotheosis of friendship sets the scene for *Les Amies*, dominated by a series of women; it has something of the mood of a symphonic slow movement, and its interest in women's emancipation anticipates *L'Ame enchantée*.[18] The main subject is Olivier's marriage to a Parisian who, though superior to her world, cannot escape its corruption. Rolland scrupulously makes Jacqueline Langeais as unlike Clotilde as possible, and his portrayal is by no means unsympathetic, but a number of intimate touches reveal Clotilde's presence; the death of Jacqueline's aunt reflects Clotilde's bereavements in 1892, and the coolness between Christophe and Olivier hints at the rift with Suarès to which Clotilde contributed. After the collapse of the marriage, Christophe tries to help Olivier but is too full of life not to be irritated by his friend's grief: 'Comme le vanneur trie le grain, il range d'un côté ce qui veut vivre, de l'autre ce qui veut mourir' (*JC*:1235). The difference between them is clear, and it hints at how Rolland uses Olivier to exorcize his negative feelings. Olivier is what must die in him, and Christophe what must survive. Christophe himself befriends the singer Cécile Fleury and Mme Arnaud, a married woman whose happiness is more apparent than real, and he has an affair with Françoise Oudon, an actress combining elements of Eleonora Duse and Suzanne Després, Lugné-Poë's wife; both, however, are too strong personalities to give themselves completely in love. Only in the closing pages does Christophe encounter love in its purest form. In one of the novel's great climaxes, Grazia reappears as a distant protector, in a moment of eye-contact in a mirror which leads into a scene with clear allusions to the death of Rolland's sister (*JC*:1238). Grazia is married and cannot be Christophe's, but the stage is set for their love in the final volume.

At this point in the 1903 plan, Christophe was to depart for England and come under the influence of a revolutionary based on Mazzini. In a later version, this episode was rescheduled to take place after Olivier's death, and an elaborate scenario was worked out showing Christophe involved in revolutionary action.[19] In the finished work, however, the political content is confined to the first part of *Le Buisson ardent*. Rolland never fully explained his change of plan. His visit in 1906 confirmed his lack of sympathy with England, and he decided after visiting Spain in 1907 to confine himself to the Franco-German axis rather than attempt a wider portrayal of Europe, which would overstretch his plan.[20] Yet considerations of size had not stopped him from adding *La Révolte* at a time when his prospects were much less secure; it seems more likely that he no longer felt able to write his political volume. By 1909 his interest in Mazzini had cooled, and he was less enthusiastic about revolutionary activity.[21] What interested him now was less the heroic presentation of revolution than the attitude to it of artists who are not primarily men of action, Olivier because he is weak and above the mêlée, Christophe because he senses his role is as an individual, not as part of a mass movement. This theme could be treated without the Mazzini figure and without leaving Paris.

Olivier as a Frenchman has a mystic attachment to revolution (*JC*:1274), and senses before Christophe that the tide of history is running towards socialism. The individuals carried by the tide are, however, often mediocre, and it is to the revolutionary elite that he is drawn:

> Le regard et le cœur d'Olivier étaient attirés par des îlôts d'indépendants, les petits groupes de vrais croyants, qui émergeaient çà et là, comme des fleurs sur l'eau. L'élite a beau vouloir se mêler à la foule; elle va toujours à l'élite – l'élite de toutes les classes et de tous les partis – , ceux qui portent le feu. (*JC*:1293)

Even in a mass movement individuals count, and Olivier's interest goes to the crippled child Emmanuel. He dies shielding this child in a riot, but not before transmitting his faith to him. Emmanuel has been brought up a materialist, but Olivier broadens his horizons with his own 'foi idéaliste [. . .] qui n'a ni commencement ni fin, et dont les milliards d'êtres et les milliards d'instants ne sont que les rayons de l'unique soleil' (*JC*:1307).

Olivier expresses Rolland's pantheism, and its presence demonstrates the unity of the two disparate parts of *Le Buisson ardent*; both are concerned with awakening the divinity in man.

The second part of the volume, sketched at a very early stage, was painful to write. At times one senses a return to an earlier manner, notably in the chronology. Christophe's departure from Paris, we have seen, marks the point where the work leaves the present for a mythical future, but the Basle episodes seem to be set, like the early volumes, in an unspecified past when, we are told, the city carnival took a different form from the one it takes at present (*JC*:1390). The tragic vision of man in the grip of destiny which is the episode's main theme has more in common with the Revolutionary dramas than with the world of *Les Amies*, and the concern with the dangerous power of music can be traced to Rolland's student projects. Yet the volume is essential to the novel's architecture, the crisis Christophe must go through to release the divine within himself.

Christophe's killing of a policeman shows him possessed by uncontrollable forces, and the process goes further in Basle, where he commits adultery with his protector's wife and is saved from suicide only when a revolver fails to fire. This episode is not autobiographical; it was inspired by Tolstoy's *Kreutzer Sonata* and a story told to Rolland by an acquaintance familiar with the narrow Calvinism of the Basle bourgeoisie.[22] Despite Anna Braun's efforts to conform and Christophe's horror of adultery, their emotions overwhelm them, and it is music that releases Anna's repressed instincts:

> O musique, qui ouvres les abîmes de l'âme! Tu ruines l'équilibre habituel de l'esprit. Dans la vie ordinaire, les âmes ordinaires sont des chambres fermées [. . .] Mais la musique tient le magique rameau qui fait tomber les serrures. Les portes s'ouvrent. Les démons du cœur paraissent. (*JC*:1377)

Music releases the divine in man, but the divine can take a demonic form. Christophe escapes and buries himself in the country, but nature brings no solace and the winter scene reflects the drying up of his creativity. The environment itself is rent by demonic forces; Christophe confronts the tragedy of nature red in tooth and claw, in which all life is a struggle against other life forms. The very trees in the forest form armies attacking each other (*JC*:1413).

Life returns with Easter, season of resurrection, and the *foehn* brings with it a dialogue between Christophe and his God which explains the volume's title. It carries the novel's central profession of faith:

> Dieu n'était pas pour lui le Créateur impassible, le Néron qui contemple, du haut de sa tour d'airain, l'incendie de la Ville que lui-même alluma. Dieu souffre. Dieu combat. Avec ceux qui combattent et avec tous ceux qui souffrent. Car il est la Vie, la goutte de lumière qui, tombée dans la nuit, s'étend et boit la nuit. Mais la nuit est sans bornes, et le combat divin ne s'arrête jamais; et nul ne peut savoir quelle en sera l'issue. Symphonie héroïque, où les dissonances mêmes qui se heurtent et se mêlent forment un concert serein! Comme la forêt de hêtres qui livre dans le silence des combats furieux, ainsi la Vie guerroie dans l'éternelle paix. (*JC*:1422)

The tragedy of nature makes sense when seen as the battle waged by a pantheist God, identified with life and intimately associated with his creation, not detached from it. Life, however, does not comprehend everything:

> Je ne suis pas tout ce qui est. Je suis la Vie qui combat le Néant. Je ne suis pas le Néant. Je suis le Feu qui brûle dans la Nuit. Je ne suis pas la Nuit. Je suis le Combat éternel; et nul destin éternel ne plane sur le combat. Je suis la Volonté libre, qui lutte éternellement. Lutte et brûle avec moi! (*JC*:1420)

God struggles for victory over 'le Néant' in a conflict of which the outcome is uncertain. Responsibility for victory does not lie with destiny, but with God-bearers such as Christophe, who pit their will against the void which they find in such places as the Paris 'foire'. Life is identified with struggle, and in that struggle the individual may be overcome, but he has played his part in the great symphony which becomes perceptible to the truly serene. In this way he becomes a victor, revealing the cosmic dimension of the 'vaincu vainqueur' paradox. Now that Christophe is again in contact with God, his music returns. He is still prey to demons, but this time it is 'das Dämonische', the force driving a creator to create, which springs from the divine life within him:

> Il était en proie à ce délire d'esprit, que connaît tout génie, à cette volonté indépendante de la volonté, '*cette énigme indicible du monde et de la vie*' que Goethe appelait '*le démoniaque*' et contre laquelle il restait armé, mais qui le soumettait. (*JC*:1425)

His art is transformed. As in Beethoven's late works, the subservience to old musical language is gone, he passes beyond what the public can understand and his works reflect, in Novalis's words, '*les yeux du chaos qui luisent à travers le voile de l'ordre*' (*JC*:1426). Order will, however, be reconquered in the final volume.

The Rolland of *La Nouvelle Journée* was very different from the Rolland of *L'Aube*. Successful, independent and recovered from his road accident, he had, like Christophe, survived a shattering experience, and this volume is about the world he found on his return. Christophe has conquered serenity. Like Michelangelo's *Moses*, he combines two selves, the fighter and the man of calm:

> Il porte en son âme deux âmes. L'une est un haut plateau, battu des vents et des nuages. L'autre, qui la domire, est un sommet neigeux qui baigne dans la lumière. On n'y peut séjourner; mais quand on est glacé par les brouillards d'en bas, on connaît le chemin qui monte vers le soleil. (*JC*:1433)

The agent of his transformation is Grazia, whom he meets in the Alps as did Rolland and Sofia in 1901. True, the character was planned long before; she features in the earliest plans and owes something to Eleonora Duse and Beethoven's beloved, Theresa von Brunsvik. Yet by now he and Sofia had ten years of friendship behind them, and in his unpublished *Mémoires* he covers Sofia's identity by calling her Grazia. The relationship is platonic; Grazia's calm irony, matured by suffering, keeps Christophe at arm's length, but later, drawn together by her son's illness, they function almost as a married couple and one senses a certain idealization on Rolland's part. This, perhaps, is what he would have liked to achieve with Sofia.

Grazia draws Christophe to Italy, which charms him as it charmed the young Rolland, and she works on him by the same transmigration of souls as he experienced with Olivier:

> Grazia lui apportait en dot le trésor le plus rare, que jamais Olivier n'avait possédé; la joie. La joie de l'âme et des yeux. La lumière. Le sourire de ce ciel latin, qui baigne la laideur des plus humbles choses, qui fleurit les pierres des vieux murs, et communique à la tristesse même son calme rayonnement. (*JC*:1461)

Through her, Christophe realizes Beethoven's 'Durch Leiden Freude'. The transmigration is completed when Grazia herself dies and communicates her peace to Christophe; his last tie with suffering is broken and he composes his serenest works:

> Il était libéré. La lutte était finie. Sorti de la zone des combats et du cercle où régnait le dieu des mêlées héroïques, *Dominus Deus Sabaoth*, il regardait à ses pieds s'effacer dans la nuit la torche du Buisson Ardent. (*JC*:1556)

The order which escaped him in the previous volume is reconquered; he is above the mêlée, and death itself holds no terrors.

Before this, he has other tasks to fulfil. Returning to Paris, he finds both it and himself changed; 'la Foire' is still there, but he faces it with new calm. His music is unfashionable, but he is more drawn to the new generation opposed to him than to his disciples, as Rolland himself often was. The house which represents France has grown, and despite the fuss and apparent chaos, something solid lies beneath; France has achieved her symphonic unity in disunity: 'Sous leur anarchie, il y a des instincts communs, il y a une logique de race qui leur tient lieu de discipline' (*JC*:1471–2). Christophe does not approve of everything; as an individualist he resists the temptation to lock himself into a specific faith which is what fashion requires, but he communicates his serenity to a few of his juniors. Something of Olivier has passed into Emmanuel, now a visionary poet modelled on Péguy, a more powerful creator than Olivier but also more turbulent; Christophe helps him to face critical attacks calmly. Olivier's son Georges, an anti-intellectual tearaway typical of modern youth, also profits from Christophe's restraint. Christophe favours Georges's union with Grazia's symbolically named daughter Aurora, and the marriage of a Frenchman and an Italian woman under the aegis of a German reflects his last compositions, which 'réalise[nt. . .] l'union des plus belles forces musicales de son temps: la pensée affectueuse et savante d'Allemagne aux replis ombreux, la mélodie passionnée d'Italie et le vif esprit de France, riche de rythmes fins et d'harmonies nuancées' (*JC*:1557–8). As war clouds rise, Christophe achieves the international vision which only Olivier achieved in *Dans la maison*, and he owes it to the transmigration of souls which Rolland considered essential to the work's message:

C'est là le mystère de la transmigration de l'esprit sans frontières de l'Olivier français dans le corps plus robuste du Christophe d'Occident, sous l'illumination de la Grâce, messagère divine, – Grazia la Mantouane, de la terre de Virgile, – c'est ce mystère, célébré dans le '*Ludus Amoris et Mortis*': '*La Nouvelle Journée*', qui constitue le troisième élément – le plus pur – de mon '*Jean-Christophe*'. (*VI*:262)

It remains only for Christophe to die, which he does apparently alone but in fact rich in companions. Music stays with him, as he fights his supreme battle with an invisible orchestra to find the perfect resolution to an elusive harmony. The departed souls who have passed into him are also there, and so is the Rhine, flowing into the ocean where all souls are united and the Empedoclean antithesis of love and hatred is resolved:

Et le grondement du fleuve, et la mer bruissante chantèrent avec lui: – Tu renaîtras. Repose! Tout n'est plus qu'un seul choeur. Sourire de la nuit et du jour enlacés. Harmonie, couple auguste de l'amour et de la haine! Je chanterai le Dieu aux deux puissantes ailes. Hosanna à la vie! Hosanna à la mort! (*JC*:1593)

Christophe becomes St Christopher, crossing the river with the divine child who proclaims the new dawn: 'Je suis le jour qui va naître' (*JC*:1594). Christophe is the precursor of the new generation, and death is conquered on both the political and religious level. One understands why Rolland asserted that in *Jean-Christophe* 'je n'écris pas une œuvre de littérature. J'écris une œuvre de foi' (*JC*:xiv).

This survey, concentrating on the novel's religious trajectory, has passed lightly over a number of themes requiring more comment. First, the evolution of Christophe's art deserves a glance, for it tells us much about how Rolland saw his own creation.

Christophe's first artistic crisis is over the issue of sincerity. Forced by his father to be a court amuser, he composes conventional music whose hollowness is exposed by Gottfried:

Tu as écrit pour écrire. Tu as écrit pour être un grand musicien, pour qu'on t'admirât. Tu as été orgueilleux, tu as menti; tu as été puni. . . Voilà! On est toujours puni, lorsqu'on est orgueilleux et qu'on ment. La musique veut être modeste et sincère. (*JC*:95–6)

Music, for Gottfried, is the expression of feeling, not mere virtuosity, and *La Révolte* shows that Christophe has taken the message. Surveying his earlier works, he is repelled by their hollowness:

Ce qui l'exaspérait surtout dans ces œuvres, c'était leur mensonge. Rien de senti. Une phraséologie apprise par cœur, une rhétorique d'écolier [. . .] Il s'était toujours efforcé d'être sincère. Mais il ne s'agit pas de vouloir être sincère: il faut pouvoir l'être. (*JC*:380–1)

He needs to find a style which will say no more and no less than what he means, to build his art into an expressive language. This is why the crisis of *Le Buisson ardent* is important; before he can achieve the serene mastery of his last compositions, he must break with convention and find his own voice.

This is, however, only half the story, for that voice must communicate: 'Certes, il est de grands artistes qui n'expriment que soi. Mais les plus grands de tous sont ceux dont le cœur bat pour tous' (*JC*:1138). Art must break barriers, as Christophe asserts in *Les Amies*, where he calls for a sincere unadorned style:

> Ne t'inquiète point des recherches subtiles où s'énerve la force des artistes d'aujourd'hui. Tu parles à tous: use du langage de tous. Il n'est de mots ni nobles, ni vulgaires; il n'est que ceux qui disent ou ne disent pas exactement ce qu'ils ont à dire. Sois tout entier dans tout ce que tu fais; pense ce que tu penses, et sens ce que tu sens. Que le rythme de ton cœur emporte tes écrits! Le style, c'est l'âme. (*JC*:1140)

This ideal of simplicity owes something to Handel, on whom Rolland was working at the time, but it is also very much his own ideal, asserted in a letter to Séché refuting a suggestion that he is not an artist. He denies this, but detaches himself from contemporaries to whom the finely chiselled detail is all-important:

> J'attache plus d'importance au mouvement général du morceau qu'au détail de la phrase, aux grandes lignes de la composition qu'aux nuances fines; mais chaque volume a son rythme; et si, dans le récit, les passages intermédiaires sont traités parfois avec une certaine négligence (due à la hâte que j'ai d'arriver à la fin de l'œuvre, avant de crever), les sommets de l'action ne sont jamais sacrifiés [. . .] Je crois qu'il serait plus juste de dire que je ne regarde pas l'art comme une fin, mais comme un moyen, comme une langue expressive. (*C13*:61)

This brings together many aspects of the way Rolland sees his art: the sense of developmental process, the importance attached to overall structure, the impatience to finish, the desire to communicate and the reaction against excess refinement. One understands the coolness between Rolland and the *Nouvelle Revue Française*; Gide found Rolland's writing inelegant, while Rolland considered Gide a mere man of letters lacking broader human sympathies. Proust attacked Rolland's style on similar grounds in *Contre Sainte-Beuve*. Rolland's insistence on the primacy of content helped to create the myth that he was an author without style.[23]

Art, by communicating, brings people together. Though the German Christophe cannot create it, he envisages a symphony of French marching songs which would cement national unity (*JC*:1053), and his last serene works contribute to European harmony. These are, however, different types of unity, and the question arises of what influence Rolland hoped to achieve in an age of looming conflict. When Rolland started his novel he was still committed to a Revolutionary theatre aimed at galvanizing

French national energies, but he was already forming elitist and internationalist ideals. In 1901, he wrote to Sofia of an ambition he would voice frequently over the years:

> Il faut fonder un Weimar nouveau et agrandi, une patrie intellectuelle et morale, où se crée enfin l'âme *européenne* [. . .] C'est notre devoir de créer maintenant un centre moral de l'Europe, une capitale de l'élite européenne, une aire d'aigle, où se reforme à l'abri des tempêtes politiques, et dominant le torrent aveugle des foules, la conscience supérieure de la civilisation. (*C10*:19-20)

Elitism is not contrary to Rolland's socialism; the divine spirit could hardly be rekindled in a materialist mass movement without an elite to bear the flame, and Rolland saw no inconsistency in such an elite working to restimulate national energy. Yet the Goethean Weimar ideal suggests a different kind of elite, detached from mass movements, preserving civilization against a people on the march which has taken a wrong turning. In this, there does seem to be an inconsistency.

In both France and Germany, Christophe confronts a bogus elite claiming falsely to represent the nation before he can reach the true elite: in Germany it is the mendacious idealism of the musical establishment and the materialism of the Empire, in France the chattering 'foire' and the politicians who pervert the republican ideal. Jews feature prominently in the false elite; intelligent and flexible, they adopt features of their host nation and carry them to caricatural extremes. Jews in *Jean-Christophe* are portrayed with some hostility, reflecting Rolland's marital experience. Even Olivier's measured voice suggests they should be kept in their place:

> Non que je croie leur race inférieure à la nôtre: (ces questions de suprématie des races sont niaises et dégoûtantes). – Mais il est inadmissible qu'une race étrangère, qui ne s'est pas encore fondue dans la nôtre, ait la prétention de connaître mieux ce qui nous convient, que nous-mêmes [. . .] Les Juifs sont comme les femmes: excellents, quand on les tient en bride; mais leur domination, à celles-ci et à ceux-là, est exécrable. (*JC*:1007)

This stops short of anti-Semitism; it is no more and no less than what Rolland says of any group seeking to impose its personality at the cost of suppressing others. What Rolland seeks is not imperial unity, with everything subjected to one dominant force, but harmonic unity, in which all elements play their role. This is postulated in *Dans la maison*, where the best are separated by the national proclivity for militant faith which sets them at each other's throats. Christophe appreciates 'la grandeur de ce fanatisme' (*JC*:957), but since Dreyfus and the 1905 separation of

Church and State, internecine conflict has become self-destructive. Christophe's house is inhabited by all that is best in the France of the day: the modernist priest, the Protestant Dreyfusards, the self-made worker, the schoolteacher, the old Communard, the Jewish intellectual, the retired colonial army officer. All are men of good will, but they mistrust each other; only Christophe can break the barriers.

Rolland's position vis-à-vis these camps resists easy definition. As in the Dreyfus case, he was too aware of the strengths and weaknesses of all sides to be partisan, and he felt his task as novelist was to create characters rather than project ideas. As he wrote in 1913:

> Pas un seul, parmi les critiques, n'a remarqué *les êtres*, dans mon œuvre. Ils ne parlent que des *idées*! Les idées, qui n'existent, dans *Jean-Christophe*, qu'en fonction des personnages! [. . .] D'où ces contradictions qu'on m'a reprochées, – et dont je jouis. Ma pensée à moi, je ne l'exprime pas dans des formules. Je l'exprime dans des êtres, dont les attractions et les heurts forment une symphonie. Les rythmes et les accords, dans l'univers des âmes, voilà le plan sur lequel meut ma pensée. (*C15*:211)

This statement, remarkably close to his 1890 musical novel project, can be misleading; Rolland's omniscient narratorial voice gives plenty of ammunition to those who seek to reduce him to a series of formulae. Yet he does create a galaxy of admirable characters in all camps, and their dialogue does not lead to a neat conclusion.

The constant element is respect for individuals who refuse to be swamped by party. Liberty is essential to France, and in the two militant faiths of Catholicism and socialism, Rolland admires those who retain it. Such a one is the Abbé Corneille, the censured modernist priest who keeps silence in a spirit of discipline but continues to think his own thoughts (*JC*:964). When Rolland praises 'le magnifique mouvement de rénovation catholique' (*JC*:955), he has the modernists in mind, and he regretted the papal condemnation of them;[24] rigid attitudes within the Church delayed his rapprochement with it for another thirty years. Of the conflicts of 1905 the novel says little; allusions in his letters suggest that Rolland could not decide whether to take them as a magnificent example of militant French faith or as the petty squabbles of 'la foire' (*C10*:252, 283).

Though Rolland's condemnation of the triumphant Dreyfusards was less trenchant than Péguy's, it is striking that his main political targets, Roussin and Lévy-Cœur, are socialists. There is little in *La Foire sur la place* to suggest sympathy with the Left, so much so that Rolland was solicited by *L'Action Française* before *Dans la maison* made it clear that

Rolland did not share its ideas (*VI*:261). Christophe prefers syndicalism to political socialism:

> Sa raison approuvait le puissant effort de ces groupements corporatifs, dont la hache à double tranchant frappe à la fois l'abstraction morte de l'Etat socialiste et l'individualisme infécond. (*JC*:1285)

In the aftermath of the Amiens Charter, syndicalism seemed a remedy both to statist tyranny and individualist isolation, and Rolland's letters show signs of sympathy with the waves of strikes which took place in these years.[25] His sympathy has become rather distant, however, in *Le Buisson ardent*; syndicalist regimentation poses problems for Christophe, who is committed to the oppressed but insists on serving them in his own way. *Jean-Christophe* is essentially about an individual struggling to realize his own divinity; the problem of the artist caught between dream and action remains unresolved.

This is never clearer than when war threatens. In *Dans la maison*, the Balkan crisis of 1908 inspires a prophetic portrayal of the 'union sacrée' of 1914; even the most pacific of the tenants in the house feel a patriotic fervour seemingly involving an obscure historical force operating at a deeper level than individual will: 'Une obscure volonté veut contre votre volonté. Et l'on découvre alors le Maître inconnu, cette Force invisible, dont les lois gouvernent l'Océan humaine. . .' (*JC*:1065). A wave of Empedoclean hatred is flowing, and even Christophe thinks of returning to Germany to fight, in the name of life itself. Only Olivier resists, seeking, like Rolland's Weimar elite, to preserve the spirit of love. Less full of life than Christophe, he asks questions about where vitality is leading, and Christophe's answer is inconclusive:

> – La vie, répéta Olivier, qu'est-ce que la vie?
> – Une tragédie, fit Christophe. Hourrah! (*JC*:1072)

There is nobility in this acceptance of cosmic tragedy, which echoes *Danton*'s Saint-Just; it anticipates the call in *Le Buisson ardent* to side with life against death. Yet this is an aesthetic response to a practical problem, and it answers none of the questions about what to do in wartime.

La Nouvelle Journée begins to answer some of them. In another prophetic passage evoking the drift to war, the dead Olivier's spirit and Grazia's serenity have passed into Christophe and he takes the position of Olivier in 1908; he refuses to hate and, conscious of the attraction of French culture even among Germans, he asserts the two nations' interdependence:

> Nous sommes les deux ailes de l'Occident. Qui brise l'une, le vol de l'autre est brisé. Vienne la guerre! Elle ne rompra point l'étreinte de nos mains et l'essor de nos génies fraternels. (*JC*:1562)

He does not claim he can stop war, and even accepts its advent, but he has faith that an elite will preserve the flame until times improve. This exactly prefigures Rolland's action in 1914, which can readily be seen as an attempt to remain true to *Jean-Christophe*. What the novel does not foretell is the difficulty Rolland would find in constituting his elite, and the problem the novel does not solve is how the policy can be translated into action.

Moreover, the work contains a metaphysical inconsistency which in 1914 became a practical problem. In *Le Buisson ardent*, we have seen, life's victory over death is not inevitable; it depends on the free will of the bearers of life, and 'nul destin éternel ne plane sur le combat'. Yet in the same passage, the conflict is evoked in symphonic imagery in which all dissonances contribute to a 'concert serein' (*JC*:1420–2). This, taken in conjunction with the passage quoted above which evokes war fever in terms of an 'obscure volonté' and a 'Maître inconnu', suggests that there is indeed a supernatural force above individual will at work. Rolland appears to have no clear vision of the relationship between the individual and the collective, the human and the divine. Individualism is the essence of Christophe's heroism, but the novel also concedes the need to play a collective role. Marxist readings tend to disparage *Jean-Christophe* on these grounds, as an immature work which Rolland would later surpass; a non-Marxist reading, conscious that it remains Rolland's most read work, might see the conflict of dream and action as a creative tension making the work superior in aesthetic terms to later work in which he made some claim to have resolved it. *Jean-Christophe* is the climax of a stage of Rolland's career; it is not the end.

Notes

1. Quoted in Duchatelet (1975), p.437.
2. Duchatelet's researches into the genesis of *Jean-Christophe*, to which this chapter owes much, have found no document explicitly linking it to the principles of the musical novel.

3. Quoted in Duchatelet (1975), p.212.
4. This phrase, Rolland's own, is the title of Séché's book of extracts from *Jean-Christophe*. See *C13*:60–1.
5. Letter to Malwida von Meysenbug, 24 February 1897; quoted in Duchatelet (1975), p.258.
6. *Mémoires* 4, feuille 33.
7. Letter to E. Marchand, 4 March 1910. Quoted in Duret (1992), p.513.
8. See for instance, the letter to Elsa Wolff in which he playfully refers to the reaction of his two friends Christophe and Raphael to her latest book (*C14*:151–2). Raphael is clearly the painter, but the name was intended for Olivier.
9. See Duchatelet (1975), p.371.
10. See the preface to Gillet's abandoned book on Rolland, in *Europe*, 439–40 (1965), pp.123–35.
11. Quoted in Motyleva (1976), p.100.
12. See Duchatelet (1975), p.705.
13. See *Mémoires* 4, feuille 39.
14. See Duchatelet (1975), p.705.
15. Duret (1992, p.453) sees in this an allusion to Orpheus's loss of Eurydice. The analogy is suggestive, as the descending and rising pattern of the novel has much in common with the theme of Orphic descent.
16. See Duchatelet (1975), pp.697–8.
17. See *Mémoires* 4, feuille 46.
18. See the important planning document quoted in Duchatelet (1997), pp.106–7.
19. Quoted extensively in Duchatelet (1976).
20. See *Mémoires* 4, feuille 47.
21. See Duchatelet (1978).
22. See Duchatelet (1975), p.404ff.
23. The growth of this myth is studied in Jeanneret (1982).
24. See a letter to Gillet in which he welcomes an expression of sympathy from the modernist Sangnier (*C2*:240).
25. See his letters to Elsa Wolff in 1909, declaring his sympathy with a postal strike (*C14*:208, 213).

–6–

Colas Breugnon

On ne peut être un artiste qu'à condition d'être tout entier dans tout ce qu'on crée, mais de s'en détacher totalement après, avec la puissance d'indifférence et d'oubli que possède la nature. – Je puis me rendre cette justice qu'à présent le cordon est coupé entre Christophe et moi. (*C15*:127)

As he finished *Jean-Christophe*, Rolland's circumstances looked unusually bright. He was free to take new directions, famous and 'presque honteux' at the money he was making (*C11*:20). His independence assured, he moved to a larger apartment in the Rue Boissonnade. He was in the grips of 'un instinct animal de renouvellement [qui] me pousse à briser tout ce qui me gêne du passé' (*JCCB*:67), and ready to rethink all social and moral ideologies.

By this date, his circle of friends had changed. He rarely saw Suarès, and relations with Péguy had suffered from a 1905 clash over Ollendorff's bid to publish *Jean-Christophe*. Péguy, who financed the *Cahiers* edition, and Rolland, who received no fees for it, both felt they had rights to the text, but after some dispute it was agreed that the commercial edition of each volume would follow shortly after Péguy's. This was to Rolland's advantage, and Péguy, in financial difficulties himself, knew it. After the 1905 Moroccan crisis their political views diverged; Péguy moved towards the nationalist Catholic right while Rolland's internationalism intensified. In 1911 they were run against each other, reluctantly on Rolland's part, for the French Academy prize, and Rolland's chief backer, his university colleague Ernest Lavisse, was a target of Péguy's polemics. Neither was awarded the prize, but Rolland won it in 1913 when the two were not in direct contention. Relations remained correct and often cordial, but Rolland was uneasy about Péguy's poetry (*C2*:257), and on the eve of war he was attacked by Péguy's associate René Johannot.[1] As to Gillet, the two men met less after Gillet's marriage, and Gillet's right-wing Catholic views were always a possible source of difficulty, but it was he that Rolland suggested when, in 1913, Ollendorff sought an editor for an anthology of Rolland's writings.

His closest new friend was Alphonse de Châteaubriant, whom he met in 1906, warming to the younger man's sensitive poetic nature. Another younger admirer was Jean-Richard Bloch, whose periodical *L'Effort* brought Rolland into contact with a group of writers many of whom became his supporters during the war. *Jean-Christophe* won allies abroad; in Italy he corresponded with the writers of *La Voce*, he was praised by H.G. Wells, his Swiss friend Paul Seippel published the first book on his work in 1913 and the same year saw the beginning of his friendship with Stefan Zweig. D'Annunzio, Verhaeren, Van Eeden, Ramuz and Rilke also figured among his contacts. In the musical world he continued to correspond with Strauss, and he launched the career of Paul Dupin, a self-taught musician of humble origin.

Friendships with women were particularly important. He gleaned some German material for *Jean-Christophe* from his correspondence with the young novelist Elsa Wolff, begun in 1906, which has something of the tone of his letters to Sofia, but their friendship did not develop after they met, and the war ended it. Esther Marchand, who worked for musical charities and followed his lectures, also began to correspond with him in 1906; though her inquisitiveness irritated him, they exchanged letters until his death. She supported his efforts on behalf of Dupin; so too did Louise Cruppi, wife of a prominent Radical politician, who devoted her considerable energy and contacts to charitable works and literary projects. When in 1909 her son died suddenly, she found solace in the unorthodox faith with which Rolland sought to console her, and despite different temperaments they became close friends. Other relationships were less platonic. Hélène Barrère, daughter of the French Ambassador in Rome, was for a time in love with him, but he did not encourage her, sensing she was too young. In 1909 he thought of marrying Ethel Sidgwick, an English friend of his sister, but was discouraged by his lack of sympathy with the English character: 'Il y a entre une vraie âme anglaise et une vraie âme française un rideau de brumes qu'il est si difficile de pénétrer!' (*C11*:52) Only after completing *Jean-Christophe* did he fall in love again. The details remain obscure, as Rolland was discreet on these matters, but the 'petite crise de passion' he mentions in September 1912 (*C26*:153) appears to allude to a Belgian aristocrat, Olga de Lichtervelde. Some published pages of his diary suggest that she, Châteaubriant and others were with him in a Swiss hotel in the summer of 1913, and that, as with Clotilde, he was battling against the lady's *mondain* tendencies (*JCCB*:148ff). More important, in 1914 he began a liaison with an Irish-American actress with literary ambitions, Helena Van Brugh de Kay, to whom he refers as T, standing for Thalie, the tragic muse. He told Châteaubriant of her 'folie anglo-saxonne qui converse tranquillement avec Dieu et tranquillement vous traduit en anglais ce qu'ils ont dit ensemble'; her 'intrépidité souriante, qui ne la fait douter du succès d'aucune entreprise' he found both 'comique et charmant' (*C26*:239).

La Nouvelle Journée shows Rolland sensing new vitality in Paris. Like Christophe, he did not approve of all of it, but he was persuaded to undertake a 'chronique parisienne' for a Swiss periodical, the *Bibliothèque universelle de Genève*,[2] in which Rolland viewed Paris in a new light:

> Je ne puis supporter Paris; tout me froisse et me blesse, dans mes moindres contacts, avec le monde et l'art. Et à peine commencé-je à prendre la plume pour décrire ce qui m'entoure que je comprends et j'admire. J'ai une intelligence qui ne m'appartient pas; elle est indépendante de mon cœur et de mon corps; elle n'a pas de patrie; elle est faite pour tout comprendre. (*C26*:156)

With a characteristic separation of heart and mind, he surveyed areas of the Paris world from which he had previously held aloof and found grounds to praise a wide range of figures: Bergson, Péguy, the Catholic revival, Verhaeren, Bloch and his friends, a new generation of women writers, the Impressionists, the plays of Henri Bataille and Claudel, even Agathon and Gaston Riou, his ideological opponents. He enjoyed stepping for a while outside his combative role and adopting a serener vision which he evokes in the fateful phrase 'au-dessus de la mêlèe'.[3] This 'chronique' lasted from November 1912 to March 1913, after which he relinquished it to a young protégé, Henri Bachelin.

Rolland's attitude did not appeal to everyone. For those who saw faith as an exclusive commitment, he seemed a dilettante. André Beaunier dismissed him as a 'Don Juan des idées' (*VI*:261), and Henri Massis was already attacking him in 1913 in an article entitled 'Romain Rolland ou le dilettantisme de la foi'.[4] Nationalists resented his choice of a German hero, and the wounds of *La Foire sur la place* still festered. Critics nurtured on rationality and clear ideas, or who lacked musical awareness, found him imprecise and emotional. Fastidious stylists objected to his preference for expressivity over fine writing, and acclaim came slower in France than elsewhere. One might have expected him to consort with pacifists and internationalists, but he kept his distance. In 1912 he refused to join a 'Comité de rapprochement intellectuel franco-allemand' (*JG*:530, 1849), also a Tolstoy Committee organized by Paul-Hyacinthe Loyson, who did not forgive him. He even refused Bloch's request to sign a petition against the extension of military service to three years, arguing that once the decision had been announced, it would be against national security not to pursue it (*C15*:186). These are not the reactions of an integral pacifist, but of an independent resisting regimentation.

In April 1913, Rolland left Paris for the summer. Most of it was spent in Switzerland, but, following a family funeral in March which took him to Clamecy for the first time in years, he also toured his home province. His response to its landscapes was not uniformly enthusiastic, but the visit awakened nostalgia, and during this summer he surprised himself by conceiving and writing much of *Colas Breugnon*, in such euphoria that he lapsed into total insomnia and had to suspend work for a while on doctor's orders.

The projects he intended to follow *Jean-Christophe* were a study of the modern family from the woman's point of view, a series of works in the harmonious vein of *La Nouvelle Journée* and a theatrical *Polichinelle* (*JCCB*:29-30). *L'Ame enchantée* and *Liluli* are there in embryo, but not *Colas Breugnon*, though hints of it can be seen in a desire expressed in 1908 to write 'la vie d'un *grand homme gai*' (*C10*:353), and in 'le paysan Patience', a character in a Rabelaisian epic by Christophe and Olivier who keeps cheerful through many disasters (*JC*:1072). Rolland saw this novel as something he needed to work out of his system, an outburst from deep national and family roots, the paternal side of his personality suppressed by the influence of his mother:

> Du côté maternel, la musique, le sérieux moral, ces tendances jansénistes et puritaines [. . .] Du côté paternel, la forte vitalité et l'optimisme foncier, instinctif, invincible, malgré toutes les raisons de tristesse et les accablements passagers, – la vie bonne malgré tout [. . .] Si de [ma mère] je tiens peut-être la meilleure de ma personnalité artistique et morale, c'est pourtant l'autre qui m'a sauvé, plus d'une fois dans la vie. (*C2*:272)

The work differed disconcertingly from his previous writings. Never offered to Péguy, it was intended for Lavisse's *Revue de Paris*, but Lavisse found it too shocking to print. The war interrupted the Ollendorff edition, but it was finally released unchanged in 1919.

The novel covers one year, 1616, fiftieth in the life of the hero, a wood carver of Clamecy. This makes Colas exactly three centuries older than Rolland and situates the action at the end of the religious wars, just before the age of seventeenth-century classicism, which Rolland saw as a repressive imperialism. Colas voices an older tradition which Rolland celebrated in a 1912 letter to Paul Amann:

La France d'avant le XVIe siècle est infiniment plus vaste et plus profonde:
et cette France vit toujours dans le cœur et dans l'esprit de nos races provin-
ciales [. . .] Si vous alliez dans le Morvan nivernais ou bourguignon, mon
pays, vous verriez autour des cathédrales de Vézelay et d'Autun se promener
et causer les types qui servirent de modèles aux sculpteurs des cathédrales
[. . .] C'est là que sont nos réserves; et j'espère bien qu'un jour, au lieu de
les économiser prudemment, en silence, nous les répandrons sur le monde.
(*C17*:100)

Colas's style recalls Rabelais, epitome of a linguistic wealth stifled by
classicism. He carries to extremes a tendency to use alexandrines often
found in Rolland's prose, enriched in this instance by rhyme. This intro-
duces a ludic element to the work, irritating to the purist but appealing in
its relish of the musical potential of language, and showing the influence
of Paul Fort (*C26*:188).

Rolland described this novel as his *Meistersinger*;[5] Colas, like Hans
Sachs, is a middle-aged craftsman who cannot have the woman he loves,
but radiates personal warmth and acceptance of life. The subtitle is
Bonhomme vit encore, and Colas's heroism lies in his survival of an *annus
horribilis*. He faces civil war, learns that he could have had the sweetheart
of his youth instead of his present shrewish wife, survives the plague
only to see his wife die, his house burned and his life's work ruined,
breaks his ankle and is crippled. Yet his mood is buoyant:

Lorsque, à la fin, j'établis ma balance, je me trouve aussi riche qu'avant!
[. . .] En somme, l'homme est un brave animal. Tout lui est bon. Il s'ajuste
aussi bien au bonheur, à la peine, à la bombance, à la disette. Donnez-lui
quatre jambes, ou prenez-lui ses deux, faites-le sourd, aveugle, muet, il trouvera
moyen de s'en accommoder [. . .] Et c'est beau de sentir qu'on a cette souplesse
dans l'esprit et dans les jarrets, que l'on peut aussi bien être poisson dans
l'eau, oiseau dans l'air, dans le feu salamandre, et sur la terre un homme qui
lutte joyeusement avec les quatre éléments. (*CB*:319)

His secret is a paradoxical combination of harmony with his environment
and willingness to fight against it. As a comic hero, he resolves relatively
painlessly the constant dilemma of Rolland's heroes, whether or not to
accept his destiny.

On the one hand is an adaptability rooted in nature, which helps him
make the best of his lot. In despair after meeting his old love, he tells his
woes to a tree at whose foot he sleeps, but is consoled by the ensuing
dawn chorus:

> Aussitôt que se rouvre le rideau de la nuit, dès que le rire pâle de l'aurore lointaine commence à ranimer le visage glacé et les lèvres blanchies de la vie. . . , *oy ty, oy ty, la la-ï, la la la, laderi, la rifla*. . . , de quels cris, mes amis, de quels transports d'amour ils célèbrent le jour! Tout ce qu'on a souffert, ce qu'on a redouté, l'épouvante muette et le sommeil glacé, la nuit, tout, *oy ty*, tout. . .*frrtt*. . . est oublié. (*CB*:137–8)

Similar cosmic forces are at work when Colas overcomes the plague after a delirious night in his garden, plunged in 'ma bonne terre grasse et molle' and sustained by bottles of Burgundian wine brought by his friends (*CB*:173–6). A good trencherman, Colas absorbs the vital spirits he needs from the wine of his native soil. With its pagan sense of divine forces permeating nature, the passage recalls the forest conflicts of *Le Buisson ardent*; Rolland's pantheism has rarely been more vividly expressed.

Equally Colas asserts himself against his environment. He is the archetypal French individualist, the little man clinging to his independence, coping with a civil war in which he must withstand a siege and hide his last bottles of Chablis from the soldiers billeted on him. He readily fraternizes with the enemy once peace is concluded, and seems more concerned about being exploited by his supposed protectors: 'Pauvres moutons! Si nous n'avons à nous défendre que du loup, nous saurions bien nous en garder. Mais qui nous gardera du berger?' (*CB*:46) This mistrust of authority does not imply disloyalty to his king, but he insists that if the king visited him in his house, he would welcome him as an equal: 'Cousin, un roi vaut un autre. Chaque Français est roi. Et bonhomme est maître chez soi' (*CB*:323).

Individualism and closeness to the god within are features Colas shares with Christophe, and they are further united by their uneasy involvement in action. Colas does not hesitate to lead his fellow citizens against a band of pillagers when the civic authorities fail in their duty, even though it involves burning down a building where the bandits are trapped. He tempers ruthlessness with the heroic rescue of a former friend, but on the morning after he does not like what he sees in himself or his fellow men: 'On s'était trop bien vu [. . .]; la nature humaine avait été surprise sans chemise: ça n'est pas beau!' (*CB*:247). Even life-enhancing characters release destructive forces, Colas as much as Orsino or the French Revolutionaries. It is interesting to read this passage in the light of the coming war; it suggests reluctant acceptance of the occasional need to fight, rejection of integral pacifism and a desire to conduct conflict humanely.

Essentially, however, Colas's vitality is a radiant force. Though his art is humble and utilitarian, it is rooted in human needs, those of bringing people together and expressing their aspirations: 'L'art est pour nous quelqu'un de la famille, le génie du foyer, l'ami, le compagnon, et qui dit mieux que nous ce que tous nous sentons' (*CB*:107). One of his worst trials is seeing his prospects of immortality destroyed by an employer who vandalizes his masterpiece, but he is consoled by a brave young apprentice who saves one of his master's works from his burning house: 'Voilà mon plus beau travail: les âmes que j'ai sculptées. Ils ne me les prendront pas' (*CB*:215). For Rolland no work of art is eternal; what matters is the creative process and its transmission from man to man. Colas is on the receiving end of this transmission when, as a cripple, he reads Plutarch, writer of heroic lives, and is enriched by these figures from another age with whom he shares his humanity and divinity (*CB*:295–6).

More than an artist, Colas is a harmonizer. Like Rolland's father a Burgundian who argues his case with verve, he respects his adversary and cheerfully reconciles all differences over a meal and a bottle. This emerges in the wildly pantheistic religious debate of his friends, the priest Chamaille and the rationalist Paillard. After listening to them, Colas declares he agrees with both: 'Je suis pour tous vos dieux, les païens, les chrétiens, et pour le dieu raison, par-dessus le marché' (*CB*:65). Like the young Rolland, cheerfully willing to be both materialist and idealist, Colas scorns orderly belief in a single God:

> Je suis un vieux gaulois: beaucoup de chefs, beaucoup de lois, tous frères, et chacun pour soi [. . .] Et surtout, mon ami, ne touche pas aux dieux! Il en bout, il en pleut, d'en haut, d'en bas, dessus nos nez, dessous nos pieds [. . .] Je les estime tous. Et je vous autorise à m'en apporter d'autres. (*CB*:66)

Order returns to this merry chaos in the notion of a '*plus grand bon Dieu*, [que nul n'a] encore vu' (*CB*:67), but the debate ends with the three singing a 'cantique à Bacchus', assimilating Christ himself to the god of wine (*CB*:69). Colas's eclecticism does not exclude revolt; his sick grand-daughter inspires him to ask how any God can tolerate the pain of innocent children, but once she is cured he thanks all the gods, not knowing where credit is due: 'Je rends grâces (c'est plus sûr) à toute la compagnie, en y ajoutant même ceux que je ne connais point' (*CB*:194).

This jovial harmony is a comic expression of the priority of the psycho-logical force of faith over its precise content. In harmonizing men of differing faiths, Colas goes further. Sharing a meal with his sons who take opposing sides in the conflicts of the day, Colas imposes peace with an assurance that their country needs them all:

> A chacun son royaume. Le ciel à Dieu, à nous la terre. La rendre, s'il se peut, plus habitable est notre affaire. On n'est pas trop de tous, pour en venir à bout. Croyez-vous qu'on pourrait se passer d'un de vous? Vous êtes tous les quatre utiles au pays [. . .] Qu'un seul fléchisse et la maison s'écroulera. (*CB*:314)

The image of the house recalls *Dans la maison*; France functions best when the individuals composing it show solidarity without loss of individuality. The nation may be rent by civil war, but a shared culture and Gallic laughter help to make war humane (*CB*:36).

Such passages make *Colas Breugnon* an important reflection of what France means to Rolland. His vision of the nation as a many-roomed house which best functions as a harmony is developed in letters of the period, especially to non-French correspondents, such as the letter to Amann quoted above. The key to the problem lies in a 1907 letter to Sofia:

> Ce n'est pas un peuple. C'est une armée. Ce ne sont pas tant les liens de sang qui unissent ces millions d'hommes. Ce sont les liens de l'histoire, de l'action en commun, et de la stricte discipline. Cette discipline ne doit jamais se relâcher, dans l'intérêt de tous.
>
> [. . .] La France est, par essence, un Empire. Quelle que soit la forme de son gouvernement, elle garde, elle doit garder ce caractère. La République française doit être impérialiste, ou n'être point. Elle oscille entre deux forces opposées, essentielles toutes deux: une extrême liberté, une autorité extrême. Il faut une grande prudence pour les harmoniser: sinon – en fin de compte, c'est l'autorité seule, et sans contrepoids, qui règne, en broyant tout le reste. (*C10*:305–6)

Rolland knows how France was built by assimilating provinces of differing character, and accepts the need for a unifying authority. The danger is that it may operate by suppression rather than harmonization, and the aspects of France that Rolland attacks are usually repressive authorities: the Paris of *La Foire sur la place*, a prescriptive literary culture based on seventeenth-century classicism, or a Third Republic establishment in which the rhetoric of southern politicians and the *Action Française* impose an exclusively Latin image on France at the expense of its Germanic elements. In this, Rolland's image of France differs only in complexity from his image of Germany and Italy, deformed by Prussians and Piedmontese respectively.

Rolland does not reject these authorities from the harmony of France. Just before the war, arguing against Seippel who had written a book contrasting the Roman and Germanic elements of France and giving preference to the latter, Rolland claims:

> Je ne crois pas à une vraie France germanique et gauloise, et à une fausse France romaine, qui déforme la première. L'élément latin me paraît aussi essentiel et nécessaire que les deux autres; et la vraie France est celle qui les harmonise [. . .] La renaissance de l'esprit celto-germanique (évidente depuis 30 ans, dans la poésie française et dans les autres arts, comme la peinture impressionniste) vaut surtout comme réaction contre la domination écrasante de l'esprit classique. Mais elle ne doit pas l'écraser à son tour [. . .]
>
> – Non, je ne crains pas le 'chaos ethnique', je l'appelle et j'y travaille. Je ne veux pas d'une pureté d'eau filtrée et de vie raréfiée. Je veux d'abord le plus de vie possible et toutes les eaux de l'univers mêlée en un fleuve immense. (*C17*:121–3)

This text gives a good idea of Rolland's catholicity; its willingness to see good in all the elements of France and to give oppressed elements their share of the limelight are typical of his attitude at this time. Rolland's tragedy was that, just as he was arriving at this mellow breadth of vision, France herself was about to succumb to a new imperial authority.

Notes

1. See Robichez (1961), p.67 and Cheval (1963), p.20.
2. For this episode, see Stelling-Michaud (1970).
3. 'Il est bon, de temps en temps, sans abdiquer sa foi, de s'élever au-dessus de la mêlée, – ou mieux, d'y promener [. . .] une curiosité allègre et affectueuse' (*Bibliothèque Universelle de Genève*, 68, November 1912, p.396).
4. See Cheval (1963), p.18.
5. See Stelling-Michaud (1966), p.226.

–7–

War

J'étais alors en Suisse. Je sortais d'un long rêve, qui m'enivrait. Les mains de l'amour, où s'appuyaient mes yeux, m'avaient caché les nuages s'amassant en ces juin et juillet du merveilleux été [. . .] Quand s'écartèlent les doigts de la bien-aimée, c'était la nuit du monde. (*EL*:18)

This was how Rolland recalled Sarajevo in the 1931 preface to his wartime articles, but he simplifies. Certainly he was with Helena on holiday in Switzerland and too happy to pay much attention to the event, but a 1929 attachment to his war diaries admits that Helena left shortly afterwards and that on 28 July, anticipating a long absence, he returned briefly to Paris to pick up important papers: 'Je n'accepte donc pas l'excuse de certains de mes amis qui disent que c'est le hasard qui m'a bloqué en Suisse. Le hasard a bien pu me faire venir en Suisse, avant les événements. Mais ma volonté seule m'y a maintenu'.[1] During the war he discouraged mention of this episode (*C20*:180); by choosing not to admit it in 1931, he shows that the rectification of his image was for posterity, not contemporaries.

Rolland had predicted war for years. In January 1914, he declared himself 'convaincu de l'imminence de la guerre franco-allemande', which he saw as 'la lutte [. . .] entre la Liberté et le Pouvoir absolu, entre le progrès du monde et le passé féodal'.[2] His sympathies were thus firmly with libertarian France, and on 30 July he could even write that 'l'esprit d'insolence et de rapine des deux monarchies allemandes appelle un châtiment' (*C2*:286). Yet he sensed that war marked the ruin of his life's work, and the question was how to respond. He did not see himself as a politician, did not want a leadership role he knew would be uncomfortable, and longed for some public figure to take a lead he could follow, but the lead never came. Shocked by the unanimous war fever, all he could do was stay in Switzerland until he saw his way clear.

This was within his rights. He was just old enough to avoid military obligations and his broken arm made him unfit, so residence in Switzerland was not, technically, a desertion. Nor did he decide immediately to stay for the whole war. In January 1915 he was still debating whether to return (*C20*:67), and he admitted he would do so in a family emergency. Yet it became clear that in France he would be silenced, deprived of impartial information and perhaps unsafe, so until 1919 he led a nomadic existence in Swiss hotels. He found he could work well in their impersonal atmosphere, he hesitated before the public commitment of taking an apartment and he could afford the expense. Paradoxically, the years of his vilification were those of his greatest prosperity; despite everything his books remained profitable.

Rolland made no public statement before late August, but two intimate texts show his thought evolving. The first is a meditation dated 5–7 August, in which he re-examines his relationship with the God who is undoubtedly behind the present tumult; he insists that his personality is 'essentiellement religieuse', but he cannot accept the divinity of evil:

> Si le bien existe en moi et non en lui, c'est donc qu'*il est en moi un divin supérieur à Dieu même. Et je le crois*. Il y a Dieu le Père. Et il y a le Fils de Dieu. Le Fils de Dieu, c'est nous qui, sortis de la souche divine, sommes ses fleurs et ses fruits. Nous sommes ce qu'il doit être, ce qu'il faut qu'il devienne, ce qu'il sera *peut-être*. . . car rien n'est fatal dans l'univers, et notre volonté libre est l'élément essentiel de l'avenir. Dieu est force et justice, au sens strict et impitoyable du mot. Nous, ses fils [. . .], nous voulons que de ce vieil arbre noueux et noir fleurisse l'amour.
>
> La lutte qui se livre en moi n'est donc pas entre Dieu et le monde, mais entre Dieu et Dieu, entre la Force éternelle qui se reflète dans mon esprit, et l'Idéal d'harmonie qui est inscrit dans mon cœur. (*JG*:34–5)

The Empedoclean cycle, the sense of a God-bearing humanity and Christophe's heroic vision of life fighting against the void are merely steps towards this supreme assertion of Rolland's pantheism. God is in the destructive collective movement, and there were discouraged moments when Rolland was tempted to let destiny take its course, moments, too, in which he accepted the working of destiny in his life.[3] Yet there is another, superior God struggling for realization in man, and Rolland espoused that struggle. In this sense he, or anybody, can be son of God; he had recently reread the Gospels, and his phrase suggests a sense of kinship with Christ which later became explicit. 'Ara Pacis', written in late August, carries a similar religious message. It is an ode to peace and harmony, in which he declares his refusal to be contaminated by hatred:

> Quand je resterais seul, je te serai fidèle. Je ne prendrai point place à la communion sacrilège du sang. Je ne mangerai point ma part du Fils de

> l'Homme. Je suis frère de tous, et je vous aime tous, hommes, vivants d'une
> heure, qui vous volez cette heure. (*EL*:185)

Just as the young Rolland rejected Catholicism, he now rejects a debased
faith in his desire to realize a higher one, even if it means he must face a
hostile humanity alone.

Rolland was still convinced of the justice of the French cause, and his
relief at the victory on the Marne in September was palpable: 'Pour la
première fois depuis un mois, je peux *voir* les choses et les gens' (*JG*:49).
Yet he was sickened by the victors' crude triumphalism and a butchery
whose victims included Péguy, and once the immediate danger was over,
he released 'Au-dessus de la mêlée'. It was preceded in late August by
an open letter to Gerhardt Hauptmann denouncing German brutality, but
this more radical text became the keynote of a series of articles published
in the *Journal de Genève* which made Rolland a central figure in the
opposition to the war.

Four main lines of argument emerge from them, beginning with an
attack on German militarism. Rolland felt later that 'ces articles pèchent
[. . .] par leur partialité en faveur de la France' (*EL*:26), but at the time
the invasion of Belgium and the bombardment of Reims Cathedral
dominated his thoughts. He was appalled by the destruction of works of
art, and one of his first initiatives was a petition circulated among Allied
intellectuals against the Louvain atrocities. In his letter to Hauptmann
and his 'Pro Aris', he could pass for an orthodox French nationalist. Even
'Les Idoles', an attack on intellectuals written in December when he was
more critical of France, is still unbalanced in that he names his German
targets – Häckel, Ostwald, Thomas Mann, Harden – but no French figure.
In 'Des Deux Maux, le moindre', his attack is more nuanced; imperialism
rather than Germany is the enemy, it also affects Russia and will need to
be fought there, but German imperialism is worse and must be conquered
first. Seeking to drive a wedge between German intellectuals and Prussian
militarism, he asks Hauptmann: 'Etes-vous les petits-fils de Goethe, ou
ceux d'Attila?' (*EL*:64). The response was disappointing; intellectuals
on both sides rallied to national causes, Rolland was attacked in Germany
as a French nationalist, and in France for entertaining the mere possibility
of a civilized German response. As time passed, however, he discovered
a handful of German intellectuals opposed to the war, whom he celebrates
in 'Littérature de guerre' and 'Le Meurtre des élites'.

The second theme of these articles is praise of the sacrificial heroism
of both armies. 'Au-dessus de la mêlée' begins by eulogizing the 'jeunesse
héroïque du monde', engaged on a war of 'revanche de la foi contre tous

les égoïsmes des sens et de l'esprit' (*EL*:76–7). For this Rolland felt some responsibility. He had always sought to revive faith as a quality in itself, and he could consistently celebrate the faith of both sides. He had many friends at the front, and was moved when the mother of a young admirer killed in battle wrote to praise him for the heroism he had inspired in her son (*EL*:16). Yet Rolland saw the limitations of his achievement. He had not done enough to direct what he sought to inspire: 'Cette génération héroïque de 1914, c'étaient nos jeunes frères, nos disciples, nos enfants. Nous les avions formés. Mais nous n'avions pas eu le temps de leur apprendre le chemin' (*EL*:17). His failure, he later claimed, was to believe it possible to harmonize the ideals of 'patrie' and 'humanité'; when forced to choose between them, it was too late to provide leadership. He evoked this failure in *Liluli*, in which 'la Vie', the force celebrated in *Le Buisson ardent*, becomes a headless man leading the people to ruin; 'Le Périple' makes it explicit that this headless man is Christophe (*VI*:259-60). Once war started, Rolland had few remedies beyond the strategy of *Les Loups*, celebrating men of good faith on each side. One of his projects, sadly never realized, was an article in which 'je mettrais en opposition, non pas [. . .] l'idéal d'un des camps avec les vices de l'autre, mais l'idéal de l'un avec l'idéal de l'autre. Je voudrais restaurer la grandeur totale du combat' (*JG*:259).

Rolland's third theme is an attack on opinion leaders. War, he asserts, is not a matter of fatality, but a failure of leadership, of statesmen, and of Christianity and socialism: 'Ces apôtres rivaux de l'internationalisme religieux ou laïque se sont montrés soudain les plus ardents nationalistes' (*EL*:81–2). The two official idealisms proved inadequate in a crisis, and Rolland castigates their capitulation to war fever. His harshest words are directed at intellectuals, his so-called peers who toed the patriotic line so unanimously. Their dessicated rationalism and weakness of character have led to collective madness and murderous distortions of noble ideals. This is the theme of 'Les Idoles', where he begins to target France in a style recalling *La Foire sur la place*, which began to harden Paris opinion against him (*JG*:188).

The final theme of these articles is to 'défendre au moins l'indépendance de l'esprit et d'humaniser la guerre' (*EL*:22). He could not stop hostilities, but he might moderate them, by showing people the better side of the enemy, informing the French of free-minded Germans, contradicting exaggerated atrocity stories and helping prisoners of war and aliens trapped in enemy territory. To this end he did voluntary work for the Red Cross in the first year of the war. His massive correspondence trying to put prisoners in contact with their families convinced him that their condition was not as dire as rumour suggested; 'Inter Arma Caritas' strives to put the record straight, and 'Notre prochain, l'ennemi' highlights charitable works on both sides. His central theme was an attack on hatred:

> L'amour de la patrie ne pourrait fleurir que dans la haine des autres patries et le massacre de ceux qui se livrent à leur défense? Il y a dans cette proposition une féroce absurdité et je ne sais quel dilettantisme néronien, qui me répugnent, qui me répugnent jusqu'au fond de mon être. Non, l'amour de la patrie ne veut pas que je haïsse et que je tue les âmes pieuses et fidèles qui aiment les autres patries. (*EL*:83)

These sentiments arise from a lifetime's effort to use art to inspire love and harmony. *Au-dessus de la haine* was one of the titles he considered for his collected articles, and it might have been less abrasive than *Au-dessus de la mêlée*, with its misleading hint of the smug moral superiority of the non-combattant. One understands why Rolland preferred the latter title, a phrase he often used to express the vision born of the Janiculum 'éclair', but there is no denying that the attack on hatred is the core of his wartime writings.

Conspicuous by its absence is any attempt to stop the fighting. Writing in 1915 to a soldier unable to hate Germany, he refuses to give such advice: 'Je ne veux vous donner qu'un conseil que vous *puissiez* suivre' (*JG*:267), which is to fight with as little hatred as possible and keep his mind clear for the post-war struggle for liberation. Rolland already sensed what would be the problem with Gandhism; conscientious objection would be harshly repressed, and needed the support of a religious spirit of sacrifice that Rolland did not feel he could demand:

> Avec une foi insuffisante, ou soufflée du dehors, il est absurde, et ne peut faire que du mal. Il serait criminel d'y engager les autres, et surtout d'en faire un article de propagande, en temps de guerre [. . .] Qui se sent la vocation du Christ, qu'il se fasse crucifier! Mais que jamais il ne fasse crucifier les autres! (*JG*:1467)

Such sacrifice would require disciplined leadership of which Rolland saw no prospect. Troop mutinies were no answer; the *Action Française* was better organized for a *coup d'état* than the left, and a mutiny might play into its hands (*JG*:799–800). Diplomacy to shorten the war could and should be attempted, but Rolland opposed anything less than a just peace based on German reparation and the self-determination of peoples; only thus could future revanchist wars be avoided. He did not, strictly speaking, consider himself a pacifist, and rejected pacifist attempts to annex him:

> Je ne combats pas la guerre. (Cela me paraît impossible, et ce serait mal à propos, injuste même, si elle devait cesser brusquement, aujourd'hui, avec le *statu quo*). Je combats la haine. Je tâche de maintenir, au milieu de la guerre, une lueur de raison, de justice, de piété. (*C20*:124)

The distinction was illustrated in 1918, when the pacifist Jean Debrit refused to criticize poison gas on the grounds that to single out any one weapon implicitly legitimized the rest. Rolland rejected this 'doctrinarisme intransigeant qui [. . .] se refuse à tout progrès qui ne soit *absolu*' (*JG*:1403); an attack on the use of gas could be part of an attempt to humanize conflict without trying quixotically to stop it.

Another recourse lay in the international elite which for years had been Rolland's ideal. He envisaged 'une Haute Cour morale [. . .], un tribunal de consciences, qui veille et qui prononce sur toutes les violations faites aux droits des gens' (*EL*:86). In this, he wanted to involve the neutrals; he had hopes of the USA, corresponded with the Dutch writer Friedrich Van Eeden and welcomed initiatives from belligerents such as the British Union of Democratic Control. From Switzerland he had an overview of worldwide initiatives for peace, and he used his position to act as a channel of communication. Little of this could be publicly voiced; much depended on personal contacts, and he used his diaries to record the process, making them a repository for documents which would stand as testimony of the European mind in wartime, both the good and the bad sides. In this he sought to be both inspiration and scribe of the elite.

Rolland's public stance in the first year of the war fell short of unconditional pacifism, was essentially pro-French, did not encourage desertion and attracted much support from the front. Articles in the Swiss press, however, were slow to reach the French public. They did not appear in book form until late 1915, and by then their impact had been blunted by constant attacks. There was nothing surprising in opposition from the nationalist right, men such as Frédéric Masson and Rolland's pre-war opponent Massis; old scores were settled by enemies of *La Foire sur la place* such as Henry Bérenger, attacked in 'Le Poison idéaliste' (*JG*:187) and Willy, who, '[avait] eu la sottise de se reconnaître, sous les traits de Goujart' (*JG*:594). Less predictable was the onslaught from potential allies on the left. The first printed attack was by a respected Sorbonne colleague, the historian Alphonse Aulard, and his most implacable enemy was a man who had once solicited his support. Rolland had made his distaste for Loyson rather too clear, but had been right to dismiss him as a fairweather pacifist. Ensconced in the military information service, Loyson had access through the censor to Rolland's mail and mounted a well-informed campaign, cleverly mixing half-truths with hypocritical claims to friendship, and with contacts in Britain and America he drew in names as distinguished as H.G.Wells. This was sustained throughout the war, and crudely echoed by gross libels in the gutter press, insulting letters and death threats.

Rolland replied only to assailants he esteemed. In January 1915, he wrote a long private response to Gabriel Séailles, a former friend on the fringe of Loyson's campaign whose criticisms were expressed 'avec une loyauté et une sympathie qui me touchent' (*JG*:212), but he refused to give Loyson himself the satisfaction of being drawn into debate. He authorized friends in Paris to refute the worst factual distortions, but minimized his personal involvement:

> Je pourrais déjouer ces équivoques [. . .] Mais si je le fais, dans un moment où la presse est achetée ou muselée, où la censure coupera le principal de mon argumentation, [. . .] c'est la lutte au couteau, et la lutte pour des années, car il faudra continuer, répondre, toujours répondre [. . .] Adieu, tout travail de l'esprit, tout recueillement de l'âme dans la création artistique et la vue objective. Et j'hésite. Car je sais que j'ai une tâche d'Au-delà de la Mêlée'. (*JG*:855)

Not wishing to dissipate his energy on polemic, he opted for dignified silence.

In mid-1915, Rolland stopped writing articles. The early months of that year, a time of great personal distress, marked what he called 'un rude tournant de pensée' (*EL*:34). The war was longer than expected, the 'flot de haine' among French intellectuals was rising just as the fury of the Germans was abating (*EL*:31), and his reading of British diplomacy on the eve of the war, which suggested that Grey's duplicity had contributed to its outbreak, undermined his sense of the justice of the Allied cause (*JG*:200). Now that the issue seemed the bankruptcy of the nation state rather than the conflict of liberty and imperialism, Rolland found it hard to conduct a focused campaign. His thought was becoming more complex when the public demanded crude simplicities, and he was often misunderstood. A friend of a German moderate he praised required him to retract his remarks. Zweig, loyalest of friends but with an irritating tendency to encourage Rolland in stances he lacked the courage to take himself, detected a return to French nationalism in 'Le Meurtre des élites' (*JG*:426). He was seriously embarrassed when the *Bund Neues Vaterland*, a moderate German organization, publicized a guarded letter from him in terms suggesting that he was a member.[4] Nationalism in the French and German communities made Switzerland less hospitable, and the conservative *Journal de Genève*, on whose staff Seippel was Rolland's only supporter, became reluctant to carry his articles, especially a tribute to Jaurès on the anniversary of his death. By the time it appeared, Rolland had left Geneva for the mountains, sensing defeat. He had saved his own faith, but not given it to others:

> Pas une minute, depuis douze mois, ma foi n'a été ébranlée. Mais je sens l'inutilité de la répéter à des hommes qui se sont bouché les oreilles pour ne pas entendre. La mêlée européenne m'apparaît de plus en plus comme une crise cosmique, un phénomène de pathologie collective, qui a ses racines dans les lois mystérieuses de la chimie des peuples et de leurs mélanges catastrophiques, peut-être même au-delà. (*JG*:431)

This gloomy text contrasts strikingly with the heroic meditation of a year earlier in which he denied that war was a matter of fatality. It now appears a cosmic movement, a tragic upheaval like the Revolution as portrayed in his dramas, or the wars of religion which had fascinated him as a student.

His main desire now was to withdraw into his inner world. He took some consolation from books; an abortive invitation to lecture in London on the tercentenary of Shakespeare's death rekindled his interest in an old favourite, he discovered the poems of Spitteler and he made his first contact with India when Ananda Coomaraswamy sent him his book on Indian arts and crafts. All of these helped to inspire a serene sense of a larger cosmic existence. He tried to resume his personal work; he planned, though never finished, a volume on Shakespeare and his contemporaries, and began to sketch *Liluli* and *Clerambault*. Both were on the stocks by 1916, but progress was slow; this was the closest he ever came to a writer's block.

The war brought major changes in Rolland's personal and professional relationships. He faced serious difficulties of communication, especially later in the war when frontiers were often closed and the censorship forced him to use code in private correspondence. His family was a particular worry. Though intensely loyal to each other, the four Rollands each had their own life, and his father was a stubborn patriot who insisted on staying in Paris, resisting his son's attempts to bring the family to Switzerland for anything other than holidays. The two women had to shuttle between father and son, facing difficult journeys and divided loyalties, and it placed a strain on his aging parents' health, but Rolland had the support of his mother, who had no strong views on the war but was totally loyal to her children, and Madeleine was an active sympathizer, herself involved in anti-war work. Their separation was a factor in Rolland's decision to suspend his articles: 'Il y a longtemps que j'aurais écrit des articles d'une bien autre portée que ceux qu'on connaît, – sans vous, et mon désir de vous ménager. Vous êtes des otages pour moi dans les mains de la Foire sur la Place'.[5]

Helena de Kay was another problem. She visited him late in 1914, but then returned to America and contact became difficult. Letters were intercepted, and Rolland was furious at the censors' interest in a totally unpolitical correspondence. She was a consolation, but it was not clear where their relationship was going. Their differences were considerable, he mistrusted her Christian Scientist principles which, he felt, made her over-confident, he worried about her latent instability, and when marriage was discussed he faced opposition from his mother, whose reservations about Clotilde had proved correct and who now echoed his own doubts. In August 1916, Helena returned to Europe and Rolland arranged a meeting with the family, at which his mother's reaction was to determine whether they should marry: 'Si elle te déplaisait vraiment, ce serait une raison suffisante pour renoncer au projet. Il est bien entendu que je ne veux pas, cette fois, d'une femme qui ne serait pas pour vous une fille et une sœur' (*C20*:368). No written record of this meeting has emerged, but it was clearly not a success; he seems to have tried to warn Helena in advance not to expect too much of it.[6] Helena departed to Italy, where she had relations, with marriage apparently ruled out, and Rolland admits that the ensuing discord with his mother soured her last years. This episode is probably what Rolland had in mind when writing to Sofia in October 1916:

> J'ai eu à traverser certaines crises intimes assez douloureuses. Grâce à Dieu, j'en suis sorti; et il faut croire que je suis élastique, car au lieu de me laisser courbaturé, pour quelque temps, elles semblent m'avoir donné un nouvel élan de vie et de pensée. (*C11*:246–7)

This suggests that taking a decision about Helena helped to end his writer's block; it was now that he started to write articles again.

Rolland frequently complained that the war lost him his friends. With one or two exceptions, he tends not to name names; many were colleagues with whom he was not intimate, and he seems to have been wounded by the general phenomenon as much as by particular cases. Lavisse was an exception; a scene between Lavisse and Julien Davy in *L'Ame enchantée* expresses Rolland's grief at alienating one of his few elders in France whom he respected. Communication with friends in the Army caused the worst problems. Bloch wanted to fight the war to a finish, Rolland found him 'plus enthousiaste que perspicace' (*JG*:567), and relations were strained until after the Armistice. Châteaubriant, disturbed by his experiences, underwent a crisis of mysticism and his thought moved away from Rolland's. Their differences were not aired, but letters went unanswered and Rolland worried about him.

Worst was the break with Gillet, who withdrew the anthology prepared before the war, by now on the point of publication. He was apologetic, and tried to explain his position in a series of letters which did not lack reason and moderation, arguing that he had claimed since hostilities began that the text would at least need modification. It was unfortunate that, due to postal breakdown, Rolland first heard of this through his publisher, but there was enough in the letters he did receive to suggest that Gillet had misunderstood Rolland's attitude to Germany in *Jean-Christophe* and that he was judging Rolland's articles before reading them. Grieved at such incomprehension from an old friend and sensing that Gillet was under pressure from his father-in-law, the Academician René Doumic, Rolland curtly released him and did not write to him again. This Rolland regarded as 'une des plus grandes tristesses de ma vie' (*JG*:385). A letter to Louise Cruppi suggests that he acted more in sorrow than in anger, and he rightly sensed that Gillet would be sorry:

> Je trouve très naturel qu'on ne pense pas comme moi [. . .] et que l'on condamne mes idées. Mais ce qui m'a été pénible, chez un vieil ami et chez un homme *très brave physiquement*, ç'a été la poltronnerie morale que montrait sa démarche précipitée [. . .] Il l'a senti lui-même, depuis. – Je ne lui en fais pas un crime [. . .] Héroïsme et caractère sont deux. La France a peut-être montré le plus d'héroïsme dans cette guerre, mais le moins de caractère.[7]

Rolland's friendships could withstand intellectual differences, but not the loss of respect.

This rupture was not publicized, and Gillet was spared the outbursts of which Rolland was capable when angry rather than sorrowful. Jacques Copeau was the target of one such, an overreaction to false reports that Copeau had slandered him. Rolland tried to make amends on discovering his error (*C27*:26, 166), but it did not take many such episodes to make him look touchy, splenetic and obsessed by personal grievances at a time when others were suffering worse than he. His situation was certainly precarious; he received several death threats, which his diary shows him facing with some stoicism: 'Je dirai même que j'y goûterais un certain plaisir: de toutes les façons de prendre congé de l'humanité, celle-ci s'accommode le mieux du dégoût mêlé de pitié que j'ai pour elle' (*JG*:1502–3). Yet there is a touch of theatricality in this, and he did exaggerate his sense that the whole world was against him. The tension shows in the working title of *Clerambault*, *L'Un contre tous*, whose tactlessness he recognized in time to change it before publication. It is revealing that in alluding to Gillet's betrayal he uses the words 'renier' and 'reniement' (*JG*:385, 1090), echoing Peter's denial of Christ; he did indeed sometimes think of himself as suffering Christ-like martyrdom.

In fact he was never totally isolated. In Paris he had vocal defenders with whom he communicated through his sister. Humblot, Ollendorff's chief executive, remained faithful despite initial misgivings. A pre-war friend, Gaston Thiesson, published a series of testimonies in his favour (*JG*:539), and he was supported by a number of figures he had barely known before the war, such as the art critic Jacques Mesnil, the poets René Arcos and Marcel Martinet, who replaced Gillet as editor of the Ollendorff anthology, the journalist Georges Pioch and a number of syndicalists hostile to the war. Later, he saw something of his younger self in Jean de Saint-Prix, who wrote a series of articles defending him before dying at the age of twenty-two. Most helpful of all was Louise Cruppi. Troubled in mind after losing a second son, in growing sympathy with Rolland's ideas and free to cross frontiers, she used her influence to keep Rolland in touch with his family and apparently to protect him in official circles, especially late in 1916 when he risked facing conscription (*JG*:1014).

His main new friends were two young writers exiled in Switzerland. Pierre-Jean Jouve, a sensitive poetic nature akin to Châteaubriant in whom he found 'un jeune frère du même race, qui vous comprend à demi-mot' (*JG*:827), became his main confidant of the war years. Jouve's post-war book on Rolland, produced with a rare authorization from its subject to print extracts from letters, is a major source of Rolland's wartime thought. Where Jouve was a Tolstoyan pacifist, Henri Guilbeaux was editor of the revolutionary review *Demain*, which published Rolland's articles when no one else would. Rolland appreciated his upright independence, but found him impulsive and outspoken, and frequently pleaded with him to tone down the eulogies which Guilbeaux printed alongside texts with which he disagreed (*JG*:1247). This became a serious problem in 1918, when Guilbeaux was condemned to death on a trumped-up treason charge which forced him to flee to Russia. Loyson's team exploited Guilbeaux's links with Rolland, hoping either to compromise Rolland or force the two into an open break. Rolland, sure of his friend's innocence, supported him in French diplomatic circles in Switzerland with which he never completely lost contact. Guilbeaux and Jouve did not get on, and the constant need to reconcile and encourage them was a drain on Rolland's emotional resources: 'Chacun vient me demander de la force et du calme. Et moi-même, à qui en demanderai-je?' (*JG*:1417).

Outside France, Rolland had a growing number of contacts. In Switzerland he remained on good terms with Seippel despite growing differences, and with Dr Ferrière of the Red Cross. He corresponded with German dissidents such as Einstein, Wilhelm Förster, Alfred Fried, Georg Friedrich Nicolai and Hermann Hesse. Though less close than Guilbeaux to the Russian revolutionaries in Switzerland, he was on cordial terms with Lunacharsky and began to correspond with Gorky. Few of these became intimate friends, not least because he was wary of close contacts with the enemy. Reluctant to abuse Swiss hospitality, he avoided comment on Swiss affairs and he was especially wary of German involvements after the *Bund Neues Vaterland* affair. Anything smacking of a business deal with Germany was excluded; he refused to allow even a Swiss German translation of *Au-dessus de la mêlée* (*JG*:599), which did not appear in German until 1952. Involvements with neutrals could equally be compromising, and he was embarrassed rather than pleased to be offered the 1915 Nobel Prize for literature. A decision on the award was postponed until what he thought would be the end of the war, but he was unpleasantly surprised to find it confirmed in November 1916. 'J'aurais prié qu'on ne fît pas choix de moi,' he writes to Seippel, 'afin de garder intacte la force de mon action solitaire'; anything he said from then on would be interpreted as 'une quittance du prix' (*JG*:970). He felt bound to accept in the interests of the ideals for which he was fighting, but resolved to keep no money for himself, and the full sum was distributed to the Red Cross and other charities. The net financial effect to him was detrimental when the tax authorities demanded a belated cut.

Independence was the key to his wartime action, and he defended it against friend and foe alike. He refused to join committees or give lectures, and he regretted the one interview he gave, to a German dissident, Hermann Fernau, who distorted his ideas. As he wrote to Chapiro, an importunate friend eager to publish an article to express Rolland's true thought:

> J'exprime dans mes articles tout ce que je crois devoir, ou pouvoir, dire de mes idées politiques ou sociales. Le reste est à moi, et nul n'a le droit de parler pour moi. L'unique chose que j'autorise des amis à repéter, à mon sujet, c'est que je suis un indépendant ombrageux, irréductible, qui n'admet pas qu'on l'embrigade. (*JG*:1331)

Rolland never liked people to speak in his name. He quibbled over details with friends who wrote books on him and disconcerted several generations of sympathizers who thought they knew him but found his thought had moved on. His need for independence was elevated to a policy during these years when a certain mistrust was forced on him, and it ensured that part of his solitude was of his own making.

In April 1918, surveying the long campaign against him, he sensed logic behind its apparent injustice:

> Je n'ai jamais écrit que des paroles modérées [. . .] Mais on dirait que l'opinion a flairé mes pensées, qui sont en vérité beaucoup plus subversives et ne respectent aucun des idéals régnants. Les sectateurs fanatiques du passé sentent en moi l'ennemi; et je le suis, vraiment [. . .] Je ne crois à *rien*, à *rien* de ce qu'ils adorent. (*JG*:1443)

This reveals both how far his ideas had travelled and the gap between his public and private thinking. Apart from personal reasons for caution, he was restrained by a strong sense that he could not at present voice the only solution he could envisage. Responding in some irritation in 1917 to a correspondent who criticized him for merely attacking war rather than seeking a just peace, he reiterates that he supports the self-determination of peoples, but given that both sides have their repressed nations, he does not feel that the present war can serve that cause. A complete social reorganization would be needed, a revolution which Rolland cannot recommend to a demoralized, ill-prepared people, but which nevertheless seems inevitable. These ideas cannot be publicly expressed:

> J'aime trop mon pays pour risquer de lui nuire, en fournissant à la presse impérialiste allemande des arguments dont sa mauvaise foi abuserait [. . .] Les hommes comme nous, qui gardent leur pensée libre, sommes bâillonnés à la fois par la censure française [. . .] – et par le respect même et l'amour que nous avons pour [notre pays]. C'est pourquoi nous devons nous borner à une argumentation vague et sentimentale, à une condamnation évangélique et tolstoïenne de la guerre en général. (*JG*:1180)

This is the answer to those who condemn Rolland's articles for unrealistic idealism; he was aware of their limitations, which were self-imposed. Behind lay a bleaker vision, painfully reached after rejecting much of his past thought.

Its first public expression was 'Aux peuples assassinés', late in 1916.

In 'Au-dessus de la mêlée' he had hailed the peoples of Europe sacrificing themselves for noble causes, but now he pities the way others sacrifice them to two far from noble causes. The first of these, the nation state, no longer represents any kind of ideal. Already before the war Rolland sensed how nations fall prey to imperialist authorities suppressing everything alien to themselves. War carries the process to extremes, and the peoples of Europe are left with no voice:

> *Les nations n'existent plus*, comme personnalités. Un quartiron de politiciens, quelques boisseaux de journalistes parlent insolemment, au nom de l'une ou de l'autre. Ils n'en ont aucun droit. Ils ne représentent rien qu'eux-mêmes. (*EL*:198)

This is not a matter of fatality, but a collective abdication for which all are to blame. In 1914 the nation still, just, seemed a channel for dynamic faith; in 1916 this was no longer so, and the conclusion was painful since Rolland's love of France was undiminished. He mistrusted dissidents who attacked their own nation more than others, fearing Guilbeaux might assist the enemy by attacking France alone for faults shared by both sides (*JG*:927), and criticizing Förster, who seemed to be wishing suffering on the Germans by way of expiation for their crimes (*JG*:940).[8] In a 1916 letter, he dissociates himself from those who reject their own nation:

> Je ne maudis pas la patrie. J'étais son hôte, hier. La patrie, la religion sont de grandes flammes. Sont criminels ceux qui s'en servent pour brûler les autres, au lieu de s'en réchauffer. Il faut passer par l'étage de la patrie pour arriver à celui de l'humanité. J'y suis. Ce n'est pas une raison pour que je crache sur la tête de ceux qui sont à l'étage au-dessous. (*JG*:884)

The insufficiency of the national ideal is none the less clear; only a pan-humanist ideal suits the needs of the time.

Even Europe is insufficient. 'Aux peuples assassinés' quotes Tagore's Tokyo speech attacking European civilization, together with a list of the colonial wars which had stained Europe's reputation before 1914 (*EL*:195–7). Europe had abdicated all moral advantage, and Rolland looked beyond. Apart from the Indians, he had hopes of the USA, but they were tempered by growing awareness of the covert role of American business, and they evaporated when Wilson brought the USA into the war and failed to live up to his idealistic image at the peace conference. Japan, too, interested him, his main informant being a young correspondent, Seichi Narusei, but the picture Narusei painted was disturbing rather than encouraging, leading Rolland to predict clashes with America

(*JG*:1554). Rolland was remarkably prescient in recognizing the future world role of non-Europeans, but they presented problems as well as opportunities.

The second, profounder cause to which peoples are sacrificed is money. For some time Rolland had been collecting evidence of the profits accruing to international capitalism from armaments and its interest in prolonging the war: 'Les peuples qui se sacrifient, meurent pour des idées. Mais ceux qui les sacrifient vivent par des intérêts. Et ce sont, par conséquent, les intérêts qui survivent aux idées' (*EL*:201). War becomes a finance-driven affair in which the debased peoples conniving in it are hardly less culpable than the occult world of high finance. This bitter article voices a conspiratorial view of capitalist society which dominated Rolland's thought for the rest of his life.

'Aux peuples assassinés' offers no remedy. Its revolutionary thrust is clear, but in 1916 Rolland was reluctant to preach a revolution which would merely make a bad situation worse.[9] Yet he welcomed the Russian Revolution; in an article dated 1 May 1917 he called on the Russian people to place itself in the vanguard of progress, as the French had done in 1789. Rolland was too imbued with the spirit of 1789 not to respond to its apparent renewal, but he was not blind to the problems. Knowing that democracies could be as bellicose as autocracies, he foresaw no end to the war from the fall of the Tsar (*JG*:1097). He was forewarned by Guilbeaux and Lunacharsky of Lenin's return to Russia, and even invited to be a witness of his departure, but he disapproved, feeling that the Bolsheviks' deal with German imperialism would contaminate their cause (*JG*:1130). Nor did he approve of the Treaty of Brest-Litovsk, which would release German troops for an offensive against France (*JG*:1390).

He soon became aware that the Bolsheviks were men of violence. As he wrote to Guilbeaux in August 1918, he saw in them

> un côté négateur, destructeur, niveleur, implacablement fanatique [. . .] Ma nature, à moi, et mon rôle dans la crise mondiale, sont tout autres [. . .] Je ne suis ni ne serai jamais l'homme d'*une* nature, ni d'*une* classe. La meilleure est mauvaise, si elle veut écraser tout le reste. (*JG*:1580)

The Bolsheviks sought to impose imperial rather than harmonic unity; the dictatorship of the proletariat appealed no more to Rolland than any other dictatorship. They seemed unlikely to respect Rolland's cherished role as a free intellectual; their work was '*nécessaire*, mais insuffisante dans le domaine de l'esprit. Et trop souvent, ils foulent aux pieds cette liberté morale qui, pour moi, donne à la vie son seul prix' (*JG*:1389). Yet in a letter to Bloch, discussing German revolution in October 1918, his reservations are qualified:

> Les hommes qui dirigent le mouvement bolchevique me semblent de grands jacobins marxistes, qui tentent héroïquement une expérience grandiose. Je comprends qu'on les combatte. Je ne comprends pas qu'on les méconnaisse aussi aveuglément. Une bonne partie de leurs pires erreurs vient de ce qu'au lieu de les modérer et de les encadrer, les Alliés les ont rejetés, outragés, acculés à des situations et à des partis désespérés. – Pour en revenir à l'Allemagne, qui ne voit que, si nous avions voulu, ils (les bolch.) auraient pu être, contre elle, nos meilleurs alliés, par leur propagande révolutionnaire? (*C15*:379)

The allusion to the Jacobins recalls 1793, when another centralizing revolutionary party violently reconstructed a nation to counter a foreign threat. Rolland's dramas show that he could respond to the Terror's tragic heroism without ignoring its unsavoury side, and there was still hope that the Bolsheviks could avoid the mistakes of the Jacobins. At least they deserved space to try, and Rolland condemns the Allies' attempt to destroy them without even having the strategic sense to use them against German imperialism, which Rolland thought best toppled by German revolution. Despite everything, Rolland supported Bolshevik social reconstruction and opposed its enemies.

The last year of the war was particularly painful. Communications with his family were worse than ever and the Guilbeaux case made his situation in Switzerland perilous; rumours circulated that he might be expelled. The trials of Clemenceau's political opponents and the jailing of E. D. Morel in England on a trumped-up charge of smuggling documents to Rolland underlined the dangers he faced. Factional fighting in France brought new problems. He hated being called a defeatist, with its implications of passivity; arguing against Zweig, who relished the term, he distanced himself from that attitude as expressed by Lux in *Le Triomphe de la raison* (*JG*:1533–4). Yet he objected equally when Fernau's interview, twisting his words into support for a crusade against German imperialism, made him appear a 'jusqu'au boutiste'. The fluctuating fortunes of war, with the Germans threatening Paris before their final collapse, engaged his sympathies both for his own people and for the defeated Germans. The armistice did little to improve matters. The silence which met his plea for reconciliation in an open letter to Wilson was as disappointing as it was predictable (*JG*:1645), and the harsh terms imposed on Germany seemed disastrous. The spirit of Bismarck had passed into the opposite camp, and Rolland saw no more in the peace treaty than an 'entr'acte dériscire entre deux massacres de peuples' (*JG*:1832). The murder of Liebknecht and Rosa Luxemburg inspired a series of articles for *L'Humanité* on the German revolution, aimed at warning the French against a harsh policy which might drive Germany back into military reaction. He chose these articles to open his 1935 collection, *Quinze ans de combat*.

All this gloom should not, however, mask another side of Rolland's thought, his blending of short-term pessimism with long-term optimism. As Zweig put it, he had a capacity 'd'être pessimiste dans l'intimité, de connaître le doute pour soi, et de donner en même temps l'espérance aux autres' (*JG*:1659). It sprang from his religious faith, coupled with his historian's long view of human affairs. 'N'ayant jamais cru dans les progrès, je ne suis pas étonné des retours de barbarie,' he wrote to Châteaubriant (*C30*:66); having had a low view of his contemporaries before the war, he had little to be disillusioned about, and his reading was wide enough to show grounds for hope. They are expressed in 'La Route en lacets qui monte', an article published at about the same time as 'Aux peuples assassinés'; the two are disconcertingly different, but it was typical of Rolland to work simultaneously on contrasting texts.

In it, he hopes to 'rappeler aux frères ennemis d'Europe non ce qu'ils ont de pire, mais ce qu'ils ont de meilleur, – les motifs d'espérer en une humanité plus sage et plus aimante' (*EL*:189). The present carnage is not new; other, similar ages have passed, stimulating in their passage the cause of human unity. France herself owed her unity to conflict between her provinces; the present war anticipates European unity, and behind can be glimpsed the union of Europe and Asia. Rolland hails Erwin Hanslik's Viennese *Institut für Kulturforschung*, devoted to the comparative study of civilizations, whose task is 'd'éveiller à la conscience la beauté qui réside en toute individualité humaine, en tout peuple, et [. . .] de trouver les bases scientifiques d'accord entre les peuples' (*EL*:193); from such a body a true harmonic unity might emerge. The move towards unity is a cosmic process, springing from 'le rythme de l'histoire' rather than 'le bon sens des humains' (*EL*:190), but it is furthered by the 'âmes libres de tous les temps': Socrates, Erasmus, More, Voltaire and of course Renan who provided the image of the winding mountain road. The union of such men over the ages is 'l'armature de fer qui tient la molle glaise humaine, cette statue d'argile, la Civilisation' (*EL*:194). This article stands apart from Rolland's wartime writings so far considered. He does not often cite Erasmus and Voltaire, for whose ironic good sense his regard had risen, but who seemed to him limited, and the trust placed in historic process rather than human will runs counter to his refusal to abdicate to fatality. This lofty detachment in the year of Verdun could well appear a step too far above the mêlée, and in the intense political engagement of his 1931 preface to *L'Esprit libre*, this article is not even mentioned.[10] Yet, as Jouve asserts,[11] it is a calculated complement to 'Aux peuples assassinés'; together they express a double vision akin to the Janiculum 'éclair', of renewed indignation and reasserted faith. From it springs the revival in late 1916 of Rolland's urge to write, and it provides the key to aspects of his wartime writing yet to be discussed.

Rolland's second collection of wartime articles, *Les Précurseurs*, celebrates '[les] hommes de courage qui, dans tous les pays, ont su maintenir leur pensée libre et leur foi internationale' (*EL*:183). They include combattants who have kept or recovered their humanitarian faith, sometimes at the cost of their lives, such as Petzold and Marc de Larréguy, witnesses to the horrors of war such as Barbusse, whose *Le Feu* combines documentation of trench life with a declaration of faith in the future, and men imprisoned for their ideals, such as Ernst Toller and E. D. Morel. These men prepare the unity announced in 'La Route en lacets'.

Part of the same strategy are texts on two old favourites whose message had become relevant. Four articles are all that remain of his projected Shakespeare volume, and they celebrate qualities needed by a world at war. Shakespeare, like Tolstoy, is master of 'l'universelle sympathie' (*CR*:69), the ability to penetrate pityingly the souls of a wide diversity of individuals. He is the master satirist, devising ways of telling the truth despite political constraints. Through Coriolanus, the Fool in *Lear*, Hamlet and Timon, he denounces hypocrisy and greed and anticipates future revolutions. Above all, he carries out the artist's essential task, 'la libération de l'esprit' (*CR*:94). His themes are tragic, yet through creative dream he engenders a 'forte joie de la douleur':

> Jeu suprême de l'esprit, qui s'affranchit des lois cruelles de la vie, en se faisant lui-même créateur de la vie et maître des lois qui gouvernent l'univers modelé par lui, à l'image du réel. Des plaines du Simoïs où s'affrontent les guerriers, l'esprit s'élève auprès de Zeus qui les contemple et ressent leurs passions, mais de loin, apaisé, et sans que reste en lui leur aiguillon empoisonné. (*CR*:95)

The release can only be momentary, but its analogy with the lofty vision of 'La Route en lacets' is obvious.

At the height of the German offensive of April 1918, Rolland returned to Empedocles. The pre-Socratic world had much in common with the present, with its ceaseless wars, confused migrations and intermingling of the thought of East and West, but Empedocles, most human of the pre-Socratics, realized an ideal dear to Rolland, 'unir et harmoniser toutes les forces de l'âme' (*CR*:25). In the Empedoclean alternation of hatred and love, Rolland identifies the present with the stage of the cycle at which the world is conquered by hatred. The vision offers hope, in that love will eventually return; it is tempered by the knowledge that the cycle will begin again, but Empedocles revolts against the iron law of fate which determines the recurrence of the cycle: 'Il cherchait à y échapper, à briser l'Anagké [. . .] Il avait beau reconnaître l'égal pouvoir alternant de l'Amour et de la Haine. C'est pour l'Amour seul qu'il prend parti' (*CR*:48). Like Rolland in 1914, he defies fate in the name of a higher god, with whom he is in touch through his 'âme supranaturelle, mystique, qu'il appelle "*le démon*"' (*CR*:54). A believer in the transmigration of souls, Empedocles works for the good of his fellow men and strives to free himself of hatred, hoping to transmit his conquest beyond his present incarnation. The resultant vision of a future pan-humanity is both a consolation and a spur to action. A serene grasp of universal rhythms combines with a combative desire to modify them.[12]

This vision receives support from science. Rolland disliked the science of Taine and Berthelot, which was contaminated by the anti-religious materialism of the 1880s, but he now began to sense a less dogmatic, more adventurous spirit among scientists. He was captivated by their explorations of the unknown and their scrupulous regard for truth, and two scientists figure prominently in *Les Précurseurs*. The entomologist Auguste Forel's study of ants inspired consoling reflections on collective life. The ants' nest has much in common with a democracy at war, but it demonstrates that the urge to fight is not a basic instinct; peace can, in the right circumstances, be made between warring colonies. This proves 'l'erreur funeste de ceux qui croient à l'immuabilité sacrée des instincts, et qui, après y avoir inscrit l'instinct de la guerre, y voient une fatalité imposée' (*EL*:326). Evolution away from warfare is at least not impossible.

Nicolai points the same way, and the longest article in *Les Précurseurs* studies this biologist who was also a leading German dissident. In his *Biologie des Krieges*, Rolland finds fresh support for the view that the warlike instinct can be eradicated. It exists, but it corresponds to man's needs at an earlier stage of evolution, and if man is to progress, he can and must outgrow it, struggling in its place for the conquest of nature (*EL*:279). Nicolai's thesis is 'une étrange vision de panthéisme matérialiste et dynamiste: l'Humanité, considéré comme un corps et une âme en perpétuel mouvement', a vision in which 'le monde terrestre est un seul organisme, possédant une conscience commune' (*EL*:292). Such a world should permit the growing together of humanity in a new stage of evolution. Rolland pressed this case harder than Nicolai himself; though Nicolai provided evidence against the concept of race, he showed little regard for non-Europeans, and Rolland was pained by his indifference to victims of colonialism (*JG*:1760). Yet this remarkably prophetic thinker pointed in the same direction as Empedocles, Hanslik and Forel; war can perhaps mark a step towards higher unity.

Explaining his 1915 retreat to Jouve, Rolland declares that it was 'non pas pour renoncer, mais au contraire pour exprimer ma pensée toute entiere. Il n'y a que dans l'art qu'on le peut'.[13] Only the cyclic structures of art could fully express his blend of indignation at the present and faith in the future. He published no artistic work while hostilities lasted; *Liluli*, though finished six months earlier, was symbolically dated November 1918.[14] Neither it nor *Clerambault* were easy to write; the one wartime work he wrote fairly quickly was his novella, *Pierre et Luce*, inspired by the 1918 bombardment of Paris. Its central characters are two lovers who die in the shelling of the church of Saint Gervais on Good Friday, an atrocity in which a young woman known to Rolland was killed (*JG*:1438). The atmosphere of the work recalls *Le Siège de Mantoue* in its portrayal of doomed youths in the death throes of an old civilization.[15] Pierre, a bourgeois with the sensitive charm often found in Rolland's adolescents, clutches at a fleeting happiness with Luce, of lower social origins, as he unenthusiastically awaits conscription, but Luce, more realistic than he, knows that society will never let them marry; it is always clear that their love is hopeless. Set against the military threat to a France which is also succumbing to the imperial order of Clemenceau, their fragile affair reflects the doom of the refined, gentler side of France embodied in Debussy, the lovers' favourite composer who dies in the same week as they. This unusually conciliatory evocation of Debussy is part of a sympathetic portrayal of Paris at its moment of danger; the lovers are Parisians through and through, and Rolland seems touched by rare nostalgia for the city he often criticized. He resists the temptation in this novella to enlarge on his anti-war thought; it is a restrained, succinct work in which the story speaks for itself.

The origins of *Liluli* predate the war. Rolland planned an Aristophanean farce for his Revolutionary cycle, the orgiastic debasement of an ideal in *Le Triomphe de la raison* anticipates some of its scenes, and in 1912 he meditated a *Polichinelle*. The Rabelaisian accumulations and rhymed prose of *Colas Breugnon* is applied to a satirical vision as sharp as that of *La Foire sur la place*, and the result is by far his most original play. Its imaginative visual effects make almost impossible staging demands, but it is based on a highly precise visual imagination, ironically reflecting Renan's 'route en lacets'.

Two tribes, the Gallipoulets and Hurluberloches, seek the high ground after floods destroy their valley homes, and their routes converge on two sides of a ravine. Their instinct is to build a bridge and fraternize, but they are seduced into battle by the rich, seeking to maintain their property, by diplomats extolling peace while preparing for war, and by intellectuals ready to serve any cause. Ideals appear in caricatural form: Life is a headless man with an animal stench, Reason is blindfold, Love is beautiful only after she has passed by, Peace is an armed warrior, Liberty and Equality slave-drivers and Fraternity a cannibal. Even God is Maître-Dieu, a charlatan who, after urging one side to fight, changes uniform and crosses to the other, leaving his voice behind on a gramophone. Liluli, spirit of Illusion, rules supreme, a young girl who sings like a bird, floats in the air and entices both sides, a perverted version of Goethe's *Ewig-Weibliche*. She alone prevents the debased ideals from being unmasked, and her charm works strongest on the idealistic. Seducing two Raphael-esque brothers, Altaïr and Antares, she watches them slaughter each other in battle.

Resistance comes only from common sense. Polichinelle, representing laughter, sees through Liluli, but fails to support Truth, a gypsy held captive by Maître-Dieu who hides her while pretending to revere her. Polichinelle is too scared to help her escape, and she denounces his cowardice:

Ainsi que tes grands-pères, les grands Polichinelles, les maîtres de la libre ironie et du rire, comme Erasme et Voltaire, tu es prudent, prudent, ta grande bouche est fermée sur ton ricanement. Ils sont beaux, mes amants! Pourvu qu'ils aient sauvé leur esprit et leurs grègues, il ne leur chaut de ceux des autres. Mon amour les fait libres; mais moi, ils me laissent captive. (*LI*:123)

This reveals the limitations of 'la Route en lacets', where Rolland associates himself with Erasmus and Voltaire, and indeed of *Liluli* itself. To save one's own skin by irony is not enough; active involvement is necessary. After Polichinelle's failure, the last hope for peace is peasant inertia, and to overcome it Liluli invokes Llôp'ih, or public opinion, a hideous idol emitting wordless roars. She provokes the final disaster as two peaceful peasants refuse to give way to each other on the bridge; both collapse into the abyss, followed by the warring armies.

The implications of this work are so negative that Rolland himself was worried. He knew he risked shocking with his portrayal of Maître-Dieu, an attack on the various national churches' contribution to the war which might suggest that God himself is the target. In 1919 he even turned down an invitation from the Archbishop of Uppsala to lecture on a religious subject because 'je trouve peu franc de me prêter à cette exhibition religieuse, au moment où je publie *Liluli* et *Colas Breugnon*' (*JG*:1730). *Liluli* does not, however, signal the crumbling of Rolland's faith.[16] Like many of his works, it was conceived as part of a cycle, the second of three plays in which the dominant idea was 'consolante [et] baignée de foi' (*VI*:274). In the third play, Prometheus was to unmask Maître-Dieu and Liluli as caricatural representations of Hope and the true God. In its central position, *Liluli* corresponds to *La Foire sur la place* in *Jean-Christophe*, the satirical low point of a curve of decline and rise. In a 1920 letter, Rolland explains that he was publishing it separately to shock people out of complacency and make them think:

> On ne sauve pas les autres. Il faut que les autres – chacun des autres – se sauve soi-même. Et pour l'y amener, il faut jeter en lui le doute et l'angoisse qui l'arracherait à sa quiétude, lui révéler le mensonge dans lequel il vit. La vraie foi n'est pas une formule commode sur quoi il est permis de se reposer, toute sa vie. Il faut la mériter, en la conquérant sans cesse. (*C17*:164–5)

Rolland was pleased with *Liluli*. Writing it was a release, and in its elements of pure artistic play it is the work of his which most aspires to the condition of music. Rolland himself compared it to Offenbach: 'Vous me direz que de l'Offenbach sans musique. . . Oui, je sais bien. . . Mais je tâche que ce soit aussi de la musique'.[17] It strains at the limits of theatrical art and has been little performed, though in 1923 it was staged with a combination of actors and Chinese shadows designed by the Belgian engraver Frans Masereel, who became one of Rolland's loyallest friends. Masereel also illustrated the edition of *Liluli*, effectively capturing its tone of macabre caricature.

Rolland was far less pleased with the 'méditations grises et crépuscu-laires' of *Clerambault*.[18] This work, started in 1916, was hard to write; Rolland delayed finishing it until the war's end, and the final stages were written in the aftermath of his mother's death. His thought changed in process of composition, with the important character of Edme Froment added at a very late stage.[19] Though cast as a novel, it attempted a synthesis of his wartime thought and he saw its value as essentially intellectual: 'A défaut de la valeur d'art, cela peut avoir une valeur d'acte et d'idée'.[20] Clerambault's age and literary status in 1914 are comparable to Rolland's, as are the flaws in his pre-war thought; 'avec ses dons lyriques et une intelligence moyenne, que le cœur dominait' (*CL*:36), he appears naïve, more eloquent and generous than intelligent. Yet Clerambault is not Rolland; he stays in France, faces family tensions that Rolland avoided, is more implicated in a traitor's trial than Rolland was with Guilbeaux's and is eventually murdered by a nationalist. The articles Rolland attributes to him are more rhetorical, more sentimental and less measured than Rolland's own, and his tactical sense is weak; he drifts into futile debates with his attackers which Rolland avoided (*CL*:175). Through Clerambault, Rolland castigates some of his own errors, particularly his failure to give better leadership before the war, and by giving Clerambault a longer and harder road to travel than his own, Rolland elevates him into a martyr.

The five-part work follows a familiar pattern of descent and rise. In the first part, Clerambault, possessed by 'l'Ame multitudinaire' (*CL*:23) in the heyday of unanimism, is infected by war fever, but the result is alienation, leaving him 'dépersonnalisé, anesthésié pour ce qui se passait au fond de lui, déshabitué de sa propre conscience, étranger dans sa maison, – son moi' (*CL*:26). His warlike verse is applauded, but he is estranged from his son, who dies in battle leaving his bereft father with a sense of 'mensonge intérieur' (*CL*:64), of having seen but refused to recognize the horror in his son's eyes. He revolts against the idea of the nation, and in the second part he considers how far he can express this.

His central debate is with Hippolyte Perrotin, a Renanesque academic who takes a long view of history. Though under no illusions about the war, Perrotin will not express his views publicly. Deeply pessimistic about the present, he sees no possibility of man making an act of will against fatality: 'Cette pauvre pensée européenne est une épave comme les autres. Le courant l'entraîne; elle ne fait pas le courant' (*CL*:81). In the long term it is a different matter; Perrotin rehearses, in almost caricatural form, the vision of future unity expressed in 'La Route en lacets', seasoned with references to the Empedoclean cycle and to Shiva, Hindu god of destruction who unleashes essential transformation. The ideas are Rolland's, but the use to which they are put is not: 'La sagesse affranchit. Pour les Hindous, Bouddhâ délivre. Pour mon compte, la curiosité m'est un suffisant adjuvant' (*CL*:113). Perrotin stands revealed as an ironist who saves himself but not others. His advice to Clerambault is to avoid risks, but Clerambault finds Buddhist detachment selfish, and longs to be 'ce Bodhisattvâ, [le] Maître de la Pitié, qui a fait le serment de ne pas [. . .] se réfugier dans le Nirvâna libérateur, avant d'avoir guéri tous les maux!' (*CL*:113) Humanity advances only through men who, like Christ, sacrifice themselves. Clerambault's instincts are confirmed by Aimé

Courtois, the wounded farmhand who embodies the virtue of patience, admirable in the humble heroes of *Jean-Christophe* and *Colas Breugnon*, but now simply inviting exploitation. Irritated by Courtois's 'résignation héroïque et imbécile' (*CL*:124), Clerambault goes public.

In the third part, the low point of the cycle in which many of the satirical themes of *Liluli* recur, Clerambault suffers worse rejection than Rolland. He alienates his family, including his daughter who sympathizes with his views but sees no reason why he should voice them, and her fiancé, a traditional scientist who sees the war in determinist terms, whereas for Clerambault recent developments suggest that even scientific laws are capable of transformation. In this, Clerambault anticipates an argument Rolland later used against Barbusse. Sympathizers are rare; he is offered support by a Schulz-like provincial schoolteacher who dies before he can be contacted, and the case of Mme Mairet, a friend's widow, reveals how little Clerambault can do for those who need to believe their loved ones died in a noble cause: 'Il ne fut pas loin d'approuver sa révolte contre lui. Il vit l'immense douleur cachée et l'inefficacité de la vérité qu'il apportait pour y remédier' (*CL*:196). It is the dilemma of the *Vie de Michel-Ange*, which helps to explain why Rolland was reluctant to publish during the war; harsh truths wound the unheroic.

In the fourth part, Clerambault finds allies among revolutionaries. Like Rolland in his dealings with Jouve and Zweig, Clerambault radiates a force which gives his friends a strength and encouragement he is far from feeling himself:

> Cette sécurité de l'âme, cette harmonie intérieure, que les yeux de Julien Moreau cherchaient dans les yeux de Clerambault, Clerambault, tourmenté, ne la possédait point... Ne le possédait-il point? ... – Or, regardant Julien en souriant humblement, pour s'excuser, il vit ... il vit que Julien l'avait trouvé en lui... Et voici que, de même qu'en montant au milieu du brouillard on est soudain dans la lumière, il vit que la lumière était en lui. (*CL*:213)

The discovery is encouraging, but it enhances his problem of how to tell hard truths, especially to the young who need something to live for. The only answer is to be truthful but kind:

> Tu n'es pas le maître du destin, mais tu es aussi le destin, tu es une de ses voix. Parle donc! C'est ta loi. Dis toute ta pensée, mais dis-la avec bonté. Sois comme une bonne mère, à qui il n'est pas donné de faire de ses enfants des hommes, mais qui leur enseigne patiemment à le devenir, s'ils veulent. (*CL*:224)

Destiny, as ever, is ambivalent. Here, Clerambault as one of its voices has a duty to speak, but cannot impose his will; as an individualist, his role is to make it possible for others to further their own individuality.

Clerambault does not support the Bolsheviks. He respects their iron logic, but is fearful of men just as oppressive as those they have overthrown. He mistrusts fanatics who destroy everything falling short of their ideal, even themselves if they do not attain it (*CL*:235); Rolland now viewed the Saint-Just of *Danton* with distaste (*JG*:350). Besides, even if history compels revolution, it is not Clerambault's role to accede to it:

> Il y a là une *Diké* d'airain, que reconnaît l'esprit, qu'il peut même honorer comme une Loi de l'univers. Mais le cœur ne l'accepte pas. Le cœur refuse de s'y soumettre. Sa mission est de rompre la Loi de guerre éternelle [. . .] Il est clair que son espoir, son valoir, sortent de l'ordre naturel. Sa mission est d'ordre surnaturel, et proprement *religieux*. (*CL*:236)

Destiny changes sense again, and we are back with the Rolland of August 1914 and the Empedocles of 1918. Clerambault's role is not to follow history and be a revolutionary, but to break with the law which condemns man to eternal violence. The God within man strives to realize himself against the fatality of the universe.

Clerambault's religious role dominates the fifth part. Though alone, he feels closer than ever to his fellow beings, in a process of harmonization and Tolstoyan love, recognizing the individuality within everyone in terms recalling the *Credo quia Verum*:

> Sur la sombre rivière du Destin qui emporte l'humanité, et qu'il avait confondue avec elle, lui apparaissaient les millions d'épaves vivantes qui se débattaient, – les hommes. Et chaque homme était soi, à lui seul un monde de joies et de souffrances, de rêves et d'efforts. Et chaque homme était *moi*. (*CL*:254)

Despite the hostility he inspires, he experiences some return of fraternity, from his family and the paralyzed Edme Froment, who in his living death has become an intellectual leader of his generation and realized Rolland's ambition of creating an international elite. Froment goes further than Clerambault in asserting the individualist ideal:

> La foi de notre temps voit dans le groupe social le faîte de l'évolution humaine. Qui le prouve? Moi, je vois [. . .] ce faîte dans l'individualité supérieure [. . .] [La nature] dépense des peuples, pour créer un Jésus, un Bouddhâ, un Eschyle,

> un Vinci, un Newton, un Beethoven [. . .] Nous ne relevons pas l'idéal égoïste
> du Surhomme. Un homme qui est grand est grand *pour* tous les hommes. Son
> individualité exprime des millions d'hommes, et souvent elle les guide [. . .]
> Le seul fait qu'un homme a été Christ, a exalté, soulevé au-dessus de la terre,
> des siècles d'humanité et a versé en eux des énergies divines [. . .] L'idéal
> individualiste ainsi compris est plus fécond pour la société humaine que l'idéal
> communiste, qui conduit à la perfection mécanique de la fourmilière. (*CL*:280)

In this, the most extreme statement of Rolland's heroism, the individual
is the force which shatters the determinist laws of history, of which
communism is the latest manifestation. Though apparently opposed to
the masses, the great individual works for them by setting an ideal,
unrealizable maybe, but a necessary inspiration: 'Penser sincèrement,
même si c'est *contre* tous, c'est encore *pour* tous' (*CL*:8). Such men,
like Christophe, are God-bearers, and like Christ they face martyrdom.
Clerambault faces it calmly, and in his meditation before his death he
synthesizes the liberty which has been his guiding spirit with a higher law
of necessity:

> Le mot de Liberté n'exprime qu'un des ordres – haut et clair – de l'invisible
> Souveraine qui régit les mondes, – la Nécessité. C'est elle qui suscite la révolte
> des Précurseurs et qui les met aux prises avec le lourd passé, que traînent les
> aveugles multitudes. Car elle est le champ de bataille de l'éternel Présent, où
> luttent éternellement le Passé et l'Avenir. (*CL*:305)

This interpretation of his life in terms of cosmic conflict is in the tradition
of *Le Buisson ardent* and of Rolland's revolt in August 1914, but though
it asserts faith in the free individual, it nevertheless suggests that freedom
is itself part of a higher destiny. Rolland was to move closer still to that
position in the coming years, but in the conclusion to this work the
individual most to the fore is Christ. Clerambault dies shortly after the
Good Friday on which Pierre and Luce are killed, and in his death he is
compared to Christ as 'le principe éternel de la non-soumission de l'Esprit
à César' (*CL*:318).

Never before has Rolland stated so forcefully the presence of the divine
in man, carried to its extreme by the forces which compel it to martyrdom.
The processes leading to this position are, of course, visible in his earlier
work. His Tolstoyan realism, his cyclic view of history, his cult of heroism,
his internationalism and his rejection of orthodoxy in the name of a higher
faith all converge to produce this result, and *Clerambault* can be seen as
the end of a long evolution, written into the very fabric of Rolland's
previous thought. Yet this statement is so extreme, so arrogant even in

its analogy with Christ, that it is hard to see where else it could lead. Hints are already visible that the individualist in revolt against destiny is in fact fulfilling destiny, and Rolland moved further towards this position in the post-war world.

Notes

1. See Stelling-Michaud (1967), pp.26–7.
2. Quoted in Stelling-Michaud (1966), pp.226–7.
3. In a letter to Zweig, he admits that '[le Destin] m'a fait ce que je suis, bien plus que je me suis fait. A trois ou quatre moments décisifs, il a choisi pour moi, m'orientant durement, mais justement, dans une voie qui m'était imprévue, et qui était pourtant la seule vraie' (*JG*:1478). This self-analysis became the theme of Zweig's biography of Rolland, in its subject's view one of the best to appear in his lifetime.
4. For this episode, see Cheval (1963), p.442ff.
5. Letter to Madeleine, 28 January 1916.
6. This is the probable sense of a letter to her dated 17 June 1916, but only fragments of this correspondence survive.
7. Letter to Louise Cruppi, 7 July 1915.
8. See Cheval (1963), pp.577, 654.
9. Jouve (1920, p.213) claims that in October 1916 Rolland explicitly stated that revolution was not at present the answer and that 'Aux peuples assassinés' was not for publication. It was his friends who persuaded him to change his mind.
10. See Cheval (1963), p.606.
11. See Jouve (1920), p.213.
12. See Duret (1992), p.666.
13. See Jouve (1920), p.193.
14. See Duret (1992), p.674.
15. See Starr (1971), p.171.
16. See his rather grumpy letter to J-R. Bloch, 20 December 1921, responding to a review in which Bloch claimed that *Liluli* signalled Rolland's loss of faith.
17. Letter to Louise Cruppi, 3 September 1919.
18. Letter to Louise Cruppi, 25 February 1919.
19. See Duret (1992), p.687.
20. Letter to Madeleine, 28 February 1919.

–8–

Failed Heroes (I): France and India

In November 1918 Rolland contracted influenza, and though it did not seem serious at the time, his health was permanently affected. Old tubercular lesions were reactivated, and intestinal complications developed. For the rest of his life he was under doctors' orders; he had to be careful with diet and travel plans, and the least cold was a threat. Yet he lived another quarter century, sustained by 'une extrême vitalité de l'esprit, qui, loin de se ralentir, s'accroît toujours, et paraît même rajeunir, avec l'âge. (Je suis convaincu que c'est l'esprit qui soutient le corps, et qui, vingt fois, l'a sauvé.)' (*C28*:231–2). His mother was with him at the time; though herself affected, she nursed him to health before returning to Paris. This was his last memory of her, for in May 1919 she suffered a hemiplegic stroke. Rolland rushed to her bedside, crossing the frontier without hindrance, and after a harrowing three weeks she died. This loss was a turning point in his life, leaving him with a sense of detachment from a world in which he increasingly felt out of place: 'Je ne tiens plus au sol que par l'extrémité de mes profondes racines' (*VI*:105).

His bereavement left him ill-prepared to meet Helena de Kay when he returned to Switzerland in July 1919. A year before, on the very day of the bombardment of Saint Gervais, Helena had given birth to a daughter, conceived during a brief liaison in Italy. The child lived only six weeks, but the mother intended to bring her up by herself. This caused Rolland great emotional confusion. Feeling responsible as well as betrayed, he helped her with money and advice, and tried to rebuild the relationship on platonic lines, advising her on publications and a lecture tour on which she hoped to base an American career, but although his emotion was by no means dead, he ruled out marriage, mindful of his mother's dying wish that he and his sister should look after each other.[1] Helena went back to America, intending to return the following summer, but in 1920 she was admitted to a mental hospital and by 1921 it was clear that she would be confined indefinitely. Her family claimed that her relationship with Rolland contributed to her condition; Rolland himself could merely bewail his powerlessness to help and assert, perhaps more than he felt, that his conscience was clear.[2] Their correspondence continued sporadically until 1939, but to little effect. The whole tragic episode, which Rolland kept a deep secret, shaped the genesis of *L'Ame enchantée* and possibly influenced his later relationships.

Rolland returned to Paris in November 1919, but was unhappy. He felt he needed Paris, but was profoundly out of sympathy with its literary world. Some of his friends had died, notably Humblot, a sad loss when his new works faced a conspiracy of silence so complete that even paid advertisements could not be placed. For the first time he met wartime allies such as Duhamel, Barbusse, Bertrand Russell and Tagore, but no one in Paris offered much support in the causes he wanted to fight. Duhamel, though an estimably level-headed moderate, had a tendency to compromise which pointed to a 'manque de hardiesse morale';[3] Barbusse, hand in glove with figures Rolland mistrusted, was annoyingly reluctant to give straight answers to questions (*JG*:1824–9). Even the loyal Bloch would not write 'les redoutables Confessions d'un grand combattant, héroïque et lucide, – que *vous seul, vous seul en France pouvez – devez* écrire'.[4] With his distinguished war record, Bloch's testimony was a text Rolland wanted to see written, but like many lesser talents, Bloch seemed merely to want to put the war behind him.

Before the war, Rolland had named Péguy as his literary executor; now, in the event of anything happening to his sister, he entrusted the task to Châteaubriant and Jouve. His two friends were hypersensitive poetic natures in whom he appreciated 'l'absolue loyauté d'une âme passionnée, qui se donne toute entière à ce qu'elle aime et croit' (*C30*:193), but both were evolving away from him. When Jouve's marriage broke up, his art took new directions which Rolland did not appreciate; Rolland supported his wife and the rift became permanent in 1927 when Jouve, determined to shake off Rolland's influence, destroyed all his letters after a supposed slight.[5] With Châteaubriant, relations were cordial but infrequent. Rolland sensed that Châteaubriant was avoiding him, he was saddened when his old friend, without telling him, decided to collaborate with Massis, and he was painfully aware that since 1914 Châteaubriant had never publicly supported him. Rolland waited until Châteaubriant published his long-gestating novel, *La Brière*, then took the initiative in gently pointing out how far they had drifted apart (*C30*:281–3). Châteaubriant finally declared support for Rolland during his sixtieth birthday celebrations in 1926; their friendship did not die, but it was much cooled.

His most reliable Parisian friend, until her sudden death in 1925, remained Louise Cruppi. With Châteaubriant, he visited her home near

Toulouse in the summer of 1920, and she persuaded him to think of taking a house in the south-west. Seeking a permanent residence outside Paris, he considered Pau, well-known to tuberculosis sufferers. Finally, however, he opted for Switzerland, and he and Madeleine rented two villas in the grounds of the Hôtel Byron in Villeneuve, a favourite from the war years. There were financial problems due to the unfavourable exchange rate, but the view of lake and mountains was superb, and they moved in during the summer of 1921, accompanied by their father, who survived until 1931.

Rolland returned to Paris for one more winter, largely to maintain contact with his friends, but the effort was barely worthwhile. Friends eluded him, letters went unanswered,[6] and in April 1922 he vacated his flat. As he wrote to Mme Cruppi: 'J'ai passé six mois dans une lutte vaine de tous les jours contre l'apathie, l'aboulie, le déséquilibre mental des uns ou des autres'.[7] By now launched on *L'Ame enchantée*, he needed space to work and Villeneuve gave it to him; the coming decade was highly productive. Yet he was far from cut off: 'L'éloignement [. . .] de Paris m'a rapproché du reste du monde' (*QC*:xxix). Villeneuve was on one of Europe's main north-south axes, and Rolland was besieged by visitors and correspondents, seeking advice, soliciting signatures for petitions or simply scalp-hunting celebrities. Conscious of Tolstoy's example, Rolland tried to respond, but he mourned for his privacy. He dreaded the possible consequences when Zweig's biography proclaimed that he never left letters unanswered,[8] and in the summer, when travellers were numerous, he often fled to mountain retreats.

Irksome as they were, these contacts were important. More than ever, the war had proved the need for an international elite, and Rolland still struggled to form one, but the task was not easy, and Parisian apathy was a major hurdle. His first effort, in the spring of 1919, was the 'Déclaration de l'indépendance de l'esprit', in which he petitioned the world's intellectuals to put wartime errors behind them and rally to their traditional duty to 'maintenir un point fixe, de montrer l'étoile polaire, au milieu du tourbillon des passions dans la nuit'. Truth should be their master, and though they should also serve men, their allegiance is to humanity, not to one people: 'C'est afin que [les peuples] prennent, comme nous, conscience de cette fraternité, que nous élevons au-dessus de leurs luttes aveugles l'Arche d'Alliance, – l'Esprit libre, un et multiple, éternel' (*EL*:344). This was circulated widely for signature, but the response was disappointing. Some nations were under-represented, notably Britain and Russia, where communication was difficult, and there was no massive adhesion in France outside Rolland's group of friends. The lack of university support was saddening, and some distinguished names declined to sign. Châteaubriant signed, then withdrew, Anatole France refused to reply, Max Eastman would not sign a non-communist document and Bernard Shaw, allergic to what was sentimental and moralistic in Rolland's style, felt it would be hypocritical to sign. Shaw's refusal at least generated an interesting correspondence, which helped Rolland, he later claimed, to decide in what sense he was 'au-dessus de la mêlée' (*PR*:15). Others quibbled over the wording; Russell wanted a less abrasive text to win over waverers who might be regretting their wartime behaviour. Rolland sensed the nobility of this, but was unwilling to forgive time-servers, and in the end the text published was close to the first draft.

Rolland's task was not made easier by his reluctance to join organizations. His sister worked for the International Women's League for Peace and Liberty, and he occasionally went to its conferences, but any body he supported had to be supported freely. To please Louise Cruppi, he joined the new PEN Club, though as an honorary member of the British branch, not the French branch, which would not have admitted him, and he travelled to the inaugural dinner in London in 1923, where he immediately threatened to resign in protest against the Belgian blackballing of German members (*QC*:59ff). After Mme Cruppi's death his membership lapsed; though well-meaning, the PEN Club did not meet his uncompromising standards.

The sharpest challenge to his individualism came from *Clarté*. He was suspicious of Barbusse, the *Clarté* team seemed to him a disorganized body in which some admirable figures mingled with suspect Parisian literati, and he and some of his friends refused to join. After the split in the French left in 1920, *Clarté* became militantly communist; in Rolland's view 'elle ne s'arracha au confusionnisme que pour faire un brusque bond dans l'extrémisme intolerant' (*QC*:xvi). Late in 1921, Barbusse used it to attack intellectuals who refused to accept the logic of revolution. Though naming no names and specifically excluding Rolland himself, he castigated his targets as 'Rollandistes'. Rolland recognized no such group and had no wish to head one, but felt bound to reply, and the result was an important polemic.

For Barbusse, the best shield against war was revolution, whose advent he regarded as an inflexible scientific law. A measure of violence, which he preferred to call constraint, seemed to him inevitable in any society, and by rejecting it, the Rollandists condemned themselves to impotence. Individualists and moralists could not prevent war, and the Rollandists were therefore instruments of reaction. In short, Barbusse adopted to communist use the old argument that all who are not with us are against us.

Rolland's attitude to the Soviets was nuanced. He opposed the 1919 blockade, arguing that they should be left to pursue their social experiment, but he remained critical of their abuses. Having refused to see the 1914 war as a product of destiny, he was not prepared to accept the inevitability of Soviet revolution. He assimilated Marxist theory to a positivist science he considered superseded, and his notion of a scientific law was not that of Barbusse:

> Il n'y a pas de lois dans la nature. Elle ne nous livre que des rapports entre des faits; et la loi vient de nous, de nous seuls. Si vous croyez que les lois naturelles ont une existence concrète, au livre de la nature, vous êtes, Barbusse, un mystique sans le savoir. (*AL*:217)[9]

Nature provides facts, but the laws explaining them are products of the fallible human mind, not the 'géométrie sociale' which Barbusse claimed (*AL*:218). This made Rolland reluctant to tolerate Soviet error. 'Les chefs de l'ordre nouveau ont sacrifié trop souvent, de propos délibéré, les plus hautes valeurs morales: l'humanité, la liberté, et – la plus précieuse de toutes – la vérité' (*AL*:202). Means do not justify ends; violence and tyranny, however provisional in intent, will never remain so because of their effect on their perpetrators. War-weary Europe is in any case not fit for revolution, which needs 'des greniers pleins de la santé robuste et de l'espoir joyeux d'une race' (*AL*:211). Rolland's hopes therefore lie elsewhere. He pins some trust on 'la lutte intrépide de l'esprit [. . .] pour voir, contrôler, juger les actes de pouvoir', taking as models the Union of Democratic Control and 'l'ironie acharnée de Voltaire et des Encyclopédistes, qui ont plus fait pour la chute de la royauté que la poignée d'écervelés qui ont pris la Bastille' (*AL*:213). This is consistent with his elite-forming ambitions, but it sits oddly with his mistrust of Voltaire and his celebration of the crowd in *Le Quatorze Juillet*. More tellingly, he praises the rejection of violence practised by British conscientious objectors and by Gandhi, cited here by Rolland for the first time.

Barbusse retaliated by denying the value of the critical mind as a weapon and detecting as much constraint in Gandhism as in any mass movement. Rolland rejoined that his concern was not with the immediate situation. Despite a gloomy view of the present, his view of the future was positive:

> Je suis habitué par l'histoire à embrasser de plus vastes espaces; et je sais que Paris n'a pas été bâti en un jour, que l'unité humaine ne le sera pas en un siècle. Je n'en crois pas moins en elle. J'y crois même beaucoup plus, puisque les échecs passagers ne peuvent m'ébranler. (*AL*:212)

The key to the transformation of humanity lay in two factors:

> D'abord [. . .] *le sacrifice*, qui est l'exemple héroïque de cette transformation, accomplie par un homme, accomplie par nous-mêmes, – et, en second lieu, *le temps*, le maître-maçon qui bâtit avec la peine et le sang des genérations. (*AL*:214)

As in *Clerambault*, this lifts the problem out of politics and places it in the lap of the self-sacrificing individual. Barbusse claims to be the voice of realism against idealism and sentimentality, but for Rolland, idealism and sentimentality can be potent forces. He therefore supports the Soviets only insofar as they are enemies of tyranny: 'Avec vous et les Révolutionnaires, contre les tyrannies du passé! Avec les opprimés de demain, contre les tyrannies de demain!' (*AL*:205)

In later years, Rolland praised the lofty tone and mutual esteem which prevailed during this polemic, and condemned his own failure to find effective formulae for action (*QC*:xix, xxv-xxvii). This, however, understates his irritation at Barbusse's shiftiness; Barbusse's refusal to print Rolland's rejoinders in *Clarté* forced him to use Paul Colin's Belgian periodical, *L'Art libre*, and the tone of the exchanges became sharper when Martinet intervened on Barbusse's side, but the two men remained on good enough terms to collaborate in later years. Like the Sartre-Camus polemic a generation later, this debate on means and ends raised important issues for the left. It provoked a series of exchanges in *L'Art libre*, with most participants supporting Rolland, but with Trotsky himself declaring for Barbusse. Rolland, however, had no taste for polemic. 'Le problème présent est de trouver une harmonie où s'accordent les exigences légitimes de la Révolution économico-sociale, et celles non moins légitimes de la liberté spirituelle' (*AL*:231). His quest was for harmony, for making men of different outlook work together, rather than fomenting discord. This debate, last flowering of his heroic individualism, was not his chosen *modus operandi*, and the time and effort it absorbed during the 1921–2 winter strengthened his resolve to leave Paris.

What Rolland sought in Paris was a successor to Péguy's *Cahiers*, a review of broader sympathies than *Clarté* which would open its doors to international contributors,

> une grande revue française de pensée libre et vraiment internationale, – en dehors de tout parti politique ou social, et même en laissant la politique résolument de côté. Nous voudrions qu'elle fût un centre de ralliement pour la pensée littéraire, scientifique, artistique, philosophique, dans ce qu'elle a d'universellement humain.[10]

This was to be *Europe*, which first appeared in 1923 under the editorship of Arcos and Colin. Rolland, by now in Switzerland, was not on the editorial team, but was a guiding spirit in its foundation; it became his main point of contact with literary Paris. *Europe*, however, lacked a Péguy. The board included men Rolland considered suspect, especially when Arcos and Colin were downgraded by Albert Crémieux, director of the review's publishing house, Rieder, who moved *Europe* towards partisan politics and weakened its literary character. Rolland's friends Bloch, Arcos, Vildrac and Duhamel faded into the background, and the team was weakened by the early death of two of its best members, Bazalgette in 1929 and Robertfrance in 1932. 'Le vigoureux honnêteté de l'esprit et le sérieux moral' of Jean Guéhenno had echoes of Péguy,[11] and Rolland supported him as editor until 1936, when he backed the changes which gave the review a more communist character. Yet there was constant friction; *Europe* refused works by Tagore and Gorky that Rolland had recommended, and when in 1930 it carried an article by André Thérive, who had recently attacked him, he threatened to withdraw all support. Yet by April 1931 he was again placing articles with *Europe*; for all its faults he needed it.

The problem was that *Europe* 'a toujours déplorablement manqué, non seulement de foi, mais de vraie, profonde, brûlante vie intérieure'.[12] This condemned it to mediocrity, and though Paris would have been poorer without it, it was symptomatic of the failure of French literary circles to renew themselves. The revival of 1912 had dissipated, and Rolland lost his faith in the ability of independent intellectuals to act:

> Ce fut [. . .] ma principale erreur et ma déception la plus cuisante, en ces années, d'avoir surévalué ces 'esprits libres', ces 'individualistes', dont le plus grand nombre [. . .] s'éclipsèrent devant les risques et se replièrent derrière l'ordre social existant. (*QC*:xxxviii)

Their failure was an important part of the process which drove him into the arms of the communists. Before that, however, he devoted much of the 1920s to supporting non-communist action in India.

His interest in India dated from the war, when Coomaraswamy introduced him to Indian culture and Tagore's Tokyo speech suggested that Asia was ready to assume world moral leadership. What India meant to him can be seen in his 1922 preface to Coomaraswamy's book *La Danse de Çiva*, in which he celebrates the sheer magnitude of this ancient civilization which realizes his ideal of harmony:

> Chaque chose a sa place, chaque être a sa fonction, et tous associés au concert
> divin, faisant de leurs voix divers et des dissonances mêmes, selon le mot
> d'Héraclite, la plus belle harmonie. Tandis qu'en Occident une forte et froide
> logique sépare le dissemblable, [. . .] l'Inde, en tenant compte des différences
> naturelles des êtres et des pensées, cherche à les combiner entre elles, pour
> rétablir en sa plénitude la totale Unité. (*I*:600–1)

Religion, poetry, science and even sexuality blend in a synthesis suggesting both Empedocles in its long, cyclic vision and the discoveries of Einsteinian science:

> Lorsque [. . .] je rentre dans mon siècle et que j'y trouve les prodigieuses
> tentatives de cosmogonie nouvelle, issues du génie d'Einstein, [. . .] je ne
> m'y sens pas dépaysé. J'entends [. . .] résonner encore la symphonie cosmique
> des mondes qui succèdent, s'éteignent et se rallument, avec leurs âmes vivantes,
> leurs humanités et leurs Dieux, selon la loi de l'Eternel Devenir, le Samsâra
> brahmanique, – j'entends Çiva qui danse, dans le cœur du monde, – dans
> mon cœur. (*I*:601–2)

The image of Shiva's dance evokes a world whose vitality depends on transformation, where contemporary problems are subsumed in a cosmic vision blending dynamism and serenity. It is related to the struggle against 'le Néant' in *Le Buisson ardent*, and it anticipates the attraction that Goethe's motto, 'Stirb und Werde!', held for Rolland in the 1930s.

Rolland soon developed a network of Indian contacts. He met Tagore in 1921 and became friendly with the musician Dilip Kumar Roy and Kalidas Nag, a student in Paris who later held an academic post in Tagore's circle. Later, he was fascinated by the scientist Sir Jagadis Chunder Bose, whose studies of 'la vie psychique, la sensibilité des plantes et des minéraux' supported the pantheistic vision of nature expressed in *Le Buisson ardent* (*I*:215–18). He also met Charles Andrews and W. W. Pearson, British supporters of the independence movement who brought him news of Gandhi. Unlike most French writers on India, Rolland supported Indian independence from the start,[13] and his biography of Gandhi, produced in 1923, did much to make Europe aware of the Mahatma.

Gandhi answered questions that Rolland had failed to answer during the war, transforming pacifism into an effective non-Bolshevik mass movement:

> Deux sortes de pacifisme: le pacifisme par renoncement, par pauvreté de vie.
> Et le pacifisme par tranquille confiance en sa force, par surabondance de vie.
> Ce dernier pacifisme, l'Inde seule [. . .] peut se payer le luxe de le mettre en
> pratique. (*I*:70–1)

Rolland rejects negative definitions of Satyagraha as passive resistance or non-violence; Gandhi's struggle is full of 'l'énergie enflammée de l'amour, de la foi et du sacrifice' (*MG*:50). Based on religious tradition, it reacts against Western materialism, it shows that a nationalist movement led by an 'apôtre du monde' is, after all, possible (*MG*:131), and also that a whole people may unite in a sacrificial movement, accepting suffering, even setbacks such as the suspension of the campaign after the violence at Chauri-Chaura, rather than compromising its principles. Reluctance to believe this possible had prevented Rolland from calling for disobedience during the war; now Gandhi offered a new model, and Rolland sought ways of transmitting it to Europe.

This, however, was not easy. Rolland knew it had to be based on religious faith, which was stronger in India than in the West; even in India it required an educative element to make it work (*MG*:92–3). Moreover, Rolland was unhappy about narrowly Hindu aspects of Gandhism like the cult of the cow and the spinning wheel and the boycott of foreign goods, which appeared to reject progress (*MG*:49). Gandhi himself might rise above such limitations, but Rolland feared his disciples who denatured his thought by systematizing it:

> Dieu préserve un grand homme de ces amis qui ne saisissent qu'une partie de sa pensée! En la codifiant, ils détruisent l'harmonie, qui est le principal bienfait de son âme vivante! (*MG*:137)

Here, Rolland ruefully recalls his difficulties with his own supporters; life is to be found in the great personality who harmonizes contrasts, not in any purely intellectual synthesis. Worst of all, Gandhi is essentially nationalist rather than internationalist. This was why Rolland refused, in 1922, to write an introduction to a collection of Gandhi's articles:

> Je vois en lui le type le plus haut, le plus pur du nationalisme spiritualisé [. . .] qu'il faudrait offrir en modèle aux nationalistes égoïstes et matérialisés de l'Europe actuelle. Je compte le faire; [. . .] mais je ne le pourrais dans une Introduction au volume, car je ne serais pas aussi libre de la discuter et de marquer en quoi je m'en sépare. (*I*:34)

Rolland's study aimed to be critical, and the instrument of criticism is a comparison with Tagore, who differed from the Mahatma on grounds which reflected Rolland's own debate between dream and action. Of all living artists, Tagore best embodied Rolland's ideal of harmony. An internationalist wounded by the idea of non-co-operation with the West,

Tagore sensed an 'intolérance mesquine' in Gandhian circles which might spawn the excesses of a mass movement (*MG*:121), and Rolland shared his worries. He could not forget the damage done in the war by misplaced faith in mass movements, and after the Barbusse polemic he felt closer to the individualist Tagore than to Gandhi's activist approach. He even regretted that Gandhi had become political leader of the independence movement; he would have preferred him as 'chef de la minorité, de l'élite morale' (*MG*:29), a role more in harmony with Rolland's own preferred mode of action.

It was therefore with Tagore that Rolland sought to work. Tagore's university of Santiniketan was a model for the elite that Rolland wanted to create, and he hoped to build a European counterpart, centred on the publishing house of his Zürich friend Emil Roniger, who planned a 'Maison de l'Amitié' devoted to collaboration between Europe and Asia. Rolland tried to bring the two men together to discuss the scheme, but the process proved frustrating. Tagore had embarked on a series of long and, in Rolland's view, pointless world tours, and Rolland had difficulty in persuading him to come to Switzerland. After a series of broken arrangements, a meeting planned for 1922 finally took place in June 1926, when Tagore and his retinue descended on Villeneuve, and it was not a success. The discussions on poetry and music were cordial enough, but Tagore had recently visited Italy, where pro-fascist Indophiles had inveigled him into making statements appearing to favour Mussolini. Concerned to maintain Tagore's credit in Europe, Rolland tried to open his guest's eyes to fascism's ugly realities, but found it hard to overcome what he saw as a characteristic Indian indifference to the nuances of Western politics, and was inhibited by the ailing poet's manifest distress at facing harsh facts. Tagore promised to clarify his views, but the article he drafted was disappointingly non-committal (*I*:140). The whole issue took far too much time, and there was no opportunity to discuss practical co-operation. Rolland was unimpressed by the organizational abilities of Tagore's entourage, and felt that the poet himself had failed to harmonize his roles as artist and man of action:

Sa nature est éternellement partagée entre ses aspirations poétiques, qui sont les plus profondes, ce qui lui est inné, – et le rôle social prophétique, que les circonstances lui ont commandé d'assumer. Ce rôle est grandiose; et Tagore, par moments d'inspiration passionnée, s'est trouvé à la hauteur. Mais il ne s'y maintient pas. (*I*:155–6)

Tagore had, in effect, opted out of action; the aristocrat in him had lost touch with the people. Matters were not eased by the constant criticisms of Gandhi which Tagore seemed unable to suppress. Rolland found them so discouraging that they put him off his ambition of travelling to India: 'J'y serais écartelé entre les deux groupes rivaux. Chacun chercherait à se servir de moi' (*I*:180). In losing hope of collaborating with Tagore, Rolland became disillusioned about the prospect of forming any elite based on men of letters. From then on, his hopes lay in collective action; the failure of this meeting, on the eve of his reconciliation with communism, was an important turning point in his evolution away from individualism.

Rolland's Indian interests took a new turn when he discovered Ramakrishna and Vivekananda, who became the subject of works to be treated in a later chapter. In the political arena he moved closer to Gandhi, largely thanks to Madeleine Slade. This daughter of an English admiral had been drawn to Rolland by an interest in Beethoven, and to Gandhi through Rolland. In 1925 she sailed to India to become one of Gandhi's closest disciples, thus furnishing Gandhi's camp with a warm admirer of Rolland, and a correspondence developed. Their relationship needed careful defining; there were debates on points of discord, such as Gandhi's support from the British war effort in 1914-18, and when Gandhi expressed a wish to visit Europe specifically to discuss the matter, Rolland felt bound to dissuade him, sensing that Gandhi saw him more as a religious and moral authority than as an artist (*C19*:45). Though Rolland felt it wrong to bring Gandhi to Europe purely to meet him, he did want Gandhi to carry his message to the West, and he pressed him to accept other invitations. The young needed to be told what the practical consequences of a pacifist movement would be, reassured that their sacrifice would contribute to the overall well-being of mankind (*C19*:21, 48), and this, Rolland felt, could be done by Gandhi better than any European.

When Gandhi did come, in 1931, it was for the London Round Table Conference, but for Rolland, convinced now that the best way to prevent war was by social transformation on the Soviet model, it was too late. Writing to Edmond Privat in May 1931, he deplored Gandhi's blindness to Russia: 'Ce qu'il a récemment publié [. . .] montre qu'il ignore presque tout de la nouvelle phase où s'est engagé la marche sanglante du monde' (*PR*:74). Given the urgent threat of war in an increasingly fascist Europe, Rolland felt that for want of the right religious atmosphere there was no time to organize non-violence, and he was as reluctant to demand the sacrifices involved as he had been in 1915. The rather different sacrifice required by a Leninist movement, offering the prospect of triumph and progress, seemed more in harmony with the times, and indeed more human:

> Bien qu'incapable, pour mon compte, de tremper mes mains dans la violence, combien l'attitude d'un Lénine, risquant sa vie et l'infamie ou les malédictions, m'a paru [. . .] non seulement plus virile, mais même plus véritablement aimante et conforme à la loi intérieure du sacrifice pour le service de l'humanité! (*PR*:76)

What Rolland wanted of Gandhi was a recognition that Gandhism and Leninism shared a common cause, and he argued the case when Gandhi visited Villeneuve in December 1931.

Rolland's record of their meeting is a striking human document, mingling ironic observation of Gandhi's motley crowd of camp-followers with reverence for the Mahatma himself. As with Tagore, the personal meeting of minds was more successful than the political. Rolland responded to Gandhi's sincerity and humour, but could not elicit the support he wanted. Blending humility and stubbornness, Gandhi worked only from personal experience; he did not feel he knew the West well enough to preach to it, but was too convinced of the universal validity of non-violence to accept revolutionary socialism (*C19*:83). He hinted that he would favour labour over capital in any conflict between them, which allowed Rolland to claim that Gandhi would be on the side of revolution when it came,[14] but in practice all Gandhi offered was a promise to study the problem further. As with Tagore, Italy complicated their meeting. Gandhi planned to visit Rome on the way to his ship in Brindisi, and Rolland struggled to discourage him from doing anything which might be considered pro-fascist. More cunning than Tagore and confident in his faith, Gandhi was convinced he could visit Rome without contamination. He agreed to stay with Sofia Bertolini's friend General Moris rather than accept official hospitality, but he accepted an audience with Mussolini, and Rolland was left to explain to his Western friends that this did not amount to support for fascism. Apart from these tensions, their meeting produced many interesting discussions. Rolland responded to Gandhi's 'esprit [. . .] qui est en constante, mais patiente évolution' (*C19*:298). He liked the way Gandhi had reshaped his maxim, 'God is Truth', into 'Truth is God', which, by opening the way to any thought sincerely seeking truth, favoured Rolland's ideal of harmony. Some of their most fruitful conversations touched on the problem faced by their mutual master Tolstoy, that of how to state the truth when it risks causing pain to weak minds. Both agreed that unpleasant truths must be stated; Rolland had some success in arguing that joy and artistic beauty should be regarded as emanations of the divine, but rather less in making Gandhi appreciate Beethoven (*C19*:106–11). Their personal affection survived, but Rolland was again left with a sense of how different he was from his Indian guest and a certain irritation at Indian ways.

Gandhi's subsequent imprisonment curtailed their correspondence. Rolland resisted an attempt in 1933 by Saumyendranath Tagore, the poet's communist nephew, to draw him into an attack on Gandhi; seeking harmony as ever, he tried to persuade the youth to work for a collaboration between Gandhists and communists in the independence struggle. By 1935, however, it was clear that this could not be, and that Gandhi's promise to study socialism had led to nothing. Rolland declined Subhas Chandra Bose's call to dissociate himself publicly from Gandhi, believing still that non-violence was appropriate to India (*C19*:342–3), but by publishing the letter to Privat quoted above in *Par la Révolution, la paix* he did give public expression to his reservations. Gandhi's message now seemed to lack universal validity; it was 'très pur et très haut, mais pas assez large pour embrasser l'humanité en marche vers des horizons nouveaux' (*C19*:341). Leadership of the Indian movement had passed to Nehru, more open to socialist ideals. In 1939, in a homage for Gandhi's seventieth birthday, Rolland saw his doctrine playing 'le rôle des grands monastères du Moyen Age chrétien', providing an island of peace in a troubled world, but in other respects declared it inappropriate to Europe (*C19*:421).

The meetings with Tagore and Gandhi mark the beginning and end of an evolution which led Rolland away from individualism to almost total espousal of communism, and they contributed to that evolution by revealing that practical collaboration with the great Indians would not be possible. Neither Tagore nor Gandhi offered a satisfactory alternative to alliance with the Soviets. He retained his sympathy for the Indian independence movement, but it faded from the forefront of his mind in the 1930s as the movement itself went through a quiet period and other problems seemed more urgent.

Notes

1. See letter to Helena de Kay, 28 May 1919.
2. See letter to Madeleine, 6 August 1921.

3. Diary 17 December 1919. See *Europe* 439-40 (1966), p.187.
4. Letter to J-R. Bloch, 17 September 1919.
5. See Leuwers (1981). Jouve attempted to resume contact with Rolland in 1940.
6. See letter to J-R. Bloch, 6 April 1922.
7. Letter to Louise Cruppi, 16 April 1922.
8. Letter to Zweig, 10 June 1920. See Nedeljkovic (1970), p.279.
9. Rolland's letters appear in *Quinze ans de combat*, but they and a number of other inter-war articles are quoted from the more accessible Albertini anthology, which has the advantage of setting them alongside Barbusse's letters.
10. Letter to Einstein, 21 April 1922. Quoted in Kvapil (1971), p.86.
11. Letter to M. Martinet, 15 September 1934. See Kvapil (1971), p.100.
12. Letter to J. Robertfrance, 16 November 1927. Quoted by Kvapil (1971), p.95.
13. See Fisher (1988), p.116. This volume gives the fullest account of Rolland's inter-war political evolution.
14. See Francis (1975), p.302.

–9–

Failed Heroes (II): Russia

> Je me souviens d'un jour lointain de mes vingt ans à Rome [. . .] Nouvellement arrivé en Italie, une magique soirée après une course de tout le jour dans la Sabine, j'eus brusquement des larmes de bonheur au spectacle d'une telle beauté, au sentiment que le bonheur était donc possible sur terre [. . .]
>
> Quand j'ai reconnu, ces dernières années, en U.R.S.S., que le grand rêve social pouvait être réalisé, j'aurais pu de nouveau connaître ces larmes de bonheur, si mes vieux yeux ne s'étaient déshabitués de pleurs. (*CG*:29)

These words from a 1936 polemic may exaggerate, but they show the emotional intensity with which Rolland embraced communism, after a soul-searching evolution which has led some communist critics to cite him as a model bourgeois intellectual convert.[1] He never was a party member, nor pressed to become one;[2] the party accepted that he was more useful as a fellow-traveller. Yet throughout the 1930s he showed a partisan commitment which would previously have been unthinkable.

Even the self-critical 'Panorama' prefacing *Quinze ans de combat* does not present this change as a total rupture: 'Je n'ai pas besoin, pour être ce que je suis aujourd'hui, de rien abdiquer de ce que j'ai été' (*QC*:lvii). It was a continuous evolution, and he stresses the continuity by defining himself as a revolutionary in never-ending movement:

> J'ai toujours écrit *pour ceux qui marchent*. Car j'ai toujours été en marche, et j'espère bien ne m'arrêter qu'à la mort [. . .] – Et c'est pourquoi je suis avec les peuples et les classes qui fraient la route au fleuve de l'humanité [. . .] Ils sont portés par l'élan irrésistible de l'évolution historique. Et j'obéis au même Destin. (*QC*:237–8)

The process has, however, become a historical movement rather than an individual reaction; instead of defying destiny, as in 1914, Rolland espouses its flow. This is the crucial change, apparently springing from an 'éclair' which, in an enigmatic allusion in *Le Voyage intérieur*, he situates in January 1926.[3] Its effects can be traced in several texts of that period to which I shall later return. Its character is essentially religious, involving serene acceptance of a cosmic process now perceived as beneficial. It has analogies with Marxist determinism, and in some texts, such as the Introduction to *Compagnons de route*, he accepts the affiliation (*CR*:15). Yet what mattered to him was not systematic Marxism, with which he was imperfectly familiar, but the faith it inspired and the quality of the faithful. When he came to admire Lenin, it was as a great individual rather than as a Marxist (*QC*:65). He turned to collective movements in search of heroic qualities which 1920s intellectuals could not match; in this, he could justly claim continuity with his pre-war thought.

The degenerating world situation was another factor. Rolland watched it with unceasing concern, devoting more and more time to highlighting dangers and denouncing capitalist, imperialist and fascist crimes. With a constant fear that Germany would be driven back into militarism, he criticized the occupation of the Ruhr, supported appeals to relieve German economic distress and frequently called for revision of the post-war treaties. Indian independence was just one of the anti-imperialist causes he supported; he attacked the French in Indo-China and the Dutch in the East Indies (*QC*:191), and saw in America the potential to be the worst imperialist power of all (*QC*:72–3). As he worked for Eurasian harmony, the quest for European unity came to appear insufficient. Despite a guarded early welcome (*VI*:391), in 1929 he denounced Count Coudenhove-Kalergi's Pan-Europa as a tool of reaction (*PR*:19–26). In a 1931 exchange with Gaston Riou, a supporter of Pan-Europa whose idealism Rolland respected, he argued that without the USSR, 'cette pseudo-Europe ne peut être [. . .] qu'une *Sainte-Alliance* de la grosse Démocratie d'affaires internationale, qui se sert de votre idéalisme comme d'un appât' (*QC*:125–6).

Since 1916 Rolland had seen international capitalism as a threat to peace. It dominated the Western democracies, and lurked behind the new threat of fascism. As early as 1922 Rolland experienced fascist violence when blackshirts forced his sister's International Women's League to relocate a conference from Varese to Lugano; the fascist climate prevented Rolland from ever again visiting Italy, and it clouded his correspondence with Sofia Bertolini, who was drawn in widowhood to Catholicism and Mussolini. His first attacks on fascism, dating from 1926, concentrate on the threats to peace and liberty and the murder of Matteotti and Amendola, but as time passed he placed more emphasis on fascism as a tool of reaction, a superficially revolutionary movement led by class traitors serving capitalist ends. Mussolini 'arrachait les derniers scrupules qui paralysaient l'esprit "au-dessus de la mêlée". Qui combattait la guerre devait entrer dans le combat contre ses agents provocateurs' (*QC*:xl).

Anti-fascism drew the crusader for peace into wider social conflict, and late in 1926 he organized an anti-fascist committee with Einstein and Barbusse.

He tried to keep this apolitical; reluctant to head a Moscow front organization, he was determined to attack Russian as well as Italian abuses. He mistrusted Soviet propagandists who used his name without authorization; one such episode threatened his position in Switzerland by falsely attributing to him a critical article on Swiss politics (*QC*:xlii). Capitalist plots, however, seemed more serious, and by 1927 Rolland was convinced of an international conspiracy against the USSR. Invited by an anarchist review, *Libertaire*, to attack Soviet repression, he declared himself perfectly willing to believe the worst of it, but warned that '*la Russie est en danger*' and called for solidarity among all parties of the left. Despite everything, the USSR was the world's best hope, and its defeat would mean war and tyranny: 'Si elle est écrasée, ce ne sera pas seulement le prolétariat du monde qui sera asservi, mais toute liberté, sociale ou individuelle' (*QC*:79–80). Rolland had been saying similar things ever since 1917, but the urgent tone is new, also the sense that defence of Russia takes priority over purist condemnation of its errors. This was noticed by Lunacharsky, now Soviet Commissar for Public Instruction, responsible for cultivating Western sympathizers. He invited Rolland to contribute to a Soviet review; though disagreeing with some of Rolland's opinions, he promised that Rolland's copy would be printed even if it was against editorial policy. Only a year before, Lunacharsky had attacked *Le Jeu de l'amour et de la mort* and a Leningrad edition of Rolland's works had been banned, but now the signals indicated more openness, and Rolland responded.

It helped, as with other fellow-travellers, that Stalin was concentrating on socialism in one country rather than world revolution. This was in line with Rolland's advice in a letter to the Russian press on the tenth anniversary of 1917 (*QC*:xlvi). He was wary of Stalin, whom he rated lower than Lenin; in July 1927 he was still declaring in private that 'la Révolution russe a été [. . .] l'œuvre d'un seul homme: elle est morte avec lui'.[4] Yet he preferred Stalinism to Trotskyism; the exhausted West still seemed unfit for revolution, and in all his calls for unity of the left he never sought to include Trotskyists, accepting Moscow's line that they were in league with reactionary forces. The heroic Russian people building its future within its own frontiers offered a much more appealing image, and Rolland was eager to find out how true it was. Reliable information was hard to obtain, but he cited enthusiastic eye-witnesses among the stream of visitors to Villeneuve (*C28*:178, *QC*:88), and the flow was dominated by two Russians who made it their business to supply favourable data.

Gorky had been a correspondent since 1916. They did not meet until 1935, neither spoke the other's language, and it is doubtful how well they understood each other, but each supported the other at difficult moments. Their attitude to the USSR evolved in harmony; Gorky left Russia at about the time of Rolland's debate with Barbusse, in which Rolland claimed Gorky's support,[5] and returned in 1928 just as Rolland was becoming a fellow-traveller, rallying to a leadership apparently inspired by dynamic Western ideals. As semi-official leader of Soviet culture he fed Rolland with enthusiastic details of Soviet achievements, and Rolland used him as a channel for humanitarian pleas to the Soviet authorities.

Neither of these operations ran smoothly. Rolland, though open to persuasion, sensed the propagandist in Gorky, and as late as 1930 was privately critical of Gorky's 'optimisme béat laudateur de tout ce qui se fait à Moscou' (*C28*:462). When Gorky extolled the White Sea Canal, an atrocious slave labour project, as a model work of penal reform, Rolland reflected that his correspondent 'ne dit pas un mot des souffrances et des révoltes' (*C28*:568). At other moments, however, Rolland perceived a certain grandeur in this 'œuvre à la Cheops',[6] and he kept his reservations to himself. Nor was he prepared to be used as Gorky's mouthpiece. When in 1927 Balmont and Bunin, two Russian *émigré* writers, appealed for support, Rolland responded by expressing personal sympathy but insisting that the future lay with the Soviets (*QC*:86–96). Gorky wrote to Rolland with unflattering information about both writers, apparently so that Rolland could publicize it, but that was not Rolland's style and he dissuaded Gorky from pursuing the matter (*C28*:198–9). To this extent he avoided complete subjugation.

Rolland felt that in making representations through Gorky about human rights abuses he could at once serve humanitarian causes and help the USSR win Western friends. Sometimes he succeeded; Oskar Hartoch, a doctor whose sister Else was a family friend, was released from prison in 1931 on Stalin's direct order, Stalin having recognized that Rolland's approval was worth cultivating.[7] Gorky, however, was not always helpful. Their friendship nearly ended when he took offence at Rolland's support of Francesco Ghezzi, an Italian anarchist imprisoned in Russia (*C28*:206–7), and he rejected Rolland's plea on behalf of forty-eight prisoners executed for sabotage of the food supply industry, after confessions which Rolland thought must have been extracted by torture (*C28*:463). Gorky insisted that a regime in an effective state of civil war had the right to defend itself (*C28*:211–12), and Rolland capitulated: 'Aux "48" je ne m'intéresse point: je ne les connais point. Je ne réponds que de ceux que je connais. – Si vous, Gorki, vous vous faites garant de la justice de l'arrêt, c'est bien: j'y crois' (*C28*:214). Henceforth he was content to accept Gorky's guidance, confining himself to private advocacy of cases of which he had personal knowledge. Where in the 1920s his model had been Tagore, the elitist harmonizer, in the next decade it was Gorky, the artist as revolutionary.

Much harder to measure was the influence of Maria Koudacheva. The illegitimate daughter of a French mother and a Russian father she never knew, she went through harrowing times in the Revolution. Left a widow by an officer of princely rank in the White army, her background made her suspect to the Bolsheviks, yet she became an ardent supporter. Her fascination with literary figures older than herself, with some of whom she had affairs, indicates a quest for a surrogate father. She was briefly secretary to Guilbeaux, then to the academic Piotr Kogan. She wrote to Rolland in 1923, sending him some of her poems, but broke off when he disapproved of her affair with Kogan. Acting as his official guide, she set her cap unsuccessfully at Duhamel on his visit to Moscow in 1927. Correspondence with Rolland resumed in 1928; with their thirty-year age difference he made an ideal father figure, and he, as so often, was happy to exchange affectionate letters with an interesting and ardent woman, apparently responding to her passionate revolutionary faith.[8] There was already a sense that the relationship was special when she visited him in 1929, ostensibly to prepare a Russian edition of his works. She returned in 1930, and by 1931 was permanently installed at Villeneuve. In April 1934 they married; it might have been sooner but for the need to respect Madeleine's sensibilities. Keeping the peace between the two women often taxed Rolland's ingenuity.

In 1937 Guilbeaux, who was well placed to know and had turned against Stalin, alleged that Maria Koudacheva was a Soviet agent, detailed to counteract Madeleine's influence and keep Rolland faithful to the party line. From such an unbalanced source the claim might be disregarded, but it is supported by Willi Münzenberg's widow, Babette Gross, who alleges that she was attached to the Comintern network headed by Münzenberg and Louis Gibarti, which manipulated fellow-travellers while letting them think they were operating independently.[9] Duhamel's diary, published in 1983, portrays a harrowing encounter with her in 1930, when her marriage prospects were far from certain, at which she more or less admitted she was being pressurized into manipulating Rolland and fearful of the consequences of failure.[10] It is therefore hard to avoid concluding that she was some kind of agent; the question is what kind. Guilbeaux claimed she had been trained for the task from the early 1920s, but this is unproven and there are signs of Soviet uncertainty as to how to use her. Her 1929 visit to him nearly collapsed, as she had difficulty obtaining an exit visa until Gorky intervened; she thought the delay was caused by Kogan, who wanted her to attract Rolland to Russia, not to have her visit him.[11] This may be explained by bad communication within the system, but it argues against a long-planned operation. She easily obtained her visa on later visits, but by then the situation had changed, and it would be surprising if the authorities had not recognized her value and put pressure on her to work for them. Her son Serge, a teenage student staying behind in Moscow, was an ideal hostage.

The evidence points to a reluctant accomplice of the authorities rather than a professional agent. Her support for the Revolution was sincere, but so were her literary enthusiasms, which were enough in themselves to make her throw herself at Rolland. She told Duhamel that she was being blackmailed, and convinced him of the genuineness of her fear. Rolland noticed it too, and it made him more rather than less sensitive to the regime's oppressive nature. As he wrote to Madeleine in 1931, after disappointing both Maria and the Soviet authorities by declining an invitation to visit Russia: 'Je suis certain maintenant que toutes mes lettres sont lues là-bas; et de là, les terreurs de Macha, qui tremble qu'on ne se venge sur elle de mes libertés de langage ou de mes irrévérences à l'égard de l'U.R.S.S'.[12] Duhamel drew similar conclusions, which suggests at the very least that if she was an agent, she was not very competent. She was certainly ill-fitted for the role. In later years she referred to herself jokingly as a mixture of French organization and Russian disorganization; when Rolland knew her she was moody and prone to emotional scenes, with strong, if confused opinions which she would argue tenaciously against all comers.[13] This does not suggest a professional agent trained in prolonged dissimulation.

It is harder still to say how aware Rolland was of her role. He could easily be dismissed as an old man besotted by this unexpected autumnal affair; Duhamel and Guilbeaux, both of them irritated at Rolland's increasingly shrill pro-Soviet statements, suspected as much. Yet his faculties appear to have remained intact. The war had left him ultra-sensitive to possible conspiracies against his independence, and the role of which Maria Koudacheva is accused is precisely that kind of threat. It seems likelier that he knew something of her role and was prepared to take her in spite of it; certainly Duhamel relates a conversation which suggests that Rolland had a shrewd awareness of what she had confessed to him.[14]

It is possible, too, that Rolland felt some responsibility for her and did not want a worse repetition of the tragedy which befell Helena after she went home. Of the two scenarios, a professional agent deceiving an old man in his dotage or an agent *malgré elle* accepted by Rolland for her real qualities, the second seems more plausible. Duhamel shared this view:

> J'ai toujours pensé que si Marie était manipulée par les Soviets, ce qui est indiscutable (même sous la forme d'un simple chantage, ce qu'elle admet), elle a surtout travaillé pour elle-même, pour son amour de la littérature et des littérateurs, et qu'elle a trouvé sa voie en épousant Romain Rolland.[15]

The role of Assia in *L'Ame enchantée*, clearly inspired by Maria Koudacheva, points in the same direction. If Marc returns to her after her adultery with a Comintern official who exhorts her to try to convert him, it is a sign that at least in a fictional context Rolland could envisage an agent still being an acceptable wife. A final clue is in Rolland's response to Guilbeaux's attack, published in 1983 as a riposte to Duhamel's diary.[16] The text was edited by the lady herself and therefore suspect, but she would hardly have suppressed any evidence exculpating her, and none such is cited. Instead, Rolland concentrates on another issue, the integrity of his personal papers; he assures future readers that his diaries have been placed in safe keeping, under the joint charge of his wife and sister, in conditions protecting them from the doctoring by his wife that Guilbeaux feared. It is as if he accepted there was no point in denying his wife's role as agent, but had taken measures to protect his literary estate.

Marie proved a fiercely loyal wife. As well as providing more secretarial support than Rolland had ever enjoyed before, she took charge of his household and physical well-being. His health had been bad since 1929; after their marriage it improved, and without her it is unlikely that he would have survived as long as he did. She lived until 1985, devoting herself to furthering his reputation and publishing his papers. Questions might be asked about her selection and editing of documents, and she could be difficult, but she earned the respect and gratitude of a generation of researchers for the access she offered to what remained unpublished. She was, however, well placed to serve the Soviets in Rolland's household. Anything in Russian passed through her hands, he trusted her enough to let her draft some documents and she could keep visitors at bay and sift his mail. We do not know how she used these powers, but anti-Soviet letters from disillusioned friends such as Guilbeaux, Mesnil and Martinet went unanswered, and Zweig and Masereel found that, when visiting, they could not see him alone.[17] Zweig had differences of opinion with Marie over the politicizing of Rolland's seventieth birthday celebrations in 1936. There had been coolness between the two friends ever since Rolland had rallied to the Soviets, and Rolland suspected Zweig of feeding evidence to Guilbeaux for his attack on Marie, a charge which Zweig denied. There is an uncomfortable ring of truth in the testimony of Eugene Lyons, a disaffected American fellow-traveller who visited Rolland in 1934 and found him embarrassed, even panic-stricken, when confronted with criticism of Russia. Lyons spotted the Stalinist in Marie and sensed she was shielding her husband from a true knowledge of the state of Russia.[18]

Rolland was confident that Marie did not influence his thought. Helena's Christian Science had not done so during the war, he argued,[19] he was well on the way to engagement before they met, and later events show that he did not follow wherever she went; he could accommodate intellectual differences with those he loved. Her control of the information flow, however, was certainly important, on the artistic level she made her mark on *L'Ame enchantée*, and her personality made the greatest impact of all. People mattered more to Rolland than ideas, and Marie and Gorky were two people of faith, each with reason to be hostile to the Soviets, who had nevertheless rallied to them. Their example counted for more than their powers of persuasion.

If a single moment must be selected when his Soviet commitment became total, it is his illness late in 1930, when he nearly lost the will to live,[20] but emerged with an enhanced will to fight against the old society. During this illness he saw his way to the completion of *L'Ame enchantée*, over which he had hesitated, and his first two writings after it, the response to Gaston Riou quoted above and the preface to the projected German edition of his wartime articles, signalled a clear break with the past. The latter in particular, pointedly titled 'Adieu au passé', aimed to show how far he had travelled since 1914.

David Fisher considers that Rolland swung from critical to uncritical support of the USSR in the mid-1930s, under the influence of fascism and the Popular Front,[21] but signs of the swing are visible much earlier in one of the saddest of his broken friendships. Rolland first encountered Panaït Istrati in 1921, helping to launch his literary career after a failed suicide attempt. He admired the brilliant but unstable Romanian's gift for story-telling and observation, but when Istrati visited Russia and saw the regime's effects on the lives of ordinary people, these gifts led him to a vision which began to frighten Rolland. Istrati did not help by over-using Rolland's name in protests; Rolland did not like his limited credit wasted in causes not of his choosing, and was suspicious of Istrati's friends. One of them, Victor Serge, was an anarchist who had fallen foul of the Soviet authorities, and his Russian father-in-law Russakov was being harassed on his account. Rolland had little time for anarchists, especially Serge, who had attacked him during the Barbusse polemic, and feared being drawn into fruitless factional struggles (*IS*:309–10).

More seriously, Rolland discouraged Istrati from pursuing his own action. Istrati wrote twice to the GPU in support of Russakov, denouncing officials' abuse of authority and demanding the right to criticize. These letters were dignified and basically supportive of the Revolution, and Rolland recognized as much. Yet he pleaded with Istrati not to publish:

> Ces pages sont sacrées. Elles doivent être conservées dans les archives de la *Révolution éternelle*. Dans son livre d'or. Nous vous aimons encore plus et *vous vénérons*, de les avoir écrites. *Mais ne les publiez pas!* [. . .] Cela ne servirait en rien à la Révolution russe – mais à la réaction européenne, dont les oppositionnistes font aveuglément le jeu. (*IS*:319–20)

Rolland was concerned for Russia's image in the West and understandably reluctant to hand her enemies a propaganda success, but his willingness to veil an individual injustice for political reasons reveals how far he had travelled since the Barbusse polemic. Istrati, despite a quasi-filial reverence for Rolland, could not understand, and at the time of this exchange, late in 1929, he was one of the first to accuse Rolland of becoming 'officiellement soviétique' (*IS*:339). Against Rolland's advice, he published his criticisms and their friendship foundered on some disparaging remarks he made about Maria Koudacheva, whose close attachment to Rolland was not known to him. Rolland refused to write to Istrati until these were withdrawn, which he did only when he was dying, in 1935. Rolland is not at his best in his often hectoring letters to Istrati, which hint at a desire to hide from himself that he is defending the indefensible.

Rolland knew that all was not perfect in Russia; his dealings with Maria Koudacheva made him intimately aware of an oppressive regime based on espionage and informants. Yet she convinced him that 'on a rétabli dans la doctrine le respect des individualités [. . .] Ce n'est plus le dogme de la communauté aveugle et tyrannique qui engloutit les individualités'.[22] There seemed to be movement towards the respect for the individual which had been the cornerstone of Rolland's thought; a synthesis of individualism and collectivism began to appear possible. He wrote in July 1931:

> [L'U.R.S.S.] n'a certes rien d'idyllique. Mais elle est saine, virile, héroïque. C'est le seul pays du monde, à l'heure actuelle, où des milliers d'hommes et de femmes – toute une jeunesse – se sacrifient joyeusement pour bâtir, au moins les assises d'un monde meilleur. Et leur élan est mené, d'une main ferme, par des contremaîtres d'Etat, qui savent ce qu'ils veulent et qui le font. Evidemment, c'est aux dépens de beaucoup de biens dont on jouit en Occident; mais l'Occident les achète, aujourd'hui, de tant de complaisances morales et de lâchetés, d'une telle abdication inconsciente, que, pour mon compte, il ne m'est plus possible d'y respirer. (*C29*:63)

Russia was forging a revolutionary people whose joyful self-sacrifice recalls that of Gandhi's India, though in a different mode; more hope emanated from Russia than ever could from the stagnant West. Recalling in 1935 the conclusion to his *Théâtre du peuple*, thirty years ago, in which he had asserted that, 'pour avoir un art du peuple, il faut "*commencer par avoir un peuple*"', he could now assert that: 'L'U.R.S.S. a fait son peuple. Elle a fait l'Action' (*AL*:302–3).

Part of the anti-Soviet plot was to 'empêcher qu'on connaisse en Occident l'existence d'une Russie non-violente, résolument opposée à la guerre'.[23] Stalin's Russia needed and wanted peace, and Rolland sought to harmonize support for Russia with other means of pursuing peace, especially Gandhism. The keystone of that policy was the Amsterdam-Pleyel movement of 1932. The idea of an all-party conference against imperialist war emanated from the Münzenberg propaganda machine, hiding behind a front organization headed by Barbusse, and it was he who drew Rolland into the preparatory work. Rolland accepted, but disliked Barbusse's methods and constantly complained about unanswered letters, abuse of his name and evasiveness about their differences.[24] Rolland does not appear to have grasped the extent of Münzenberg's involvement; a letter to Barbusse before the conference shows him complaining rather naïvely of the way Münzenberg had taken over 'notre Congrès'.[25] His own role was limited, especially as the conference, first planned for Geneva, had to relocate to Amsterdam and his health prevented him from attending; soliciting support and organizing publicity were his main contributions.

Rolland aimed to keep the conference an all-party event, leading to a loose grouping of anti-war parties each acting in its own way rather than a centralized disciplined organization. 'Le Refus de service pour objection de conscience est une sape à la forteresse du même ennemi, que les armées prolétariennes vont assaillir en bataille rangée' (*PR*:46); different kinds of activist should complement and respect each other. Rolland was no longer fearful of Barbusse's communism. If anything, he felt more rather than less intransigent than his shifty colleague: 'Je ne crains pas, – *je ne crains plus* – le trop de hardiesse communiste de Barbusse. *J'en suis arrivé à de tout autres doutes* – bien inattendues! Je me demande s'il ne triche pas avec le communisme'.[26] Yet, as he wrote to Barbusse: 'La signification de mon nom allié au vôtre [. . .] repose sur le fait que j'apporte (symboliquement) aux armées prolétariennes le renfort des deux armées de la Conscience individuelle et de la Conscience collective' (*PR*:62). He recognized that the public perceived him as an independent harmonizer, and he worked to involve non-communist counterweights to Barbusse, such as the pacifist Félicien Challaye and Madeleine's colleague in the International Women's League, Gabrielle Duchêne; he also tried to bring together himself, Barbusse and the Austrian socialist Friedrich Adler to ensure socialist participation. Barbusse and Adler did meet, but without Rolland, and it ended acrimoniously, with the socialists excluded. Rolland, disgusted with the politicians' deviousness, hoped to appeal over their heads to a wider public seeking a broad union against war, a Popular Front policy *avant la lettre*:

> La tactique du *'front unique'* [. . .], c'est justement là ce que j'entends revendiquer, au Congrès. Front unique de tous les peuples pour la guerre, – sans passer par l'intermédiaire des caporaux et des sergents, qui disposent de leur volonté.[27]

Such was the tenor of the message he sent to be read to the congress by Gabrielle Duchêne, taking precautions that the text would not be deformed. After its close he wrote a review (*PR*:50–60), denying that the congress had been taken over by the communists, and he challenged Barbusse over the text of the ensuing manifesto, threatening to resign if Gandhists and conscientious objectors were not accepted as allies (*PR*:61– 4). He carried his point, but it was one of his last public gestures of support for pacifism.

The reason for this was that after Amsterdam it became impossible to ignore the Nazis. Unlike many fellow-travellers, Rolland was committed to the Soviets well in advance of 1933, but Hitler's advent strengthened his commitment. Rolland's attacks on the Nazis began from the moment Hitler took power, and despite his rudeness about Jews in earlier writings, he immediately fastened on the evil of anti-Semitism (*QC*:202).[28] The Nazis attempted to win him over; he was offered the prestigious Goethe Prize, and an article in the *Kölnische Zeitung* appealed to his former love of Germany, but he declined the prize and to the newspaper he reasserted his 1914 distinction between the old and the new Germany (*QC*:205). Later, he campaigned to free the defendants in the Reichstag fire trial. All this was at some personal cost; his plays, previously popular in Germany, were banned, and even Roniger in Zürich was scared into dropping the German edition of his wartime articles. At a time when depression was playing havoc with the book market and he was already donating to Russia all proceeds from his work there, this was a financial blow.

Rolland hoped that Nazism would prove unstable. Stalin needed peace for his reconstruction programme, but Hitler depended on the threat of war to unite his nation around him, and could be destabilized by a European order imposing peace:

> Ce n'est pas la guerre, c'est la paix qui est mortelle pour l'Hitlérisme, incapable de résoudre par les moyens ordinaires les difficultés économiques et sociales qui le serrent à la gorge. Il suffit qu'il trouve autour de lui une Europe ferme et calme, résolue à l'obliger à la paix [. . .]
>
> La Paix est l'épreuve victorieuse des Etats qui ont bonne conscience et une organisation saine. L'U.R.S.S. n'a besoin de rien autre, pour prouver sa raison d'être. (*PR*:170)

This is the sense of the title of *Par la Révolution, la paix*, a collection of Rolland's articles on peace and the Amsterdam conference, arguing the case that peace was best achieved by mass organization, to which end only the Soviet model was effective. As early as 1930, he challenged Einstein's view that European pacifism could become a mass movement (*PR*:32–4), and he criticized pacifists who failed to admit that conscientious objection involved self-sacrifice of a type better suited to India than to Europe (*PR*:69). In March 1933 he resigned from the presidency of the Ligue Internationale des Combattants de la Paix, which offered no answer to the problem of how to resist oppression, asserting that though he would himself continue to practise non-violence, he would not argue against Stalin's military organization, and would side with Stalin in any armed conflict between the dictators (*PR*:83). His best hope, however, was in the diplomatic field, a defensive alliance of the USSR with the Western democracies. This was one of the topics discussed when Rolland met Stalin.

Rolland had hoped to visit Russia almost yearly since 1928, but only in 1935 did he feel fit for the journey. With a military agreement with France recently initialled, the moment seemed propitious; the murder of Kirov was still only a small cloud in an atmosphere which seemed more open. His health gave him little opportunity to explore; after a few days in Moscow, most of his month's stay was spent at Gorky's country house, near enough to Moscow to let him receive visitors. As Gorky's guest he went to some lengths to preserve his independence; he resisted official hospitality offered by Arosev, president of V.O.K.S., and avoided accepting gifts (*C29*:288). He insisted that his constitution would not stand public ceremony, but that did not prevent the authorities from doing their utmost to impress him and publicize his presence. He was cheered in the theatre, cheered at a sports festival, shown countless films, besieged by delegations of young workers, authors, parachutists, reformed criminals and the like, and had opportunities to meet and drink with, or witness the drinking of the leading politicians. After a lifetime of ostracism and vilification, Rolland was undoubtedly touched, and formed a high opinion of Russian vitality, but he was not altogether its dupe. He was uneasy at being on show and overwhelmed by the sheer excess of it all: 'Ces Russes ne connaissent pas le "ne quid nimis". Ils n'en ont jamais assez' (*C29*: 179). He was aware that much of it might have been staged for his benefit: 'On n'arrive pas à démêler, dans ces apologies, ce qui est spontané, de ce qui est commandé,' he commented after a particularly enthusiastic speech by a worker on the Moscow Métro (*C29*:171). His diary account shows he had not lost his gift for shrewd observation.

In meetings with politicians, language was an obstacle; only Bukharin, whom Rolland liked, and Radek, whom he did not, spoke French, and he depended on Marie, whom he trusted, and official translators, whom he did not. The suspect Arosev assisted Marie during a two-hour meeting with Stalin, and it is hard to assess how much the language barrier accounted for Rolland's failure to see through him. Rolland had a long list of points to discuss; too long, as his protracted exposition took too much time and had to be cut, but as far as it went, the discussion throws much light on Rolland's worries about the Soviets.

First to be raised were humanitarian issues. Rolland complained that 'la politique de l'U.R.S.S. ne se préoccupe pas assez de donner à ses amis étrangers les raisons de son action' (*C29*:128); the West would be happier about the executions following Kirov's murder if charges were made public, and the detention of Victor Serge on no published grounds was also bad publicity. Rolland did not esteem Serge, but they had mutual friends, and it was against Soviet interests to make him a martyr. Rolland further worried about the extension of the death penalty to children of twelve; he accepted there might be a reason, but felt the world should know it. With hindsight, these issues may be seen as the first signs of the coming repressions, and Stalin's response was to weep crocodile tears. He justified the extended death penalty, arguing that it was a response to 'la vieille Russie barbare, atroce, qui subsiste encore' (*C29*:132). Over the Kirov conspiracy, Stalin conceded that he might have been hasty; the Serge case he did not know well enough to comment, but he referred it to the appropriate authorities. Finally, Rolland mentioned the confusion among French communists and pacifists in face of the recent political and military rapprochement with France. Rolland, we have seen, felt that this was the right policy; different types of war should be resisted in different ways, and he understood that the Soviets could not be integral pacifists. There were, however, 'de grosses questions de dialectique et de tactique révolutionnaire à élucider' (*C29*:130) and Rolland looked to Stalin for a lead. Stalin replied that alliance with capitalist powers had never been excluded from Soviet tactics; each national party must find its own way and resisting Hitler need not stop French communists from resisting capitalism at home.

Rolland was eager to publish this interview and disappointed when permission was withheld, concluding later that Stalin's frankness would have given his Western enemies too many arms against him (*C29*:293). Personally, Stalin impressed him; he showed 'une parfaite, une absolue simplicité, loyauté, véracité' (*C29*:130), with every sign of being an approachable human being. Yet there were already signs of a cult of personality. Watching him take the salute at the sports festival, Rolland sensed an enigma: 'Je n'arrive pas à mettre d'accord le Staline de mon entretien d'avant-hier, au Kremlin, et celui qui se laisse faire, pendant six heures, une apothéose d'empereur romain' (*C29*:140). Stalin cunningly showed Rolland what he wanted to see, but could not hide his more sinister side. Just as enigmatic was the police chief Yagoda, the Soviet Fouché, as Rolland called him, with whom Rolland's discussions brought about Victor Serge's release once the Soviet bureaucracy had ground its way through the case. Yagoda seemed an idealist, a lover of books and flowers, convinced of the reformative value of his harsh penal system, yet blandly denying that Rolland's mail was tampered with when Rolland knew full well that it was (*C29*:174).[29] Other troubling evidence came from the Koudachev family, supporters of the Whites in the civil war, who gave him glimpses of the regime's harsher side (*C29*:182). Marie's student son Serge voiced a discontent with officialdom which reminded Rolland of his own rebellious youth (*C29*:199).

More disturbing, though not mentioned in his diary at the time, was a certain unease about Gorky. Rolland could never see him alone; the house was always full, they needed an interpreter and could never have intimate conversations. Gorky played his role well, but Rolland sensed submerged tensions:

> Comme il est pâle, comme ses yeux sont tristes et affectueux. Il est sûrement un homme très bon et faible; il force sa nature, il se raidit pour ne point désapprouver, souvent les fautes de ses grands amis politiques. Il se livre en lui de durs combats, dont nul ne sait rien. (*C29*:200)

Rolland sensed that what Gorky found on returning to Russia was not what he had hoped to find, and suspected his secretary Kruchkov of manipulating him in the interests of the party. Rolland's final reaction was one of sympathy: 'Il me semble que, si nous avions pu [être seuls] ensemble, (et que cette barrière des langues fût brisé), il eût pu m'étreindre et sangloter longuement, sans parler' (*C29*:231). At the hour of his triumph, Gorky was after all a 'vainqueur vaincu'.

Rolland's main public statement on his visit was 'Retour de Moscou', published in *Commune* in October 1935 (*C29*:211–23). Its tone was eulogistic, but it was in fact a truncated version of a more nuanced text. Rolland expresses admiration for Soviet vitality, which seemed to go beyond what could convincingly be rigged, also for the Soviet leaders, who combined faith, realism and firmness. He supported Stalin's policy of alliances, arguing that its nationalism and sometimes mendacious propaganda were acceptable risks in an age which demanded action. He was, however, worried by the regime's violent methods, attributable though they may be to an unresolved civil war, and aware that the party risked becoming a privileged class; he sensed it in the eyes of the ordinary people watching him sweep past in official cars, and he knew that the privileges he enjoyed disqualified him as a witness. Much in this document is prophetic. He knew he had not seen enough to make authoritative statements, and was divided between the need to preserve his integrity and reluctance to criticize Russia at a difficult hour. He therefore said much less in public than he thought.

A year after being lionized in Russia, Rolland found himself lionized in France. He had long encouraged a broad anti-fascist alliance, the communists had come round to his view, and he found himself prophet of the Popular Front, working with a whole new range of political and literary figures. He was on good terms with Thorez, Cachin and Vaillant-Couturier, gave a rare press interview to Aragon and headed committees with Malraux and even Gide, now an unlikely ally. The two men met in 1934, 'deux sur-individualistes [qui] ont dû reconnaître que l'individualisme absolu et le dogme de l'indépendance de l'esprit n'offraient plus une base suffisante' (*C27*:266–7). Their conversation was friendly, but they avoided discussing their artistic differences. In January 1936,

Rolland's seventieth birthday was celebrated by a meeting at the Mutualité, and 14 July saw a revival of *Le Quatorze Juillet*, with a glittering cast, music by six leading composers and a curtain by Picasso. For this Rolland made one of his rare visits to Paris and even rarer public appearances. His private reaction was cool; performances of his plays invariably disappointed him, and the rousing reception did not turn his head: 'Une belle revanche officielle, après 35 ans de silence. – Mais à 70 ans, c'est trop tard. L'esprit était absent. – Tout de même, assez content'.[30] On the same visit, he was granted an interview with Léon Blum, in which they acted out the reconciliation of Christophe and Lévy-Cœur.

The Rollands went on to visit Clamecy, and next year they returned to look for a house. The reasons for this were complex, one element undoubtedly being solidarity with a France facing hard times under a relatively congenial government, but this must not be overstated. Popular Front euphoria was much diminished in 1937, and his widow insisted that the main reason was difficulties with the Swiss authorities, who had recently banned the import of communist literature. Rolland avoided public discussion of Swiss politics, but was privately critical of its bourgeois parochialism. He was befriended by the eminent Swiss politician Heinz Haeberlin, to whom he successfully turned for support on several occasions, but could never be sure the authorities would not turn against him. The situation was worse for Marie, for whom entering Switzerland had been almost as hard as leaving Russia; one of the reasons why the couple married was to protect her against expulsion. The decision to move to France was part of the same process:

> Il était devenu difficile pour moi d'envisager une continuation de ma vie en Suisse, où ma liberté de lecture et de travail (au moins, social) était gênée, sans nul égard, et pouvait être peu à peu annihilée [. . .] – A cela se joignaient les craintes (peut-être exagérées) de Macha, de se trouver, après ma mort, sous une menace d'expulsion, de la part d'autorités que ne retiendraient même plus ma présence.[31]

Marie did not relish the prospect of being sent back to Russia; residence in France, where she would have rights, was more appealing. The tone of Rolland's letters to Madeleine, as he and Marie went house-hunting, suggests that Marie was the more enthusiastic of the two. Madeleine objected to the move, suspecting that Marie was trying to take her brother away from her. Marie denied it, and Rolland made ceaseless attempts to reassure his sister, but in the end Madeleine decided to stay in Switzerland. The house-hunting did not go well, despite the help of the Nivernais municipal authorities, most of which were run by Popular Front politicians, but they finally fell in love with a house in Vézelay, which they purchased and occupied in the summer of 1938. They kept the lease on the Villeneuve villa, but Rolland aimed to make France his main residence. As he wrote to Madeleine during the Munich crisis:

> Si la guerre venait, nous resterions à Vézelay. Mes chers amis les pacifistes intégraux m'ont trop de fois insulté [. . .] en écrivant que je suis entré dans la mêlée, '*depuis que je ne suis plus mobilisable* (comme si je l'avais été en 1914!). Je tiens à partager le sort de mon pays.[32]

This shows a distinct change from Amsterdam, where he had battled to unite pacifists and communists. Many pacifists had become appeasers, and in two 1936 articles, forming the brochure *Comment empêcher la guerre?*, he turned on Challaye and Bertrand Russell, seeing no place in the Popular Front for a group whose anti-fascism was so insecure. Peace was best served by alliance with Soviet Russia, and if the worst came to the worst, some wars were worth fighting; a just society was more important than peace at any price. Rolland had, of course, never been an integral pacifist. The pessimistic realist, the fighter for justice and the lover of action could not be satisfied with a peace which in 1936 looked like acceptance of evil. During the Spanish Civil War, he urged Blum to intervene to support the Republic, and he again sided with what could be construed as the war party by attacking the Munich settlement. On both issues, successive French governments failed to live up to Popular Front ideals, and Rolland entered 1939 disappointed and disillusioned.

Rolland had high hopes of Spain as an extension of the revolutionary spirit into Western Europe:

> Le grand esprit de la Révolution est maintenant passé de l'U.R.S.S. en Occident, et [. . .] c'est en Espagne que se livre la plus grande bataille d'aujourd'hui [. . .] C'est la première fois que la Révolution s'accomplit chez et par un peuple de haute culture. (*C29*:90)

This 1936 note is interesting not just for what it says about Spain, but for its implied criticism of Russia. Gorky had died, and with him Rolland's influence at a time when humanitarian voices were sorely needed; henceforth Rolland complained that his letters to Stalin went unheeded as the old Bolsheviks were destroyed in the show trials, which brought down Arosev, Kruchkov, Yagoda, Bukharin and others Rolland had met in Moscow. Rolland was at a loss to know how to react, and in 1938, as members of Gorky's entourage were tried for his alleged murder, he attempted to reassess the notes taken during his visit. He was inclined to believe that there had been conspiracies; like many contemporaries he found it hard to accept that the detailed confessions torn from the defendants might be completely false, but the sheer horror of the situation reduced him to a silence which has been held against him.[33]

This silence was compounded by his evasive attitude towards criticisms of the Soviets. He ignored letters trying to make him aware of what was happening, and when he did respond, it was often in *ad hominem* terms. He sensed the voice of the mistrusted Victor Serge in many criticisms, and when Gide launched his *Retour de l'U.R.S.S.*, Rolland's response, in a letter carried by *L'Humanité* in January 1937, was a virulent attack on the man which Fisher castigates as spiteful and slanderous.[34] It is certainly one of his harshest attacks on a named individual, accusing Gide of treachery and hypocrisy. It was not, however, meant for publication in France, but an answer to an inquiry from a group of foreign labourers working in Russia;[35] Rolland was happy for his text to be printed in Russia, but does not appear to have seen it as a review suitable for the French press. Fisher suggests that Rolland was jealous of Gide's success; if so, it was an emotion he had rarely voiced in his career, but Rolland certainly had suspicions that Gide was jealous of his own success in Russia:

> Il aurait voulu être le premier écrivain français, dans l'opinion de l'URSS et l'estime des chefs. Il a trouvé en URSS la place prise par moi, et ses avances auprès de Staline ont été rejetées, d'une façon mortifiante. Alors il se retourne vers Trotsky et il sera le premier de son camp. (*C27*:312)

Gide's rejoinder to the *Humanité* attack, equally *ad hominem* but telling, was to compare the aged Rolland unfavourably with the Rolland of *Au-dessus de la mêlée*; Rolland reflected that Gide in 1914 had hardly appreciated that work. That was the end of their working relationship; the episode does neither much credit.

As to the Soviet trials, the best that can be said is that Rolland could not be persuaded to support them publicly, although he did do so in some private letters (*C29*:318–22). His attitude is expressed in his 1938 reflections on his visit to Moscow, in a passage inspired by the fact that his departing letter to Stalin had not attempted a flattery which he assumed Stalin would not want:

> Moi qui, par la suite, m'étonnai du silence de Staline, je ne pensais pas qu'il avait pu être secrètement déçu et froissé [. . .] En effet, toutes les lettres que je lui ai, depuis, adressées, étaient pour plaider la cause ou demander la grâce

des conjurés qu'il avait fait arrêter [. . .] Et je me suis toujours dérobé aux demandes répétées, qui m'ont été faites de divers côtés, de joindre ma voix à celles qui flétrissaient les condamnées du procès [. . .] Staline a bien dû voir que je n'avais jamais dit un mot qui pût nuire à la cause de l'U.R.S.S. et à la sienne. Mais rien non plus pour lui. Et cependant, je suis pour lui, dans la mesure où je puis connaître et contrôler les faits. Mais il ne me plaît pas de fouler aux pieds les vaincus, dont plusieurs, – comme Boukharine – conservent mon affection et mon estime, – ni de donner mon approbation à la répression implacable de la conjuration; [. . .] car, sans parler des raisons d'humanité, elle a été ruineuse pour le régime soviétique et pour la cause de la Révolution, dans l'opinion du monde. (*C29*:289–90)

Several points emerge from this. Rolland now sees more clearly the Stalinist cult of personality, he feels sympathy for the victims of the trials, many of whom he tried privately to help, and he refuses to be dragooned into supporting the trials in public. All this amounts to considerable private misgivings. Yet his public stance remains pro-Soviet; he is as concerned as ever with Russia's image in the West, and expresses general support for Stalin's right to resist conspiracies against him.[36]

Once it is accepted that Rolland believed there was a conspiracy, his silence becomes understandable, and it must also be judged in the light of the Nazi threat. Rolland saw this as the main priority, and the arguments in favour of a Franco-Soviet military alliance were in no way changed by the trials. Fisher concludes that his anti-fascism took priority over all else, overriding instincts which at other times would have caused him to protest.[37] In this Rolland was not alone in his generation, and his reaction can be classed as a desperate response to a desperate time. There is a hint of tragic vision in it; as dramatist of the French Revolution he was aware of the individual sufferings necessarily generated by historical upheavals. There is also, as Duchatelet has noted, a personal dimension; Marie's son and the Koudachev family were still in Russia, and vulnerable if Rolland turned against Stalin (*C29*:85). In this, the end of Rolland's public life resembles its beginning in the Dreyfus case; his expression of his thought was inhibited by his wife's family.

The year 1939 saw Rolland drifting away from the French communists. His view of the Munich crisis from Vézelay differed from what it might have been in Villeneuve; as an ex-pacifist and a current supporter of the war party, he was doubly suspect to the local populace, he received threats, and he was even pressurized into signing a petition for peace, brought to him open by the local postmaster, alongside the suspect pacifists Alain and Giono. Writing to explain this to Bloch, he complained that the communists had missed the mood of the nation:

> Il fallait tenir davantage compte de cette passion de la paix qui tient anxieuse-
> ment des millions de simples Français des petites villes et des campagnes; et
> c'était sur elle (sur cette passion ancrée) qu'il fallait s'établir solidement.[38]

Communist reaction to Munich seemed counterproductively shrill. Daladier
had miscalculated, but the only defence against Hitler now was national
unity, in which the communists should be working with Daladier, not
pursuing vendettas against him.[39] Rolland wrote in this sense to Thorez
and others, seeking allies 'parmi les honnêtes gens de la bourgeoisie
républicaine modérée' (*C29*:98) whose support he had not solicited for
years. After the collapse of the Popular Front, he sought another grouping
on which to build a harmonic French unity; the one man against all of
1914 had become the advocate of a new 'union sacrée'. He sensed a
growing distance between himself and his allies. 'Les amis de Paris font
le silence,' he complained. 'Je crois que ceux de gauche me boudent, depuis
que j'ai désapprouvé certaines de leurs violences de politique, que je
jugeais absolument inopportunes et même funestes pour leur parti.'[40]

Nothing came of this in public, but Rolland's last pre-war article,
celebrating the hundred and fiftieth anniversary of the fall of the Bastille,
drops suggestive hints.[41] That event, he declares, was the moment when
free men made themselves masters of destiny: 'L'homme échappe à
l'empire de la nécessité aveugle. Il a pénétré les lois de l'évolution et
il prend en main la direction [. . .] C'est une rupture avec les temps
d'asservissement de l'homme au destin' (p.292). The Revolution was
the expression of 'la libre raison'; revolutionaries of today regard this
with a 'méfiance peureuse' (p.295), but Rolland distances himself from
'les doctrines d'aujourd'hui [. . . qui] font de l'esprit un des produits des
conditions sociales et économiques, dont il partage l'évolution' (p.298).
He agrees with the Marxists that social and intellectual evolution are
linked, but the thrust of this article privileges the latter, and the process
must continue. Everything is subject to change, and a more politically
mature people must continue the ceaseless progress prophesied by
Condorcet, Rolland's hero of twenty years earlier.[42] As Rolland evokes
Condorcet declaring faith in the future while planning suicide to avoid
the guillotine, he may well have been thinking of his own situation on
the eve of war. Nowhere in this article are the Soviets mentioned, but it
reads as a coded statement that Revolutionary dynamism has deserted the
sclerotic Soviet camp.

Rolland's disaffection from the Soviets thus pre-dated the Nazi-Soviet
pact, which shattered his last hopes. He had feared some such development
since Molotov replaced Litvinov as Foreign Minister, but the shock was

still considerable. The pact ended hopes of encircling Hitler, and though he could see its benefits from a purely Russian point of view, he sensed that Stalin had abandoned the Western communists to become a pan-Slavic imperialist, and judged that the main need was to oppose Hitler rather than support Stalin. Again, he made no public reaction, but privately he urged that *Europe* should suspend publication and he resigned from the Association of Friends of the Soviet Union. His one public gesture, when war was declared, was an open letter to Daladier declaring support for the Western democracies. It was his last act of political engagement. He had thoughts of writing a new 'Au-dessus de la mêlée', 'beaucoup plus vigoureux et vengeur que le premier' (*C29*:101), attacking Hitler, fascism, the Soviet Union and the tergiversations of the British and French, but was discouraged by the difficulty of obtaining information and the prospect of being censored or having to suppress part of his thought, and he also had an uncomfortable sense of having forfeited his authority. He entered the war totally disillusioned with public life and the men who took part in it. Throughout the inter-war years he had sought to fend off a disaster written into the heart of the Treaty of Versailles, but everyone in whom he had vested any hope had disappointed him. Yet the end of his active career was not the end of everything. Used to combining short-term pessimism with long-term optimism, he had other resources to sustain him, and they could be found in his art.

Notes

1. The best such study is Motyleva (1976).
2. See the correspondence between J. Albertini and M. Thorez, cited in Chagny-Sève (1995), pp.287–9. An accompanying note states that in 1949 Thorez failed to respond to a public request from Rolland's widow to confirm that Rolland was not a card-carrier. Thorez's claim that only practical considerations prevented Rolland from being a member is therefore suspect.
3. See below, p.202.
4. Letter to Madeleine, 21 July 1927.
5. J. Perus, however, considers this claim dubiously based (*C28*:15–17).
6. Letter to Madeleine, 18 August 1933.
7. See letters to Madeleine, 3 February and 13 June 1931.

8. Rolland's will specifies that this correspondence cannot be opened to researchers until 2004.
9. See Koch (1994), pp.21–2.
10. See Duhamel (1983), pp.152, 187ff. This volume includes a record of Duhamel's son's discussion of these allegations with Madame Rolland in the last years of her life.
11. See Duhamel (1983), p.417.
12. Letter to Madeleine, 13 June 1931.
13. Rolland describes her in Moscow in 1935, taking a stubbornly independent line in argument against Gorky (*C29*:85).
14. See Duhamel (1983), p.191.
15. See Duhamel (1983), p.185.
16. *BAARR* 139–42 (1983), pp.53–6.
17. See Vermorel (1993), p.426.
18. See Lyons (1937), pp.617-21.
19. Letter to Zweig, 26 September 1937.
20. Letter to Zweig, 5 February 1931.
21. See Fisher (1988), p.264.
22. Letter to Madeleine, 23 July 1930.
23. Letter to Madeleine, 8 August 1928.
24. See Duchatelet (1983b).
25. See Gross (1974), p.224.
26. Letter to Madeleine, 16 August 1932.
27. Letter to Madeleine, 18 August 1932.
28. Fisher (1988, p.180) points out that Rolland was earlier than most to see the importance of this issue.
29. This is why his letters to Madeleine from Russia are bland and carefully phrased; he avoids naming names or making criticisms.
30. Letter to Madeleine, 2 August 1936.
31. Letter to Madeleine, 15 August 1937.
32. Letter to Madeleine, 15 September 1938.
33. See especially Fisher (1988), p.286.
34. Fisher (1988), p.269.
35. Duchatelet (*C29*:91) senses official prompting in the stilted rhetoric of this query, which Rolland would not publish in France as he considered it too insulting. See Harris (1973), p.158.
36. As late as 1942, Rolland interpreted the easy passage that the Trotskyist Martinet had in a Gestapo interrogation as evidence of collusion in the 1930s between the Soviet opposition and fascism; see letter to Madeleine, 26 January 1942.
37. See Fisher (1988), p.286.

38. Letter to J-R. Bloch, 2 October 1938.
39. See Fisher (1988), p.283.
40. Letter to Madeleine, 15 May 1939.
41. 'Nécessité de la Révolution', *Europe*, 50, 15 July 1939, pp.289–302.
42. See Lelow, p.166.

Art and Revolution (I): The Dramas

Rolland's political activities, like his pre-war university work, kept him from his artistic projects for longer than he liked, but his inter-war output is prolific, including two film scenarios, four plays, a novel cycle, an autobiography, three Indian biographies and three volumes on Beethoven. The momentum was less sustained in the 1930s, but he never lost his ability to juggle several large projects at once.

Rolland's view of his art was not radically modified by political engagement, but there were changes of emphasis. The artist, he now felt, should be a revolutionary, espousing a historical process which appeared, as it did not in 1914, to be working in basically the right direction. In an important 1935 article, 'Du rôle de l'écrivain dans la société d'aujourd'hui', he resumes his attack on the kind of elite which abstains from action. The artist may be part of the avant-garde, but he is not detached from the main body of the army:

> C'est le privilège de l'artiste – ou ce doit l'être – de voir plus loin, de vivre plus à fond ce que les autres vivent et voient. C'est par là même qu'ils sont appelés à constituer un état-major de l'armée, ou, comme Staline l'a formulé, un corps d'élite, 'les ingénieurs des âmes'. Mais qu'ils gagnent leurs galons, dans le rang! (*AL*:303)

Rolland seeks the 'cohésion indispensable de l'écrivain et des masses' which characterized Greek and Elizabethan theatre (*AL*:302) and exhorts the artist to speak a language comprehensible to all. This need not prevent him from expanding his expressive capacities; Bach's example demonstrates that an innovative artist can also serve the everyday needs of his community. Moreover, the artist's struggle for self-realization reflects the revolutionary people's struggle to shape its destiny: 'L'homme, les hommes y sont à eux-mêmes leur fatum. C'est leur volonté passionnée qui les mène, et, avec eux, elle mène l'œuvre d'art' (*AL*:305). Artistic dream and political action are thus reconciled, in a way which is further explored in the introduction to the 1936 collection of articles,

Compagnons de route, centred on the artistic figures who helped Rolland towards revolutionary commitment.

Here, he redefines the conflict of dream and action as that of 'les aspirations d'un idéalisme individualiste et l'objectivisme souverain de la Nature, qui impose ses lois à l'esprit' (*CR*:9). It relates to the conflict of optimism and pessimism; his 'optimisme révolutionnaire' has won (*CR*:12), but only after conquering bourgeois passivity, Christian pessimism and a heroic individualism '[qui] tranche ses liens d'avec la communauté' (*CR*:11). His conclusion, despite abiding worries about presenting harsh truths to an unheroic public, is that a tragic vision encourages action as well as a hopeful one; pessimism and optimism both have a role:

> La vision tragique des injustices et des souffrances du monde présent n'est pas un moindre adjuvant pour l'action que la certitude illuminée de l'avenir meilleur. On n'est pas bien prêt à vaincre et à mourir, si l'optimisme de l'élan ne s'appuie pas sur la résolution désespérée de ne jamais revenir en arrière. (*CR*:13)

Shakespeare is the supreme expression of the tragic vision, but its static character has a dynamic counterpart in Goethe. Rolland came late to Goethe, whose cold serenity seemed too close to the fleshless idealism that disturbed him in Malwida. Now, however, he found in Goethe an acceptance that man and society are in perpetual transformation:

> '*Stirb und Werde!*'. . . L'élément dynamique est entré dans le champ de regard du génie. Et avec lui, le puissant optimisme de l'armée en marche, le conquérant. L'ordre Apollinien de l'homme de Weimar couve l'esprit de la Révolution. (*CR*:15)

A willingness to ride with destiny, 'l'assimilation de l'esprit Goethéen avec les forces et les lois du Devenir éternel' (*CR*:15), makes Goethe a revolutionary. A line of influence runs from him through Hegel and Marx to Lenin; Rolland finds quotations from Goethe the dreamer to justify action, and from Lenin the man of action to justify dream. The dreamer fosters action by espousing the rhythms of history.

The Soviets, however, had not yet evolved a satisfactory revolutionary art. Socialist realism seemed to Rolland just as insufficient as the realism of 1880, and he called on the revolutionary artist to surpass it by cultivating 'les grandes provinces de la vie intérieure'. Whatever the demands of collectivism, human dynamism is rooted in the individual, and the artist releases it by facing it in himself. Even Soviet artists must dream:

Il s'agit de forer l'écorce de la vie, jusqu'aux nappes profondes des passions. Car elles sont et resteront, quel que soit le régime de vie sociale, la substance intime de la vie. Camarades soviétiques, votre saine habitude de vivre ensemble ne doit pas vous priver de vivre chacun en soi. Vous devez, dans l'entraînement de l'action et des passions communes, vous ménager une cabine d'isolation, pour vous y enfermer seul avec vous-même [. . .], pour méditer, vous concentrer, pour reprendre contact avec la terre. (*AL*:305–6)

Similar views are expressed in a 1930 letter to Armin T.Wegner, in which Rolland defines his role in terms recalling the *Credo quia Verum*, distinguishing between his 'moi d'un jour' and 'Moi de toujours'. The latter is the oceanic sentiment which unites him to God and 'la marche même du Cosmos, du Moi éternel', now identified with revolution. His individual role, however, is not confined by the violent processes of revolution:

Le moi individuel que je suis n'a rien à sacrifier de ses Lois propres. Si la loi du flux sauvage de la révolution est la violence pour accomplir le progrès relatif que réclame l'heure présente de révolution sociale, par quel non-sens renoncerais-je à ma loi propre, qui est de créer en moi l'harmonie, et de tâcher de la répandre sur ceux qui m'entourent? (*C17*:290)

As in 1914, Rolland still sees a role for himself distinct from the onward march of history, and he identifies it with the quest for harmony. The implication is that the artist has two roles, one outward-looking, one inward-looking. The former requires him to espouse historical processes which as a visionary he recognizes before others; the latter requires him to cultivate his inner resources and by mastering them exert a beneficial influence. These functions combine in his works in a variety of ways; broadly speaking, the outward-looking role dominates his dramas and political writing, the inward-looking role is expressed in his biographical studies and *L'Ame enchantée* attempts to harmonize both.

Rolland's plays had always strained the resources of the stage, and in two unfinished projects he tried to apply the techniques of *Liluli* in the cinema. In the summer of 1921 he worked with Masereel on a film scenario, *La Révolte des machines*, in which a caricatural society confronts a group of machines running amok in response to anti-social instincts in their creator's subconscious mind. Rolland did not object to mechanical progress as such; his target is its abuse in the service of man's vices and the abdication of liberty before an iron social determinism which can and should be resisted. As well as expressing horror at the mechanization of war, this work anticipates Rolland's attack on Barbusse's notion of social evolution based on inevitable laws. Rolland was not satisfied with the work, however, and it was never produced.

His second flirtation with cinema was another summer project. In 1929, a Berlin film company asked him for a scenario on the history of music, and he was interested enough to produce a first draft and approach Ernest Bloch for a soundtrack. The film company pulled out, perhaps frightened by his ambitious ideas, but the resultant sketch, *Mélusine*, is full of interest. In the manner of Spitteler, Rolland creates a personal mythology round a fairy from French folklore, who becomes a spirit of music, charming and frightening, exercising a Liluli-like power over Alcyon, 'la grande individualité, le poète musicien', and Orion, expressing 'la veine popu-laire'.[1] The three pass through many incarnations illustrating the basic elements of music, Alcyon being embodied in the great composers from Orpheus to Beethoven, and Orion in a variety of roles from Harlequin to revolutionary leader. Alcyon is brother to Altaïr and Antarès in *Liluli*, while Orion, in the line of Polichinelle, Colas and Sylvie in *L'Ame enchantée*, is more down-to-earth and with occasionally sounder instincts. Their relationship reflects the pervasive tension between the individual and the collective. The work reflects the study of artistic inspiration in *Beethoven*, and the imagery has Indian elements recalling Rolland's recent study of Ramakrishna; one of Mélusine's incarnations is the goddess Kâlî, Ramakrishna's patroness, mistress of the process of transformation which music reflects. Music is a dynamic force reflecting the revolutionary process, but the final emphasis is on human unity, expressed in the concept of harmony.

More important than these was the continued Revolutionary cycle. Its inspiration came from Germany, where Rolland's plays were popular following the 1919 revolutions; Zweig encouraged him, and the imme-diate stimulus came in 1923, when he rediscovered his twenty-year-old sketch for *Le Jeu de l'amour et de la mort*. Rolland added four plays to his cycle; each reflects his political thinking at the time of writing.

During the war, Rolland became wary of the Revolution. It had inspired too much nationalism and fanaticism; the extremists Adam Lux and Saint-Just no longer appealed to him, and in 1916 he declared his solidarity with Condorcet, Lavoisier and Chénier, moderate victims of Revolution:

> Quand je pense qu'il m'a fallu cette guerre pour m'ouvrir tout à fait les yeux sur le passé! N'ai-je pas à m'accuser moi aussi de n'avoir pas tenu compte des trois noms que je viens de dire – (les trois plus grands du temps!) – dans mes jugements fascinés par la Révolution![2]

These were the figures who inspired *Le Jeu de l'amour et de la mort* in 1924. This one-act play, restrained in staging demands, lends itself well to traditional stage resources, and when Gémier produced it at the Odéon in 1928 it was the first of Rolland's plays to reach a major French stage. It portrays no public events, the whole action takes place in a drawing room and the subject is love and sacrifice during the Terror.

The plot is based on the Tristan and Isolde story, the Isolde being Sophie de Courvoisier, torn between her lover, Vallée, and her elderly husband, Jérôme. Vallée is a proscribed Girondin modelled on Louvet de Couvray, who has secretly returned to Paris to see her; the husband is a distinguished scientist who has protested against the Terror by refusing to vote for Danton's arrest. Courvoisier's friend Carnot warns him that his life depends on his support for the government's measures; Courvoisier withholds it, and tries to give the passports for his escape to Sophie and Vallée. Sophie, however, puts duty before love and is arrested with her husband.

The centrepiece of the play, a debate between Carnot and Courvoisier, recalls both *Les Loups* and the Barbusse polemic. Carnot, like Barbusse, believes in 'l'inexorabilité des lois de la Nature' (*JAM*:147); though revolted by violence, he considers he is on the side of history and must fight for the cause by whatever means necessary: 'Le progrès de l'humanité vaut quelques saloperies – et, s'il le faut, des crimes'. Courvoisier, however, shares Rolland's scepticism over what pass for laws:

> Je suis trop homme de science pour croire sans réserves à une de mes hypothèses (car ce n'est rien de plus). Et si flatteuse qu'elle soit pour le génie de l'homme et son ardent espoir, je n'en ferai jamais un dieu sur un autel, qui se nourrit de l'odeur sanglante des sacrifices.

Sacrificing the present to the future makes no sense: 'sacrifier à l'avenir la vérité, l'amour, toutes les vertus humaines, et l'estime de soi-même, c'est sacrifier l'avenir' (*JAM*:148). Truth and love transcend expediency.

As a weary old man who has already made his act of defiance, Courvoisier is less central to the action than his wife, on whose decision the play turns. Many of Rolland's Revolutionary dramas contain women facing similar dilemmas, but none more acutely than Sophie; she longs for the happiness offered by Vallée, but shares her husband's faith and reminds him that the road to progress is a 'route en lacets' which promises no quick victory:

> Vous avez eu la force de monter assez haut pour embrasser en une large vision la terre d'au-delà des monts et le fleuve qui serpente, le Progrès de l'Esprit humain. Vous n'avez jamais cru que, pour suivre son cours, quelques années suffisent; vous prévoyiez des siècles, avec plus d'un arrêt et d'un retour en arrière. Nous, nous ne verrons pas, de nos yeux, la Terre Promise. Mais n'est-ce pas beaucoup déjà de savoir où elle est et d'en montrer la route? (*JAM*:107)

This faith prepares her decision to share her husband's fate, and the final scene is a moving review of their lost hopes, allied with an elegy to departing youth. None of Rolland's plays better encapsulates a Revolutionary issue in an individual dilemma; this tragedy of an intellectual in a movement of which he approves the general thrust but not the detail is the main artistic expression of Rolland's preoccupations in the early 1920s. By 1939, when the Comédie Française at last recognized Rolland's existence and staged this play, Rolland's position had changed and he amended the text to make Carnot's role more attractive, but in the same months he was writing 'Nécessité de la Révolution', in which, we have seen, Courvoisier's inspirer Condorcet plays a leading role.

The prologue and epilogue to the Revolutionary cycle had long been planned, and it was on these that Rolland worked next. Based on the same set of characters, they mark the beginning and end of the Revolution as a historical movement, and behind it they reveal the changing attitude to destiny which determined Rolland's Soviet commitment.

In 1925 Rolland worked on *Pâques-Fleuries*, which shows revolution looming in 1774, in the family of the Prince de Courtenay, based on Rousseau's patron, the Prince de Conti. Rolland found more distinction in Louis XV's nobles than in Louis XVI's, and the prospect of pitting them against the great Revolutionaries appealed to his dramatic sense. The Prince, who shares Rolland's openness to strong ideas other than his own, favours the noble reaction against the crown, and is about to disinherit his royalist son, the Comte d'Avallon, in favour of an illegitimate son, the Chevalier de Trie, a feckless youth incarnating the doomed charm of the Ancien Régime. The Revolutionary forces include the lawyer Popelin, representative of the moneyed bourgeoisie which is already taking over the Prince's mortgaged estate, a process expressed, as in Chekhov's *Cherry Orchard*, by the felling of trees in the park. This class was present in the earlier Revolutionary dramas, but Rolland's dislike of the power of money had intensified, and its nefarious role is thrown into relief by contrasting Popelin with his nephew Mathieu Regnault, the future Jacobin to whom 'l'argent n'est qu'un moyen, l'instrument qui délivre' (*PF*:80). Regnault discovers the Comte's complicity in the murder of the Chevalier by a peasant whose mistress he has stolen.

The central scene features the Prince's protégé, Rousseau; previously unenthusiastic about him, Rolland found a kindred spirit in this 'Précurseur halluciné' (*PF*:10). Rolland claimed visionary power for himself, and Rousseau is portrayed as a half-mad visionary, barely aware of his surroundings but prophesying the doom of the old world. Like Rolland, Rousseau sees conspiracies everywhere and is tormented by the hatred he attracts. He senses the God within him, but knows that the message he bears is of hatred; though grieved to foretell a destructive phase of the Empedoclean cycle, he is, like everyone in the play, carried by forces bigger than himself:

> Ah! je le vois maintenant, un plus fort qu'eux les mène, et ils ne le voient pas. . . J'avais depuis longtemps senti sa main puissante, qui s'acharnait sur moi. . . Mais je ne suis donc pas seul! . . . Il me mène. . . Il mène le persécuté et les persécuteurs. Tous ceux qui sont ici, il les mène. . . (*PF*:179–80)

The Chevalier's death is merely the first tragedy of an age rich in them; Rousseau voices the tragedy of the individual within the movement.

Les Léonides dates from 1927, after the third volume of *L'Ame enchantée*. Rolland claimed that his idea for this play had been 'la première cellule d'où germa tout le cycle' (*LE*:8-9), but the immediate impulse was his exchange with Balmont and Bunin, which directed his attention to the human problems of *émigrés*. The setting is Switzerland; its scenery dominates a work steeped in natural forces, and the clash of conservatives and revolutionaries in a small canton is one of Rolland's rare hints of his private opinion of petty Swiss politics. This comic-opera society is about to be swept away by Bonaparte, who for Rolland was not the fulfilment of the Revolution but the imperial authority betraying it, a rapacious military dictator and an enemy of harmonic unity. He is a sullied force of nature, 'fruit de l'accouplement orgiaque du despotisme et de la liberté'; he causes history to advance, but is proof that 'la Force invisible, qui nous tient, use, pour ses fins et le progrès, quand il lui plaît, des plus bas instruments' (*LE*:217–19). In this, he recalls Mussolini, and the Bolshevik leaders as Rolland still saw them in 1927.

Bonaparte has demanded the expulsion of all *émigrés*, and dislike of Bonaparte unites Regnault and the former Comte, now himself Prince de Courtenay, both exiled in the canton. They are old; Regnault is a 'colosse brisé' after his labours in the Terror (*LE*:55), and weaker in health than the Prince, who, brought up according to Rousseau's principles, has supported himself by the work of his hands, building roads and 'occupant l'ardeur inassouvie de son activité [. . .] à soumettre la nature, à lutter corps-à-corps avec la pierre et l'eau, la montagne et le torrent – et, dans ce duel silencieux, s'identifiant avec les lois éternelles qui font tourner le monde' (*LE*:8). He fights the battle to master nature which in Nicolai's view should supersede warfare. Both men have been instruments of the forces moulding history, both love France, and on this basis they are gradually reconciled. Each knows the other has sinned, Regnault has married the mother of the murdered Chevalier's daughter, and this child falls in love with the Prince's son. Together they depart to a new life in America.

Regnault's own son Jean-Jacques is a weakly adolescent in the line of Aert and Olivier. Acutely sensitive to hatred, he bears the sins of the world heavily on his shoulders and longs to redeem them: 'Comme ce serait beau, pourtant, de pouvoir par sa souffrance racheter au moins une partie de ces cruautés' (*LE*:190–1). His death cements the alliance of the former rivals, but they depart at the end in different directions. Like the meteor shower of the play's title, they are 'les débris d'une constellation, la poussière héroïque d'un monde détruit'. Last representatives of a great historical moment, their role is to disperse its spark through the rest of the world:

> Nous nous étions trop habitués à croire que la vie est une sage rivière de chez nous qui sinue pour toujours dans le même vallon, entre les mêmes prés. Nous sommes peut-être faits pour être dispersés à tous les coins de la terre, afin que se propagent notre sang et notre pensée. . . Eh bien, nous sommes prêts! Nous ferons comme nos grands-pères, du temps des Migrations [. . .] Nous reprendrons l'Exode. (*LE*:247)

The Revolution has spent itself in a shower of individual tragedies, but it has furthered the process of history and enhanced the life of humanity. Images of the heavens and of fertilization dominate the close of the play as they do the close of *L'Ame enchantée*.

Rolland regarded *Les Léonides* as 'le plus achevé de toutes mes pièces',[3] and it is an important statement on his attitude to revolution. It reflects his new-found submission to the laws of history, and it views the Revolution as a whole as a movement beneficial in its overall effect despite the tragedies it spawned; its characters have reached the moment of lucidity when they recognize that they are involved in a tragic process whose laws they must follow. As such, this play expresses Rolland's mood as he stands on the brink of political engagement, and it marks an important step towards his acceptance of the Russian Revolution.

Rolland's long-planned play on Robespierre's fall was delayed until 1938, when the Moscow trials made the collapse of revolution topical. It is long and ambitious, using cinematic techniques and vast crowd scenes; Rolland's indifference to the problems of performance had if anything intensified, and the work has rarely been staged.

In the 1890s, Rolland had already judged Robespierre the clearest mind and purest representative of the Revolution, and Albert Mathiez's research had strengthened this picture. Rolland's Robespierre is no saint; like the rest of the Committee of Public Safety, he has been affected by the long hot summer of 1794, beset by war, plots and rumours. Though eager to end the Terror, his susceptible temperament exacerbates differences with colleagues. He will work with no one whose virtue he does not trust, which in practice means almost everyone, and he is known to be willing to eliminate those who fail to meet his standards. Though rightly mistrustful of Fouché, Carrier and Tallien, the proconsuls who carried the Terror to the provinces, he fails to build on the genuine love of the Republic which his adversaries share. The collapse of the Republic is a tragic story of men of goodwill who cannot work together: 'Tous les hommes que je mets en scène [. . .] sont de sincères et passionnés Républicains [. . .] Et cependant, ils vont s'acharner à détruire leur œuvre' (*R*:7–8). The analogy with the Bolshevik old guard is inescapable.

Robespierre genuinely wishes to improve the people's lot, and his readiness to die for the people is none the less sincere for being rhetorically expressed. Yet he senses that the Revolution is dying. The real profiteers are the bourgeoisie, 'cette classe éhontée de trafiquants et d'exploitants de la Révolution [. . . qui] fera tout pour mettre le peuple sous son joug et pour étouffer les progrès de la Révolution' (*R*:60). The people have gained little from the Revolution, as Robespierre learns from an old woman he meets on a country walk; the ceaseless grind of peasant life is unchanged. Worse, the demagogue Hébert has corrupted the people as a revolutionary force, and the process is accelerated by atheism. Robespierre denounces Fouché and others who have destroyed the people's faith:

> Les pauvres gens, les gens de bien, tous ceux qui mènent le combat quotidien, l'âpre combat meurtri et décevant, contre la misère et les méchants, ont besoin de s'appuyer sur la pensée d'une Providence qui veille sur l'innocence opprimée et qui punit le crime triomphant. Nous leur devons de sauvegarder cette espérance qui les fait vivre. (*R*:25)

Robespierre shares Rolland's sense of the dynamic force of faith, is sympathetic to ordinary people clinging to hope, and aware that the peoples of the West need a material objective if they are to be galvanized into action. At the hour of crisis, however, when Robespierre flees to the Hôtel de Ville and needs to appeal to the people, there are signs that support is fading. There has been too much bloodshed, the Parisians are too concerned for their pockets, and drunkenness and inefficiency prevail. Revolutionary Paris is no more.

Crucially, however, the call to the people never comes. This is both Robespierre's doom and his glory, the key point which distinguishes him from Stalin. He is tempted by a cult of personality; as he surveys the crowd at the Festival of the Supreme Being, as he speaks in the Jacobin Club before an audience hanging on his lips, he is moved by the intense devotion he inspires, and at some moments he seems willing to appeal directly to the people against the government. Yet he never mounts his *coup d'état*. Despite pressure from Couthon and Saint-Just, he refuses to make himself a dictator:

> Moi vivant, nul homme, si sûr soit-il, ne mettra la main sur les faisceaux de la dictature! Même s'il était un Cincinnatus, qui abdique volontairement après l'action, la République et la nation demeureraient flétries, d'avoir consenti cette atteinte dégradante à leur souveraineté. (*R*:286)

The end, he knows, would be military dictatorship; he will operate within the law, through the sole power of truth, and if he fails he will sacrifice himself. Unlike Stalin, he avoids the corruptions of power at the last gasp; he is Rolland's last 'vaincu vainqueur'.

Yet he is not untainted; Rolland comments that he prefers the 'lucide et intrépide opposant' that was Robespierre before 1793 to the man of power of 1794, and Robespierre himself is nostalgic for his past:

> Heureux, le temps où j'étais seul, seul opposant, contre l'hostilité de toute une Assemblée! Aujourd'hui, que le pouvoir est dans mes mains, je ne suis pas moins seul, et je suis beaucoup moins libre. . . (*R*:67)

These words recall Rolland's wish to see Gandhi leader of a moral elite rather than a mass movement, and one senses a nostalgia for the Rolland of 1914, alone but uncompromised. This is supported by Rolland's veiled confession in the preface that he has been 'pris moi-même par la grande vague' which carried the men of 1794 (*R*:8). Entangled in the revolutions of his own day, Rolland strives to dominate them by viewing them as a tragedian.

One of Rolland's main points is that the Revolution was destroyed by its supporters. Though royalist plotters lurk, the tragedy springs from the clash of republicans, and Robespierre contends with a large cast of fellow revolutionaries. Mathieu Regnault is present, forced to work for Robespierre's fall to save himself; so is Billaud-Varenne, who hates Robespierre but senses that their dissent is harmful, and Carnot, at odds with Saint-Just over the conduct of the war. The architect of Robespierre's fall is Fouché, the time-server who assembles the motley coalition which drowns Robespierre's voice in the Convention, but even Fouché is a sincere revolutionary, humanized by the background presence of his dying daughter. This theme emphasises the tragic inevitability of the action.

In his closing words on the play, Rolland dwells on the role of Saint-Just, the heroic pessimist who sees clearly that without dictatorial powers they are doomed, but who stands by his leader to the last. He fights with 'ce puissant détachement de jeune héros de la Gîta', and 'son pessimisme du présent était en somme un optimisme à longue échéance'. Like Rolland, he owes his combination of short-term pessimism and long-term optimism to 'une conscience exaltée de son identification [. . .] avec les Lois qui mènent l'histoire humaine' (*R*:316–17). During the war, Rolland had been out of sympathy with Saint-Just's words at the end of *Danton*: 'Les peuples meurent, pour que Dieu vive'. Now, as the aging Rolland prepares to pass into history himself, he shares Saint-Just's heroic resignation, and the play ends with a visionary passage in which reactionary forces turn on the last great Jacobins, who vest their hopes in an appeal to 'la Révolution immortelle'. Rolland asks for closing music in which the *Marseillaise* yields to 'une puissante *Internationale* qui, enfantée d'elle, la recouvrît et l'absorbât' (*R*:309–10); as in *Les Léonides*, the emphasis is on a Revolutionary spirit which, in defeat, fertilizes the course of history. The message for 1938 is that the revolutionary spirit, exploded in Thermidor and paralysed by Stalin, is not destroyed, but moves on to another place and time. It is a message which in 1940 would salvage Rolland's faith in the future.

Notes

1. Quoted in Francis (1967), p.34.
2. Jouve (1920), pp.176–7.
3. Letter to Madeleine, 15 September 1938.

–11–

Art and Revolution (II):
L'Ame enchantée

If the Revolutionary dramas are a tragic reflection of man's assimilation into the rhythms of history, *L'Ame enchantée* is its epic reflection, and more besides. Though planned to be shorter, it came to equal *Jean-Christophe* in length, but has never attracted as much critical favour; the obtrusive political passages in the final volumes tend to cause it to be judged on polemic rather than artistic grounds. These passages were in fact a late addition to a plan whose main concern was the heroine's inner life and its religious implications.[1] Rolland wrote to Zweig in the early stages:

> Ne me demandez pas de faire un second *Jean-Christophe*, avec beaucoup de vie extérieure, de nombreux personnages, le spectacle aux mille décors du monde contemporain! Mon intention, ma volonté est tout autre. Je veux me concentrer dans l'univers intérieur d'une 'âme enchantée'.[2]

Later, the work did become a portrait of society like *Jean-Christophe*, but it never loses its focus on the inner world.

Rolland's interest in women's emancipation dates from the 1890s. Both Malwida and Clotilde supported it, and a novel on the theme was projected in 1912. The tragedy of Helena and her baby, coupled with the death of Rolland's mother, directed him towards a celebration of motherhood, and when he began work in 1921, he saw it as a return to the mainstream of his evolution, after the 'arrêt [. . .] dans la marche naturelle de ma vie intérieure' caused by the war (*VI*:270). The original title was *Fas ac Nefas*, and the aim was to attempt 'une totale révision des valeurs sociales et morales du temps' (*VI*:266), centred on '[une] femme tranquille, honnête et raisonnable, [. . .] habitée, à son insu, par un Eros invisible, qui ne connaît pas les limites du *Fas* et du *Nefas*' (*AE*:x). This desire, deeper than all morality, takes the form of a rich inner river, as the heroine's name, Annette Rivière, suggests. It flows beneath the superficial events of life, surfaces into consciousness at privileged moments, sets her at odds with convention and unites her with universal life in a sense which emerges only at her death. Being a woman, not an artist, and as such 'ne pouvant être libérée de l'afflux de la passion par les incessantes décharges de la création de l'esprit' (*AE*:ix), Annette is the victim of her sub-conscious. Freud and William James had familiarized Rolland with this notion since before the war, but he had his own understanding of it, as the original God-bearing dynamic force in humanity. Where Christophe expressed his subconscious in music, Annette expresses hers in relation-ships. Creativity, for her, is essentially maternity: 'Elle crée des êtres, rarement des oeuvres' (*AE*:xi). As Rolland wrote to Helena in 1919:

> Si la femme savait capter pour l'art les sources de poésie et d'intelligence qui sont en elles, – quelles grandes œuvres surgiraient! Mais la vie quotidienne en aspire le meilleur [. . .] L'enfant prend, dans la vie des femmes, la place de l'œuvre, dans celle des hommes.[3]

Artistic creation and procreation are analogous, and as the novel leads her into a growing web of relationships, Annette becomes mother to the whole 'petit enfant Monde' (*AE*:xii).

Behind these relationships, the novel is governed by a pattern to which its enigmatic title is the key. Its sense lies in the concept of illusion, revealed in *Liluli* as the force behind the world's errors and related to the Hindu concept of Mâyâ, which hides the ultimate truth, but within which mankind must live:

> '*L'Ame enchantée*' se dépouille, au long de sa vie, des tissus d'illusions qui la recouvrent. A chaque tissu qui tombe, elle se croit nue. Mais un autre tissu se substitue au précédent. Chaque volume est un compartiment de la grande illusion. L'*enchantée*', qui de ses mains fiévreuses, s'arrache au rêve, tombe de rêve en rêve, jusqu'au dernier – (est-ce le dernier?) – où l'agonie tranche l'ultime cordon. (*AE*:xi)

The enchantments of illusion must be stripped away layer by layer, like Peer Gynt's onion, until death brings the ultimate revelation. Rolland envisaged five stages to the process; Annette undergoes illusions of love for her father, her sister, her son, 'une pitié passionnée pour l'humanité outragée' during the war, and finally, 'quand le grand tournant de la vie est passé, ce sont les profondeurs abyssales de l'âme, qu'aspire l'Infini' (*AE*:x). Where Rolland's earlier novels follow a pattern of decline and rise, this one offers a spiralling cycle of illusion and disillusion, each coil embracing a wider circle than the last. This plan does not anticipate the political elements of the final volume which amounts to half the work's length, but though they distort the work's proportions, they do not change the plan. The following study will focus on Annette's progressive discovery of the meaning of her life.

The first volume, *Annette et Sylvie*, is, like *L'Aube*, a 'prélude printanier' (*AE*:xii), showing Annette still under all her illusions. This calm, self-possessed young woman 'qui avait sa volonté et son libre jugement, [. . .] n'avait eu, jusqu'ici, nulle occasion d'en user contre les règles établies' (*AE*:7), but her father's death, in breaking the first illusion, releases unknown forces. In an opening Freudian dream, Annette bathes in a forest pool and finds herself trapped by creepers and mud from which she must fight free; these represent the ambivalent illusion surrounding her, the negative aspects of the world with which she must battle to realize her destiny. The process begins when she discovers that her father's vitality had not been contained by conventional morality; she seeks out her illegitimate sister, Sylvie, in a first defiance of convention, and builds a new illusion round her. Much of *Annette et Sylvie* focuses on the sisters' struggle to control each other; their affectionate clash appears to reflect an ambivalent image of Helena, in whom Rolland saw, 'd'une part, un fond de *conservatisme social*, [. . .] et qui m'a souvent étonné, – de l'autre, une *extrême liberté morale* de sentiment et de fait, [. . .] qui m'a aussi étonné quelquefois'.[4] A streetwise Parisian *couturière*, inspired in part by the working-class writers Marguerite Audoux and Simone Bodève,[5] Sylvie has an easy-going sexuality which Annette admits more easily in theory than in practice. Like Colas and Luce, she represents the vitality of the people of France, and specifically of Paris. A confirmed extrovert, she cannot strip away the layers of Mâyâ as Annette does, and self-awareness eludes her: 'Elle n'avait peut-être pas une vie intérieure moins étrange [. . .], mais elle ne s'en doutait pas, et elle ne s'y intéressait pas' (*AE*:83). Her common sense, however, shields her from dangers that Annette cannot avoid. Their affection survives a clash when each tries to captivate the same man, but Annette's sexual awakening reveals a tragic seriousness of which Sylvie is incapable, 'l'Eros en cage, aux yeux bandés, inquiet, avide, et affamé' (*AE*:70). She is ripe for her encounter with Roger Brissot.

The tragedy of this relationship lies in an observation that emancipated women, in 1900, were evolving faster than men:

> La femme qui, s'efforçant de rompre avec les errements du passé, s'engageait sur un des sentiers qui menaient à la société nouvelle, y rencontrait rarement l'homme qui voulait aussi fonder le monde nouveau [. . .] L'esprit féminin,

plus longtemps retenu en arrière, était en train de prendre, depuis quelques années, une soudaine avance, dont les hommes d'alors ne se rendaient pas compte. (*AE*:93)

Brissot, a centre-left politician of the class that did well out of Dreyfus, is as progressive as can be expected of a rhetorician too fond of his own voice, but ill-equipped to cope with Annette, for whom the tragedy of love is that it requires the complete gift of a self which is not hers to give: 'Mon âme libre ne m'appartient pas. C'est moi qui appartiens à mon âme libre [. . .] Sauver sa liberté est beaucoup plus qu'un droit, c'est un devoir religieux' (*AE*:86–7). Annette clings to the freedom which makes her a God-bearer. She is willing to commit herself to Brissot, but their union must be a harmony, not a surrender to authority. Brissot cannot understand and Annette breaks with him, rejecting the convention which requires the wife to mutilate herself: 'La seule vraie morale, selon la vie vraie, serait une morale d'harmonie. Mais la société humaine n'a jamais connu jusqu'à présent qu'une morale d'oppression et de renoncement' (*AE*:139). Harmony, however, eludes her in the inner life she is beginning to discover:

[Ces oscillations inattendues] provenaient de la complexité de sa riche substance, dont la neuve harmonie ne pourrait que lentement se réaliser par la vie; mais, en attendant, elles risquaient de la livrer à toutes les surprises de la violence, de la faiblesse, de la chair, de la pensée, aux hasards insidieux du destin embusqué. (*AE*:137)

Destiny works through her ill-harmonized urgings and provokes her ultimate defiance of convention; she gives herself freely to Brissot, and her resulting pregnancy creates a new illusion of perfect, self-contained love. The whole episode, together with Annette's decision to bring up her child alone, is a projection of the future not vouchsafed to Helena de Kay.

Pregnancy and lactation are fulfilling creative acts, but 'chaque période créatrice a son champ limité; et sa force ascensionnelle suit une trajectoire, qui forcément retombe' (*AE*:185). Once born, Marc develops away from Annette, and *L'Eté*, on which Rolland worked in 1923, charts the uneasy relationship between the possessive mother and the child aspiring to independence. Marc's childhood owes much to Rolland's; he is mother-dominated, lonely, sickly and afraid of death, which erupts violently into the novel with the fall from a window of Sylvie's daughter Odette, an affectionate child recalling Rolland's first sister, who sacrificially transmits to Marc the sense of the time-transcending immensity of inner life which characterizes childhood as in *Jean-Christophe* and *Le Voyage intérieur*:

> Tout est déja dans l'enfance, dès la petite enfance, tout ce qu'on est et sera, le double Etre du présent et de l'avenir (pour ne rien dire du Passé, immense, impénétrable, qui commande l'un et l'autre) (*AE*:305–6)

Marc shares this rich inner life with his mother. Occasionally it draws them together, but the emphasis is on separation, and at the climax of the volume, when Marc glimpses Annette's passionate side in the fragments of her poem, the chance to communicate is missed (*AE*:424–5). Much of this reflects Rolland's relationship with his mother; *Le Voyage intérieur* states that the dominant impression of his childhood was of imprisonment, and affectionate intimacy with his mother came only later, as it does for Marc. Now, as he sucks nourishment from Annette, he is portrayed as a hungry little animal,[6] eager to be his own person, protecting himself with 'une aptitude remarquable à dissimuler' (*AE*:277–8) and manipulating the contrasting affections of Annette and Sylvie.

Annette's status as single mother is precarious. She is ostracized, loses friends, cannot find work in state schools with their narrow 'morale civique' (*AE*:204), is assumed easy prey by her cynical Jewish friend Marcel Franck, another incarnation of Léon Blum, and is ruined financially. This makes her face social realities and see for herself 'le mensonge de la société moderne, dont, si sincère que fût Annette, elle ne s'apercevait pas, aussi longtemps qu'elle en faisait partie' (*AE*:xii). Social as well as passionate illusions are stripped away, but in the process she discovers the new morality of work:

> Travail: le seul titre de noblesse authentique! La force et la joie essentielle de l'être créateur, c'est-à-dire du seul qui soit vraiment vivant, – du seul qui participe aux forces éternelles. (*AE*:xiii)

The novel's revaluation of moral values moves from the erotic to the social field, as Annette's hard work and integrity gradually command respect.

Maternity, for Annette, does not end with Marc's birth. She has a religious responsibility towards her free soul, whose development is not just a matter of stripping away illusions, but also of self-creation, through a series of births and rebirths: 'C'était aussi une maternité: celle de l'âme cachée' (*AE*:217–18). The consequence is two relationships with contrasting men which help her to define her inner world:

> Les deux amants [. . .] lui montrent l'impossible union qui sauvegarde les deux pôles de l'axe de sa vie: Pitié et Vérité. Le faible (Julien) ne peut supporter la vérité nue, il faut la lui voiler. Le fort (Philippe) n'a pas de bonté, il marche sur les vaincus. Annette ne peut leur consentir le sacrifice, ni de la vérité, ni de la pitié. (*AE*:xiii)

Recalling the principles of the musical novel, these two men's strengths and weaknesses represent forces with which Annette contends. The problem of reconciling truth and pity is familiar from the *Vie de Michel-Ange* and *Clerambault*, and the contrast of the two men echoes that of Sabine and Ada in *Jean-Christophe*.

Julien Davy, the bourgeois academic scarred by the joyless Catholicism denounced in the *Vie de Michel-Ange*, is cousin to Olivier Jeannin. Annette offers him vitality, but he does not profit because he cannot come to terms with her frankly accepted free maternity, just as Rolland struggled to come to terms with Helena's. His attitudes are reinforced by his mother, whose dislike of Annette echoes Rolland's mother's mistrust of Helena. Julien has qualities; he initiates Annette into recent scientific thought and returns revivified in a later volume, but for the present the hope he offers of a calm marriage comes to nothing.

Philippe Villard, by contrast, a doctor who responds to social and individual ills alike with ruthless surgery, is prepared to face brutal truths, but as a lover he is misogynistic, selfish, a conqueror rather than a harmonizer. In their intense affair, Annette risks subjugation by a 'démon sensuel' (*AE*:395), and to save her soul she must struggle against it. As with Julien, her frankness ends the relationship; she requires Villard to break with his wife, which he is not prepared to do, and she is weakened by pity for Noemi. The crisis brings her close to suicide, but in the climactic scene of the volume, in which another new soul is born in her, she discharges her grief by writing a poem. 'Seuls vainquent la douleur ceux qui osent embrasser l'excès de la douleur, lui dire: "Je te prends. Tu enfanteras par moi"'; by plumbing the depths of her pain, she transforms it into a creative experience. Following this feminine version of *Durch Leiden Freude*, Annette has a brief vision of 'cette chaîne de servitudes, dont l'âme se déleste lentement, une à une, à travers la série des existences' (*AE*:421). It does not complete her disenchantment, but for the moment she is happy. As war is declared, her outer and inner lives are in harmony.

Mère et fils was written in the important transitional year of 1926. Its subject was a difficult one; Rolland had not enjoyed writing *Clerambault*, and hoped to 'échapper à l'écrasement de la guerre, qui pèse sur le pacifisme d'un Clerambault' (*AE*:xv). The solution lay in his two focalizers, neither of whom are essentially pacifists; Marc's war coincides with a turbulent adolescence, while Annette, devoted like Rolland's mother to loved ones more than ideas, develops a reaction based on pity, not ideas. This helps Rolland to avoid the sermonesque tone of *Clerambault*, and the central episode, Annette's rescue of a German prisoner, is close in subject-matter to a conventional adventure novel. As the title suggests, the mother-son relationship is a central theme; they separate in the war's first year and go their own ways until reaching a new understanding in 1918, thus renewing Rolland's characteristic pattern of descent and rise.

At first neither opposes the war. The apolitical Annette, whose old-fashioned notion of scientific laws recalls Barbusse in 1921, simply accepts its inevitability:

> Tranquillement imbue de son éducation scientifique officielle, des temps où la relativité n'avait pas encore tout fait chanceler, Annette est habituée à accepter ce qui est [. . .] La guerre fait partie des lois de la nature. (*AE*:449)

In Marc, for whom war parallels sexual awakening, dark instincts are released, transforming him into a 'Machiavel de collège' who sees through official ideals but is cynically willing to exploit them. This Annette roundly condemns in terms echoing Rolland's conflict with the intellectuals in 1914:

> 'Une chose [. . .] je ne pardonne pas: l'hypocrisie. Jouer une croyance qu'on n'a pas, mentir à soi et aux idées, faire le Tartuffe de la foi, – mieux vaudrait n'être jamais né!' (*AE*:470–1)

They quarrel, and Marc is confined to a Paris *lycée* while Annette takes a job in the provinces. Separation allows them to focalize different aspects of France at war, but first, Rolland returns to the scenario of *Dans la maison*, taking their house as a cross-section of France. The union welded in Christophe's house is now 'l'union sacrée', and as the volume begins, the men joyfully issue forth to fight, but the war takes its toll, solidarity collapses and at the Armistice nothing is left; the 'silence tragique' of a house in mourning 'contraste avec la kermesse de la rue' (*AE*:733). The survivors are walled in their rooms, communicating no more than Christophe's neighbours before his arrival. The cycle has run its course.

Wartime Paris is in moral decline, and Marc catches the mood. He is saved from corruption by a certain inner purity and by Sylvie, herself affected but sensible enough to set herself limits. Few details are given; Marc later confesses shameful things to his mother, but we are not told what (*AE*:688). His only associates to be evoked more than superficially are the anarchists and syndicalists who begin his political education. His friendship with Pitan hints at a revolutionary alliance of worker and intellectual, but he cannot achieve revolutionary self-abnegation: 'Il en percevait bien la grandeur. Mais il était trop jeune encore pour y aspirer. . . "Non! Pas être mangé! . . . Manger!"' (*AE*:505). Still as hungry as when he was a nurseling, Marc is fully occupied with growing up.

Annette exchanges the fever of Paris for soporific indifference. Small-town life offers peace of a sort, but not her sort, for, in the words of Spinoza which forms the volume's epigraph: 'La paix, ce n'est pas l'absence de guerre. C'est la vertu qui naît de la vigueur de l'âme' (*AE*:431). Annette reacts against this bogus calm when a group of German prisoners, whom she defends against the town's hostility, trigger a universalized maternal instinct in a new moment of self-discovery:

> Et brusquement, s'était dressée contre la nature sauvage sa propre nature reniée et bâillonnée, sa nature trahie, inassouvie, qui se venge et s'affranchit. Et ses seins comprimés par les liens barbares brisent les liens, respirent. Elle réclame son droit, sa loi, sa joie, – et sa souffrance aussi, mais sa souffrance sienne – la Maternité.
>
> Toute la Maternité. Pas seulement celle du fils! . . . Vous êtes tous mes fils. Fils heureux, malheureux, vous vous déchirez. Mais je vous étreins tous. (*AE*:538)

Maternity widens to embrace all suffering humanity, and leads Annette to fight against war, not, like Madeleine Rolland, in pacifist or charitable organizations, but by a futile gesture, arranging the escape of a German prisoner. It is a mad venture, in which she risks far more than any good she can do, and she is just as much one against all as was Clerambault:

> Elle affrontait le visage menaçant de la patrie. Elle se sentait sous le pied des grandes Déesses irritées. Mais si elles pouvaient l'anéantir, elles ne pouvaient la soumettre. Elle ne croyait plus en elles. A partir du moment où elle avait retrouvé, foulées par les colosses inhumains, les affections primitives et sacrées: l'amitié et l'amour, – tout le reste avait disparu [. . .]
>
> Folie, – soit! Mais à ce compte, folie est aussi l'âme. Par cette folie je vis, je marche sur l'abîme, comme l'apôtre sur les eaux. (*AE*:582)

Her aim, the reunion of two friends, seems ludicrously small in face of the world's problems, but her apparently narrow, individualistic vision would, if generalized, be a panacea: 'Si chacun faisait de même, dans son domaine restreint, ce serait la plus grande Révolution de l'humanité' (*AE*:589). The revolt of Annette's soul against force mirrors Rolland's stance against destiny in 1914, as well as his growing engagement in 1926.

Germain Chavannes, the instigator of the plan, is a crippled soldier-philosopher who superficially recalls Edme Froment but is in fact closer to Perrotin: 'Il avait le don funeste de dire oui à sa pensée, et de ne pas dire non à la pensée des autres; car il la comprenait' (*AE*:547). He helps Annette by showing her the merits of both sides of the world's conflicts, but he knows that his breadth has inhibited his development. He has lost his capacity for action, and advises Annette not to let Marc follow his example:

> 'Qu'il *préfère*! . . . Il est beau d'être juste. Mais la vraie justice ne demeure pas assise devant sa balance, à regarder osciller les plateaux. Elle juge et exécute l'arrêt. Qu'il tranche! . . . Assez rêvé! . . . Vienne l'éveil! . . . Adieu, Songe! . . .' (*AE*:627)

Germain has erred by dreaming too much; his call to action echoes through the rest of the novel, and his self-castigation anticipates Rolland's in *Quinze ans de combat*. His pre-war friendship with Franz recalls Olivier and Christophe, but Franz is no Beethoven. He is a childlike egoist who holds his friends' loyalty by charm, and Annette is exploited by both men. In organizing Franz's escape, she approaches Marc's world by working with Pitan, but cannot involve Marc himself, and their chance meeting in Paris while she waits for the escape train, at which she is obliged to exclude him sharply from her life, marks the lowest point of their separation.

When the friends are reunited in Switzerland, illusion is again to the fore. They need it to rebuild their relationship after the inevitably disappointing reunion, Germain all the more so because he is dying. Annette, too, lacks a clear perception of her motives, and is chastened to discover that her feelings for Franz are sexual rather than maternal. Struggling to overcome them, she feels defeated, 'l'éternelle esclave [. . .] qui suit avidement, comme une chienne, le désir' (*AE*:675), fighting the same battle for her soul as she had fought against Villard. An encounter with a blind wounded soldier, however, leads her to a tragic acceptance of her role in the wartime world, in a passage whose image of crushed grapes anticipates the novel's close:

> Non, ce n'est pas pour rien que nous sommes lacérés, piétinés, et broyés, comme une grappe de raisin! Et même si ce n'est pour rien, n'est-ce rien d'être le vin? Cette Force qui nous boit, que serait-elle sans nous? Quelle terrifiante grandeur! . . .
>
> Penchée sur l'aveugle, elle dit, à voix basse et brûlante:
>
> 'Tous les dévouements sont dupes. Peut-être . . . Eh bien, il est mieux d'être dupe! Moi aussi, je l'ai été. Je recommencerais. Et vous?' (*AE*:676–7)

In this variation on the theme of the 'vaincu vainqueur', the ambivalence of illusion is clear. On the one hand it engages humanity in futile causes. On the other, it keeps the world moving; to escape is to cease to live.

Annette returns to find Marc ready for a new relationship. The silent intimacy of their nocturnal vigils recalls Rolland's last days with his mother in January 1919 (*AE*:688, *VI*:103), and their bond survives two trials which dominate the closing stages of the volume. First, Marc tries to contact his father, Annette having made no attempt to hide that he would be welcome. Brissot, however, is in Clemenceau's cabinet, and Marc, repelled by his hypocritical panegyric to the youths he sends to the front, decides he has no wish to know him. Finally, the two must face Marc's imminent conscription. Neither see themselves as pacifists, but both are opposed to war, Annette because of its cruelty, Marc because of its hypocrisy, and Marc is determined to refuse conscription. Annette wants to spare him this sacrifice; she seeks to remain apolitical and confine her role to the level of pity:

> Tous les devoirs sociaux [. . .] comptent peu, à mes yeux, auprès des affections sacrées – amour, maternité, – immuables, éternelles. Qui les blesse me blesse. Je suis prête à les défendre, partout où elles sont menacées. Mais je ne vais pas plus loin. (*AE*:728)

Marc, however, sees the weakness of the old order, and wishes to break all restraints, both social and moral, in the name of joy and freedom:

> Il faut briser, pour refaire l'ordre plus haut, plus vaste, à la mesure des hommes qui viennent, qui sont venus, – des hommes: nous! De l'air! Plus d'air! Elargissons le bien et le mal! ils ont grandi avec nous. . . (*AE*:729)

This is barely a social programme, but he seeks to be in the vanguard of those building a new world, and invites his mother, if he falls, to project her maternal instincts on to all men. To decline this role would be unworthy of her, and he forces her to confess that she repents none of her precarious past. In the event, the Armistice spares him the decision, but the spirit behind the next volume is in place, even if its direction is not. For Annette, as the crowds celebrate, the emphasis is still on illusion:

> Ils sont tous, avec elle, livrés aux rets de l'Illusion [. . .] Pour les uns, c'est le drapeau, la fureur sacrée de la patrie. Pour les autres, c'est la foi en la fraternité des hommes et en l'amour. . . Et son fils, qui prétend n'être dupe de rien, le mépriseur des 'illusions de mots', n'est-il pas de tous le plus illusionné, lui qui est prêt à sacrifier elle et soi à la chimère d'être vrai contre tous? (*AE*: 733–4)

Clerambault's martyrdom is placed in perspective by an illusion which denies absolute value to any terrestrial ideal. Yet it is clear that this will prevent neither mother nor son from pursuing ideals. They face the post-war world knowing that engagement is illusion, but equally knowing that only through it can they be true to themselves. In this they reflect Rolland's evolution in this crucial year of 1926; reliving the war set him on the road from individualism to social engagement.

When Rolland began *L'Annonciatrice* in 1929, he had travelled further down this road. A 1921 note hints at a conclusion akin to *La Nouvelle Journée*: 'La fin doit faire entendre une harmonie belle, paisible et pleine. C'est le soir d'un beau jour. Une grande vie de femme est accomplie. C'est la sérénité d'un lumineux automne'.[7] This, however, was overtaken by events, and Rolland described the emerging work as 'à la fois une *Foire sur la place* (mais beaucoup plus touffue et plus crue) et un *Buisson ardent*'.[8] Yet the comparison itself suggests that there is more to *L'Annonciatrice* than political diatribe. He had been exploring religious and creative processes in his studies of Beethoven and the Vedantists, and *L'Annonciatrice* marries these developments to his political thought. The project was ambitious, and Rolland took his time over a work intended as a testamentary statement.

Its key lies with Maria Koudacheva. He resumed work shortly after their first meeting, and although both of them denied it, it is hard not to see her in Assia, who plays a pivotal role in a familiar pattern of decline and rise. The work is in two parts, the first, *La Mort d'un monde*, being a social satire, with Assia, the neighbour nursing Marc through an illness, appearing in circumstances recalling Sidonie in *La Foire sur la place*. In *L'Enfantement*, Assia becomes the embodiment of revolution, steering Marc into political engagement, whilst the aging Annette delves deeper into her inner life. The work's composition was complex and hesitant;[9] it was not until his illness in December 1930 that Rolland saw precisely how to carry it through.

La Mort d'un monde was easier to write than *L'Enfantement*, and in Rolland's view 'très inférieur'.[10] Of its three parts, the first, 'Les Sept contre Thèbes', belongs to Marc and the second, 'Annette dans la jungle', to Annette, while the third, 'Le Vent du crime', draws themes from both to a tragic conclusion. The first part shows Marc and six student friends confronting Paris society, a financially and morally insecure world where leadership is sadly lacking. The returning troops merely want to resume normal life, Wilson's authority collapses and there is little help to be had from bourgeois intellectuals. Rolland now goes beyond *La Foire sur la place* and names names; Anatole France is a pathetic old man out of his depth, the stoic Alain is admirable but no leader. Even 'ceux qui avaient porté au-dessus de la mêlée l'étendard de leur opinion' have been disqualified by the epithet of defeatism, which they were too moderate to turn into a banner of defiance (*AE*:765); Rolland did not now regard his 1920s self as an effective leader of youth. As to the literary avant-garde, splenetically attacked in the persons of Proust, Joyce and Pirandello, it makes matters worse by encouraging 'une conscience exacerbée, désagrégée, qui perdait son moi, ou le retrouvait multiplié, par morceaux, en tourbillons vertigineux, sans point fixe' (*AE*:961). Rolland was attached to a heroic conception of the personality based on will, and mistrusted these new movements tending to break it down.

In face of this confusion, escapism is a temptation. One possibility is hedonism; Sylvie is one of the organizers of the pleasures of Paris, and as in *Mère et fils* she tries to take possession of Marc, but with only temporary success; he flees from this dangerous mixture of 'petite bourgeoise' and anarchist 'pétroleuse' (*AE*:811). For those less balanced, sexual excess is ruinous; even Marc's strong friend, Henriette Ruche, leaves Paris after failing to preserve her integrity. Others escape into safe careers, but not before Marc's circle of friends is shattered; Véron cynically incites Bouchard, the easily duped peasant, to revolutionary violence, and in a scenario recalling Bourget's *Disciple*, saves his own skin while Bouchard dies on the scaffold.

Marc himself is still the hungry, vulpine adolescent with few social graces; before his marriage Annette notes ominously that 'il manquait de frein et d'équilibre, il manquait de prudence et de justice, il manquait de bonté et de vraie humanité' (*AE*:1005). Yet she knows his saving integrity: 'On y voyait passer d'assez vilains animaux, de cruels et d'avides, haine, orgueil et luxure, tous les vices de violence, mais [. . .] aucun vice de bassesse' (*AE*:773). Marc is sustained by a willingness to struggle against his worst instincts and a vague sense of direction which keeps him struggling even at the worst times:

> Qu'est-ce que le nord? Une banquise? Un trou d'abîme dans les glaces éternelles? Je n'en sais rien. Mais le nord est là. Et il faut que j'aille au nord. La force aveugle veut pour moi. Elle veut pour moi. Ma liberté est de vouloir ce qu'elle veut. (*AE*:819)

This identification of liberty and destiny is characteristic of Rolland's later work, but as yet it takes no political form. Marc is no Marxist; 'son individualisme indiscipliné se cabre devant l'implacable nécessité de ce matérialisme historique' (*AE*:787). Yet he carries a desire to 'sauver les autres' (*AE*:797); he tries to save Bouchard and supports Ruche. The potential for Gandhian self-sacrifice is there.

Annette's orientation is even less clear. She embraces the post-war world with euphoric detachment thanks to her growing awareness of illusion, which she now accepts and enjoys as part of herself, since it is mankind's destiny to live in it. As such, she is not averse to risky involvements. She flirts with danger in a brief spell as a governess in Romania, where she escapes her sexually predatory employer by plunging into a muddy marsh whose symbolism recalls the novel's opening dream. The symbolic impact of this episode seems more important than its social content; it could be set in any country where feudal landlords make their own law. Romania merely anticipates a much wilder jungle in which Annette's guide is Timon, the press magnate. Through his shady dealings, international capitalism enters the novel. In his willingness to fight for the sake of fighting rather than for any precise goal, he recalls Orsino, and is even described as a 'condottiere' (*AE*:862), which helps explain why this potentially odious figure is portrayed with some sympathy. To work for him, Annette must suspend her scruples, but she is attracted by his energy and a strong curiosity:

> Quels duels de forces! Quel bestiaire! [. . .] La riche époque. . . Oui, elle n'est pas très confortable. Elle râpe la peau et elle l'écorche. Le sang y coule, comme de l'eau. Mais c'est tellement intéressant! (*AE*:879)

This ominously echoes Christophe's insufficient 'La vie est une tragédie. Hourrah!', but she does influence Timon, curbing his excesses and communicating her instinctive support for the Soviets. This she does effectively enough to make Timon suspect in the international anti-communist conspiracy; it is hinted that his fatal fall from an aeroplane is no accident.

Marc's failure to find love with Ruche or Sylvie's protégée Bernadette, combined with the trauma of Bouchard's trial, forms the prelude to the illness from which Assia saves him. As with Jacqueline and Grazia in *Jean-Christophe*, Rolland minimizes detailed allusions to the woman who inspires them, but the parallels with Maria Koudacheva are inescapable: the horrors of the Russian Revolution leaving her with reason to hate the Bolsheviks, the violent mood swings, the fiercely honest self-analysis, above all the intense vitality and 'l'intégrité de l'âme, sincère et sûre' (*AE*:1004). At first she has no firm sense of political direction. She does not identify with her fellow *émigrés*, but has too much 'fierté individualiste' to surrender to her instinctive support for the Revolution (*AE*:972). Love enslaves her to illusion as much as anyone, but she shares Annette's feminine ability to give birth to a new soul. As Annette tells her, this can cause problems:

> [Les hommes] veulent que nous gardions, pourrissantes sous notre peau, nos vieilles âmes que nous avons, grâce à Dieu! laissées tomber, à mesure que nous nous renouvelons. Les hommes sont incapables de comprendre, ma fille, cette force qui est en nous [. . .] de rajeunissement éternal. (*AE*:1002)

Women are more in touch than men with the principle of 'Stirb und Werde!', and Annette rightly senses that this will be the lovers' tragedy. As Marc and Assia marry, the future seems gloomy. 'Mais j'y entends aussi, déjà, vagir l'enfant' (*AE*:1009); renewal will come in the final volume.

L'Enfantement is again divided into three parts, each corresponding to a phase of the renewal which the three main characters take turns at leading. In 'Le Combat', Assia leads; transforming herself more rapidly than Marc, she provokes a marital crisis which furthers their political evolution. In this, Rolland has some success in embodying his political message in the interplay of relationships. According to a note dated 6 December 1930, during his crucial illness, this evolution leads from 'l'individualisme libre et sincère' to 'l'individualisme social' (*C29*:60), reflecting Rolland's progress described in *Quinze ans de combat*. Both Assia and Marc feel trapped in marriage. In terms echoing Annette's difficulties with Brissot, Assia finds depths in herself which she may not give to her husband: '"Mon corps, mon cœur est à toi. Mais '*l'âme*', non. '*L'âme*' est à moi. . . Est-elle à moi? Ou à elle, moi?"' (*AE*:1019). Nostalgic for Russia and not greatly squeamish about violence, she cannot avoid 'des comparaisons entre la stérilité d'opposition de Marc et la féconde énergie de l'U.R.S.S.' (*AE*:1046), and is subjugated when Soviet force presents itself in Djanelidze, the Comintern emissary, who sweeps her into the flow of a collective movement. During the Revolution she had resisted the current, like Rolland in 1914, but now she moves with it, and the result is a brief sexual relationship. Assia does not consider the physical act important, but Marc, still conditioned by traditional notions, rejects her. Echoes of Helena and her Italian liaison can perhaps again be felt here.

Marc is slave to the once-glorious ideal of individualism which is now official ideology. He cannot accept party discipline, and resists the historical flow to which Assia submits:

> Ah! si la Révolution était – comme autrefois, où elle avortait en feux d'artifice – un libre jaillissement de révoltés, où l'on met tous dans le tas commun, chacun la sienne! Mais ils l'ont aujourd'hui militarisée. (*AE*:1044)

This condemns him to futility, and his failure to find an effective mode of action diminishes him in Assia's eyes. After their split, however, he sees the flaws of individualism. In his scientist friend Félicien Lerond, loyal to the regime that abuses his work, Marc sees a caricature of his own illusory liberty; the ideals of the war years have been made to work for a capitalist conspiracy which can use a profitable peace and an anti-communist Europe. Individualism is vital, Marc concludes, only if rooted in the community: 'Ce moi n'avait de sève et de durée que grâce aux canaux qui montaient du *soi* de la communauté' (*AE*:1092). He wants to serve this community, but the only possible alternative to collective struggle is a difficult religious way, 'un combat plus difficile encore, en transposant le combat sur un plan d'éternité; il y faut un renoncement, un sacrifice entier, "au-dessus de mes forces"' (*AE*:1092). He admires Gandhism, but sees its difficulties, and to find his way he needs to meet Romain Rolland himself.

The author makes a few brief appearances in this volume, always as a harbinger of sacrifice and death. Marc asks his advice, and Rolland is not sure whether to direct this violent Gandhist to India or Russia (*AE*:1105). The answer is found in two of Rolland's favourite quotations, one from Heraclitus, one from Goethe. First, Marc must try to harmonize his inner conflicts, for the finest harmonies are born of dissonances: 'Ne rejetez rien! Gardez tout! Souffrez, cherchez la plus belle harmonie, celle qui est le miel noir des dissonances! "ἐχ τῶν διαψερόντων χαλλιστην ἀρμονίαν"' (*AE*:1106). He must forge his inner unity, just as Rolland himself tried to reconcile Gandhi and Lenin:

> Il s'agissait de ne rien renier des forces profondes de sa nature [. . .] L'indépendance de l'individu et le sacrifice à la communauté. Marx et Gandhi.

> La *still voice* de l'âme éternelle, fille de Dieu, et la grandiose *Ananké* du matérialisme historique avec l'enclume et le marteau, qui forge et reforge la société. (*AE*:1108)

To this end, sacrifice must be accepted: 'Meurs, mon petit! *Stirb und werde!*' declares Rolland, and Marc agrees to die, asking only that his sacrifice be useful to others. It is, however, some way ahead. The immediate consequence is a reconciliation with Assia, triggered by his involvement with Bernadette and Colombe, another brief irruption of Sylvie's world. His infidelity makes him humble, news of it revives Assia's desire for him and they are reunited under Annette's watchful eye.

In 'Mai florentin', ironically named after Rolland's youthful *Mai romain*, Annette's beneficent influence draws in new characters; as in *L'Eté*, she forms relationships with two contrasting men. The first is a regenerated Julien Davy, who has outgrown his traditionalism to become a leader of advanced thought. Though no activist by temperament, he is drawn into opposition to the war by a scientist's regard for truth which makes him break with his fellow intellectuals; a quarrel with his dying tutor Lavisse reflects one of Rolland's more painful wartime ruptures. Silenced by the censor, Julien avoids the vilification that Rolland faced; instead, he writes on the history of science, expressing the 'pessimisme héroïque aux yeux vaillants, fixant en face la tragique réalité et n'espérant point la transformer' which Rolland associates with Spitteler and Thomas Hardy (*AE*:1175), also with the cautious Duhamel, identified in a preparatory note as the source of some of Julien's features.[11] Julien owes his transformation to Annette, who recognizes herself in his writings, and they are reunited by his daughter George, who contains more of her than of Julien's colourless wife. George's tomboyish dynamism and disrespectful loyalty recall Olivier's similarly named son.

If Julien is Annette's Olivier, Bruno Chiarenza, combining Italian serenity with Indian wisdom, is her Grazia. Like Rolland's friend Gaetano Salvemini, Bruno loses his family in the Messina earthquake of 1908, and is left with an awareness of the natural forces evoked by the Orphic creation myth in which the god Dionysos is killed and reborn. After an attempt to resurrect his family in the child Athanase, whose life he fails to save, he discovers the myth's true meaning:

> Le sauveur sacrifié, [. . .] qui, vingt-cinq siècles avant le '*Durch Leiden Freude*' de nos héros, apprit aux hommes, par son exemple, à conquerir, par la douleur et par la mort, l'éternité, – le dieu qui rompt la roue des naissances pour réintégrer ses élus dans la plénitude et la joie de l'Un. (*AE*:1208)

This echoes Rolland's essay on that other Sicilian, Empedocles; the theme of a demigod sacrificing himself for his fellow men and for cosmic unity has its relevance in the closing stages of this novel. Bruno learns resignation from the 'vues tragiques et sereines' of the Ionian thinkers, and achieves the Heraclitean conquest of harmony out of dissonance:

> S'il ne pouvait empêcher les blessures de se rouvrir dans la nuit – (combien de nuits) – la nuit seule en était le témoin: [. . .] la victime, couché sur le dos, sans un mouvement, pressant son cœur avec les mains, offrait son sang en sacrifice à la céleste Harmonie dont il était un accord poignant. Et quand le jour revenait, le jour indifférent éclairait aux yeux des hommes, non la douleur du passage, mais l'Harmonie. (*AE*:1210)

He visits India and meditates among the Himalayan peaks, but the effect, as with Vivekananda, is to send him back to the world of men. He does ambulance service in the war, and his social work in southern Italy falls foul of the fascists. It is his serenity amidst disaster which draws Annette to him, when he comes to her aid after a railway accident.

Where Julien is the pessimist, slow to express his thought for fear of discouraging others, Bruno is an optimist, espousing the laws of nature which contain more vitality than the rational constructions of man and the sclerotic moral rules which this novel has constantly denounced:

> Cet optimisme [. . .] répondait aux lois profondes de la 'Nature naturante', qui veut vivre, sans se soucier du bien, du mal, de la souffrance, de l'inutilité des efforts; il voulait vivre et il vivait, en dépit des lois morales et rationnelles, qui sont celles de la 'Nature naturée', de l'homme logique, qui n'a pas la sagesse de lâcher le fil de son fuseau. (*AE*:1234)

Bruno's ability to '[se délester] de l'humanité dans le rêve illuminé d'un Cosmos océanique' is admittedly 'trop commode' (*AE*:1240), but it corresponds to Rolland's ability to set his role aside and rise 'au-dessus de la mêlée'. As to the two men's relationship with Annette, the difference is that, while she has given to Julien, Bruno has given to her:

> [Si son cœur] eût suivi son seul penchant, c'était vers Bruno qu'il eût incliné. Bruno avait plus à lui donner. – Mais elle avait plus à donner à Julien. Et pour une femme de son espèce, donner est le besoin le plus fort. (*AE*:1241)

None of the three mentions marriage, but this is why she refuses to think of marrying Bruno when Marc forces her to face her feelings (*AE*:1273).

Julien and Bruno are of an older generation than Marc, do not engage in action more than they must, and cannot define Marc's way for him. His love for Assia helps him more, by freeing him from individualist illusion:

> L'amour l'amenait à se dépouiller de l'égoïsme de l'esprit – le plus mortel – celui de ses idéologies et de ses absolus de pensée. Il l'aidait à passer d'un plan de vie à l'autre plan, de l'individuel au social. (*AE*:1139)

Yet though committed to the masses, he still does not know how to serve them. He fears violence, knowing his own violent temperament, but the alternative, sacrifice, is still no easy option. He is drawn to the Soviets, but equally to Gandhist and other anti-fascist causes, 'sans se décider à prendre position nette entre ces diverses formations de combat, mais en tâchant de se faire le lien entre ces armées et de les amener (rêve utopique) au front unique' (*AE*:1151). Bruno helps, by admitting the inevitability of violence in any conflict (*AE*:1238), but like Germain, he knows his detachment is not appropriate to Marc and does not try to inspire it. Bruno's 'confiance en la montée du monde vers l'unité' (*AE*:1256) no more solves Marc's problems than 'La Route en lacets' solved Rolland's in 1916. What he and Julien do give Marc is a sense of being on 'la route royale du grand Destin', the 'Via Sacra' which gives its name to the volume's third part (*AE*:1245).

Marc accepts destiny, but surpasses Bruno in heroically accepting personal responsibility for it:

> Il était résolu maintenant à servir, à tous les postes où sa consigne de combat le placerait, l'armée des opprimés qui doit briser le vieux ordre d'injustice sociale. Les injustices nouvelles et les souffrances, que causerait fatalement le combat, il les savait inévitables, – donc nécessaires. (*AE*:1257)

While accepting that violence must accompany change, he prays that destiny will spare him from shedding blood, but his fears are confirmed when, in a scuffle at a meeting, he kills a right-wing demonstrator in self-defence. Assia, who does not share his scruples, is proud of him, but Marc knows he has been defeated; his deed was an ambivalent instinctive response rather than an act of justice. To take his mind off this unresolved problem, he is persuaded to take the holiday on which he dies, and it is Rolland's intention that he should die with his problems unresolved. As the note of 6 December 1930 expresses it:

Il n'arrivera pas à trouver son équilibre, – (comme moi) défendant à tout moment la Révolution russe contre l'indignité des attaques de l'Europe, – et, dans le fond du cœur, mal à l'aise, déchiré, révolté par les abus du pouvoir en U.R.S.S. Ce dernier sentiment est renforcé par sa condamnation des mêmes violences dans le fascisme italien, – et par les souffrances personnelles que lui cause Dacha.[12] Il mourra, sans avoir résolu cette tragique antonomie, de l'âme libre qui lutte pour assurer la victoire de l'énorme Machine sociale multitudinaire instaurée par la Révolution russe. (*C29*:61)

In the three years separating this from the final text, the intention to make Marc criticize Soviet abuses has disappeared, but the basic scenario remains. Marc does not achieve harmony; the fate of an individual trying to espouse a historical movement remains as tragic as in Rolland's theatre. Marc's end reflects reservations about revolution which stayed with Rolland well after he ceased to express them publicly.

In Switzerland, the family encounters the fascist banker Zara, whose daughter's life Annette saves in a gesture which Zara cannot reciprocate. Zara portrays Mussolini as a Neronian *artifex* obsessed with action for action's sake, a gambler staking the future on 'une construction sociale qui reposait sur le génie violent d'un seul homme' (*AE*:1281). Marc is not attracted to this exacerbated individualism: 'Jamais il n'aurait pu se sacrifier pour un homme', but Assia has 'un fond de sympathie pour l'adversaire qui était de taille' (*AE*:1283), and they decide to visit Italy. Marc, the northern barbarian, is as charmed as Christophe by its light and beauty, but Italian society is dominated by informers and *agents provocateurs*, with the British Intelligence Service, nerve centre of the capitalist plot, brooding in the background. Marc's death, in a scuffle in which he helps an old man and a boy attacked by fascist thugs, has every appearance of being planned. He dies gallantly, but ambiguously. His sacrifice is not for the masses, but for an individual, admittedly a more attractive one than Mussolini, but the principle is arguably the same. Like Annette in the war, he stakes everything on a futile gesture, and it is far from clear whether his intervention is an act of principle or the same instinctive violence which led him to kill in Paris. The impression is one of incomplete harmonization. Only Annette at the close achieves perfect harmony.

In 'Via Sacra', after the death of the betrayed hero on a journey to the south, a woman finishes his work and her death restores cosmic harmony in face of collapsing world order. Rolland's Wagnerism had waned, but the scenario recalls *Götterdämmerung* as surely as the cataclysms of his early plays. The task Rolland set himself, that of showing the religious basis of Revolutionary fervour, is one of the greatest artistic challenges he faced, and the process recalls *Jean-Christophe*; just as Antoinette, Olivier and Grazia are harmonized by Christophe after their death, Marc passes into the souls of the survivors and directs them.

First affected is Ruche, saved by Marc's support, who contracts the free marriage to which Annette aspired a generation earlier. Assia, eager to complete Marc's mission, re-enters the world of illusion: 'Quand est nécessaire l'illusion pour qu'on reprenne pied dans l'agissante réalité, c'est donc que l'illusion est un morceau aussi de la réalité' (*AE*:1346). She remarries and throws herself into worldwide action, inspiring an American revolutionary circle and leaving her son behind just as Maria Koudacheva left Serge in Russia. She leads her followers to suffering and sacrifice, finally returning to Russia and deserting a mission to come to Annette's deathbed, an individualist gesture which is not appreciated in Moscow (*AE*:1454). Significantly, this concluding reference to Soviet Russia is one of the few in the volume to show its sinister side.

For Annette, Marc's death shatters yet another illusion. Bruno tries to console her with a parable of Vivekananda's: Narada lives a whole life of joys and sufferings in the space of the half-hour during which Krishna has sent him to fetch water (*AE*:1336–7). The implication is that life is Mâyâ, an evanescent dream, but Annette rejects the proffered consolation and Bruno, returning to India, fades from the scene. She prefers the view which has prevailed for most of the novel: Mâyâ is the fabric of life, and man must live it to the full:

> Pourquoi le verre d'eau serait-il plus vrai que mon pauvre Marc englouti? Ou ma douleur est illusion, ainsi que l'Un; et tout n'est rien. Ou tout est vrai, tout est réel, le mal et le bien, la mort et l'Un. Et puis-je trancher entre les deux? [. . .] Que j'aie le courage de ne rien savoir, et de faire face au: 'Quoi que tu sois – ou Rien, ou Tout, – j'irai jusqu'au bout de mon destin!' (*AE*:1338)

She decides therefore to complete Marc's work, and becomes a public speaker and activist, working to build the united front of the left which was Rolland's hope as it was Marc's: 'Indifférente aux étiquettes et au formalisme bureaucratique, elle obligeait ceux des deux Internationales, sœurs et ennemies, à se compter sur le terrain de l'action. On discuterait plus tard la théorie!' (*AE*:1361). She is remarkable for the spirit of calm with which she acts, which she owes to being in touch with ultimate religious truths:

> Loin de se retirer dans le rêve de l'Un, que lui avait ouvert la flûte du chevrier,
> elle en puisait, par ses racines, du fond de la terre, les énergies; et elle les
> transfusait dans l'action. Que serait l'Un, si le sang de l'action n'y circulait
> point? L'Un est un acte. L'Un est en marche. S'il s'arrêtait un seul moment,
> tout croulerait. (*AE*:1358–59)

As usual, Rolland's God is a God in movement, best served by action; Bruno's dreams help Annette only insofar as she can fuse dream and action and make dreams a source of strength.

This period is, however, passed over rapidly. Annette's and Assia's action are things of which we are told, rather than shown, and in Annette's case ill-health curtails her activities. As in *Jean-Christophe*, Rolland shies away from portraying revolutionary action in the modern world, probably out of reluctance to address a subject of which his experience was limited, and which left him more uneasy than he was prepared to admit. In 'Via Sacra' the political rhetoric fades; the focus is more on Annette's inner life and her immediate circle. This has political implications, but the fact remains that Marc's political heritage is not translated into anything more specific than generalized support for revolution and a broad left front. Russia may be the ideal, but it is kept at arm's length.

Annette in the closing stages is described as 'une constellation' (*AE*:1408) whose stars are the younger generation she has moulded: Marc's son Vania, George, now his guardian, Assia and her American son Waldo, Bernadette's daughter Marcelle: 'Ils sont tous sortis d'elle. Et la même force qui la mène les lancera tous, en losange, dans le grand ciel, vers le même but lointain' (*AE*:1423). They are a dynamic brood, making their way to the stars like the survivors at the end of *Les Léonides*, and much of 'Via Sacra' is devoted to their first steps on the way, which leads through revolution. The one who flies highest is Silvio, the Florentine boy whose life Marc saved. Having absorbed Marc's ideal of sacrifice, he emulates Lauro de Bosis, who died scattering anti-fascist literature over Rome from the air, '[voulant], par ce sacrifice, racheter la honte et rallumer la flamme "*du peuple de Mazzini*"' (*AE*:1451). Annette recognizes her influence in his act, and in a deathbed vision she sees George, Vania and Assia facing the same sacrificial destiny:

> Ils étaient tous voués à la mort exaltée dans la flamme. Et cette flamme, elle
> avait, aveugle, jour après jour, travaillé à l'allumer [. . .] Sa mission avait eté,
> à son insu, de porter dans ses mains calmes, pour éclairer sa pensée, la torche
> de l'action, que d'autres mains avaient saisie, et que le vent rabattait sur sa
> propre maison. . . L'Ame Enchantée et sa couvée, comme le phénix, étaient

destinées au bûcher. Gloire au bûcher, si de leurs cendres, comme du phénix, renaît une plus haute humanité! . . . (*AE*:1452–3)

Death, like the holocaust of *Götterdämmerung* and *Le Siège de Mantoue*, will purge and renew humanity, and Annette welcomes it. 'La route en lacets' becomes the Via Sacra, a triumphal way but also the road to martyrdom.

Annette is preceded in death by Sylvie, who despite a growing awareness of inner life through music, maintains the contrast with her sister by dying without knowing what is happening to her. Annette, meanwhile, withdraws into inner life, living, like the aging Christophe, on two levels:

L'une, sur le plan des jours qui passent et dont elle faisait encore partie, comme de l'équipage d'un bateau l'homme à la proue, qui fend les flots, – l'autre, au sein du gouffre intérieur, où elle descendait en planant, comme la feuille d'un noyer dont le corps se penche au flanc d'une pente. (*AE*:1428)

In a last meeting with the author, she describes how the dream of the opening pages has returned, but now she escapes from the pond and is carried away by the river: 'Le flot de l'eau d'or, de l'eau qui dort – et moi, dedans – s'est écoulé dans l'eau vivante, dans la rivière. Et la rivière s'écoule vers la mer' (*AE*:1447). Images of river and ocean prevail at Annette's death as at Christophe's, but Annette's is more richly orchestrated, reinforced by Rolland's recent studies of mysticism. Duchatelet identifies the influence of Cécile Vé, described by the psychologist Théodore Flournoy, and a near-death vision recorded by William James.[13]

The scene begins with images of fire and battle; her death is assimilated to the demise of the old world:

Le gouffre du monde se creusait; les grosses fumées montaient de tous les corps du logis: Europe, Asie, partout les guerres et les Révolutions: l'humanité brûlait, aux quatre coins. (*AE*:1457)

As the barriers fall between self and universal life, images of fire yield, as in *Götterdämmerung*, to that of the river, but one which flows upwards to an oceanic sky, a 'route en lacets' whose bends become the coils of the serpent which, biting its tail, signifies the union of past, present and future:

'Rivière suis [. . .] – Rivière de l'Etre, Rivière des êtres, Rivière des âges, qui gravit, en serpentant, les flancs escarpés du mont. Au-dessous de moi, en me penchant, je vois les anneaux indéfinis qui se déroulent et qui s'enroulent. Et au-dessus, la tête allongée du serpent, qui s'érige frayant son chemin, tâtant les aspérités des rocs qui surplombent, et s'y hissant. Et tout au haut, et tout au fond, au-delà des cimes, l'abîme du ciel océan. . .' (*AE*:1459)

The river freezes into a ladder on the mountainside; individual lives are its rungs, and destiny climbs, crushing each rung in passing and pressing the juice from it like a treader of grapes. Destiny and the individual are united at the moment of death, and it is then that the last illusion collapses:

Elle était une maille de l'échelle, jetée par-dessus le vide, à un tournant. Et quand le pas qui monte s'appuie sur elle, en le broyant, l'échelon tient bon, en tournant; et le Maître franchit, sur l'arc tendu de son corps, l'abîme. Toute la douleur de sa vie a été l'angle d'infléchissement de la marche en avant du Destin. . .

 – 'Destin! avance! Merci de m'avoir prise pour marchepied! . . . Et je te suis. Destin je suis'. (*AE*:1461)

Annette accepts destiny, but her life has changed destiny's course; Rolland's imagery harmonizes the relationship between destiny and the individual and creates a religious context for revolutionary action. In dying, Annette fertilizes the heavens and the serpent of infinity becomes the Milky Way, combining the sidereal and procreation imagery which have featured throughout:

L'Ame Enchantée avait fusé – jet de semence dans le sillon que creuse la Mort, vers le trou du ciel, au haut du mont – la grande écluse par où s'écoule la Voie Lactée, collier des nuits, serpent des mondes, qui déroule dans la prairie de l'Infini ses anneaux d'Etre. . . (*AE*:1461)

Rolland laboured long over this scene, which attempts as complex a synthesis as anything in his work: 'J'aurais voulu que fussent mariés, en ce dernier morceau de la symphonie [. . .], les grands motifs musicaux de toute mon œuvre'. Rolland sensed that the harmonization was incomplete: 'L'œuvre réalise moins ce grand dessein, trop vaste pour que nos bras puissent le ceinturer, que l'aspiration pathétique de l'époque'. His reach had perhaps exceeded his grasp in a project which he came to see, as he saw *Jean-Christophe*, as the portrayal of the aspirations of a generation. Yet he insists on the musical character of his achievement: 'l'œuvre est musique' (*AE*:xix), and he was convinced of its special testamentary importance. He returned in later works to the problem of destiny and the individual, but does not depart far from the synthesis suggested in the novel's last pages. Its lukewarm reception disappointed him, and his hopes that posterity would be kinder have not yet been realized. As a work of imagination, its best parts stand comparison with *Jean-Christophe* and often sound more modern in their approach to the human personality, though feminist criticism has yet to come to terms with its ambitious attempt to understand the psychology of a woman. It will best be appreciated by those who, like Rolland himself, value the creative act above the end product, and in his remaining works, study of the creative act becomes the central theme.

Notes

1. See Duchatelet (1987a).
2. Letter to Zweig, 3 March 1924. Quoted in Duchatelet (1987a), p.50.
3. Letter to Helena de Kay, 3 January 1919.
4. Letter to Helena de Kay, 21 December 1917.
5. See Duchatelet (1997), pp.179-89.
6. For animal imagery in this novel, see Melet (1976), p.17.
7. Quoted by Duchatelet (1985), p.61.
8. Letter to Madeleine, 3 September 1932.
9. See Duchatelet (1985).
10. Letter to L. Price, 22 December 1934. Quoted in Duchatelet (1987a), p.54.
11. See Duchatelet (1997), p.243.
12. This was Assia's original name.
13. See Duchatelet (1985).

<h1 style="text-align:center">–12–</h1>

The Voyage Within

In 1921, Rolland had criticized Barbusse's claim to be following universal scientific laws, but in the writings that remain to be considered, he has found a kind of universal law in which he has more confidence:

> La pensée est, comme notre corps, un produit de la Nature [. . .] Elle participe à la marche générale de l'armée, au mouvement général de la vie.
>
> Il serait donc sage de la considérer comme conditionnée, sans le savoir, par les lois obscures qui régissent cette étrange aventure: l'expédition de la Vie dans le Cosmos [. . .]
>
> La pensée sera, qu'elle le veuille ou non, l'aveu de ces lois, inscrite en notre substance. Et nous ne devrons pas l'oublier. C'est ce qui peut donner à notre pensée son cachet le plus authentique de réalité. Si nous savons la laisser couler, libre, ample et naturelle, sous le regard lucide de la conscience [. . .], sa pente nous indiquera celle de la Nature et de nos destinées humaines. (*VI*:370)

The flow of thought parallels that of the laws governing the rhythms of history, and its study in certain minds reveals fundamental truths. The subjects Rolland chooses for such study usually have the heroic characteristics that interested him before the war, but he no longer approaches them in the spirit of heroic celebration. The aim is to probe the depths of their minds in search of the God within.

In *Le Voyage intérieur*, the subject is himself. Most of this 'prélude symphonique' to an autobiography (*VI*:14) was drafted between 1924 and 1926, when *L'Ame enchantée* was already pointing him towards the inner life; his meeting with Freud encouraged the process, and so did rediscovery of the lost manuscript of the *Credo quia Verum*, which showed him how close he had remained to it.[1] He conceived the work as a voyage of self-discovery in which he attempts to fathom his essential self. It is loosely structured and unfinished; like the Montaigne essay or Rousseau *rêverie*, its unity is that of the author's personality, following no preconceived pattern:

> Aucune arrière-pensée de sculpter sa propre statue, aucun système préconçue d'autoconstruction, n'ont dirigé ce '*Voyage intérieur*'; c'est en le faisant que j'ai découvert ce que j'ai écrit. (*VI*:14)

Rolland surprised himself with the extent of his self-discovery and sometimes wondered where it was leading. He admitted the work was self-indulgent, but felt he was arriving at important religious insights: 'Plus on descend au fond de sa vie intérieure, plus on y trouve l'Etre commun à tous'.[2]

In 1942, for financial reasons, Rolland published five of the most narrative chapters. Omitted were three discursive chapters, 'Le Seuil', 'Le Royaume du T' and 'La Ceinture', and a long narrative chapter, 'Le Périple', tracing the tortuous evolution of his career and the failure of public and friends alike to follow it. This was the one chapter to which he returned after setting the manuscript aside late in 1926, but the additions he made in 1940 could not appear under the Occupation. All four are reinstated in the posthumous edition, together with notes for further chapters.

The five chapters originally published have already been quoted extensively. In 'La Ratoire', the emphasis is on the 'plénitude océanique des premiers jours' (*VI*:24). Children are in touch with their inner being, and the contrast between it and their restricted individual life engenders a sense of imprisonment. Escape is possible through occasional 'éclairs', the one associated with his first sister, and those related in 'Les Trois Eclairs'. In 'L'Arbre' he considers what he owes to his father, his maternal grandfather, his great-grandfather Boniard and his mother, the latter two, the revolutionary and the Jansenist, being at the root of his rebellious temperament (*VI*:62). In 'Le Sagittaire', he traces the origin of his creativity through his adolescent dream world. 'Les Amies' sets out to cover his relationship with Malwida von Meysenbug and Louise Cruppi; it was triggered by the latter's death, but he could not bring himself to write about her, and the final text deals only with Malwida.

The initial stress is on his roots. His family is important because he sees his life as the culmination of a process lasting several generations: 'Au cours de plusieurs siècles, ces ruisseaux de vie mêlés ont frayé leur vallée; et le dernier venu n'est que la commune conscience de cette artère qui pense' (*VI*:47). Similarly, he insists on his Frenchness, which his enemies had contested:

> Vieux Français d'origine, et d'essence morale, j'ai, toute ma vie, aspiré passionnément à la compréhension – et (pourquoi ne le dirais-je pas?), à

> l'amour des meilleurs de mon peuple, – du plus antique, du plus pur de ma race, dont je me sais (*je me sais*) un pur représentant. (*VI*:330–1)

The emphasis on purity and antiquity of race points to the unlikely influence of Gobineau, whom Rolland had recently read, though with a critical eye. Rolland insists that his is an Aryan, un-Mediterranean, land-based Frenchness, born of invaders migrating from Central Asia:

> Je suis 'l'homme qui marche'; et je ne sais d'où partit mon lointain pèlerinage, si c'est de chez mes cousins du Don et de l'Oural, ou de l'au-delà mythique des hauts-plateaux d'Asie. (*VI*:127)

Even his inherent dynamism is traced to an ethnic stereotype, in a passage which later embarrassed him when he saw the Nazi abuse of racism.

In 'Le Seuil', this immense prenatal past inspires religious reflections. Unsatisfied by Catholicism, he seeks firm metaphysical ground in self-exploration, starting with the observation that, 'dès ma prime conscience inscrite, entre trois et cinq ans, si je songe à ce que je laisse derrière moi, [. . .] je vois des espaces immenses' (*VI*:183). These inner spaces are the realm of myth rather than science, and Rolland finds himself attracted to myths of other cultures. He responded to Indian myth during the war; Bruno discovering Orphic myth in *L'Ame enchantée* has a similar experience. Organized faiths making over-specific claims about past and future enter into the realms of illusion, and Rolland admits to being harsh on religions which make mendacious promises. He acknowledges, however, that Mâyâ is an essential dynamic force; even the belief in progress, today's religion which Rolland hardly shares, is 'nécessaire sans doute à la Créatrice, Nature naturante' (*VI*:192). Knowing that all is illusion, Rolland can espouse no single faith; all the tomorrows to which faith aspires collapse into a single today which is where Rolland chooses to live. This today must still renew itself: 'L'épreuve du feu est, pour les initiés, de contempler en face cet "*Aujourd'hui*" éternel, et cependant d'agir. Rien ne doit arrêter le courant qui renouvelle l'"*Aujourd'hui*". (*VI*:192)

Renewal, however, is a tragic process, and nothing guarantees that the individual will not be overwhelmed in Shiva's dance:

> Tragique est l'être. Sous la danse des formes est la douleur. Si tu la fuis, tu n'atteindras jamais au but: l'Esprit du Maître, '*la paix centrale, au cœur de l'agitation sans fin*'. (*VI*:193)

This is why death, 'le seuil' of the title, is so important; Rolland's prayer is to face it free of illusion. This reflection on the individual confronting universal dynamic processes anticipates the conclusion of *L'Ame enchantée*, which similarly embraces past and future in mystic union, and it throws light on the tragic vision underlying Rolland's communist engagement.

'Le Royaume du T' further explores Rolland's faith, starting with an attack on religious commentators with 'aucune notion directe du sens religieux' (*VI*:199) which seems to allude to Freud. Zweig had introduced the two men in 1924, but though Rolland admired Freud, he argued that Freud's atheism left him ill-equipped to understand religious experience. More fundamentally, Rolland rejected the Jewish elements of Christianity, declaring himself 'infiniment plus à l'aise dans la pensée hellénique, ou dans celle des Aryens de l'Inde primitive' (*VI*:200). The problem was not Christ, whom he reveres as a 'frère sacrifié', but the monotheistic Jahveh, whose authority is based solely on the tyrannic notion that he is 'le plus Fort'. Worst of all, Jahveh is outside the individual; his nature is sharply distinct from man's: 'Extérieur à moi. Un autre. Bien qu'il m'ait fait, dit-on, à son image, il est loin de moi, autant que je le suis de la glaise entre mes doigts' (*VI*:205). Rolland's God is within, not an imperial authority imposing his will from outside, and this essay again celebrates pantheism, which Rolland finds in the Gallo-Roman notion of '*Genius*: le dieu de chacun' (*VI*:208–9). The T of the essay's title, 'le θέοξ (Théos) et le *Tau*, qui marquait au front les maisons et les églises de Gaule, – croix du Christ, fabriqué du bois non raboté du maillet de Teutatès, le Mercure Gallique' (*VI*:198), symbolizes a divinity more Hellenic and Gallic than Judaic. In this perspective, all are united in the 'Urseele', the primordial universal soul in whom individual differences are resolved as the colours of the rainbow blend in white light (*VI*:217).

Rolland is conscious of the visionary character of this essay, and fully aware that a multiplicity of gods could be a recipe for chaos. His answer, attributed to the Gallic pantheist Colas, is 'La Nécessité' and 'Conscience de la Nécessité'; his God bids him to see, not to obey, and what he sees is the conflict of *Le Buisson ardent*, light struggling against night in a battle whose outcome is uncertain:

> Le 'génie' qui me guide [. . .] n'est pas le Dieu des armées. Il est l'armée, qui marche, qui geint, qui est blessée, mais qui avance, ensanglantée, illuminée par l'Esprit. Tous mes génies et moi [. . .], cette marée grondante sur la plage qui bruit, comme une conque, de l'Humanité, nous avançons ensemble, battus et combattant, [. . .] corps à corps avec la Nuit. (*VI*:211)

In this, man and God are free allies, not master and servant: 'Le Dieu libre et ses hommes libres, qui font le destin: le destin ne les fait pas' (*VI*:212). Man should therefore not submit to destiny imposed from outside, but collaborate with destiny experienced from within, which shapes his life in ways which harmonize with the movement of history. Hamlet's 'There's a divinity which shapes our ends, Rough-hew them how we will' is the epigraph to the whole work (*VI*:17).

In an unfinished chapter, 'Je n'accepte', Rolland planned to relate how 'ce mot, qui fut celui de mon action vivante, toute ma vie, [. . .] a fini par me mener à l'Acceptation suprême et à se confondre avec elle' (*VI*:335). In a text dated 'Nuit du 20 au 21 janvier 26', he seems to relate the change to a new 'éclair', leaving him detached from his individual role and full of 'le sentiment de soumission au Seigneur, d'indifférence à moi' (*VI*:339). Ill-health, exile and bereavement have brought him to a state in which he can 'm'élever de ma loi propre au système général de lois, à l'Harmonie totale, où trouve sa place légitime ce que rejette ma Non-acceptation et mon individualité' (*VI*:338). This is the heroic resignation he later celebrates in Beethoven, and it marks his surrender of individualism. The metaphysical ground is prepared for an identification of revolution with man-made destiny, and for the synthesis of the individual with destiny in *L'Ame enchantée*. It is a crucial turning-point.

If man is God, man creates, and Rolland values art as a creative process which matters more than the product created: 'Je n'attache aucun prix à la création (à l'œuvre créée). Mais un prix infini à l'acte créateur' (*VI*:369). In 'Le Périple', he admits that his own works fall short of his aspirations:

> Je sais, mieux que personne, la médiocrité de mes réalisations. Un très petit nombre répondait à ce que j'aurais voulu. Presque toutes sont puérilement inférieures à ce qui m'était dicté. (*VI*:249)

Yet he resorts to sidereal imagery to insist proudly on the worth of his work as a dynamic process:

> Chaque livre [. . .] doit former une unité organique, harmonieusement lié, un petit monde fini, comme un de ces grains stellaires, qui parsèment la nuit de leur flot de poussière. Mais qui ne connaît que ce grain, ne le connaît guère. Il faut connaître le flot, auquel il appartient, et voir où va ce flot, d'où il vient, de quelle main. Les étoiles d'aujourd'hui ne sont plus des clous d'or fichés dans un plafond. Ce sont des projectiles. Calcule le trajectoire! (*VI*:248–9)

This trajectory is important because it offers clues to the future. In another sketch, 'Le Démon', Rolland returns to the Goethean notion of 'das Dämonische', 'le génie des forces qui dépassent l'espèce (et surtout la société)'. It is a deeper force than the unhealthily anarchic Nietzschean Dionysiac or Freudian subconscious, and as such it works for unity (*VI*:309). It helps to direct the cosmic process, and artistic creation serves as a signpost to it. This gives art the 'rôle annonciateur' which Rolland had investigated in his musicology. Artists and thinkers do not cause historical movements, but they betray advance symptoms: 'La pensée n'est pas plus la cause de l'action, que l'action de la pensée [. . .] La cause est le cœur. Mais chaque pulsation est ou peut être l'indice des fièvres qui vont venir' (*VI*:313). Thus it was that Freud and Schönberg gave warning of the war in the preceding decade, and Rolland himself, schooled in notions of historical evolution, had sensed the mood before the event.

The artist's role is further explored in 'Le Sagittaire', where the artist is the bow waiting for the divine archer, and the arrow the work of art whose trajectory must be followed. The archer is related to the Demon, and the language evoking him is markedly sexual:

> L'Archer, mon maître, dort. Mais même en son sommeil, il ne me lâche point. Je suis couché près de lui, moi, l'arc, je sens sur mon bois lisse sa main, sa belle main, aux doigts longs, détendus; ils caressent de leur pulpe une corde qui chante dans la nuit. Je mêle mes ondes à celle de son corps; et j'attends, frémissant, la minute du réveil, où se reserrera sur moi l'étreinte du divin Archer. (*VI*:108)

Rolland is conscious of this sexuality, and situates the origins of his creativity in an erotic infantile dream world. The content of these dreams is imprecise, and Rolland admits the presence of homosexual elements. As long as they remain dreams, such instincts are untouched by morality; they are ruled by an Eros which is 'partout où jaillit le jet brûlant de l'Esprit qui s'élance et qui veut féconder de son grain de vie la rivière de vie, la Voie Lactée' (*VI*:116–17). This acceptance of the protean forms of love recalls the *Credo quia Verum*, and the imagery anticipates the sexual ambivalence of Annette's death, in which she becomes a drop of semen fertilizing the Milky Way. Only one erotic dream is denied: the Oedipus complex. Rolland was not convinced that valid conclusions could be drawn from Freud's Viennese patients, and his profound respect for his mother led him to deny any erotic content to their affection (*VI*:112–13). It could of course be argued that he was reluctant to face the Oedipal elements which a Freudian could easily detect in this relationship.

These dreams are merely the raw material of creation, which depend for their realization on the Janiculum 'éclair', the discussion of which, quoted in an earlier chapter, is the climax of 'Le Sagittaire'. The separation of mind from heart at this moment is the key to aesthetic order; it allows passions to be controlled and canalized in a discipline which is further discussed in 'La Ceinture', Rolland's most important statement on morality. Like everything worthwhile, morality is the product of creative energy, 'une discipline de la vie en mouvement' by which the will masters the dynamic process (*VI*:219). Its content needs periodic reassessment and it resists codification, but its essence is the quest for a means of conducting the conflict of 'l'homme contre le néant' (*VI*:221). The key to morality is truth and will, and in the interests of the latter he rejects sexual excesses which his dreams admit. Already in 'Le Sagittaire' he insists that in practical terms he has rejected homosexuality; without actually naming Gide and Proust, he declares his dislike for the flaunting of it which characterizes the present generation (*VI*:120). In 'La Ceinture' he goes further; isolated acts of abnormality are of little consequence, but if they become habitual, they are a drain on moral energy:

> Nous devons être assez forts pour dire: 'En soi, rien n'est "*fas vel nefas*". Mais en virile liberté, je fais choix [. . .] du plus sain, du meilleur; et j'écarte avec l'épée ce qui nuit aux autres et à moi'. – Il nous faut remplacer *l'habitude morale*, dénuée de toute 'vertu' (au sens exact et plein), par l'acte vrai de vertu – de *virtus* – qui tend l'arc de la volonté, et qui décoche sa flèche au but clairement visé. (*VI*:225)

The recurrence of the arrow image underlines the parallel between moral discipline and the work of art; both are creative acts, whose essence is the will's harnessing of the subconscious.

Morality and art are impossible without truth. 'Le respect du *réel*' is essential to creation (*VI*:369), and the desire to study other souls is at the heart of Rolland's work: 'Le mouvement naturel de mon être fut, dès la première heure dont je garde conscience, – non pas d'observer les autres, – mais, instantanément, de me couler en eux' (*VI*:117). Respecting the truths of other beings through Tolstoyan realism, he aspires to create harmony from the dissonances of their individual lives. In the unfinished 'Le Maître Musicien', Rolland outlines this process in one of his clearest statements of his ideal of harmony:

> Le sens même de la vie, son héroïsme, est, pour moi, de se différencier. Que chaque être soit un être propre, tout entier! Que pas un ne soit un autre! – Et mon ennemi perpétuel est l'esprit de troupeau et sa contagion.

> Mais cette poussière d'êtres, tous différenciés, s'anéantirait elle-même, si, comme celle des étoiles, elle n'avait – et ne retrouvait – les lois de l'harmonie qui accordent ses millions de voix en une divine symphonie.
>
> Cette symphonie de millions de voix diverses, c'est, pour moi, l'Unité cosmique vers laquelle je tends mon espoir et mon désir. (*VI*:321)

To achieve this, one must step outside one's own part in the symphony which nevertheless must be played to the full, and the Janiculum 'éclair' makes this possible by freeing Rolland's vision from his personal role and letting him function on both the individual and the cosmic level.

The artist cannot avert his gaze from the modern world, but none of the planned chapters broaching the subject were completed, perhaps because Rolland's vision was so dark. Ever since youth, 'j'ai vu se renouveler [. . .] le cinquième acte qui vient de la grande tragédie d'Occident' (*VI*:345–6). This is seen not only in the war, but also in 'la désagrégation de la personnalité, forgée par des siècles de volonté' (*VI*:313). Freud, Schönberg, Proust and Joyce reflect the collapse of traditional notions of selfhood based on the will, which Rolland cherishes. His fear of the consequences is expressed in a comment on Surrealism:

> Où s'arrêtera cette désagrégation? Ne prendra-t-elle pas le caractère d'une destruction de toute autorité mentale? Ou en vue de quel nouvel équilibre des forces intérieures? Car, de toute façon, il faut un chef invisible [. . .] Car la vie est un combat. Chaque jour, chaque minute. Et qui s'abandonne, un seul comma, est terrassé pour jamais. Si le vieux chef a fait son temps, renversez-le, mais hâtez-vous d'en élever un autre sur le pavois! (*VI*:317)

If this iconoclastic movement heralds a new order, it may have value, but if not, it represents a threat, and Rolland envisages his function in pessimistic terms: 'Mon principal souci, dans le désastre inévitable que j'envisage de notre civilisation d'Europe, est de préserver ses trésors les plus rares, pour l'humanité qui viendra' (*VI*:49). Of these, the greatest is the spirit of scientific investigation; in this 1925 text, a last flickering of his individualism, he still sees his role in terms of an elite holding out against encroaching barbarity.

The hardest problem is to determine how much of this vision to share with a public too weak to bear it. This had long inhibited Rolland, and in 'La Ceinture' he battles with the problem again as he strives for a balance between truth and love, the sincerity which forbids him to 'formuler un mot de plus ou de moins de ce que l'on croit vrai' and the sympathy by which he shares the sufferings of his fellow men (*VI*:235). He finds no easy solution, but accepts that, as a leader figure, the visionary artist cannot simply pursue his own truth; since he must think for all, his action must accept certain disciplines:

> On est né chef. C'est pour servir. On appartient à ceux qui ne s'appartiennent point. On n'est pas libre de suivre la ligne de sa pensée. On pense pour soi, on agit pour tous. Comment faire? Agir pour tous est souvent agir contre sa propre vérité. Car cette vérité est pour les forts. Son alcool – son eau-de-vie [. . .] assomme les débiles [. . .]
>
> Sur le plan de l'action, quand ce n'est point la liberté de mon âme qui est en jeu, mais celle de mes mouvements, je dois donner envers moi-même l'exemple d'une rigueur, que ma pensée souvent juge avec ironie. Pour guider les peuples aveugles dans la forêt des passions, ceux qui marchent en tête [. . .] ont à imposer aux masses inorganisées une stricte discipline, dont eux, depuis longtemps, ils pourraient se passer. Mais puisqu'ils l'imposent, il ne leur est plus permis de s'en passer. (*VI*:230–1)

The artist as leader must think sincerely, but at times act against his own truth, submit to disciplines which must be imposed on others for the sake of action. This throws light on Rolland's view of the artist's elite status, but above all it justifies his later suspension of public criticism of the Soviets. Once certain needs are recognized, he must set aside private reservations; if the world needs Soviet action, he must support it at whatever cost to his scruples.[3]

Le Voyage intérieur occupies a pivotal position in Rolland's work. It continues the exploration of his roots in *Colas Breugnon* and the deeper study of the inner life in *L'Ame enchantée*, but it leads to metaphysical reflections which he had restrained since the *Credo quia Verum*. His religious meditations reassert his pantheism, his thoughts on art develop a vision of creativity based on the interaction of the subconscious and the will, and his views on artistic and moral discipline anticipate his political activities. The sketched chapters show he could have gone further, especially in his redefinition of the artist's role and his tragic vision of the contemporary world, but after 1926 he set the project aside, having found other ways of pursuing the same investigations. His political role intensified, leaving him little leisure for his personal quest, his tragic vision of the modern world found its home in his drama and fiction, his metaphysical reflection was canalized into his Indian biographies, and Beethoven offered a field where he could study the creative mind. These last two projects, dating from sudden changes of direction in 1927, are born of the reflections behind *Le Voyage intérieur*.

Rolland discovered Ramakrishna and Vivekananda late in 1926 and was immediately captivated. The two little-known Bengalis offered him no new revelation, but rather 'la clef d'un escalier perdu' (*VR*:20–1), striking confirmation of his own religious instincts, and his study of them, which occupied much of 1927 and 1928, stressed the universality of these instincts:

> Il y a dans leur riche pensée une multitude d'éléments divers [. . .] Une partie de ces éléments ont un caractère plus spécifiquement indien. Une autre est universelle. Et c'est celle-ci que je dois dégager. (*I*:213)

The task obliged him to be critical. He found a frustrating 'indifférence à l'exactitude scientifique' (*VR*:123) in his Indian sources, he was irritated by the nationalism and pedantry of Vivekananda's disciples and saw no reason to accept that Ramakrishna was an avatar; every man, for Rolland, carried an element of God, and he did not wish to 'enfermer Dieu entre les frontières d'un homme privilégié' (*VR*:25–6). Yet this study allowed him to elaborate his metaphysical thought in a way he had not attempted since his student days:

> Quand j'avais 20 ans, [. . .] j'avais eu la sagesse de m'interdire toute bâtisse métaphysique [. . .] jusqu'à ce que j'eusse éprouvé, en long et en large, la solidité de ses substructions [. . .] Interdiction de philosopher, en plein vent, avant les soixante ans [. . .] Et voyez! sans que j'ai en rien obéi au plan préconçu de mes 20 ans (je n'y songeais plus), – vers les soixante ans, la dernière partie du plan a commencé de se réaliser.[4]

In this, these volumes look like a continuation of *Le Voyage intérieur* by other means.

Rolland's two subjects offered contrasting challenges. Ramakrishna, a humble peasant who sustained for long periods the ecstasies which Rolland knew only in occasional 'éclairs', was an 'échelle de Jacob, par où monte et descend, du ciel au sol, le double flot ininterrompu du Divin dans l'homme' (*VR*:32). Intense ecstasy carries risks of madness and even death, but Ramakrishna attained exceptional mastery over it, and Rolland traces his steps to that mastery, which was combined with remarkable common sense (*I*:197). Ramakrishna was also a leader, showing psychological insight in his choice of disciples and pedagogical insight in tailoring his message to their needs. His aim was 'non pas de communiquer une foi précise, mais les énergies nécessaires à la foi' (*VR*:275), which coincided with Rolland's valuation of faith as force rather than doctrine.

Vivekananda was the Paul to Ramakrishna's Christ, the Beethoven to his Mozart, a man of heroic energy who gave the movement impetus and discipline, systematized its teaching, and carried the message to the West. He was closer to Rolland himself in his striving towards an impossible harmony:

> Ce corps trop puissant, ce cerveau trop vaste, étaient le champ de bataille désigné pour tous les heurts de l'âme orageuse. Le présent et le passé, l'Orient et l'Occident, le rêve et l'action, s'y livraient assaut. Il savait trop, il pouvait trop, pour consentir à une harmonie faite de renoncement à une partie de sa nature, à une partie de la vérité. (*VV*:15)

These tensions were known to Rolland, and Vivekananda was just as insistent, in resolving them, that social responsibility was paramount. No pure contemplative, Vivekananda felt responsible for the poor and weak, in accordance with Ramakrishna's dictum that 'la religion n'est pas pour les ventres vides' (*VV*:31). He brought Ramakrishna's message down from the heights of ecstasy to face the world's urgent needs.

Hinduism appealed to Rolland because of the variety of ways to God that it offered, and his subjects differed in their process of religious discovery. Ramakrishna started as a devotee of Kâlî, the universal mother, reverence for whom was rooted in the physical and human, but progressed to abstract Vedantist metaphysics which drew a sharp distinction between God and matter. Vivekananda, by contrast, started from an obsession with abstractions and came only later to Kâlî (*VV*:122). This difference reflects a dispute in medieval Vedantism about the nature of Mâyâ which illuminates the treatment of the theme in *L'Ame enchantée*. The Advaïta school of Sankara professed absolute monism; God, Brahma, is the sole reality and everything human is illusion, but the less strict school of Ramanuja reinstated the value of the human by accepting it as a manifestation of God (*VR*:75–6). Ramakrishna sought to reconcile these positions, arguing that God is Brahma in his eternal, inactive role, and Mâyâ in his active creative mode (*VR*:73). This authorizes a positive interpretation of Mâyâ, which is not, Rolland argues, 'le sens de totale Illusion, d'hallucination pure', which has misled many Westerners to think of Eastern religion as unworldly (*VV*:163). Rolland objected to Buddhism because it encouraged that error. For the Vedantist, Mâyâ is the necessarily limited raw material on which humanity, restricted by its senses, has to work. It is consistent with Western science and lets the individual seek his own truth. With Einstein in mind, Rolland calls it 'une forme intermédiaire entre l'Etre et le Non-Etre également absolus. Par conséquent, elle est le Relatif' (*VV*:165).

After striving for a vision of the absolute, then, Ramakrishna and Vivekananda chose to work within a world which may be Mâyâ, but not worthy of disdain:

> Le voyant, rejailli du gouffre en feu de *Brahman*, retrouve sur la rive, avec des transports, la Mère Divine, sa bien-aimée. Et il la voit avec des yeux nouveaux, car il reconnaît enfin son sens profond, son identité avec l'Absolu. Elle est l'Absolu qui se communique aux hommes, l'Impersonnel qui se fait homme – qui se fait femme. (*VR*:80)

Ramakrishna's devotion to Kâlî, and Rolland's pantheism, are validated. Through Kâlî, God is in the material universe, and man must seek ways of realizing his divinity within it, aspiring to the supreme moment when the last illusion falls, but resisting the temptation to withdraw from active life, just as Annette rejects Bruno's parable. In this, Vedantism provides metaphysical justification for engagement.

This revived polytheism displeased other Hindu reformers. Rolland sets his subjects in the wider context of the Indian revival, and voices of dissent could be heard; the leaders of the contemporary Brahmasamaj movement were austerely monotheistic, and Tagore objected to the cult of Kâlî: 'L'apparition de Ramakrishna et de son sonneur de conque, Vivekananda, rappellent la foule et l'élite à l'adoration et à l'amour de toutes ces formes d'idéal aux millions de visages, qu'ils espéraient avoir repoussés dans l'ombre!' (*VV*:263). For the author of *Colas Breugnon*, however, this protean embrace of the divine in man is a liberation, written into the central principles of Ramakrishna's Vedantism:

> 1e) *La Divinité de l'homme.*
> 2e) *La spiritualité essentielle de la vie.*
> Et les conséquences immédiates qui en découlent sont:
> 1e) que toute société, tout Etat, toute religion doivent être basés sur la reconnaissance de cette Toute-Puissance intime et latente de l'homme.
> 2e) que, pour être féconds, tous les intérêts humains doivent être guidés et contrôlés d'après cette idée ultime de la spiritualité de la vie. (*VV*:252)

This admits a whole range of ways to God, and the disciplined exploitation of these ways is yoga, a word much abused in the West. Vivekananda systematizes Vedantist reflection on the different kinds of yoga, and Rolland's exploration of the subject reveals much about his values.

Karmayoga, the way of work, is the yoga of the poor of whom Rolland sought to be champion:

> Celui qui écrit ces lignes et qui peut, à défaut d'autre mérite, attester son travail sans relâche de soixante ans de vie, est aussi le témoignage vivant de ces générations de travailleurs taciturnes, dont il a été l'œuvre et dont il est la voix [. . .] ce peuple muet dont la conscience inexprimée est la substance de mes pensées et commande à ma volonté. (*VV*:179)

The humble heroes of *Jean-Christophe* and his mute inglorious forefathers celebrated in *Le Voyage intérieur* were unwitting practitioners of Karma-yoga, as were the Soviet masses. The concept of Karmayoga helps to explain how Rolland could see their secular faith as a manifestation of God. Bhaktiyoga, the way of love, was Ramakrishna's way, involving 'l'acceptation d'une certaine forme de Dieu, dont il a fait son idéal choisi (ainsi, la Divine Mère, élue par Ramakrishna)' (*VR*:61). The young Ramakrishna could even see God in casually encountered human beings; this perhaps was excessive, but it gave him a remarkable power of sympathy, 'le génie d'épouser toutes les âmes du monde' (*VR*:38), which is close to Tolstoyan realism. Vivekananda preaches a more disciplined Bhaktiyoga, whereby love becomes the motive force of the universe and the devotee achieves liberation by complete sacrifice of self: 'Il a atteint le zone de l'Amour illimité et il est devenu UN avec lui. Plus de désirs, plus d'égoïsme, plus de moi, c'est le plein flamboiement de la Lumière' (*VV*:187). This is the way of Annette, who becomes a universal mother reminiscent of Kâlî.

Rajayoga, the psycho-physiological discipline familiar in the West, is for Vivekananda the prelude to Jnanayoga, and the quality it confers is concentration, the ability to harness mental energy by cutting oneself off from distractions and ordering the inner life. This recalls the discipline of 'La Ceinture', and Rolland is convinced that: 'Dans tous les pays et de tous les temps, savants, artistes, hommes d'action puissante et d'intense méditation, l'ont su et pratiqué' (*VV*:189). Rajayoga, with its imposition of will on the inner life, seemed relevant to Beethoven's creative processes.

Jnanayoga, the way of reason, is Vivekananda's way, and it harmonizes with Western science. Like Cartesian rationalism, it is based on 'une critique serrée des conditions de la connaissance', and some scientific theories have parallels in Vedantist cosmogony. Science and religion both undertake 'la recherche de l'Unité', and Jnanayoga bridges the gap between them; with its instinct for harmony, Indian thought seems poised to resolve one of the profoundest cleavages in Western culture. To do so, however, 'il fait appel, dans son organisme, à un nouvel ordre d'expérience que la science d'Occident n'a jamais admise'. This is subjective religious experience; Vedantists, convinced of man's spirituality, 'ont fini par découvrir qu'au noyau le plus intime de l'âme est le centre de tout l'univers' (*VV*:199-201), and Jnanayoga investigates religious truths at the heart of the individual. Rolland was convinced of the importance of such truths. Commenting on a thought of Lao-Tse which seemed in harmony with recent astronomical discoveries, he asserts the coincidence of man's inner laws with the laws governing the universe:

> Dire que cette connaissance des profondeurs psychiques ne nous apprend rien sur les réalités extérieures, c'est, chez un homme de science, obéir, sans s'en douter, à un préjugé d'incompréhension orgueilleuse [. . .] Il n'est pas *deux* réalités. Ce qui est inscrit dans l'un l'est également dans l'autre. Les lois de la substance psychique intérieure sont forcément celles de la réalité du dehors [. . .] Croyez-vous que jamais un Lao-Tse eût pu imaginer une telle pensée, si dans cette pensée n'étaient secrètement imprimées les formes de la Substance cosmique universelle et leurs lois ignorées? (*VV*:308)

This declaration of faith shows the same conception of the human mind as the quotation which opened this chapter.

Rolland worried that the scientific study of religion had not been properly addressed in the West, and in an appendix he criticizes Freud's failings. Freud had sent Rolland a copy of his *Die Zukunft einer Illusion* in 1927, and Rolland, objecting to Freud's dismissive comments on religion, advised him to undertake 'l'analyse du *sentiment religieux* spontané ou, plus exactement, de la *sensation* religieuse, qui est toute différente des *religions* proprement dites'. Citing his familiarity with 'le sentiment océanique' as an example, he considers religious sentiment a possible and appropriate subject for scientific investigation.[5] He criticizes Freud's attribution of such sentiments to the pleasure principle, and objects to Freud's description of religious sentiment as regression (*VV*:303, 309). Freud, in reply, denied that this term implied a value judgement,[6] and his 1930 essay, *Das Unbehagen in der Kultur*, was an answer to Rolland's comments. Rolland regretted that in this essay Freud had not been able to take account of his Indian researches; in the end, neither changed the other's mind.

Since the essence of religion is 'la vie intérieure', Vivekananda is opposed to established religion, but with the corollary that: 'Toutes les religions sont vraies – prises dans leur essence et dans la foi sincère de leurs croyants' (*VV*:186). Each faith '"*représente une portion de la Vérité universelle* [. . .]" Ils devraient donc s'ajouter les uns aux autres, et non s'exclure entre eux' (*VV*:232). The welcoming spirit with which the Ramakrishna movement approached other faiths was one of its most appealing features. Ramakrishna embraced Christianity and Islam by empathy, and Rolland contributed to the cause by tracing analogies between Eastern and Western mysticism. He explored Oriental elements in the Pre-Socratics (*VR*:78), and through the religious historian Henri Brémond he discovered a Christian mystic tradition previously unknown to him. He was particularly struck by the fourteenth-century Meister Eckhart and Ruysbroeck (*VV*:181), but in an appendix he chose to comment on Plotinus and Dionysus Areopagiticus, two earlier figures in whom Hellenic, Oriental and early Christian traditions meet.

He found many similarities in the experiences described; the main differences were that the more hierarchized Western tradition had a 'sens architectural' akin to the great cathedral builders (*VV*:332) and made more place for goodness and beauty:

> Ce point de vue est [. . .] bien différent de la Mystique hindoue, dont l'Absolu culmine au-dessus du bien et du mal. Et il communique à l'ensemble de la pensée de l'Aréopagite une sérénité, une joie tranquille et sûre, à sa vision de l'univers une calme lumière, que n'effleure aucune des ombres tragiques d'un Vivekananda. (*VV*:330)

This comparison is a reminder of the harsh side of Vedantism. As well as being universal mother, Kâlî, consort of Shiva, presides over the destruction which renews creation, and Vivekananda's vision embraces death and transformation (*VV*:125, 203). Rolland himself was not repelled by this, but the problem of accommodating it to a Christian tradition was akin to that of persuading the Western masses to adopt Gandhism.

Vivekananda resembles Empedocles in his willingness to step down from his contemplations, serve his fellow men and make love reign. Neither he nor Ramakrishna were charitable in the Western sense, but Vivekananda's concern with the Indian poor lay behind his missionary work. In this there was none of the condescension which underlies much Western charity, but a recognition that the God in man deserves respect even in the humblest:

> Si nous voyons Dieu dans le prochain, c'est que Dieu est en nous, nous le savons [. . .] Il ne nous dit pas: 'Prosternez-vous!' Il nous dit: 'Haut la tête! Car vous portez en vous le Dieu. Soyez-en digne! soyez-en fier!' (*VV*:239)

It is this linkage of metaphysics to social concern that made Vivekananda important to Rolland. In validating work for humanity, Vedanta offered a solution to the problem of dream and action, and though Rolland regretted that Vivekananda's and Gandhi's disciples did not co-operate more, he stressed their mutual esteem (*VV*:283). Rolland's final statement on the movement, a 1937 article for Ramakrishna's centenary entitled 'Jiva est Shiva', argues that in the belief that man is God, revolutionary action is validated. Soviet materialism is a faith to embrace like any other:

> Sans le savoir, ces peuples soulevés, même quand ils se croient sans Dieu ou contre Dieu, sont pourtant dans leur combat pour la Justice, dans leur montée vers la lumière, ils sont pourtant Dieu vivant. (*I*:610)

To describe Rolland's study of the Vedantists as a 'flight from social and political reality'[7] is therefore to misconstrue the thrust of a work subtitled *Essai sur la mystique et l'action de l'Inde vivante*. Mysticism becomes a basis for action, a means of defining man's relationship with a God who requires engagement in the world. Rolland did not seek to impose Vedantism as a system. Characteristically, he threw himself completely into studying it, but once it was mastered, he moved on:

> La griserie de l'esprit des Indes m'a possédé aussi longtemps que j'écrivais mes trois volumes [. . .]; j'en étais encore tout étourdi, quand quelques mots sages et discrets d'un jeune ami, Jacques Robertfrance, me réveillant, je m'aperçus que j'étais déjà sorti du songe. (*M*:236–7)

The phase which followed was dominated by active commitment, but in between the political activities of the 1930s, his study of Beethoven kept his inward-looking side alive.

Music since 1914 had played a diminishing part in Rolland's work. He often abandoned the piano at times of distress, and there was little live music in Villeneuve. In the 1920s he spent part of his holidays visiting music centres in Salzburg, Prague, the Rhineland and Vienna, and after 1929 the radio gave him access to broadcast music, but he did no musicological work between 1912 and 1927, when he was invited to contribute to the Beethoven centenary celebrations in Vienna. Unusually for him, he agreed to give a lecture, largely to react against political exploitation of the occasion,[8] and planned further articles. These grew into a major study, on which he worked in phases for the rest of his life, alongside other things. Sometimes he felt guilty about the effort it absorbed:

> Je m'opiniâtre, malgré tout, (Dieu sait pourquoi!) dans un travail d'excavations et de filtrage psycho-physiologico-musical, comme je n'en ai jamais fait d'aussi

acharné et aussi minutieuse [. . .] A qui, à quoi cela peut-il bien être bon, dans un pareil temps de catastrophes?[9]

Thus he wrote in the troubled times of 1937, but he had answered this question in 1934: 'C'est un travail d'éclaircissement essentiel, – en quelque sorte, testamentaire, – qui peut me servir à mieux comprendre le sens de ma vie'.[10] Rolland explored his own creative personality through Beethoven's, and from the start he saw religious significance in his project: 'Aucune religion du monde [. . .] n'a eu sur moi le dixième de l'influence et du bienfait de cet homme libre, Beethoven'.[11]

Rolland's approach is implied in the subtitle, *Les Grandes Epoques créatrices*. These 'époques' are five in number, but Rolland does not cover them all. Leaping over the early years, still relatively little known, he devotes his first volume, *De l'Héroïque à l'Appassionata*, to the Third Symphony, the early piano sonatas and *Fidelio*. These works reflect the French Revolution, and Rolland's study, dating from 1927, follows closely on his Revolutionary dramas. *Goethe et Beethoven*, written in 1929, is a digression exploring the two men's uneasy relationship. Rolland omits the middle period of Beethoven's career, between the Fourth and Eighth Symphonies, and in *Le Chant de la résurrection*, written intermittently in the mid-1930s, he concentrates on the years of faltering inspiration leading to the triumph of the last piano sonatas and the *Missa Solemnis*. This period echoes Christophe's crisis in *Le Buisson ardent*, and Rolland felt he had more to say about it than any other (*B*:428). It may be significant that he himself was in a fallow period between major works at the time. During the Occupation, he returned to the Ninth Symphony and the last quartets. Circumstances were difficult, he had limited access to recent scholarship and he was disappointed with his study of the Ninth Symphony, but the bulk of the work was finished late in 1941. The title of this study, *La Cathédrale interrompue*, reflects both the religious character of the music and Rolland's view that Beethoven's premature death had deprived the world of important projects.

Part of Rolland's agenda was to correct the oversimplifications of his earlier biography. He shows much concern with the interaction of Beethoven's art and life, and more sense of the complexity of the man than in the previous volume. Sounding a note often heard in his late works, he stresses the need to harmonize the multiple personalities present in all men, especially the greatest:

Tout grand artiste [. . .] est plus qu'un homme individuel. Il est plusieurs personnalités associés, pas toujours harmonisés, réalisant côte à côte leur essence. En cela, d'ailleurs, l'artiste ne se distingue des autres hommes que par son pouvoir d'expression. (*B*:489–90)

Critics often err by seizing on one of these personalities at the expense of others, and to avoid this Rolland adopts a free approach, using biographical material less to produce a linear narrative than to explore themes which illuminate his subject's creativity. This parallels the unstructured self-exploration of *Le Voyage intérieur*. Some of the biographical material has little relevance to the music. Rolland describes the last months of Beethoven's life simply in order to follow his old friend to the grave, and the novelist in Rolland focuses on some significant secondary characters: Schindler the amanuensis, the much-maligned nephew Karl and several women, especially Bettina Brentano, the link with Goethe, and the two Theresas, von Brunsvik and Malfatti, either of whom could have been the recipient of the famous love letter to the 'unsterbliche Geliebte', whose enigma Rolland tries lengthily, but unsuccessfully, to solve.

The longest digression concerns Goethe. The two men's one unsuccessful meeting seems scant material for a volume, but Rolland was fascinated by their failure to communicate despite Beethoven's admiration for Goethe and Goethe's sensitivity to music which, Rolland shows, was greater than often supposed. He concludes that Goethe, who had difficulty in achieving serenity, was afraid of the passions unleashed by Beethoven and not musician enough to recognize that Beethoven could control them. He therefore closed his mind to Beethoven, not an admirable response but a necessary act of self-preservation:

De Beethoven le Dionysos exalté et souvent chancelant, et de Goethe l'Olympien, c'est Goethe qui recelait la plus de faiblesse morale. Mais la force de l'esprit est de connaître sa faiblesse et de fixer les limites de son empire intérieur. (*B*:328)

Rolland could not but have been struck by the discrepancy between Goethe's timid response to Beethoven and the boldness of his principle of 'Stirb und Werde!' Rolland's ultimate preference for Beethoven helps to explain why he could never take refuge in the works of Raphaelesque serenity he longed to write; his was the road of dangerous passionate commitment.

In exploring the links between Beethoven and his age, Rolland returns to the concerns of his early musicology. As in his thesis, he argues that '[les] mouvements de la sensibilité d'un temps sont les précurseurs des grands événements de l'histoire' (*B*:430). Rolland was fascinated by the way Beethoven reflected the Revolutionary era, exploring his political views through his conversation books and examining his use of French Revolutionary music, which, he decides, influenced Beethoven in many ways. More fundamentally, Rolland attempts a deeper exploration of how a creative mind recaptures the essence of an age and, through it, universal laws. Beethoven achieves this through sonata form, the dialectic development of contrasting themes and tonalities:

> Tout, à ses yeux, se réduisait à une dualité de nature:- le masculin et le féminin, – le '*widerstrebende*' et le '*bittende*', – ce dialogue dramatique, qui anime la plupart de ses œuvres et qui répond à un antagonisme intérieur [. . .] C'est par là qu'il fut le héros représentatif de tout un âge de l'humanité. Et si cet âge, comme tous les âges, a passé, il en survit, comme de tous les âges, éternellement, des types qui sont de toutes les races, de toutes les classes, et qui se retrouvent éternellement en lui. (*B*:599)

Beethoven's sonata form marks a triumph of self over self which reflects the Revolutionary age, and also an elite which has survived its passing; for Rolland, who spent so much effort trying to assemble an elite, Beethoven becomes a rallying point. Beethoven did not invent sonata form; his achievement was to give it discipline: 'Il réalisa la perfection classique de cette forme d'art et de pensée: car le dualisme de ses principes, leur antagonisme fécond et leur synthèse, c'est la nature même de Beethoven' (*B*:431). Beethoven represents the moment of classical equilibrium at which the form becomes the perfect vehicle for a thought characteristic of an age.

Its essence lies in 'un combat Herculéen entre l'âme et le Destin' (*B*:1376), a central problem for Rolland as well as for Beethoven. Triggered by deafness, this theme pervades Beethoven's sonata movements; the contrast of a stern, demanding first subject with a gentler, pleading second subject reflects the individual's struggles against the imperatives of fate. Yet the destiny expressed in the first subject, like the God of 'Le Royaume du T', is no outside force, but part of Beethoven himself. The great adagio of the Piano Sonata Op.106 is interpreted as 'le colloque entre le Destin, ou entre cette partie de l'âme qui le reconnaît et l'accepte, – et l'autre partie, qui souffre, se plaint, se révolte, et qui finit par être brisé, ou qui s'incline religieusement' (*B*:630). With destiny identified as part of the self, the two contending elements relate to Rolland's vision of a self composed of an individual role and a 'Moi cosmique', and acceptance of destiny therefore becomes a triumph of the self; the first movement of the Ninth Symphony is compared to the conflict of Jacob and the angel, in which the human confronts the divine and triumphs in defeat (*B*:893). Beethoven's music teaches 'la résignation héroïque, la paix dans la souffrance, le renoncement d'Hercule sur le bûcher, – qui, par l'acceptation, s'élève au-dessus de son destin' (*B*:1378).

This 'mariage mystique avec le Destin' (*B*:1379) has religious significance. Though no orthodox churchman, Beethoven had a personal faith; his *Missa Solemnis* is a work of 'profonde sincérité religieuse' (*B*:672), and like his fictional double Christophe, he is a 'porteur de Dieu' (*B*:1391). His role, however, is complex:

> D'une part, il magnifie la Personne humaine, – je ne dis pas l'individu, mais l'âme essentielle et son royaume des airs, son '*Reich in der Luft*'. De l'autre, il a célébré la collectivité humaine, solidement implantée dans la terre, et les vastes espoirs promis à la fraternité de tous les peuples unis en Dieu. (*B*:869)

Parts of the *Missa Solemnis*, the last piano sonatas and especially the last quartets represent 'l'âme seule avec son Dieu' (*B*:868); they achieve moments of great serenity, especially the adagios of the Sonata Op.111 and the Quartet Op.132. Yet the absence of a full close at the end of the *Missa Solemnis* and the third movement of the Ninth Symphony suggests unresolved problems, to which the answer is the triumphant finale of the Ninth Symphony, defended by Rolland against purist opinion as a satisfactory conclusion to a unified work. Here, joy and fraternity prevail; by drawing mankind into a universal embrace before God, Beethoven succeeds in creating joy from grief. This involves no concession to a lowest common denominator of public taste; it is the transmission of a divine message in which suffering is offered as a eucharistic sacrifice:

> A l'image – très humble – du Dieu qui est en lui, il offre aux autres son propre sacrifice. Sa musique est une sorte d''*Abendmahl*', une Cène, où l'âme crucifiée, qui va ressusciter, se donne en pâture aux hommes, dans sa souffrance rachetée. (*B*:1389)

As in *L'Ame enchantée*, but in a form appropriate to the artist, sacrifice is the lot of the God-bearer.

This cannot be achieved without discipline. Beethoven releases unprecedented passions, but in ordered form: 'Le plus frappant n'est point l'énormité des armées, les flots sonores, les masses qui se lancent à l'assaut, – c'est l'esprit qui commande la raison impériale' (*B*:21). The dialectic of individual and will is paralleled, in aesthetic terms, by that of the natural origins of inspiration and the mind controlling them.

Beethoven's music is rooted in nature. Rolland sensed this from his first hearing of the Sixth Symphony, the Pastoral, and the Seventh, which he saw as 'la Symphonie de la forêt'. This is not just a matter of fields and trees; 'c'était l'Esprit qui les étreint, l'Esprit de la Terre, [. . .] celui qui ne fait qu'un avec la Vie universelle' (*B*:1348–9). Again, the laws governing the individual harmonize with those governing the universe: 'On ne voit pas de quoi serait faite l'étoffe des rêves de Beethoven, si elle n'était de l'étoffe même de cet univers, avec lequel nous faisons corps' (*B*:433). The source of his inspiration is his subconscious mind, and his work is drawn out of it by virtue of 'une violence de concentration inouïe' (*B*:1349). Rolland constantly asserts the power of Beethoven's mind; though no master of words, Beethoven had literary taste, political awareness and critical acumen, and his capacity for mental absorption recalls the disciplines of Rajayoga (*B*:1501). Rolland finds medical evidence to suggest that his deafness was caused by the excessive concentration against which Ramakrishna warned (*B*:224–6).

Above all, Beethoven's art is the triumph of will, the force that inspires his stern first subjects. The will commands the mind, and his work is born of the creative tension between subconscious and will:

> La volonté, qui, chez les artistes du second ordre, a un caractère de raison tiède et appliquée, est toujours chez Beethoven brûlante de génie, autant et plus encore que l'inspiration première. Car [. . .] le propre de ce génie étant dans son subconscient, il ne se connaît pas lui-même avant de se découvrir; et il se découvre, à chaque coup de pic dans le rocher, qui fait sauter les rudes éclats de l'enveloppe de pierre, – à chaque coup de bêche dans le limon qui engaîne l'idée, – il se déterre, à la sueur de son front. L'obscur et puissant instinct sait où il doit aller. L'esprit a repéré la direction du tunnel à creuser. (*B*:58–9)

In a footnote to this passage, Rolland promises a chapter devoted to 'l'analyse des lois qui semblent commander ce subconscient créateur'. He never wrote it, but it would probably have stressed again the identity of inner and outer laws.

The disciplined forms of Beethoven's art, his inner promptings and universal laws are all forged into a harmony, but it is not easily achieved:

> Le meilleur de Beethoven est enfoui, scellé au fond d'un sol dur et pierreux; il doit difficilement l'en déterrer. La puissante énergie Beethovenienne, qui est, pour nous, la caractéristique de son art, se dépense en partie à l'extraire de la mine. (*B*:600)

Beethoven had to labour to transform the promptings of his subconscious into finished works, and the process can be followed in his sketchbooks. Through them Rolland traces the origins of Beethoven's themes, and he finds that they often emerge in an atmosphere very different from their final form. Rolland first adopted this approach in his work on Handel; the two composers could both spend years on a theme before getting it right:

> Ce n'est qu'au terme de toute une vie que Haendel et Beethoven, en certains cas, découvrent le mot magique et donnent enfin à la phrase le coup de pouce, l'accent qui illumine la forme définitive. (*B*:76–7)

This happened with the finale of the *Eroica*, whose theme appeared in three works before achieving its final form, and especially the Sonata Op.106, the work in which Beethoven conquered his period of sterility, whose genesis reflects a prolonged uncertainty which Rolland traces in detail. The artistic labour involved is primarily a matter of simplification; 'immer simpler' is Beethoven's motto, and simplicity must be worked for, 'en la dégageant par un travail acharné de la banalité et du mensonge' (*B*:544). The result is a style in which no note is wasted, no artifice obstructs the emerging idea; Beethoven is a popular composer in the best sense, defined years ago in Rolland's thesis, speaking directly to his audience without concession.

Another Beethovenian ideal is unity. It appears in varying contexts: 'l'équilibre absolu de l'idée et de la forme' in the *Appassionata* (*B*:142), the ambitious harmony of words and music which the Credo of the *Missa Solemnis* does not quite achieve (*B*:695), the remarkable stylistic unity of the last quartets, 'fait des éléments les plus hétéroclites' (*B*:1203). Rolland's awareness of it goes back to his lessons with Breuilpont, and his attempts to define it were aided by the scholarship of Heinrich Schenker, who interpreted Beethoven's music in terms of an 'Urlinie'. This, Rolland insists, does not mean a simple musical theme; it lies rather in 'ce rythme, ces lois en quelque sorte élémentaires, qui commandent son esprit créateur, qui sont l'essence même de son être' (*B*:435). It exists at the level where Beethoven's inner world blends with musical forms, and the unity it reflects is that of structure and the subconscious. Rolland pays generous tribute to what Schenker's approach can achieve:

> Il advient qu'un grand critique [discerne ces lois] plus nettement que le grand créateur. Car nous ne connaissons pas le son de notre voix, comme l'entend l'oreille des autres hommes [. . .] Elle n'acquiert sa réalité objective que dans les autres qui nous écoutent. (*B*:436)

Rolland, however, is not a critic, but a creator. Some things, like the unity of the Ninth Symphony, cannot be understood by critics with no feeling for the creative process (*B*:941), and Schenker is one of a school of formalists who concentrate on exposing musical mechanisms without trying to interpret their meaning. Rolland constantly battles against this approach, which can never reveal more than part of music's secrets. When Schenker declares that the climax of the adagio of the Ninth Symphony is '*rien de plus* [Rolland's italics] que le passage à la sous-dominante, habituel dans les cadences', Rolland reacts sharply:

> Je le veux bien. Mais comment Beethoven opère cette '*Wendung*', et sous quelle soudaine irruption d'un flot de violence, qui l'envahit, le scrupuleux analyste des formes ne se l'est même pas demandé [. . .] Rien de plus, vraiment, que, dans la paix d'un beau jour d'été, un coup de tonnerre, – que, dans la douceur du paradis, l'apparition d'un Jéhovah, couronné de foudres!
>
> [. . .] Je devais mettre en lumière, par un exemple aussi frappant, l'insuffisance d'une analyse purement technique des formes, que ne vivifie pas l'analyse parallèle des démarches de l'âme. (*B*:920–1)

Rolland therefore offers his parallel analysis of the soul, based on personal experience of the creative process, as well as his historian's experience of interpreting works in terms of their age and using documentary evidence to solve biographical problems. Thus he fulfils his student ambition of uniting intuition with historiography.

The 'débat tragique' which underlies Beethoven's work is 'provoqué par telles circonstances précises de sa vie' (*B*:438). In each composition, the form the debate takes is influenced by biographical factors, which Rolland seeks to recapture. The scherzo of Op.106 is attributed to happy days in the country (*B*:614), aspects of the *Missa Solemnis* and the Sonata Op.110 reflect a change of mood brought about by illness, and the well-attested influence of illness on the Quartet Op.132 leads Rolland to justify his approach:

> Qu'on ne nous dise pas que toutes ces variations de l'humeur de Beethoven n'intéressent pas l'étude de son œuvre. Je sais fort bien que le génie de Beethoven était parvenu à un tel degré de concentration qu'il était, dans sa création, presque totalement détaché des événements extérieurs de sa vie. Mais il ne pouvait l'être de ses dispositions intérieures; joie ou tristesse, santé ou maladie: et il est impossible qu'on n'en retrouve pas les lumières et les ombres dans les pages qu'il écrit. (*B*:1114)

Rolland knew that care was needed in this area, and sought to avoid over-close connections between specific incidents and specific passages. He also argued against other types of over-interpretation. Beethoven was no philosopher, and Wagner was wrong to interpret the Quartet Op.131 in terms of his own 'élucubrations Schopenhauerisantes' (*B*:1201); equally Otto Baensch was wrong to impose Schelling's theosophy on the Ninth Symphony. The intellectual and emotional pattern suggested by Schelling, 'désespoir, illusion, espoir religieux [qui] s'élève à l'harmonie de l'âme réconciliée avec le destin', corresponded closely to that of the symphony, but was common enough for both men to have arrived at it independently (*B*:1018–19). Beethoven expressed emotions rather than philosophical speculations, and Rolland aims to recapture them by all means available: musical analysis, documentary study and creative intuition.

Intuition can lead Rolland into the kind of over-interpretation he seeks to avoid; the slow movement of the Quartet Op.127, for instance, is claimed to represent religious ecstasy during a starry night:

> Je vois l'homme agenouillé, dans la nuit, et, là-haut, sur les notes aiguës du premier violon, scintillent les étoiles. Ce n'est pas une image, c'est une intuition directe, j'en ai la certitude: la langue de Beethoven est transparente à ceux pour qui, depuis l'enfance, c'est la langue maternelle. (*B*:1092)

This is an extreme example of his faith in the expressive power of musical language, but even in more cautious passages he justifies literary play. After evoking Beethoven's late works as a cathedral of which they form the parts, he declares:

> Pourquoi serait-il interdit à l'écrivain de jouer – de *fantasieren* sur le beau thème qu'il s'est efforcé de comprendre et de commenter, avec application et avec amour, – l'œuvre-compagne, aux côtés de laquelle il a fait route, pendant un demi-siècle de vie! (*B*:664)

The result is a remarkable combination of musicology and creativity, a labour of love as much as science, for Rolland insists that intellectual understanding is no obstacle to loving music. Much of it was written at difficult times, and he undoubtedly found its composition therapeutic, but it would be wrong to dismiss it as escapism. Beethoven was an artist who faced problems similar to Rolland's, often more successfully, and in exploring his mind, Rolland was still pursuing a quest for self-understanding. In Christophe he had found an imaginary figure in whom he could write about both Beethoven and himself; now he has internalized Beethoven's music to such a degree that he needs no intermediary.

Above all, Beethoven's achievement has implications in action. Like the Christian mystics whom Rolland contrasts with Vivekananda, Beethoven is concerned with the link between beauty and goodness; 'das Schöne zum Guten' is one of his mottoes, and his passion for unity is 'un trait de caractère moral et musical à la fois' (*B*:685). The artistic discipline in his works has implications going beyond art:

> Le grand artiste qui est, comme Beethoven, un homme au grand cœur, ne sacrifie pas son art à son cœur; et son combat se livre sur un double plan: sur le plan moral, pour tous les hommes, – sur le plan constructif de son rêve musical, de l'Idée [. . .], pour l'élite de ses compagnons dans son art [. . .] La lutte acharnée de l'artiste, pour fondre en une harmonieuse unité les éléments chaotiques, correspond à l'assaut toujours renouvelé que livre la volonté morale aux passions aveugles, pour s'en rendre maître, et les faire concourir à son '*accomplissement*'. Beethoven l'homme est identique à Beethoven le créateur. Et l'un vaut l'autre, car l'un est l'autre. (*B*:1380)

This is an important declaration of faith. The artistic dialectic between the subconscious and the will reflects the moral dialectic by which all are called to master their passions. In this, Beethoven's art reflects the quest for discipline in action expressed in 'La Ceinture', and his artistic success is a moral triumph whose benefit Rolland and many others have personally experienced: 'Je pense que des milliers d'humbles gens, dans tous les pays, lui doivent, comme moi, d'avoir gardé les sources pures de leur vie' (*B*:1391). Beethoven's artistic discipline has transformed the force he releases into a moral force, which has implications for action on both the private and public level. In this respect, the artist's inward-looking and outward-looking role are united. Beethoven has found another solution to the problem of combining dream and action.

Notes

1. See Duret (1992), p.762.
2. Letter to L. Cruppi, 16 July 1924.
3. For the importance of this passage see Duret (1992), pp.792–6.
4. Letter to J-R. Bloch, Easter 1929.
5. Letter to Freud, 5 December 1927. Quoted in Vermorel (1993), p.304.
6. See Vermorel (1993), p.313.

7. Fisher (1988), p.138.
8. See letter to J-R. Bloch, 19 December 1926.
9. Letter to J-R. Bloch, 2 February 1937.
10. Letter to E. Marchand, 26 March 1934.
11. Letter to J-R. Bloch, 7 March 1927.

–13–

Vézelay

Rolland was optimistic as he moved to Vézelay: 'J'ai l'impression que, moralement, je suis en train de remonter sur ma bête [. . .] Il est possible que d'ici à un an (le temps que l'esprit soit acclimaté), j'entamerais une nouvelle route de travaux'.[1] His last seven years did indeed prove remarkably productive; by offering him a place he could at last call home, Vézelay stimulated a final flowering of his career. Unlike most towns where he had house-hunted, Vézelay, with its long religious history, was not dominated by the Popular Front. The clerical right was also strong, partisan spirits ran high, and Rolland joked of writing a 'roman burlesque sur Vézelay'.[2] His choice was determined by the house and its view of rolling hills and valleys, but he was probably more attuned to this centre of French faith than he would have been to a town where the authorities would have regarded him as a trophy.

Vézelay was not always comfortable. During the Munich crisis petitions were circulated to have him expelled, and he felt he was being boycotted.[3] Gradually, however, the town was won over, not least because of Marie, who turned herself into an efficient French housewife, supporting local charities, slaving in the garden and, in the war, cultivating the local peasantry in the ceaseless quest for supplies. 'La Guerre a eu beaucoup de bon pour nous; elle nous a mis en rapports intimes avec quantité de gens de la région, qu'autrement nous n'aurions jamais connus,' Rolland remarked in 1942.[4] As soon as he moved in, he felt at home, commenting to his amazed sister:

> Ce qui m'est un sentiment nouveau, et dont je ne puis dissimuler le contentement, c'est de trouver tant de ces petites gens, qui ont pour moi une affection et un respect, dont je ne m'étais jamais douté [. . .] Peut-être [les ouvriers et les paysans] m'ont-ils à peine lu. Mais je suis pour eux quelqu'un qui est leur ami, qui l'a prouvé, qui a été outragé et persécuté pour cela [. . .] Il est humain de se laisser toucher par cette affection qu'on sent sincère.[5]

Popular Front lionization had trickled down into the populace, and Rolland could at last enjoy some solidarity with his compatriots. In the months before the war, the world beat a path to his rather remote door, as in Villeneuve; his guests ranged from Maurice Thorez to Queen Elizabeth of Belgium, who admired his works on music. Vézelay itself was the home of a number of literary figures, notably Henri Petit, a correspondent of Rolland for some years and now a valued neighbour. Among new friends in the local community, Lucien Bouillé, a music teacher from Migennes, and his wife Viviane deserve special mention. Rolland enjoyed the company of this curiously old-fashioned but closely united young couple who could always be counted on for support.

Part of the reason for Rolland's move was financial. Marie often bemoaned his lack of business sense, but it would be truer to say that he had disdained to make himself rich. His income declined during the depression, Switzerland was expensive, his new house was at the upper end of what he could afford and henceforth he was never free of financial worry. In 1938 he worked on two minor commissions related to his work on Robespierre which previously he probably would not have accepted. For a series of publications for young people he wrote an account of the battle of Valmy, on which he had once considered a play, but he did not take to the genre: 'Il est bien, mais pas du tout pour enfants. Je ne sais pas "l'art d'être grand-père"'.[6] More importantly, he wrote an introduction to a Rousseau anthology for an American publisher. As well as being an apostle of freedom, a precursor of the Revolution and an influence on Tolstoy, Rousseau's visionary qualities related him to the mystics Rolland had studied, and Rolland could sympathize with the persecutions suffered by this chronically sick man whose crime was to speak out too forcefully. He was struck by the diversity of Rousseau's art and the musicianly skill with which he welded the different men within him into a harmony; Rousseau combined the rigour of an 'esprit classique' with 'un relativisme tout moderne' (*JJR*:36). Rolland planned a larger study, and was annoyed when his publisher pre-empted it by allowing his text to appear in France. The result was a poor substitute for the money-spinner he hoped would come from America, a film of *Jean-Christophe*. Several times the idea was mooted, but nothing ever came of it.

Through 1939 and 1940, Rolland worked on his *Mémoires*, the narrative autobiography that *Le Voyage intérieur* did not claim to be; he aimed to carry it to 1914, but stopped at the difficult period of his divorce. As well as drawing on his memory for it, he made extensive quotations from his diaries and notes in an attempt to give his younger self a distinctive voice alongside his narratorial self. Drawing on the observations that it had always been his habit to record, he devotes much space to portraits. Teachers, friends, politicians and socialites are recalled, giving an impression of the world he moved in as well as the inner world which was the focus of *Le Voyage intérieur*.

The most striking feature of this work is its conciliatory tone; the satirist has disappeared, the humour is indulgent and affectionate. He pays generous tribute to teachers who had irritated him, and the world of the 1890s which had inspired *La Foire sur la place* is treated with a detached amusement akin to his student reaction to Rome. Hébert of the Villa Medicis and Jules Lemaître, for instance, are portrayed much more warmly than his contemporary reaction would suggest (*M*:89, 273), and Clotilde is treated with nothing but kindness. Part of this springs from his publishing plans; though it proved impossible in the Occupation, Rolland had thoughts of publishing in his lifetime, and he did not wish to use this text to revive old vendettas. Even allowing for this, the work's tone reflects an appealing mellowness of old age.

The only person on whom he is harsh is himself. His late writings often dwell on the diversity of the human personality; several men live within the same man, and 'quand on relit, quarante ans après, le *Journal* secret de sa jeunesse, on est souvent bien étonné' (*M*:185). Rolland did not much like what he saw in this forgotten self. Surveying his student years and the 1890s, when he was constantly at odds with his environment, he was conscious of his youthful rawness:

> Il était sans doute naturel que je me trouvasse en désaccord sur beaucoup de pensées et sur ce que je faisais et voulais faire, avec ceux qui m'entouraient. Mais ce désaccord ne justifiait pas l'hostilité et l'amertume que je remâche au fond de ces notes. Je manquais trop de patience, de calme, de large et clairvoyante humanité. (*M*:187)

In the ensuing narrative he has many errors to confess; he was 'injuste envers Paris' (*M*:127), wrong to disdain teaching (*M*:114), altogether too much of a dreamer (*M*:192). More than at the time of writing his novel, he admits that he himself was Christophe in his least tolerant aspects, and confesses that it was often luck, or rather destiny, that had saved him: 'Mon seul mérite est, quand l'étoile passe, de n'avoir jamais hésité à la saisir par ses crins' (*M*:117). Rolland has not forgotten the *Credo quia Verum*; he had his role to play, and without these youthful excesses he could not have played it, but now his concern is to harmonize his various selves which in youth formed merely an 'association anarchique' (*M*:102). In this, the greatest challenge was his oscillation between Catholicism and socialism. Reacting against Beaunier's uncomfortably telling portrayal of him as a 'Don Juan des idées', he insists that he sincerely espouses each in turn, then moves on, denying nothing but pursuing an overriding search for truth which makes him seek to penetrate the constantly renewed veils of Mâyâ:

> L'on doit voir en ces noces successives de l'âme avec les 'fois' [. . .], une suite d'expériences, honnêtement tentées dans la recherche de la vérité, et qui, de l'une à l'autre, mènent un peu plus près de celle qui nous fuit et nous appelle, laissant sur le chemin quelques lambeaux de ses voiles, que, l'un après l'autre, nous lui arrachons. (*M*:238)

Recalling Gandhi's vision of life as a series of experiments with truth, Rolland uses the imagery of *L'Ame enchantée* to create a harmonized vision of his younger self. In this spirit he can contemplate his youthful battles with serenity.

Paradoxical as it may seem, this serenity was to some extent enhanced by the war. By ruling out political action, it freed him to cultivate his dream world without distraction, to be more completely 'au-dessus de la mêlée' than in 1914:

> Qu'il me soit donc permis, au terme de ma vie, de rentrer au sein de ce Songe universel, qui est la plus réelle des réalités, et d'en goûter par avance l'auguste paix! Je me détache enfin des agitations fiévreuses de la fourmilière, dont je fis partie; j'en ai gagné le droit, car j'y ai payé largement mon tribut. (*VI*:297)

This conclusion to 'Le Périple' is admittedly rather forced. The war he had fought so long to prevent left him with a feeling of failure and depression, and he knew many bad days; many of his letters express a sense of having lived too long. Yet work was his salvation. He read voraciously, renewing his acquaintance with the greatest writers; the autobiographies of Stendhal and Chateaubriand were his companions in 1939, as he drafted his own memoirs. He abandoned political rhetoric and concentrated on the artist's inward-looking role, giving a new priority to the quest for religious truth through the exploration of the creative personality.

Rolland could not count on official favour. Daladier appreciated his support, and by March 1940 he felt that he was 'en faveur auprès de ceux qui comptent dans les lettres et au gouvernement',[7] but he was watched by the local police, and since mail was censored his letters were circumspect. His daily correspondence with Madeleine, who spent the Occupation in Dijon, is a rich source of information on these years, but it treats current affairs only obliquely, if at all. Travel was restricted, but he did visit Paris in March 1940 and rented a *pied-à-terre* in his old Montparnasse haunts. He still held the lease at Villeneuve, and in May of that year he obtained a visa to go there, to consult his doctors and complete his move. Events overtook him, however; the German invasion sent him hurrying back to Vézelay, abandoning many books and papers. This time there would be no prolonging of a chance stay in Switzerland.

As the invasion and civilian exodus rolled chaotically by, Rolland seems to have kept calmer than those around him. He had contingency plans to flee to the south-west, but he resisted pressure to move and was trapped when the Germans arrived sooner than expected.[8] Beethoven, however, brought him solace:

> Dans ma tête lasse et martelée par le ronflement ininterrompu des cavaleries motorisées, sous la menace de l'ennemi, surgit (d'où? et pourquoi?) le beau chant, l'*adagio* du *Concerto en mi bémol*. Trois jours, trois nuits, il a chanté, il m'habita. Sur les ruines du monde, il planait, pur et serein: dans les ténèbres fiévreuses de l'esprit, il était comme, à travers les nuées, l'œil du ciel bleu. Je me suis demandé, par la suite, si dans de telles heures tragiques son regard n'avait point visité le cerveau de Beethoven, que martelaient le bruit des canons et l'oppression de la soldatesque de Napoléon. (*B*:1343)

Beethoven had written this serene music during Napoleon's attack on Vienna, and the knowledge helped Rolland to remain true to the spirit of the 1926 'éclair' and entrust himself to destiny:

> Ces peuples qui fuient, ces peuples à leur chasse, sont les instruments d'un '*Führer*' bien autrement puissant que celui d'en bas. Par-dessus les entrechocs des nations, les massacres, les délires furieux, la main souveraine de la Destinée et ses grandes lois mènent l'humanité à ses fins. (*VI*:296–7)

This was partly no doubt the stubbornness of an old man half detached from life, but his decision to face an enemy he had reason to fear suggests he did not lack courage. In the event, he was not greatly harassed. Life was unpleasant, with constant surveillance and shortages, but although some of his political texts were pulped, the Germans preferred to view him as the author of *Jean-Christophe* rather than the anti-Nazi. Recognizing that that work could be used in their favour, they tried to persuade him to authorize a censored edition, which he declined just as firmly as he declined a Swedish offer, later in the war, to produce an edition purged of anti-Jewish elements. Provided he did nothing to embarrass them, the Germans happily left him alone. When he and Marie burned compromising papers, they were merely warned not to attract attention with the smoke, and he was even visited by a high-ranking officer checking that all was well with him. Marie discovered after the war that it was General Speidel, later Rommel's chief of staff.

Rolland's attitude to the occupiers was consistent with his 1914 wish to see war conducted humanely and to avoid public association with the enemy. He saw no reason for the mute resistance made famous by Vercors's *Silence de la mer*; he considered that one of Madeleine's friends' refusal to attend a concert performed by Germans was needless purism[9] and he criticized the Vézelay authorities for rejecting German offers to finance public works which the French government was unlikely to match.[10] He received German officers who showed genuine interest in his writings, and apart from occasional domestic complaints he spoke quite well of the young soldiers billeted on him: 'Ils ont été extrêmement corrects et courtois, durant tout leur séjour; ils étaient eux-mêmes très toucheés qu'on fût humain pour eux'.[11] His brief letter late in the war to a naval captain, Wolfgang von Tirpitz, coolly postponing a meeting until after hostilities ceased, is less typical than its position in the centenary Cahier suggests (*C17*:378).[12]

Rolland's dealings with Gorky, Louise Cruppi and Heinz Haeberlin showed that he had never hesitated to exploit influential connections, both in others' interests and his own. During 1941 he had several meetings with Rolf Greve, a Nevers-based officer with responsibility for inter-zonal affairs who admired his work and offered hopes of helping him and Madeleine complete their move from Switzerland. Maugendre hints that this might be considered compromising (*C30*:20), but that would surely be the case only if Rolland had offered something in return, which he was careful to avoid. Practised at maintaining his independence, he declined Greve's invitation to a public reading of his works in Nevers, plausibly pleading ill-health, as he was to do on other occasions during the Occupation.[13] In the event Greve was posted elsewhere and nothing came of the move.

By 1942, the occupiers had more or less withdrawn from Vézelay. Resistance activity was increasing, but there is little trace of it in Rolland's letters. He probably had wind of clandestine activities; Vildrac, a frequent visitor, would have been in a position to give him some information, and one of his first correspondences to appear posthumously was with a young communist Resistance fighter, Elie Wallach. Most of it, however, predates the war and it offers no evidence of involvement with the Resistance. One senses that it was published to give him Resistance credentials, but if that was the only written evidence Marie could muster in 1947, it does not amount to much. In one 1943 letter there is a hint that he was opposed to acts of sabotage. Referring to an event in Auxerre which led to the imposition of a curfew, he comments:

> Ces attentats sont déplorables. Ils frappent presque toujours les innocents et ils amènent des représailles contre des innocents. Les coupables trouvent toujours moyen de décamper, et pour la plupart, sinon toujours, ce sont des gens d'un autre pays.[14]

It is not clear whether the allusion is indeed to a Resistance attack, but it suggests a wariness of activities likely to cause needless suffering while doing little to win the war. His attitude can be compared to his opposition to the use of gas in 1918; it was always worth opposing things which made war worse than it need be.

He certainly disapproved of collaboration; he passed scathing comments on local tradesmen, super-patriots before the war, who now touted for German custom.[15] In general he is more critical of his compatriots than of the Germans. Apart from a few admirable flickerings such as the 'suicide héroïque' of the French fleet at Toulon,[16] he found little to praise in a demoralized nation collapsing into petty vindictiveness. He was depressed by a series of denunciations in Vézelay in which the pro-Vichy parish priest was supposedly involved: 'L'atmosphère morale est empoisonnée dans ces misérables pays. Les vengeances, les haines, surtout les jalousies et les envies particulières se substituent aux passions publiques'.[17] Rolland himself was at one point summoned to Auxerre following a denunciation (*LB*:166); he faced more hostility from Frenchmen than from the occupiers, and a press attack by Maurice Wullens led him to reflect: 'On peut juger de ce qui nous attendait, si le pouvoir eût été aux mains, non des Allemands, mais de ces *arrabbiati* français!'[18] He had little good to say of Vichy; it was Vichy, not the Germans, who banned *Jean-Christophe* in schools. He was, however, on good terms with Maurice Brulfer, the pro-German mayor of Clamecy whose ambitious reconstruction plans upset older Clamecyçois,[19] and above all he had the support of Châteaubriant.

After 1939, when Châteaubriant found a country retreat in Burgundy, his contacts with Rolland became more frequent, and as editor of the pro-German *La Gerbe*, he was in an influential position. He appealed to Goebbels to let Rolland reside in Paris, personally guaranteeing Rolland's neutrality (*C30*:20), he persuaded Darlan to overrule the schools ban on *Jean-Christophe* (*C30*:408) and arranged for Rolland to be visited by a Swiss doctor during his illness in 1943. Rolland would not, however, let him publish a letter, now lost, which Châteaubriant felt would have raised him above suspicion 'en te situant dans la Patrie, au-dessus de tous les partis' (*C30*:399); the old independent would not make a public gesture of political neutrality. *La Gerbe* caused Rolland much distress, especially its anti-Semitism. He did not hold Châteaubriant personally responsible for all its excesses, but rightly predicted that his friend would suffer for them after the war, and was pleased when in 1942 Châteaubriant briefly abandoned journalism for creative work:

> Notre seul vrai devoir et notre mission, à nous, hommes de l'esprit [. . .] – est notre tâche de concentration et de création intellectuelle [. . .] Toute autre tâche est imparfaite [. . .] et par suite, même fautive; j'ai eu le temps de faire là-dessus mes réflexions, personnelles, depuis deux ans. (*C30*:424)

These words imply self-criticism; Rolland seems to have decided that the political role that both friends, in their way, had played was inappropriate to their poetic vocation. Too much should not be made of a letter whose recipient Rolland felt more at fault than himself, but something similar emerges from the conclusion he wrote in September 1940 to 'Le Périple'. Though not published at the time, it was meant as a public statement, and it amounts to a farewell to action. Declaring his wish to return to the world of dream and expressing confidence in the future, he surveys his inter-war political activities in a distinctly detached tone. He hints that he was wrong in 1932 to identify imperialism with fascism; the two in fact 'cherchaient à se "rouler" mutuellement'. He blames much on his illness between 1929 and 1933: 'On ne saurait s'étonner que l'esprit ait subi les fièvres du corps, et qu'il ait résonné jusqu'au paroxysme des vibrations en lui de tous les cris du monde supplicié' (*VI*:293). The fever had passed into his mind, leading him to act in an over-emotional spirit:

> Je regrette que la furie de la mêlée où je me suis trouvé engagé ne m'ait pas permis, comme je le voulais, de dominer par l'esprit le champ de bataille, comme je l'avais fait en 1914-1918, afin de pénétrer objectivement les raisons des deux camps. Hélas! le mal est partout mêlé au bien. Et c'est mal servir celui-ci, même chez les siens, que le méconnaître, ou le nier, chez l'ennemi. (*VI*:294)

He had failed to emulate the broad vision of *Au-dessus de la mêlée*; too involved in his own role, he had been too ready to take a black-and-white view of affairs. He presents his activity as essentially an anti-fascist struggle for peace; communism and Russia are not even mentioned. He appears to be passing in silence over a Soviet engagement which has failed to achieve its ends; as in *Robespierre*, there is a nostalgia for the moral simplicity of 1914.

Evidence for change in his political thought remains tenuous, but his religious thought was certainly transformed. Over the years, much had separated him from Catholicism: its sterile formalism, its pessimism, its suppression of modernists, its implication in wartime nationalism and a general distaste for Judaeo-Christian monotheism. Yet he had occasionally attracted proselytizers, and a 1908 letter to the Abbé Guerle, model for the Abbé Corneille in *Jean-Christophe*, hints that he regretted that the Church had not tried harder with him (*C17*:83). In the mid-1920s he corresponded with the intensely Catholic Jeanne Mortier, who had been helped in her youth by *Jean-Christophe* and who tried, in return, to share her faith with him. She guided his exploration of Christian mysticism in 1927, though occasionally clashing with him over his communism, and frequently visited Vézelay, helping in the house when Marie was away. An intimate of Teilhard de Chardin, she hoped, without success, to introduce him to Rolland, who was attracted by Teilhard's liberal Jesuit milieu and its attempts to conciliate faith with science (*SP*:66). In the late 1930s, Rolland was approached by several young priests, the Dominican Raymond Pichard, Jean Sainsaulieu, who took the name of Frère Romain when he became a Carmelite monk, Louis Beirnaert, a Jesuit associate of Jeanne Mortier, and another Dominican, Michel de Paillerets, who became his wife's confessor. All shared an open and tolerant Catholicism; they would have been happy to draw Rolland into the fold, but were prepared to accept his own way of being religious. The image of Catholicism that they presented encouraged him to read widely in the Scriptures, theology and religious history.

The most intimate influence came from Marie. She had been hit hard by the Nazi-Soviet pact, and was worried about her son in Moscow. Apart from snippets of news through Elsa Hartoch in Switzerland, mother and son lost touch; only after Rolland's death did she learn that he died in the defence of Moscow in 1941. She sought solace in the Church, but Rolland, though respecting her independence, did not follow her; as he watched her read the mystics he had studied ten years before, they seemed to him an 'étape dépassée' (*SP*:58). A remarkable correspondence with Claudel had begun as early as 1938;[20] once again she became infatuated with an older literary figure, he insisted on her conversion as a condition of their correspondence and she was received into the Church at Easter 1940. Her faith was never orthodox; she did not practise regularly, and she enjoyed confronting priests with embarrassing passages from the

Scriptures. Yet it helped her to cope, and Rolland, who profited from its soothing influence, was happy to accept it.

With some devious manoeuvring, Marie brought Rolland and Claudel together. They had not met since schooldays, and ideologically were poles apart; Rolland had admired *L'Annonce faite à Marie* but knew little of Claudel's post-war writings, and Claudel had never read Rolland. Yet after they met, in Paris in March 1940 and later in Vézelay, where Claudel's daughter lived, each was struck by the other's profound faith and love of Beethoven. Rolland knew Claudel's reputation as a convert-seeker, and was wary of his influence on Marie. He complained to Madeleine: 'En religion, il despotise (ou tâche de despotiser M[arie]) [. . .] J'avoue que cela m'inspire tout autre chose qu'un sentiment d'émulation'.[21] Claudel, Marie, Jeanne Mortier and Châteaubriant created an intense religious atmosphere around him which he found wearing. After a visit from Châteaubriant and his 'Egérie', Gabrielle Castelot, the Colas in him objected: 'Cinq heures durant, ils ont parlé de Dieu, avec Macha. Je crevais d'ennui. Je n'en puis plus, de ces divagations théologiques! Mon Dieu est le Dieu du charbonnier. Le bon sens est sa prime qualité'.[22] He was, however, delighted with his rediscovered friend. He worried about Claudel's desire to convert him, but chiefly because he did not want to hurt Claudel by his obduracy: 'Je ne voudrais, à aucun prix, lui apporter une déception de plus'.[23] This seems to be why he made the gesture, at the end of Claudel's visit to Vézelay, of saying the Lord's Prayer with him, stating that he did so every day, not as 'un acte de foi', but as 'un acte d'union avec ceux qui ont la foi', especially his mother. Instinct related him to the Church, but reason restrained him from believing: 'Et la raison, j'y tiens; j'y tiens d'autant plus que j'estime qu'elle est un élément divin dans l'homme' (*SP*:62–3). This persuaded Claudel that Rolland was far enough on the right road to be left to himself.

Writing to Claudel in 1941 about Père Lubac's book on Catholicism, which he admired, Rolland declares: 'Si mon esprit [. . .] s'arrête toujours au seuil de la dernière porte, qui est la mutation de ces sublimes valeurs de l'homme, en Dieu qui se fait homme, je les place bien au-dessus des conceptions "océaniques" et impersonnelles de l'Etre' (*SP*:87). This looks like a reversal of his religious thought, a rejection of his long-standing Spinozism in quest of a personal God, and he certainly expresses nostalgia for the faith of his forebears. Yet a January 1942 text makes it clear he had not crossed that last threshold of belief. Reflecting on the relationship between religion and science, he concedes that relativity has damaged religious absolutes less than might be supposed, but he still rejects revealed religion, which has never helped him make contact with God:

'Le Dieu vivant, oui, j'ai reçu, plus d'une fois, directement son toucher de feu [. . .] Mais jamais par intermédiaire d'un Dieu d'histoire sainte' (*SP*:90–1).

In May 1942, he states that what separated him from Catholicism was a certain kind of hope:

> Cette foi est avant tout un Désir immense, une brûlante Espérance, nourrie par un Amour exalté. Elle peut chercher un auxiliaire dans la raison; mais c'est toujours pour elle un serviteur, de seconde place [. . .] Ou leur 'raison' n'est qu'une accommodation des lumières du cœur passionnée aux nécessités les plus élémentaires de l'intelligence ordinaire, pas trop soucieuse de la vérité scientifique. (*SP*:103)

Reason designed purely to satisfy the heart was no reason, and Rolland had not forgotten William of Orange's motto, 'Je n'ai pas besoin d'espérer pour entreprendre', a favourite of his ever since *Aert*. In 1939, he had recalled it to Pichard:

> Un homme ne dépend pas de l'espoir, mais de plus haut que l'espoir. – Et peut-être bien, penserez-vous, que c'est là aussi une foi, – et que le *'Es muss sein'* sur lequel elle s'appuie est assez parent du: *'Fiat voluntas. . .!'* Il implique un détachement profond, au sein de l'action, même passionnée. (*SP*:55)

This suggests the heroic resignation of Beethoven. Declining the hope implicit in a Providentialist view of God, Rolland aspired to accept God's will, whatever human tragedy that implied. 'Fiat voluntas tua' was his favourite phrase of the Lord's Prayer, but 'les deux premiers mots seuls sont pour moi article de foi'. The 'tua' was merely a 'fragile promesse de la frêle petite Espérance' (*SP*:109), implying belief in the unique divinity of Christ which he rejected. As in 'Le Royaume du T', he seeks no God outside the human individual; his faith does not depend on hope of a saviour who is not already within.

Other more human reasons restrained him from conversion. He encountered some insensitive proselytizers; an advance by the Vézelay parish priest merely irritated him, and he could react sharply even to his friends if they pressed too hard. His letters to Madeleine express more of this irritation than do those published in *Au Seuil de la dernière porte*; he complains of his friends' 'simplisme',[24] is shocked by the lack of humility in Jeanne Mortier's 'absolue et tranquille certitude [. . .] de tout ce qui se passe dans les cieux',[25] and even detects a lack of charity: 'Il me paraît que ces bons Pères n'ont guère pratiqué certaines paroles de St. Paul et de l'Evangile sur l'amour du prochain'.[26] Nor did he like the complicity with Pétain which was apparent in even the best of the Church,

> la façon dont l'Eglise (et nos amis de l'Eglise, y compris Jeanne) peuvent faire cause commune avec un homme qui n'a jamais caché son athéisme, son antichristianisme, son indifférence totale aux moyens de violence et de mensonge, et son néant religieux et moral.[27]

All of these factors held him back, and it was in a spirit of sympathetic but free enquiry that he wrote *Péguy*.

Rolland frequently complained of isolation in Vézelay, and reading was important to him. As well as returning to the classics and Catholic texts, he studied the history of thought and even delved with profit into copies of the *Revue des deux mondes* that Marie's mother brought from the library. He corresponded with André George and André Sabatier, of his publisher Albin Michel's editorial team, naming them as his literary executors if his wife and sister predeceased him. They kept him supplied with books, and he keenly followed the scientific collection directed by André George, which supported his view that modern science was superior to modern literature (*C17*:370). His wide-ranging curiosity shows an undiminished intellectual vitality. Work had always been his defence, and his financial situation obliged him to publish. Paper shortages and bureaucratic restrictions cramped his publishers' style, and Arcos was disappointingly slow in producing *Beethoven*, but Albin Michel, seeing in Rolland one of his surest values, launched the first edition of *Le Voyage intérieur* and prepared a revised luxury edition of *Michel-Ange*, which, though one of Rolland's more despised early writings, explored Michelangelo's mind through his works in ways analogous to *Beethoven*.

Beethoven was substantially finished late in 1941, and Rolland sought a new project. A debate with Madeleine suggests that he thought of returning to Shakespeare; he would have liked to study the genesis of Shakespeare's works, but the plan foundered on doubts over the authorship of the plays. Rolland suspected there was a single individual behind them, but the uncertainty was inhibiting; his method required a clearly identifiable individual and firmer historical anchorage than was available. He cogitated another novel, which Robichez claims would have been based on his friendship with Claudel,[28] but the circumstances were unpropitious: 'Je ne sais pas parler pour ne rien dire. Et la consigne d'aujourd'hui est d'avaler la langue – sauf pour lécher la sainte icône de V[ichy]'.[29] In an age of censorship, a major novel was just as impossible as another *Au-dessus de la mêlée*. He toyed with writing on Vézelay during the Crusades,[30] but that too came to nothing.

Instead, he returned to 1900 and his memoirs. To recapture the atmosphere, he reread his correspondence with Péguy, Gillet and the Tharauds:

> D'excellentes lettres. Est-il possible que des amis qui me connaissaient aussi intimement et qui m'aimaient soient devenus ce qu'ils sont à présent! C'est très mélancolique [. . .] Ah! je n'ai pas gagné, à changer d'équipe, après 1914. Que les amis qui sont venus après étaient inférieurs en art et surtout en compréhension de ma vraie nature![31]

Most of his post-1914 friendships had been based on intellectual rather than temperamental affinity, and the latter seemed more important. He felt more at home with old friends than with his more recent political supporters, he took the initiative of contacting the Tharauds, and they, with Claudel, set up a reconciliation with Gillet, with whom he resumed correspondence in July 1942. Much still separated them, and Rolland's letters to Madeleine suggest a certain wariness, especially as Gillet had just published on Joyce, one of Rolland's pet aversions,[32] but they planned to meet and eventually did so in June 1943. Sadly, their reunion was fleeting. Both were in Paris for medical attention and Gillet was battling with tuberculosis, unaware of the seriousness of his condition. Rolland, himself weak, struggled to his bedside for two brief meetings and returned to Vézelay a week later to be greeted by news of Gillet's death. Rolland was left to mourn a friendship of which he had formed great hopes. He now knew that Gillet had regretted his act of 1915 within a month, and he lamented his own harshness: 'J'ai été beaucoup trop impitoyable [. . .] Ce qui m'a été funeste, tant de fois, dans la vie, ç'a été ma raideur intransigeante. C'était sans doute une forme d'autodéfense. Mais elle avait qq. chose d'inhumain'.[33]

The same return to his roots brought him back to Péguy: 'Claudel, Péguy [. . .] Du bout de la route, quand on se retourne, les deux sommets qui dominent toute l'étendue' (*C2*:322). His memoirs had reached the stage of their association, and he was moved to reread all of Péguy's writings. In 1910, Rolland had been disconcerted by Péguy's late-flowering poetic genius, and many of his contemporary comments were critical, but now he was captivated by it, and his ensuing study, though biographical in approach, is essentially an exploration of Péguy's writings.

Rolland says little of Péguy's early life and is reticent on his domestic situation. Effectively, his story starts at their first meeting, and much space is given to defining their relationship, not least because Rolland felt it had been overlooked by biographers of Péguy hostile to him. He overstates his role in the foundation of the *Cahiers de la quinzaine*, but speaks generously of their differences over the Ollendorff *Jean-Christophe*, admitting he had not been aware of Péguy's financial difficulties (*Pi*:122). He protests his innocence over their rivalry for the Académie prize and expresses grief at how badly Péguy took the refusal to offer him *Colas Breugnon*. He is under no illusions about the rough treatment he could have expected from Péguy over *Au-dessus de la mêlée*, but is convinced that Péguy the revolutionary would have rejoined him after the war, 'dans les mêmes combats contre les exploiteurs de la guerre pour le droit et pour la liberté, qui l'ont trahie et avilie, comme les faux Dreyfusistes avaient trahi et dégradé la cause sacrée' (*Pii*:121). He dwelt on the liberty of their friendship; in Péguy's words: 'Une fidélité entière dans une liberté entière, c'est l'amitié française même' (*Pi*:285), and though never intimate, that friendship survived. As editor, Péguy respected his contributors' independence, and Rolland was grateful that he had published *Jean-Christophe* despite their differences. He knew of Péguy's violent verbal assaults on almost all his friends, rightly suspected that he too was a target and makes generous allowance for it, insisting that some of their most intimate exchanges took place when their thought had already drifted apart. This celebration of a friendship between two similar temperaments transcending ideological discord is one of this study's most appealing elements.

The bulk of Rolland's work is a reading of Péguy's texts, based on the same affectionate line-by-line exposition as he devotes to Beethoven, with liberal quotation, continuing his long exploration of the creative process. This is how he justifies his approach to one of Péguy's masterpieces, the *Porche du mystère de la deuxième vertu*, a celebration of hope:

> On me reprochera peut-être de l'avoir, dans les pages qui précèdent, suivie de trop près et, pour ainsi dire, recopiée, tout en la condensant. Mais j'ai voulu faire sentir, par l'enchaînement rigoureux des parties, l'extraordinaire unité du thème [. . .] C'est un prodige de l'art, un tour de force réalisé, non par la volonté réfléchie qui serait un raidissement, mais par la puissance d'une intuition torrentielle, qui s'est emparée de tout l'être, et qui se répand, surabondante, mais selon des lois organiques, comme un grand fleuve qui se divise, sans ralentir son cours, jusqu'à l'estuaire Océanique. (*Pi*:283–4)

The tone and imagery are familiar; Rolland highlights an aesthetic unity rooted in the oceanic subconscious. The will, however, is less prominent than in Beethoven. Rather than being pitted against the subconscious, it is written into the subconscious itself and emerges in free flow, guided by an inner compass which keeps Péguy on course through all his divagations:

> Il m'apparaît que ce n'est point la volonté d'artiste qui dirige l'œuvre [. . .], mais que l'œuvre s'abandonne au rythme des vagues du subconscient, et que Péguy ne fait aucun effort pour gouverner contre vents et marées. Il sait très bien que son génie propre est dans ces vents et ces marées, qui procèdent du fond mystérieux de la vie. (*P*ii:135)

Péguy discovers himself as he writes. Like Beethoven, he initiates an idea without knowing where it will lead, but he operates by following the flow rather than by Beethoven's patient chiselling, and the result can look chaotic. Works take shapes far removed from the original plan, the obsessive repetitions may appear prolix, and in some works, notably the immense *Eve*, Rolland loses confidence in Péguy's inner compass (*P*ii:93). The result is a disconcerting changeability, but Rolland accepted the need for change, and Péguy found his justification in the thought of Bergson, whose '"*se faisant*" éternel' may not be 'propice à un développement logique et ordonné', but it legitimizes Péguy's trust in a 'développement "organique"' (*P*ii:200).

What was unique in Péguy was 'l'accent [. . .] de Confession, entière, totale, immédiate' (*P*i:8). His grasp of external realities was uncertain, but 'qui se confesse intrépidement jusqu'au fond, atteint le fond de la conscience humaine' (*P*i:85). Again, the sounding of a great soul reveals universal truths, and Péguy's interest lay in the religious implications of his creativity. He evolved dramatically from socialist polemicist to Catholic poet, and the process fascinated Rolland, himself tempted by a return to his religious roots. Péguy called this process an 'approfondissement' rather than a conversion (*P*ii:211); his faith lay deep in himself, and he discovered it by confession. Faith and poetry have the same source, and the subconscious corresponds to divine grace:

> Bien peu d'artistes français [. . .] ont connu cette emprise soudaine, totale et prolongée de l'âme par le subconscient – ces coups de la grâce [. . .] Il ne distingue plus entre la force créatrice et le verbe sacré, le Créateur. (*P*i: 200–1)

His Catholicism was sincere, and Rolland argues against his anticlerical friends who denied it (*P*i:164), but it was never orthodox and Rolland equally refutes Catholic attempts to annex him. Péguy condemned the Church's social conservatism, revolted against the notion of hell, neglected the sacraments and clashed with Thomist rationalists who placed his master Bergson's works on the Index of forbidden books. His last writings, though unmistakeably Catholic, are totally defiant of Church authority on this issue: 'Il a établi avec une douce inflexibilité son irréductible indépendance et sa foi, – les deux ensemble' (*P*ii:154). Had he lived, he would surely have been condemned by the Church; as it was, he could safely be annexed by it, and Rolland aimed to protect him from that fate.

The essence of Péguy's faith was 'l'insertion de l'éternel dans le temporel' (*P*ii:214), a reverence for the Incarnation which led him, like Ramakrishna, to find spirituality in human reality. This was the key to his poetry, and it also caused him to attribute a divine mission to France, with all the nationalistic excess that that entailed. Rolland asserts his internationalism against Péguy, but in gentle tones (*P*i:281), and he says nothing of their disharmony over the theme of hope, which was the root of what separated Rolland from Christianity. Hope was the main theme of one of Péguy's masterpieces, and Rolland celebrates his portrayal of 'cette petite fille Espérance' (*P*i:271) without showing the least sign that he does not share it. He identified strongly, however, with Péguy's emphasis on liberty. Péguy found a conciliation of liberty with necessity which was close to Rolland's own:

> La reconnaissance par Péguy de la Nécessité divine n'implique nullement, bien au contraire, une abdication de sa volonté [. . .] Car la Nécessité est la Volonté éternelle, et loin de supprimer, elle implique, elle exige, lui faisant face, la volonté propre de l'homme. (*P*ii:210–11)

Péguy's God, like destiny climbing the ladder in *L'Ame enchantée*, needs the individual to give it impetus and direction. God needs man, and Péguy is proud to be his soldier, enlisting the French nation in the cause. Liberty and grace are closely associated, and Péguy exemplifies both by serving God freely:

> Dieu veut être aimé par des hommes libres. Dieu a besoin des Français. Dieu a besoin de Péguy, pour jouir de *'la liberté, qui est le centre même de l'homme et la plus belle création de Dieu dans l'homme'* (*P*ii:225)

For Rolland, who sought to serve both God and communism freely, this struck a chord, and he found other examples of it in these years. André George, himself a broadminded Catholic, drew Rolland's attention to Louis Pasteur, a believer who rarely went to mass. The Russian émigré philosopher Nicholas Berdiaev, uncle to Marie's first husband, expressed similar views on liberty and grace; Rolland admired his work and they met in Paris in 1942. Not least Marie herself, with her willingness to stand up to priests, seemed close to Péguy in her faith (*SP*:141). Rolland may not have accepted Catholicism, but he was drawn to Péguy's idiosyncratic model of it.

Catholicism complemented rather than contradicted Péguy's social ideals. His roots were in the people, his mission within Catholicism seemed to be 'de le désembourber, en le ramenant à ses origines évangéliques, à la religion de la pauvreté et du travail' (*P*ii:229), and when he died he seemed about to return to the 'combat social' (*P*ii:231). The nationalist of 1914 was still at heart the fighter for truth Rolland had known in 1900, seeking to preserve socialist mysticism from the corruption of politics. This is important, for since 1940 Péguy's writings, suddenly fashionable, had been exploited for a variety of causes, mainly by the Church and Vichy. To counter this, Rolland insists on how alien Péguy was to partisan spirit. His role was not to lead one party, but to stimulate the best in them all, to remind Catholics of the Incarnation, socialists of justice, revolutionaries of '[les] valeurs spirituelles, que ces maladroits ont si souvent tendance à mésestimer', and nationalists of the purity of their ideal (*P*ii:262). This could only be done by an independent with a conscience; that was how Rolland saw Péguy, and it was what he sought to be himself. In making this case, then, Rolland was making his own political statement, an attack on partisan spirit of whatever complexion: 'Je [jette Péguy], avec ses contradictions furieuses, dans les jambes de tous les partis. Ils seront tous hors d'eux'.[34]

Péguy's contradictions point to a darker picture. Like most of Rolland's subjects he contained a multiplicity of selves not fully harmonized, and Rolland did not like them all. Love of justice led Péguy to harsh condemnations of his adversaries, and many of his texts were brilliant but splenetic diatribes which Rolland roundly condemned: 'Les invectives et les sarcasmes de Péguy contre Jaurès et contre Lavisse dureront autant que la prose française. S'il était moins puissant, Péguy serait moins coupable' (*P*i:261–2). Jaurès and Lavisse were not Péguy's only targets, but they were the ones who distressed Rolland most. He could understand Péguy's hatred of the intellectual hegemony of the University which inspired the attack on Lavisse, but he had been, and still was, appalled by Péguy's denunciation of Lavisse as an anti-patriot. Jaurès was a more complex case. Rolland held no particular brief for him, and knew that Péguy's quarrel with him was part of 'l'opposition des mystiques aux politiques du Dreyfusisme' in which he had been on Péguy's side (*P*ii:118). Péguy, however, had debased a noble tragic conflict into a 'mêlée fratricide'

(*P*i:77), and Rolland was sharply aware that some of his attacks could be taken as incitement to murder. He was anxious to ask Geneviève Favre about Péguy's reaction to the news of Jaurès's assassination, and the result, sadly, was not the clear-cut condemnation he wanted to hear (*P*ii:181). Though celebrating the poet in Péguy, Rolland condemns the polemicist.

This too is a political statement. We have seen that, judging by his correspondence, Rolland was concerned with the state of France; nothing troubled him more than the partisan vindictiveness which he feared would undermine post-war social harmony. Péguy the polemicist offers a terrible example of how not to fight for noble causes:

> On a le cœur serré de ces malentendus atroces entre Français, et de cette furie qui les pousse à s'exterminer en s'outrageant du nom d'ennemis de la patrie, – alors qu'à part un bien petit nombre de dévoyés, tous aiment la France d'un même cœur, en la servant, chacun selon son devoir et sa loi. (*P*ii:75)

This may be read as a warning against the post-war vendettas that Rolland correctly predicted. He knew that *Péguy* could not appear until hostilities were over, but he wanted it to appear soon afterwards, as a call to a harmonic France to live up to its ideals.

Fortunately there was enough that was positive in Péguy's France to serve as an inspiration. Militaristic it was, but this did not necessarily imply narrowness:

> Il trouve moyen d'unir en [France . . .] ses trois passions: le monde antique, le monde chrétien, et la Liberté Révolutionnaire. – Et je ne sais pas si le rêve de Péguy est vrai ou faux, mais il est grandiose, il est le plus puissant qu'ait jamais inspiré l'idéal de la France. (*P*ii:80)

Rolland's own vision of France as a harmony is not far away. Péguy's concern with the 'salut éternel de la France' (*P*i:86), his desire to 'réveiller les énergies du peuple de la France' (*P*i:184) and his celebration of those who die in a just war were causes which Rolland could appreciate. He shared Péguy's roots in Central France, and appreciated the common touch of a soldier who refused to be promoted above the rank of lieutenant. This is why Rolland is gentle in chiding Péguy's nationalism. Even in the victory which could be glimpsed as he wrote, he knew hard times lay ahead, and in Péguy he offers France a lofty image of itself:

> Pour soutenir l'assaut des forces énormes qui déferleront demain sur le globe, et dont notre petite terre risque d'être submergée, il faut que les meilleurs de son sang se rassemblent et se concentrent, dans une rude école d'énergie, où

se rallument les viriles vertus qui ont fait la France, et faute desquelles elle meurt. Auprès de nulle maître, elle ne pourra mieux les réapprendre, que de Péguy. (*P*ii:271)

The message is still that of the *Cahiers de la Quinzaine*. Péguy died heroically and tragically, and in 1914 was ready for death, but at the same time, 'c'est notre droit d'offrir aux jeunes hommes de la France et du monde, au delà de cette gloire de la mort, un but à leurs élans, d'un attrait moins funeste' (*P*ii:273). Though he could do without hope himself, Rolland concludes on a hopeful note, quoting Péguy's vision of the 'bons soldats' returning from war to a fraternal world. As well as a celebration of an old friend and a further exploration of the creative mind, *Péguy* was the best avenue for Rolland's last political message.

In January 1943, with the first draft of *Péguy* almost complete, Rolland fell ill. Cardiac problems exacerbated his other complaints, and for some days he was close to death. He was saved by the devotion of his wife and sister, but was left weaker than ever. It was a struggle to finish *Péguy*, and work on future projects was slow. He started the next phase of his memoirs; a manuscript draft exists which takes him to 1907, and he was pleased with it: 'il y avait là de mes meilleures pages, des plus intimes',[35] but he was plagued by failing memory and found writing difficult.

Though delirious during his illness, he kept his lucidity and noted visions and reflections which brought him closer still to Catholicism. He was touched that many Catholics were praying for him, and felt the idea of Christ's intercession moving in a way that impersonal pantheism could never be:

Quel soulagement pour le cœur qui, dans ces heures de détresse, ne trouve rien pour lui dans le panthéisme glacé, qui suffisait aux jours de santé. Pauvreté morale du Panthéisme... un Etre en qui tous les êtres sont absorbés. Quel intérêt, si Lui et eux sont impersonnels? (*SP*:124)

Previously Rolland had rejected a God separate from man, but now the ebbing of life convinced him that 'l'existence et moi sont deux'. He held to his reason, seeing it as a gift which he owed it to God to preserve, but was aware that his heart was working in another direction, and his brush with death convinced him of reason's inability to cope with what lay beyond.

This, he decided, was the meaning of a 'vision [. . .] singulièrement abstraite et concrète' at the height of his illness, in which he saw himself drifting above a mosaic pavement and sensed that 'au-delà d'une ligne frontière que j'entamais déjà le fil serait rompu entre moi et le monde que je quittais' (*SP*:126). Cracks in the pavement closing behind him suggested that he was at a watershed which, once crossed, would separate him from all things conceivable to humanity. Another vision pointed to the power of intercessionary prayer. He had always prayed, he confessed; to whom he was not clear, but certainly to his beloved departed. His attention had been drawn by both Claudel and Péguy to the Hail Mary, and when he experienced a vision of a swallow flying across a stretch of water with a church, he interpreted it as a fusion of the Virgin Mary with his mother. From that moment he felt his health improve, and 'mon cœur (en dehors de ma raison, qui ne se rend pas) est resté en une sorte de communion secrète et reconnaissante avec "la Mère"'. He came to use the Hail Mary himself, and it seemed to help when his wife fell under 'une grave menace' (*SP*:128–9), probably an illness shortly after his own which was suspected to be cancer.

Rolland discussed these visions with Claudel, and was impressed by his friend's broadminded attempts to interpret them, but affection blended with irritation at the revival of Claudel's proselytizing zeal. Rolland tried but failed to make Claudel give a coherent explanation of his own faith, and on his departure Rolland's wry sense of humour reasserted itself: 'Il sortira de sa visite [. . .] quelque Légende merveilleux, où Maria et moi aurons notre place d'honneur' (*SP*:132). Claudel's was the first of several attempts to convert him; Jeanne Mortier threatened to arrive with a Jesuit in tow, and Pichard wrote sermonizing letters. Only Paillerets seemed willing to take him completely on his own terms. All this he resisted, sometimes sharply. Without the rational persuasion that the Church could not provide, Rolland would not surrender his independence, and he certainly would not be bullied; Claudel's attempt to make him fear hell was counterproductive, especially when he compared it with Péguy's total revulsion against the notion (*SP*:158). The religious threshold remained stubbornly uncrossed.

In the summer of 1944, Vézelay was cut off for two months, the theatre of a minor battle as Resistance forces attacked the retreating Germans; for the first and only time, Rolland was in a war zone. Just as in 1940 he consoled himself with Beethoven, in 1944 he consoled himself with Christ, for in these months he wrote his *Entretiens sur les Evangiles*. Correspondence was impossible, and we have little evidence of how he viewed this text. The tone suggests it was meant for publication, but it is unfinished and unpolished, and he does not appear to have discussed it with his publishers.

Evidence of its genesis can be found in a 1943 letter praising the Church for recent studies of the Gospels 'd'après les méthodes de critique historique, que seules j'admets' and for its new-found preference for John over the Synoptic Gospels (*SP*:141). He exaggerates when claiming in his preface that his recent rereading of the Gospels was his first since childhood; Christ is often present in his works, especially *Clerambault*. Yet there is no reason to doubt that he had never before tried to distinguish between the Evangelists (*SP*:209), and the bulk of his manuscript is a comparative study of their reliability, as a prelude to his own portrait of Christ which remains a sketch. He was convinced of the reality of the person of Christ, feeling that the variety of the Evangelists' testimony confirms rather than denies it (*SP*:210); he also unquestioningly accepts that they were written by those to whom they were attributed. John is the testimony of an intimate disciple, Mark transmits that of another intimate, while Matthew and Luke, less close to Christ, offer the interpretations of a Jewish intellectual and a sensitive Gentile. From that basis, Rolland applies methods recalling his first ambitions as a historian, espousing the angle of approach of each witness.

Rolland's preferences follow the order in which the Gospels are mentioned above. John knows things that the others do not, especially from the beginning of Christ's ministry, and transmits some of Christ's most intimate thoughts, with no attempt at aesthetic structure and playing down the supernatural elements. John makes Christ seem more real than in the other Gospels: 'Quel frémissement particulier de la chair et de l'âme se dégage de certaines paroles et de certains gestes immortels! Imaginez ce que serait sans eux une vie de Jésus!' (*SP*:215). The emphasis is on Christ the man; Rolland significantly prefers the Gospel which makes him look most human. Mark's text, also touchingly human, reflects Peter's shame after his denial of Christ and reflects the 'antagonisme d'affection privilégié' between Peter and John (*SP*:231); it too includes apparently authentic observed details. Matthew, by contrast, attempts an intellectual synthesis, grouping events to structure a message. The Sermon on the Mount reads like an arranged narrative, and Christ appears a harsh militant marked by a 'nationalisme juif très fermé' (*SP*:239), an Old Testament prophet indulgent to the poor in spirit but to no one else. 'L'histoire connaît d'autres Amis du Peuple, qui n'étaient pas moins terribles' (*SP*:238); the allusion to Marat is hardly flattering. Luke is a milder soul, and Rolland could respond to this Gentile who senses Christ's universal message, but he finds that Luke's gentleness goes too far; his narrative is elegant and arranged, but vague. 'C'est le tempérament du conteur qui l'emporte' (*SP*:253); his Gospel is literature rather than testimony, the least reliable of the four. One senses the Rolland of *Jean-Christophe*, mistrustful of literary style when it becomes an obstacle to truth.

Rolland still thinks that Christ is divine only in the sense that all exceptional men are; his story is a 'grand drame humain', and Rolland refuses to discuss his divinity. This would be to downplay his humanity which, Rolland feels, gives the fullest value to his achievement: 'On a trop tendance à le faire toujours participant à la divinité: on ne s'aperçoit pas qu'en ce faisant [. . .], on rabaisse beaucoup son sacrifice' (*SP*:261–2). Accordingly, Rolland's portrait is of a man: an imposing orator looking maturer than his years, sensitive, indulgent to women, valuing friendship, and like all Rolland's great men a harmonizer of contradictions (*SP*:263). Some of his sayings seem to discourage work, which Rolland deplores; the old communist prefers Martha to Mary and looks in vain to the Gospels for an 'exemple du bon travail, exact et probe' (*SP*:265). He regrets the Gospels' silence on Christ's early life, and senses the influence of his mother, 'une rêveuse, illuminée, [qui] l'a trop entretenu, pendant l'enfance, de mystérieux propos sur sa naissance, sur ses royales origines, sur ses obscures et magnifiques destinées' (*SP*:267). Here too, Rolland seems to identify his own mother with the Virgin Mary.

Though there is relatively little theology, an isolated note which he may not have planned to retain finds a problem in Christ's choice of Judas as a disciple and his prophecy of the ruin of Jerusalem:

> Quel dommage que nul n'ait saisi le regard qui a élu Judas! Même en admettant qu'il ait prévu la trahison, n'a-t-il pu prévoir la damnation, le désespoir et le remords? Jusqu'à ce que le crime fût consommé, n'a-t-il point tenté, contre l'avenir écrit d'avance, de le sauver? N'exprime-t-il point sa douleur de n'avoir pu sauver Jérusalem? Comme Cassandre et Tirésias, il voit venir le Destin, qu'il voudrait et ne peut conjurer. (*SP*:260)

The passage is an unpolished draft, but the issues raised are worrying. Seeing his own prophecies of the ruin of the West fulfilled, Rolland felt close to the Christ who predicted the fall of Jerusalem, and again he reflects on whether the individual can influence destiny; even predicted disasters cannot apparently be prevented. Worse, Christ is implicated in the damnation of Judas, which would not have occurred if he had not been chosen. This raises the whole question of the place of evil in God's purpose; if Christ is omniscient but impotent, he has knowingly consigned one of his creatures to damnation.

These worries resurfaced in a debate with Pichard in the last month of Rolland's life. Pichard argued a Providentialist view of God working in mysterious ways, which Rolland rejected on account of 'les millions de victimes sur lesquelles passent les roues du char de ce Dieu'. Pichard's reply alluded to spiritual insights in some admirable letters written by victims of Nazi persecution shortly before their death, but Rolland was not impressed:

> Il a beau jeu avec les âmes fortes. Mais tous les faibles, qui sont l'immense majorité! Quel recours leur est offert, dans la misère! Et n'y eût-il qu'un seul être abandonné dans son désespoir, comment un Dieu peut-il s'en consoler? – Je préfère toujours la conception du Buisson Ardent: le Dieu qui souffre et combat avec nous. (*SP*:200)

Rolland accepted sacrifice as the lot of the elite, but still felt for the weak, unable to face the tragedy of life, just as much as in his distant conversation with Renan. He rejects a God who can accept their despair, preferring his old notion of God within man, dynamically involved in a suffering, imperfect humanity. If Jesus were God in this sense, his choice of Judas might be easier to comprehend. A similar notion emerges from what is probably the last religious reflection in Rolland's diary. He agrees with Péguy and Berdiaev; God and freedom are consubstantial, 'chaque homme partage, dans la Liberté, à la Création qui continue jusqu'à la fin des temps', and by extension 'le Christ est en agonie jusqu'à la fin des temps', not just in the traditional Christian sense of sacrifice, but also because God is implicated in human imperfection: 'L'homme participant en liberté à la libre action créatrice de Dieu, Dieu a sa part dans son péché. Et s'il le rachète, dans l'humanité, lui-même n'a-t-il pas à expier?' (*SP*:202–3). Rolland's final position is not Christian orthodoxy, but a tragic vision, in keeping with the dark days of 1944 and the pantheist views he held for most of his life.

After the Liberation, correspondence and travel resumed. Rolland's wish to see peace return was not granted; he died, after a brief attack of uraemia, on 30 December 1944, and his last letter to Madeleine, only three days before, shows him intensely worried at the German offensive in the Ardennes. All his statements aimed at a post-war audience, 'Le Périple', the end of *Péguy*, a few press declarations after the Liberation and letters to non-intimates such as the one closing the centenary *Cahier*, express confidence in France, land of liberty and noble causes: 'L'épreuve a fait resurgir la flamme du sacrifice. Et dans la littérature clandestine, comme dans la presse délivrée, on a déjà entendu de grandes voix, – pour la plupart, jeunes et émouvantes. – J'ai confiance' (*C17*:382). In private he was deeply troubled at a world where indiscriminate Allied air raids were causing unnecessary devastation and his worst predictions about post-war vindictiveness seemed to be fulfilled (*LB*:155). As in 1914, he wanted to see war conducted humanely and was bitterly disappointed. His letters begin to express political views again.

During the war he had had less contact with his left-wing friends than with the Catholic right. Moderates such as Arcos and Vildrac had visited him, Vildrac could have kept him in touch with the clandestine Comité National des Ecrivains, and he sent a message to *Les Lettres françaises* immediately after the Liberation.[36] His communist friends, however, had gone underground or to Moscow, and there was no question of active involvement, even after Hitler's invasion of Russia. References to Soviet communism, already thin in his 1939 writings, were banished from his correspondence. There are hints that he did not want his past publicly aired during the Occupation; he was worried about what compromising remarks might have been made by a former left-wing associate, Courrègel-ongue, in a public lecture about him.[37]

The signs are, however, that his social thought had changed little. His sympathies were still with the poor, and an indignant outburst against profiteers in the local meat trade suggests that he still saw social problems in terms of class conflict:

> Le principal combat n'est pas entre les nations; il est entre les égoïsmes et les profits des différentes classes ou castes, à l'intérieur de chaque nation. Il s'amasse ainsi de vigoureuses haines. Mais les nouveaux enrichis, qui ne l'ignorent pas, se disposent à filer, fortune faite, au lendemain de la guerre.[38]

Even his commentaries on Christ allude to 'nos travailleurs petits-bourgeois d'aujourd'hui, qui manifestent le plus d'inquiétudes pour la Révolution sociale, qui les avantagerait pourtant!' (*SP*:230). Such statements suggest abiding communist sympathies, but rural Vézelay gave him a model of the poor based on the peasant rather than the urban proletariat. Criticizing Vichy for taxing small food producers, he declares: 'C'est en vérité beaucoup demander de la nature humaine, qu'on s'éreinte à produire le plus possible, pour s'en voir dépouillé (au profit de qui?)'.[39] This hardly suggests he would have approved of Soviet collective farms.

Sympathy for the poor does not necessarily imply sympathy for the Soviets, and hints of evolution emerge in the survey of the world of 1900 which forms the prelude to *Péguy*. The main feature of this period was 'l'ébranlement catastrophique de la grandiose foi de l'esprit humain, qui le gouvernait depuis deux mille ans, – le mysticisme de Raison' (*Pi*:16), and for Péguy the chief rebel was Bergson, who had not been important to the young Rolland, but Bergson's notion that 'la science moderne date du jour où l'on érigea la mobilité en réalité indépendante' (*Pi*:38) was now much to his taste. Rolland includes Einstein, Max Planck, William James and Henri Poincaré in the same movement. Despite the excesses of Bergson's Catholic disciples, this movement did not appear essentially anti-intellectual: 'cet indéterminisme bouleversant pourra se résoudre un jour en un autre déterminisme plus large et plus profond' (*Pi*:29), and Rolland echoes Péguy's hopes of 'un nouveau rationalisme' (*Pi*:40), but in 1900 it was easy to view the situation as a conflict between reason and mysticism.

As a historian, Rolland found deeper sociological roots to the conflict; traditional reason was allied to the faith in progress inspired by the first phase of the Industrial Revolution, whereas Bergsonism reflects its second phase, the exploitation of electricity. Among the forces of traditional reason, Rolland lists his pet aversions, bourgeois capitalism and positivist science, but also Jaurès's socialism, which communicated faith in progress to the working classes, and Thomist tendencies in a Church suspicious of mystics, whose foremost French advocate was Jacques Maritain. In a less guarded letter to Madeleine, Rolland seems amused by this coalition of socialism and the Church: 'Cocasse, cet accord de toutes les puissances d'ordre, la papauté, l'Eglise, la Sorbonne, Jaurès, Lénine, Léon XIII, Benoît XV, etc., contre la brebis galeuse, le subjectivisme, l'irrationalisme, Kant, Bergson, James, etc.'.[40] The striking addition to this private list is Lenin, nowhere mentioned in *Péguy* but now classed with Jaurès among the forces of tradition and order, against those whom Rolland sees as the bearers of the next phase of revolution. This can be related to a passage in *Péguy* comparing the battle between Jaurès and Péguy to the rivalry of 'les socialistes marxistes et les dissidences révolutionnaires, anti-marxistes, hypermarxistes, trotzkystes, anarchistes, fascistes se réclamant de Sorel' (*Pi*:97). This is not to suggest that Rolland naïvely identified Jaurès with the Stalinists on the one hand and Péguy with the anti-Stalinist left on the other, but it does hint at a shifting attitude. Admittedly Péguy was not at his best in the conflict with Jaurès, but in the previous decade Rolland would not have accorded Trotskyists and anarchists the dignity of associating them with anyone he admired; they were the enemy, deserving no favours. As far as the evidence goes, it suggests that Rolland was less committed to a Stalinist-Leninist vision, viewing revolution as a complex phenomenon not confined to one party, especially as that party was now one of social order.

In late 1944, Rolland made a last six-week stay in Paris, to seek medical

Koudachev. For the latter purpose, the Rollands naturally approached the Soviet Embassy, which in turn invited Rolland to appear at a large reception. This he did, despite his distaste for such occasions, but he was slow to accept official hospitality and refused the offer of an Embassy car to take him to and from Vézelay. Once in Paris, however, he did accept to be driven to engagements,[41] and he let the Embassy arrange him a private showing of Soviet propaganda films portraying a victory parade after Stalingrad, to which Rolland invited about thirty friends. This shows he was prepared to associate publicly with the Soviets. There are signs that he was still willing to see current affairs through communist eyes. After meeting Aragon and Jacques Duclos, he appeared impressed by their testimony of the strength and moderation of the PCF,[42] and he seems to have taken on board Duclos's suspicions of the influence of their old enemy, the British Intelligence Service, in De Gaulle's circle;[43] in later letters critical of Churchill's policy in Greece, he expresses these judgements as if they were his own.[44] At a time when Thorez's return to France was a controversial issue, he wrote to the communist leader welcoming him back. There was still personal warmth between Rolland and his old associates.

Yet he says little on wartime Russia and its heroism. In the Stalingrad film, he praised the restraint of the crowds watching the defeated prisoners, which he did not think a French crowd would have maintained,[45] but another film viewed by Marie seemed to express 'un vent de haine et de vengeance, épouvantable',[46] precisely the triumphal vindictiveness he feared, and there were signs that French communists were infected. Rolland's last private intervention was a letter to Aragon in support of Sabatier's father, who had been arrested after incurring communist suspicion. He was disturbed, too, by an attack on Châteaubriant by Francis Jourdan (*C30*:18); it seems likely that, if he had survived, he would have faced difficult decisions about whether to give Châteaubriant public support. Two last letters suggest some detachment from communism. Writing to Sabatier, he asked to modify the pre-war arrangement whereby he ceded his profits from sales in Russia: 'Pour mes anciennes œuvres, j'avais, d'entente avec M.Albin Michel, fait l'abandon de mes droits, en faveur des Universités Soviétiques. Mais pour mes œuvres nouvelles, il doit être fait, désormais, un contrat régulier entre les Editions d'Etat, à Moscou, et nous'.[47] The reasons for this may, of course, have been purely financial; more clear-cut is one of his last letters to his sister, in which, pressed by a visitor, René Plaud, about party membership, he declares:

> C'est un de ceux qui voudraient me conquérir, me faire inscrire au Parti Comm.,
> comme vient de faire Jolliot-Curie [*sic*], – je ne le ferai *jamais*. Mais je suis
> entouré d'un double cercle – de communistes – de catholiques – qui me
> guignent. Le morceau est trop gros, pour passer dans leurs gousses.[48]

This irritated outburst was not meant to be testamentary, nor is it new; Rolland never held a party card. Yet the message is crystal clear; the old independent survived, with no intention of being annexed by either of the rival faiths on whose fringes he had lived.

One last object of faith remained: Beethoven. The Bouillés spent Christmas at Vézelay a week before Rolland's death, and Lucien Bouillé describes the old man, dejected and lethargic, taking advantage of Marie's absence at church to celebrate his own mass by playing the Sonata Op.111. For some time Rolland had confined himself to Beethoven's adagios, but now he performed the whole sonata, with the intensity that had always marked his playing. The effort exhausted him and he had to be helped back to bed, swearing his guests to secrecy like a naughty boy; Marie, no music-lover herself, had been in difficult mood. It is a sad picture, but the music was appropriate. Bouillé perceived how this work, rising from the 'tragique apocalyptique' of the stormy first movement to the 'sérénité' and the 'perfection tragique' of the Arietta, reflected Rolland's own faith rising above the tragedies of the world: 'On sentait que, libre de la laideur, libre de la mort, – comme l'homme dont le regard a mesuré trop d'abîmes – , il avait dans son cœur la calme certitude de l'éternité du maître' (*LB*:168–9). No Beethoven work better reflects the dual vision of the Janiculum 'éclair'.

Rolland's will stated that he was not a believer, but was willing to accept Catholic burial rites for the sake of his loved ones. The funeral was in Clamecy, and he was buried in the churchyard of Brèves. Aragon launched a movement to have his remains transferred to the Panthéon, and the appearance of *Péguy* in the week of his death helped to give this communist-inspired gesture a veneer of national unity. The broad-based support for it would have appealed to Rolland's sense of humour, but he had no wish to lie in the Panthéon, and the plan foundered on the coolness of the political authorities and the diversionary tactics of those who wished to see Péguy and Bergson similarly honoured. The Panthéon was no place for a man who hated to be exploited; this last attempt to annex him was a deserved failure. The Association des Amis de Romain Rolland, created by his widow with the support of both Aragon and Claudel, was much more successfully non-partisan.

Notes

1. Letter to Madeleine, 27 July 1938.
2. Letter to Madeleine, 28 November 1940.
3. Letter to Madeleine, 14 October 1938.
4. Letter to Madeleine, 3 October 1942.
5. Letter to Madeleine, 6 August 1938.
6. Letter to Madeleine, 27 July 1938.
7. Letter to Madeleine, 14 March 1940.
8. For an eye-witness account, see Arcos (1950), p.111ff.
9. Letter to Madeleine, 1 April 1941.
10. Letter to Madeleine, 21 February 1942.
11. Letter to Madeleine, 12 April 1941.
12. *C17* is a general selection from Rolland's correspondence published to mark the centenary of his birth. Of all the *Cahiers Romain Rolland*, it is the one in which his widow had most chance to create an image of her husband in the choice of material.
13. Letter to Madeleine, 10 March 1941.
14. Letter to Madeleine, 25 August 1943.
15. Letter to Madeleine, 28 April 1941.
16. Letter to Madeleine, 28 November 1942.
17. Letter to Madeleine, 1 October 1943.
18. Letter to Madeleine, 8 May 1942.
19. Letter to Madeleine, 12 April 1941.
20. For this relationship, see Antoine (1988), pp.389-414.
21. Letter to Madeleine, 15 April 1940.
22. Letter to Madeleine, 28 April 1940.
23. Letter to Madeleine, 30 March 1940.
24. Letter to Madeleine, 27 July 1939.
25. Letter to Madeleine, 20 November 1940.
26. Letter to Madeleine, 21 August 1942.
27. Letter to Madeleine, 14 May 1942.
28. Robichez (1961), pp.191–2.
29. Letter to Madeleine, 29 October 1941.
30. Letter to Madeleine, 8 November 1941.
31. Letter to Madeleine, 2 March 1942.
32. Letter to Madeleine, 12 October 1942.
33. Letter to Madeleine, 24 December 1943.
34. Letter to Madeleine, 25 September 1943.
35. Letter to Madeleine, 18 December 1944.

36. 'Un message de Romain Rolland aux "Lettres françaises"', *Les Lettres françaises*, 21, 16 September 1944.
37. Letter to Madeleine, Holy Saturday, 1944.
38. Letter to Madeleine, 5 August 1943.
39. Letter to Madeleine, 12 November 1941.
40. Letter to Madeleine, 9 December 1942.
41. See Duchatelet's comments in Chagny-Sève (1996), p.281, and letter to Madeleine, 27 November 1944.
42. Letter to Madeleine, 24 November 1944.
43. In later years, Rolland's widow hinted that he expressed guarded respect for De Gaulle himself, but the evidence is tenuous.
44. Letters to Madeleine, 9 and 15 December 1944.
45. Letter to Madeleine, 27 November 1944.
46. Letter to Madeleine, 29 November 1944.
47. Letter to A. Sabatier, 19 November 1944.
48. Letter to Madeleine, 18 December 1944.

Conclusion

Of all the accusations levelled at Rolland, the most hurtful was that of antipatriotism. He held a lofty notion of France, fame abroad was small consolation for rejection at home, and much of his mature work shows a sense of the Central French roots to which he returned in old age. Yet in his youth he reacted sharply against them; Clamecy, school, Church, Paris, all formed an environment in which he felt trapped. Ill-health, bereavement and his mother's possessiveness left him with a sense of mortality and an urge to escape, all the harder to bear because its source was a loved family whose sacrifices locked him in an education system he hated. From this situation springs his prickly love of liberty.

Art gave him a release that society could not. He sought release in books, music and writing, and there is something obsessive in the sheer quantity of his output; heavy extra-literary commitments and a desire to cheat death made him write fast and at length. Music became a substitute for faith, with Beethoven holding special significance, and his 'éclairs' confirmed the sense of being inhabited by a universal life force which the *Credo quia Verum* crystallizes. Rolland was essentially an artist, whose ideas emerged in images or formal patterns rather than abstract thought, but the pantheism of this text, which he forgot so profoundly that for years he lost the manuscript, provided a lifelong basis for his faith. Its distinction between the individual role and a universal life affording detachment from that role was transformed by the Janiculum 'éclair' into an artistic vision separating mind and heart. From this springs his ability to combine a combative sense of mission with a serenity raising him above conflict, to blend short-term pessimism with long-term optimism.

A corollary of this faith was respect for the roles of others. His tendency to value a sincere enemy above a mediocre friend is largely a matter of esteem for those who play their own role to the full, rather than imitating his and restricting his freedom in so doing. All his works express fascination with forceful personalities. Orsino's force for its own sake is tempered into the heroic ideal which dominates his pre-war work; after the war revealed its flaws, this ideal re-emerged in the probing of the God-bearing personality in his later works. His correspondence, too, shows respect for the roles of others; his letters often express messages from which the recipient can profit, rather than seeking to impose his own thought, and as such must be read with caution.

Such a faith is perforce eclectic. Though respecting reason, Rolland did not seek intellectual solutions to problems of faith, which he valued for its inspirational force rather than its precise content. He espoused a series of faiths in the spirit of the Gandhian experiment with truth, staying with them as long as they showed dynamic possibilities but abandoning them once they hardened into an establishment creed. He resisted the positivist science of the 1880s, but warmed to the post-Einsteinian scientific revolution. He objected to authoritarian Catholicism, but welcomed the post-1905 modernists and the broad-minded Catholics he encountered in the 1930s. He favoured socialism and communism insofar as they were revolutionary faiths, but not when they became parties of state order, as they did after Dreyfus and under Stalin, even though in the latter case he was slow to grasp the situation and reluctant to act upon it. The Indians offered a metaphysically congenial faith, but its translation into action was sometimes problematic. Rolland's faith is disconcerting to those who seek intellectual neatness, but once understood, it can be seen to operate remarkably consistently through his life.

Alongside it went an acute sense of the real. Some of his public pronouncements suggest a fleshless idealism, but he had plenty of shrewdness, which he related to his father's common sense. Though a rebel against the social system, he knew how to operate within it; though disdaining to follow his own best business interests, he could give sound advice. He was a good observer and a shrewd judge; his piercing blue eyes left many visitors with the sense that they were being seen through. This ability was disciplined by his historian's training; he learned how to handle evidence and solve problems, and though he resented his university work, he gradually came to appreciate it. The skills he acquired from it were indispensible to his later writings; even his diary he conceived as a historical document. Rolland's university work enriched historiography by accommodating music to it. Though in reaction against Tainean determinism, he was conscious of the links between art history and wider historical trends, and his study of artistic movements led him to see history in terms of cyclic patterns. His fascination with Empedocles gave this a metaphysical dimension, emerging in his concern with European decadence and his attempt to portray a whole historical cycle in his Revolutionary dramas. The pattern of decline and rise which dominates his novels is another expression of this vision; Rolland's imagination favoured large-scale cyclic forms, with the symphony as a model.

The problem was squaring the deterministic implications of this vision with individual freedom. It is present from the start; Orsino defies death in a gesture both futile and heroic. Saint-Just asserts the primacy of history over the individual in a way which Rolland rejected in the war but favoured again in the 1930s, and it is not clear whether the God of *Le Buisson ardent* is an inevitable force of destiny or dependent on men's free actions. In 1914 Rolland pitted the individual against war as destiny, but after 1926 he was prepared to ride with destiny incarnated in a social movement which, despite its tragic implications, seemed beneficient. Beethoven showed how resignation before destiny could become heroic, *L'Ame enchantée* portrays destiny dependent on the individual, and Péguy confirmed this by linking God and freedom.

For the individual to realize his destiny, inner coherence is needed. Rolland was conscious of the multiplicity of the self, but critical of writers who seemed to contribute to the disintegration of the human personality; this was why he kept his distance from Freud. Though against sclerotic moral codes, he valued morality as a dynamic discipline, and one of art's values was the parallel it offered to this discipline in its attempt to create order. Any order achieved, however, should be based not on repression, but on harmony. This is as true for the self as for inter-personal and international relationships; just as God depends on individuals for his realization, just as musical harmony depends on the interaction of single notes, the unity Rolland sought was one in which no individual was sacrificed but all worked for the whole.

His first marriage, university work, correspondence and political activities all distracted him from his art, for which he never felt he had enough time. He came to realize that these distractions were nourishing, but his work undoubtedly suffered from haste and discontinuity, and he sensed that he had not achieved his potential. As soon as he became known his stylistic clumsiness was attacked, and the strictures of Proust and Gide still find echoes today. It is misleading to say he lacks style; his voice is very distinctive, not easily confused with anyone else's. Yet elegance was never his objective. He preferred creative dynamism to the finished work, overall effect to individual detail and content to form. He saw his task as stylist as the forging of an expressive language through which to communicate truths; anything which obstructed truth was worse than useless, and striving for stylistic effect could be such an obstruction. He preferred simplicity to ornament, did not disdain broad rhetorical gestures or colloquialisms, and in some works developed a rhythmic prose of a type which has rarely worked well in French, although in more intimate texts he could set aside his rather overblown public manner for something more informal and entertaining. His claim to be taken seriously as an artist was based not on the chiselled detail, but on his manipulation of large structures, the juxtaposition of contrasts within patterns of overall coherence, the unifying idea holding everything together. The model is the Beethoven symphony as revealed by Breuilpont.

Since Rolland saw art as an act of faith, it followed that it should lead to action, and his dilemma was Hamlet's: how to act effectively with a dreamer's temperament. Rolland did not take easily to action; illness, the nuanced character of his thought and distaste for many aspects of society made it hard for him to engage with practical politics, he never sought power, and part of him would have been happy to withdraw into self-centred meditation. Yet his reflections on Mâyâ show him accepting that even illusion is a necessary source of dynamism, and his urge to influence events grew stronger over the years. His cult of heroism shows his admiration for those who dominate their fate sufficiently to act; Olivier Jeannin and Julien Davy, representing his weaker side, are overshadowed by the stronger Christophe and Annette, and limited or in some way punished for their passivity.

Sometimes he was restrained from action by family circumstances; divided loyalties inhibited him during the Dreyfus affair, his father's refusal to leave Paris inhibited him in 1914 and Serge Koudachev's position in Moscow affected his behaviour in the 1930s. On other occasions, however, he did not hold back from unpopular stances. *La Foire sur la place*, *Au-dessus de la mêlée* and his pro-Soviet writings were undertaken in the knowledge of the risks they entailed, and though his fears of ruin, expulsion and physical attack were not fulfilled, he was certainly boycotted, harassed and insulted, and it hurt. Though he did not court martyrdom, he lucidly accepted the possibility, considering that sacrifice was the lot of the revolutionary. His decision not to flee the Occupation in 1940 suggests a degree of physical courage which is worth recording in view of the charges of cowardice thrown at him as at all pacifists.

Rolland's love of dynamism, creativity and liberty was translated into support for revolution in whatever form it took, and his sympathies were always with the poor and weak, but he himself was unmistakeably a bourgeois intellectual whose relationship with the masses was not easy. Some of his works, *Le Quatorze Juillet* and his inter-war articles, were aimed at a mass audience, and he accepted nationalism, French, Indian or Russian, insofar as it served revolution, though at other times he attacked it. He was also concerned with fostering an elite, usually international; this was his only recourse in 1914-18, and his two longest novels are concerned with the elite within a mass movement. A true elite must show solidarity with the masses, but its manner of doing so can be problematic; the involvement of Marc and Christophe in revolutionary causes is praiseworthy, but contaminated by violence. After abandoning hopes of Gandhism, Rolland accepted that violence was inevitable in mass movements; this is clear from his Revolutionary dramas, and his rallying to communism in the 1930s is illuminated by their tragic vision, but that was not enough to reconcile him to violence, and in both wars he wished to minimize it.

Another problem faced by the elite is that of truth. The elite's duty is to discover truth and orient action accordingly, and this determined Rolland's role in 1914, when he used his position in Switzerland to see the truth more clearly than was possible in France. He refused to attempt the same role in 1939 because he lacked Swiss facilities. The problem was that the truths he saw were hard to bear. Rolland himself could face tragic visions of revolutionary sacrifice, but he feared that few could follow him; Christophe's exultant acceptance of tragedy could never be the basis for practical policy. This makes it hard for the elite to communicate the truths it sees. The problem first arose in Rolland's research into Michelangelo; failure to solve it forced him to silence much of his wartime thought, when he hesitated to preach revolution and mutiny, contenting himself with a vague idealism of whose insufficiencies he was well aware. Gandhi seemed to have mobilized a sacrificial mass movement, and Rolland convinced himself that the Russians had achieved something similar, but the fact remained that sacrifice was a difficult message to communicate to the masses.

All of this tied Rolland's hands. His pre-war work reflects on action, but in such a way as to highlight its tragedy; *Jean-Christophe* leaves major questions unanswered, and in 1914 Rolland was bitterly conscious that in stimulating action without orienting it he had left his task half done. He later felt that the war had distracted him from his proper course of inward development, which resumed with *L'Ame enchantée*, but he accepted the new responsibilities that war seemed to impose, and his 1916 conviction that social revolution was Europe's only salvation sparked an evolution towards communism. This appears to reverse many earlier principles, but it relates to much that was in his thought already; communist engagement is latent in his literary work in 1926 and 1927, just as his 1914 stance was latent in *Jean-Christophe*. His efforts to inform himself on Russia were sincerely meant, but whether because of his wife or the political pressures of the 1930s, he seems to have let his vigilance lapse, especially at the time of the show trials, and there are hints of self-deceit in his attitude. Equally there are hints that he harboured doubts. Their full extent will emerge only when his diaries are made available, but he certainly suppressed them for tactical reasons which must have rankled with a man of principle. At times in the late 1930s he seems nostalgic for his individualism of 1914, with its uncompromising moral implications. He was strongly committed to sincerity, and never was it more difficult than in those years.

September 1939 therefore came as something of a relief. Its horrors were real enough; the collapse of his efforts for peace marked the complete bankruptcy of his political action, and his withdrawal from politics is partly an acceptance that his credit had collapsed. Yet politics was merely part of the essential quest of his career, which was the realization of God in man, and he had other means of pursuing it. This is why his writings on the Vedantists, Beethoven, Péguy and Christ are so important. It would be easy to dismiss *Beethoven* in particular as a work of escapist consolation, but in fact the subjects of these texts are God-bearers just as much as the revolutionary. Retirement from public life in 1939 freed Rolland from an activity to which he was ill-suited, allowing him to pursue the inward quest which had occupied him intermittently since the beginning of *L'Ame enchantée*. All things considered, Rolland's last years were remarkably rich and his mind was clear to the end. Beethoven and Péguy both died with great works unrealized, and Rolland himself did not die exhausted.

It is not easy to pass global judgement on Rolland's career. His eclecticism poses problems for critics with strong ideological commitments, and the political and religious polarization which has so often characterized French attitudes makes it especially hard for his compatriots to come to terms with him. Rolland himself gave hostages to fortune; he made mistakes, he made enemies as readily as friends and the inflated rhetoric of his public style, not greatly to the taste of the late twentieth century, might lead readers to suppose he had an inflated opinion of himself. Yet on closer inspection a strong coherence emerges beneath the ramifications of his evolving thought, based on a firm faith and a remarkable breadth of interests and sympathies. His correspondence reveals an appealing and human figure, and whatever judgement one may form of his style, he had high ideals which are reflected in the large-scale forms he favoured. Above all, his writings give an impression of constant striving towards new truths and a firmer grasp of the real. He was idealistic but never fleshless; the starchy puritanical image he sometimes projected gives a misleading impression of a man of intense feeling and openness, with a great love of the life which sometimes seemed to him so ephemeral. Truth to himself was his objective; one may doubt whether he always achieved it, for sincerity is difficult, especially for writers whose fluency easily makes them manipulators of their own image, but the desire to be sincere is clear from the self-explorations of *Le Voyage intérieur*, the scrupulous documentation of the *Mémoires* and the veiled self-revelations of his strongly autobiographical novels. He tried hard to live up to his own demanding ideals, and rarely did anything base. The problems he raises have lost none of their actuality; the struggles of the engaged writer trying to maintain his integrity are still very much with us, and the way he harmonizes a wide range of apparently conflicting sympathies has much to offer the pluralist aspirations of the late twentieth century.

Bibliography

A. Bibliographies of the Works of Romain Rolland

Duchatelet, B. (1981), *Répertoire chronologique des lettres publiées de Romain Rolland*, Brest, Université de Bretagne Occidentale.

Starr, W.T. (1950), *A Critical Biography of the Published Works of Romain Rolland*, Evanston, Illinois, Northwestern University Press.

—— (1980), 'Romain Rolland', in *A Critical Bibliography of French Literature,* Vol.6: The Twentieth Century (I), edited by D.W. Alden & R.A. Brooks, Syracuse U.P., pp.430–72.

Vaksmakher, M.N., Paievskaia, A.V., Galperina, E.L. (1959), *Romain Rolland, Index bio-bibliographique*, Moscow, Editions du Palais du Livre de l'Union Soviétique.

See also *Bulletin de l'Association des Amis du Fonds Romain Rolland*, 1946–1985, 150 nos.

B. Works of Romain Rolland

1. Novels

Jean-Christophe, definitive edition in 1 volume, A. Michel, 1966 (First edition, Cahiers de la Quinzaine: *L'Aube* (1904), *Le Matin* (1904), *L'Adolescent* (1905), *La Révolte* (1906–7), *La Foire sur la place* (1908), *Antoinette* (1908), *Dans la maison* (1909), *Les Amies* (1910), *Le Buisson ardent* (1911), *La Nouvelle journée* (1912).

Colas Breugnon, Ollendorff, 1919.

Pierre et Luce, A. Michel, 1958 (First edition: Ollendorff, 1920)

Clerambault, A. Michel, no date (First edition: Ollendorff, 1920)

L'Ame enchantée, definitive edition in 1 volume, A. Michel, 1967 (First edition: *Annette et Sylvie*, Ollendorff, 1922, *L'Eté*, Ollendorff, 1924, *Mère et fils*, A. Michel, 1927, *L'Annonciatrice*, A. Michel, 1933).

2. *Theatre*

Savonarole (1896), in *Europe*, 109–110, 1955, pp.78–131.

Les Vaincus (1897), Antwerp, Editions Lumière, 1922.

Les Tragédies de la foi, A. Michel, 1970 (First editions: *Saint Louis*, Revue de Paris, 1897, *Aert*, Revue d'Art Dramatique, 1898, *Le Temps viendra*, Cahiers de la Quinzaine, 1903).

Le Triomphe de la raison, A. Michel, 1970 (First edition: Revue d'Art Dramatique, 1899).

Le Théâtre de la Révolution, A. Michel, 1926 (First editions: *Les Loups*, Editions G. Bellais, 1898, *Danton*, Revue d'Art Dramatique, 1899–1900, *Le Quatorze Juillet*, Cahiers de la Quinzaine, 1902). The three plays paginated separately.

La Montespan, Revue d'Art Dramatique, 1904.

Les Trois Amoureuses, in *L'Art Dramatique et Musical*, 1905, pp.169–91, 249–75, 334–48.

Liluli, A. Michel, 1926 (First edition: Editions du Sablier, 1919).

La Révolte des machines ou La Pensée déchaînée, Geneva, Editions du Sablier, 1921.

Le Jeu de l'amour et de la mort, A. Michel, 1953 (First edition: Editions du Sablier, 1925).

Pâques-Fleuries, A. Michel, 1926 (First edition: Editions du Sablier, 1926).

Les Léonides, A. Michel, 1928 (First edition: Editions du Sablier, 1928).

Robespierre, A. Michel, 1939.

3. *Biography, Historiography and Criticism*

Les Origines du théâtre lyrique moderne: Histoire de l'opéra avant Lully et Scarlatti, Du Boccard, 1931 (First edition: Thorin, 1895).

Cur ars picturae apud Italos XVI saeculi deciderit, Thorin, 1895 (See *Cahiers Romain Rolland* 9).

Millet, London, Duckworth, 1902 (Published only in English translation).

Le Théâtre du peuple, A. Michel, 1926 (First edition: Cahiers de la quinzaine, 1903).

Vie de Beethoven, Hachette, 1964 (First edition: Cahiers de la Quinzaine, 1903).

Michel-Ange, revised edition, A. Michel, 1943 (First edition: Librairie de l'art ancien et moderne, 1905).

Vie de Michel-Ange, Hachette, 1964 (First edition: Cahiers de la Quinzaine, 1906).

Musiciens d'autrefois, Hachette, 1908.
Musiciens d'aujourd'hui, Hachette, 1908.
Haendel, augmented edition A. Michel, 1951 (First edition: Alcan, 1910).
Vie de Tolstoy, Hachette, 1913 (First edition 1910).
Voyage musical au pays du passé, Hachette, 1920.
Mahatma Gandhi, augmented edition, Stock, 1930 (First edition 1924).
Beethoven, les grandes époques créatrices, definitive edition in 1 volume,
    A. Michel, 1966 (First editions, Editions du Sablier: *De l'Héroïque à
    l'Appassionata* (1928), *Goethe et Beethoven* (1930), *Le chant de la
    résurrection* (1937), *La Cathédrale interrompue: 1, La Neuvième
    Symphonie* (1943), *2, Les Derniers Quatuors* (1943), *3, Finita Comoedia*
    (1945), *Les Aimées de Beethoven* (1949).
*Essai sur la mystique et l'action de l'Inde vivante, I: La Vie de Rama-
    krishna*, Stock, 1952 (First edition 1929).
*Essai sur la mystique et l'action de l'Inde vivante, II: La Vie de Vive-
    kananda*, Stock, 1977 (First edition, 2 vols., 1930).
Compagnons de route, augmented edition, A. Michel, 1961 (First edition:
    Editions du Sablier, 1936).
Les Pages immortelles de Jean-Jacques Rousseau, Buchet-Chastel, 1962
    (First edition: Correa, 1938).
Valmy, Editions Sociales Internationales, 1938.
Péguy, 2 vols., A. Michel, 1945.

4. *Political Writings*

L'Esprit Libre, A. Michel 1953 (First edition: *Au-dessus de la mêlée*,
    Ollendorff, 1915, *Les Précurseurs*, Ollendorff, 1919).
Quinze ans de combat, Rieder, 1935.
Par la Révolution, la paix, Editions Sociales Internationales, 1935.
Comment empêcher la guerre, Bureau d'Editions, 1936.
Textes politiques, sociaux et philosophiques, edited by J. Albertini,
    Editions Sociales, 1970.

5. *Autobiography*

Le Voyage intérieur. Songe d'une vie, augmented edition A. Michel, 1959
    (First edition 1942).
Mémoires et fragments du journal, A. Michel, 1946.

6. *Posthumous Publications in Book Form*

(a) Diary Extracts

De Jean-Christophe à Colas Breugnon; diaries 1912–1913, Editions du
   Salon Carré, 1946.
Journal des années de guerre, 1914–1919, A. Michel, 1952.
Inde: Journal 1915–1943, A. Michel, 1960.

(b) Cahiers Romain Rolland (A. Michel)

1. *Choix de lettres à Malwida von Meysenbug*, preface by E. Monod-
   Herzen, 1948.
2. *Correspondance entre Louis Gillet et Romain Rolland*, preface by P.
   Claudel, 1949.
3. *Richard Strauss et Romain Rolland*, preface by G. Samazeuilh, 1950.
4. *Le Cloître de la rue d'Ulm: Journal de Romain Rolland à l'Ecole
   Normale (1886–1889)*, preface by A. George, 1952.
5. *Cette âme ardente: Choix de lettres d'André Suarès à Romain Rolland
   (1887–1891)*, edited by P. Sipriot, 1954.
6. *Printemps romain. Choix de lettres de Romain Rolland à sa mère
   (1889–1890)*, 1954.
7. *Une amitié française: Correspondance entre Charles Péguy et
   Romain Rolland*, edited by A. Saffrey, 1955.
8. *Retour au Palais Farnèse: Choix de lettres de Romain Rolland à sa
   mère (1890–1891)*, preface by S. Bertolini Guerrieri Gonzaga, 1956.
9. *De la décadence de la peinture italienne au XVIe siècle: Thèse latine
   de Romain Rolland*, preface by J. Cassou, 1957.
10. & 11. *Chère Sofia: Choix de lettres de Romain Rolland à Sofia
   Bertolini Guerrieri Gonzaga (1901–1908 & 1909–1932)*, preface by
   U. Zanotti-Bianco, 1959 & 1960.
12. *Rabindranath Tagore et Romain Rolland*, introduction by K. Nag,
   1961.
13. *Ces jours lointains: Alphonse Séché et Romain Rolland*, preface by
   A. Maurois, 1962.
14. *Fraülein Elsa: Lettres de Romain Rolland à Elsa Wolff*, edited by R.
   Cheval, 1964.
15. *Deux hommes se rencontrent: Correspondance entre Jean-Richard
   Bloch et Romain Rolland (1910–1918)*, 1964.
16. *Romain Rolland et le mouvement florentin de 'La voce'*, edited by
   H. Giordan, 1966.

17. *Un Beau Visage à tous sens: Choix de lettres de Romain Rolland (1866–1944)*, preface by A. Chamson, 1967.
18. *Salut et fraternité: Alain et Romain Rolland*, edited by H. Petit.
19. *Gandhi et Romain Rolland*, 1969.
20. *Je commence à devenir dangereux: Choix de lettres de Romain Rolland a sa mère (1914–1916)*, preface by E. Hartoch, 1971.
21. *D'une rive a l'autre: Hermann Hesse et Romain Rolland*, introduction by P. Grappin, 1972.
22. *Pour l'honneur de l'esprit: Correspondance entre Charles Péguy et Romain Rolland (1898–1914)*, edited by A. Martin, 1973.
23. *L'Indépendance de l'esprit. Correspondance entre Jean Guéhenno et Romain Rolland (1919–1944)*, 1975.
24. *Monsieur le Comte. Romain Rolland et Léon Tolstoy*, 1978.
25. *En plein vol: Correspondance entre Jean de Saint-Prix et Romain Rolland*, preface by J. de Saint-Prix, 1980.
26. *L'Un et l'autre. Choix de lettres: Alphonse de Châteaubriant et Romain Rolland (1906–1914)*, preface by L-A. Maugendre, 1983.
27. *Romain Rolland et la NRF*, edited by B. Duchatelet, 1989.
28. *Correspondance entre Romain Rolland et Maxim Gorki (1916–1936)*, edited by J. Perus, 1991.
29. *Voyage à Moscou (juin–juillet 1935)*, edited by B. Duchatelet, 1992.
30. *L'Un et l'autre II. Correspondance entre Romain Rolland et Alphonse de Châteaubriant (1914–1944)*, edited by L-A. Maugendre, 1996.

(c) Other Correspondences

Lettres de Romain Rolland à un combattant de la Résistance, Rodstein, 1947.
Jean-Christophe et Armel: Correspondance entre Romain Rolland et Jean Bodin, Lyon, Brochet, 1955.
Romain Rolland et Lugné-Poë. Correspondance 1894–1901, edited by J. Robichez, L'Arche, 1957.
Lettres de Romain Rolland à Marianne Czeke, edited by G. Safran, Budapest, Bibliotheca Academiae Scientarum Hungaricae, 1966.
Bon voisinage. Edmond Privat et Romain Rolland, edited by P. Hirsch, Neuchâtel, A la Baconnière, 1977.
Ernest Bloch – Romain Rolland. Lettres 1911–1933, edited by J-F. Tappy, Lausanne, Payot, 1984.
Romain Rolland – Stefan Zweig: Briefwechsel (1910–1940), edited by W. Klein, Berlin, Rütten & Loening, 1987. (In German translation.)
Au Seuil de la dernière porte. Correspondances avec les pères L. Beirnaert,

M. de Paillerets, R. Pichard et J. Sainsaulieu. Entretiens sur les Evan-giles, edited by B. Duchatelet, Editions du Cerf, 1989.

Correspondance intégrale. Panaït Istrati – Romain Rolland (1919–1935), edited by A. Talex, Canevas Editeur, 1989.

Romain Rolland – Lucien et Viviane Bouillé. Correspondance (1938–1944), edited by B. Duchatelet, Brest, Centre d'Etude des Corre-spondances, 1992.

Henri Bachelin. Correspondances avec André Gide et Romain Rolland, edited by B. Duchatelet, Brest, Centre d'Etude des Correspondances, 1994.

7. *Other Texts*

Articles, etc., by Rolland cited in the text and not collected in the above volumes are fully identified in footnotes.

8. *Unpublished Texts*

Of the numerous unpublished texts made available to me thanks to the generosity of Marie Romain Rolland and, more recently, the Fonds Romain Rolland in the Bibliothèque Nationale, the following should be cited:

Unpublished plays: *Orsino* (1890), *Empédocle* (1890), *Les Baglioni* (1891), *Niobé* (1892), *Caligula* (1892), *Le Siège de Mantoue* (1894), *Jeanne de Piennes* (1896).

Notes sur Hamlet (1886).

Draft scenario for *Mélusine* (1930).

Mémoires, Part IV (1944).

Correspondence: with his mother, his sister, André Suarès, Clotilde Bréal, Malwida von Meysenbug, Louise Cruppi, Jean-Richard Bloch, Esther Marchand, Helena de Kay, Jeanne Mortier, André George, André Sabatier and many others.

9. *Special Numbers of Periodicals*

Europe, 38 (1926).
Commune III, March (1936).
Le Disque Vert, 6 (1954).
Europe, 109–110 (1955).
Les Lettres Françaises, 550 (1955).

Europe, 439–440 (1965).
Etudes de Lettres, 9 (II) (1966).
Livres de France, 17 (10) (1966).
Etudes de Lettres, 3 (III) (1976).
Revue d'histoire littéraire de la France, 76 (6) (1976).

10. Works of Criticism, etc.

Hommage à Romain Rolland (1945), Lausanne, Mont-Blanc.
Liber Amicorum Romain Rolland (1926), Zürich, Rotapfel Verlag.
Romain Rolland et la Belgique (1950), Brussels, Editions du Chat qui Pêche.
Romain Rolland. Sa vie, son œuvre, 1866–1944 (1966), Archives de France.
The Universality of Man. The Message of Romain Rolland (1992), New Delhi, Sahitya Akademi.
Abraham, P. et al (1969), *Romain Rolland*, Neuchâtel, A la Baconnière.
Albertini, J. (1972), 'Romain Rolland et l'Europe', *Europe*, 513–14, pp.198–205.
—— (1973), 'Romain Rolland et les amis d'*Europe*', *Europe*, 529–30, pp.206–9.
—— (1977), 'La destinée de *L'Ame enchantée*', *Œuvres et Critiques*, 2, pp.111–19.
Alden, D.W. (1968), 'Proustian configuration in *Jean-Christophe*', *French Review*, 41, pp.262–71.
—— (1970), 'Léon Blum as a source for *L'Ame enchantée*', *Kentucky Romance Quarterly*, 17, pp.9–18.
Antoine, G. (1988), *Paul Claudel ou l'Enfer du génie*, Laffont.
Aragon, L. (1936), 'Une entrevue avec Romain Rolland, l'ingénieur des âmes', *Cahiers du Bolchevisme*, 13, pp.257–63.
Arcand, T. (1977), *Romain Rolland et les arts plastiques (1887–1906)*, thesis, University of Manitoba.
Arcos, R. (1950), *Romain Rolland*, Mercure de France.
Aucouturier, M. (1993), 'Boris Pasternak – Romain Rolland. Correspondance (1930)', *Europe*, 767, pp.104–18.
Barrère, J-B. (1950), 'Romain Rolland et Malwida, les "racines" et le "souffle"', *French Studies*, 4, pp.97–112.
—— (1955), *Romain Rolland par lui-même*, Seuil.
—— (1966), *Romain Rolland, l'âme et l'art*, A. Michel.
Bastaire, J. (1957), 'Romain Rolland et l'ombre de sa mère', *Action et pensée*, 33 (2), pp.41–7, & 34 (3), pp.76–9.

Battaglia, V. (1989), 'Romain Rolland et le théâtre de la Révolution', *Revue de l'Histoire du théâtre*, 41, pp.78–95.

Becker, J-J. (1994), 'Au-dessus de la mêlée?', *Le Monde*, 30 July, No.15398, p.2.

Blum, A. (1976), '*Les Loups* au Théâtre de l'Œuvre. Le 18 mai 1898', *Revue d'Histoire Littéraire de la France*, 76, pp.883–95.

—— (1977), *Romain Rolland, 'Les Loups' et l'Affaire Dreyfus*, thesis, University of Yale.

—— (1981), '*Les Loups* de Romain Rolland. Une étude comparative des manuscrits', *Studi francesi*, 25, pp.267–79.

—— (1993), '*Les Loups* de Romain Rolland, un jeu théâtral sur l'histoire', *French review*, 66, pp.59–68.

Bonnerot, J. (1921), *Romain Rolland, sa vie et son œuvre*, Editions du Carnet-critique.

Bresky, D. (1973), *Cathedral or Symphony? Essays on Jean-Christophe*, Bern, H. Lang.

Brunelle, M. (1953), 'L'Influence d'Ibsen sur Romain Rolland', *Revue des Sciences Humaines*, 71, pp.263–73.

Caute, D. (1964), *Communism and the French Intellectuals, 1914–1960*, London, A.Deutsch.

—— (1973), *Fellow Travellers: A Postscript to the Enlightenment*, New York, Macmillan.

Chagny-Sève, A-M. (ed.) (1995), *Permanence et pluralité de Romain Rolland. Actes du colloque tenu à Clamecy, 22–24 septembre 1994*, Conseil Général de la Nièvre.

Cheval, R. (1957), 'Romain Rolland et Nietzsche', *Deutschland-Frankreich*, 2, pp.292–308.

—— (1963), *Romain Rolland, l'Allemagne et la guerre*, PUF.

—— (1976), 'Le Prix Nobel de Romain Rolland', *Revue d'Histoire Littéraire de la France*, 76, pp.912–21.

—— (1990), *Le Coq et l'aigle*, Bern, Lang.

Chung, Seung-Hee (1994), *L'Union des contraires dans les romans de Romain Rolland*, thesis, Université de Bretagne Occidentale.

Corinne, Sœur (1953), 'La musique dans la vie de Romain Rolland', *Revue de l'Université de Laval*, 8. pp.864–79.

Cruickshank, J. (1951a), 'The nature of artistic creation in the works of Romain Rolland', *Modern Languages Review*, 46, pp.379–87.

—— (1951b), *Romain Rolland: The Content and Evolution of his Thought*, thesis, Trinity College, Dublin.

—— (1954a), 'The religious ideas of Romain Rolland', *Dublin review*, 228, pp.183–95.

—— (1954b), 'Romain Rolland: the psychological basis of political belief', *Hermathena*, 83, pp.30–47.

Dadoun, R., (1976), 'Romain Rolland, Freud et la sensation océanique', *Revue d'Histoire Littéraire de la France*, 76, pp.936–46.

—— (1990), 'Terreur et non-violence. Romain Rolland, Gandhi et la philosophie de l'"ahimsa"', *Les Temps Modernes*, 527, pp.71–81.

Descotes, M. (1948), *Romain Rolland*, Editions du Temps Présent.

Di Scanno, T., *Romain Rolland*, Parma, Guanda.

Dobossy, L. (1960), 'Lettres inédites de Romain Rolland à ses amis hongrois', *Acta Litteraria Academiae Scientiarum Hungaricae*, 3, pp.299–333.

Doisy, M. (1945), *Romain Rolland (1866–1944)*, Brussels, Editions La Boétie.

Duchatelet, B. (1966), '*Jean-Christophe* ou la symphonie héroïque', *France dans le Monde*, 5, pp.6–13.

—— (1969), 'Jean François Millet. Un ouvrage de Romain Rolland inédit en francais', *Annales de Bretagne*, 76, pp.541–83.

—— (1973), 'Romain Rolland et le théâtre français dans *La Foire sur la place*', *Revue des Sciences Humaines*, 38, pp.205–27.

—— (1975), *Les débuts de Jean-Christophe (1886–1906). Etude de genèse*, thesis, University of Paris VII.

—— (1976a), 'Présence et permanence de Romain Rolland', *Europe*, 569, pp.170–5.

—— (1976b), 'Sur la genèse du *Buisson ardent*', *Revue d'Histoire Littéraire de la France*, 76, pp.896–911.

—— (1978), 'Jean-Christophe, syndicaliste?', *Annales de Bretagne*, 85, pp.439–47.

—— (1981), 'Un canevas pour Jean-Christophe. "La Grande Passion de Jean-Christophe"', *Revue d'Histoire Littéraire de la France*, 81, pp. 970–5.

—— (1983a), 'La peinture de la société dans *Jean-Christophe à Paris*', in *Roman et société. Actes du colloque international de Valenciennes, mai 1983*, Université de Valenciennes.

—— (1983b), 'Romain Rolland et la préparation du congrès d'Amsterdam', in *La Guerre et la paix dans les lettres françaises (1925–1939)*, Presses Universitaires de Reims.

—— (1985), 'Histoire et mystique dans *L'Annonciatrice*', *Cahiers du Cerf XX*, 1, pp.59–85.

—— (1987a), 'Un titre énigme, "l'Ame enchantée"', *Cahiers du Cerf XX*, 4, pp.45–62.

—— (1987b), '"Notre sentiment d'indestructible éternité". Henri Petit et Romain Rolland', *Cahiers Henri Petit*. 7, pp.86–99.

—— (1989a), 'Notes à propos de la correspondance Jean Guéhenno – Romain Rolland', in *Mélanges offerts à Louis le Guillou*, Brest, Université de Bretagne Occidentale, pp.117–33.

—— (1989b), 'Péguy-Rolland: les débuts d'une amitié sous le signe de la Révolution', *L'Amitié Péguy*, 12, pp.219–33.

—— (1990a), 'Le dernier jugement de Romain Rolland sur Péguy', *L'Amitié Péguy*, 13, pp.54–8.

—— (1990b), 'Un roman d'amour et d'adultère, – mais à ma facon. Béroul, Wagner et le "Tristan" de Romain Rolland', *Cahiers du Cerf XX*, 6, pp.103–24.

—— (1995), 'Romain Rolland et le rêve d'une "cité d'art nouvelle": "La cathédrale de l'esprit européen"', in *Nazionalismo e Cosmopolitismo nell'opera tra '800 e '900*, pp.1–15.

—— (1997), *Romain Rolland: la pensée et l'action*, Université de Bretagne Occidentale et CNRS.

Duhamel, G. (1983), *Le Livre de l'amertume*, B. Duhamel, ed., Mercure de France.

Duret, S. (1992), *Romain Rolland: l'être et l'harmonie. Essai de biographie spirituelle*, thesis, Université de Bretagne Occidentale.

—— (1994), 'Romain Rolland face à Ernest Renan', *Revue d'Histoire Littéraire de la France*, 94, pp.74–113.

—— (1995), 'La dénonciation de l'impérialisme européen dans *Le Temps viendra* de Romain Rolland', *Littérature et Nation*, 13, pp.161–88.

Dutertre, E. (1970), 'Le credo d'un adolescent. Romain Rolland recherche sa foi', *Informations Littéraires*, 22, pp.109–19.

Elder, M. (1914), *Deux essais, Octave Mirbeau et Romain Rolland*, Crès.

Fähnrich, H. (1951), 'Romain Rollands Weg zu Goethe', *Goethe. Neue Folge des Jahrbuchs der Goethe-Gesellschaft*, 13, pp.178–202.

Fisher, D.J. (1979), 'Romain Rolland and the ideology and aesthetics of French people's theatre', *Theatre Quarterly*, 9, pp.83–103.

—— (1988), *Romain Rolland and the Politics of Intellectual Engagement*, Berkeley, California University Press.

Francis, R.A. (1967), 'Romain Rolland's *Mélusine*', *French Studies*, 21, pp.32–46.

—— (1968), *An investigation of the literary, artistic and musical opinions of Romain Rolland*, thesis, University of Oxford.

—— (1969), 'Romain Rolland and Jean-Jacques Rousseau', *Nottingham French Studies*, 8, pp.40–53.

—— (1971), 'Romain Rolland and science', *Nottingham French Studies*, 10, pp.21–32 & 74–86.

—— (1975), 'Romain Rolland and Gandhi. A study in communication', *Journal of European Studies*, 5, pp.291–307.

—— (1980a), 'La France vue par Romain Rolland', *Revue d'Histoire Littéraire de la France*, 1980, pp.602–20.

—— (1980b), 'Romain Rolland and some British intellectuals during the First World War', *Journal of European studies,* 10, 189–209.

—— (1996), 'Romain Rolland devant l'art italien', in *Studi di storia della civiltà letteraria francese. Mélanges offerts à Lionello Sozzi*, Champion, pp.863–85.

Gamarra, P. (1985), 'Marie Romain Rolland (1895–1985)', *Europe*, 674–675, pp.219–20.

Gillet, L. (1965), 'Sur *Jean-Christophe*', *Europe*, 439–40, pp.123–35.

Götzfried, H.L. (1931), *Romain Rolland*, Stuttgart, Engelhorn.

Grappin, P. (1952), *Le Bund Neues Vaterland (1914–1916), ses rapports avec Romain Rolland*, Bibliothèque de la Société des Etudes germaniques.

Grautoff, O. (1914), *Romain Rolland*, Frankfurt, Rütten & Loening.

Gross, B. (1974), *Willi Münzenberg: A Political Biography*, Michigan State U.P.

Gugenheim, S. (1955), *Romain Rolland e l'Italia*, Milan, Cisalpino.

—— (1957a), 'Roger Martin du Gard giudicato da Romain Rolland', *Rivista di Letterature Moderne Comparate*, pp.284–89.

—— (1957b), 'Spigolature Rollandiane. Romain Rolland e Mazzini; Romain Rolland e il Carducci', *Letterature Moderne*, 7, pp.226–7.

Guyon, B. (1957), 'Péguy et Romain Rolland. Mesure d'une amitié', *Les Lettres Romanes*, 11, pp.53–72, 177–87.

Hanley, D.L. (1972), *The political thought of Romain Rolland and its place in his work*, thesis, University of Warwick.

—— (1976), 'De Hobson à Lénine. Romain Rolland devant l'impérialisme', *La Pensée*, 189, pp.48–64.

Harris, F.J. (1973), *André Gide et Romain Rolland: Two Men Divided*, Rutgers U.P., New Brunswick, New Jersey.

Hewitson, L. (1970), 'Le dualisme de la nécessité et de la liberté dans l'œuvre de Romain Rolland', *Bulletin des jeunes romanistes*, 17, pp.45–50.

Hill, T.A. (1985), *Romain Rolland and the decline of the West*, thesis, University of Keele.

Ilberg, W. (1950), *Traum und Tat: Romain Rolland und sein Verhältnis zu Deutschland und zur Sowjet-Union*, Halle, Mitteldeutscher Verlag.

Jackson, C.T. (1995), *Vedanta for the West: the Ramakrishna Movement in the United States*, Indiana University Press.

Jeanneret, Y. (1982), *Un demi-siècle de réception critique de l'œuvre de Romain Rolland en France, 1898–1945*, thesis, University of Paris III.

Jouve, P.J. (1920), *Romain Rolland vivant*, Ollendorff.

Karczewska-Markiewicz, Z. (1967–68), 'Structure de *Jean-Christophe*', *Beiträge zur Romanischen Philologie*, 6, pp.266–73, & 7, pp.5–24.

—— (1969), 'Roman-autoportrait. Eléments bergsoniens dans *Jean-Christophe*', *Zagadnienia Rodzajow Literackich*, 21, pp.100–23.

Kempf, M. (1962), *Romain Rolland et l'Allemagne*, Nouvelles Editions Debresse.

Koch, S. (1994), *Double Lives: Stalin, Willi Münzenberg and the Seduction of the Intellectuals*, London, Macmillan.

Krampf, M. (1956), *La Conception de la vie héroïque dans l'oeuvre de Romain Rolland*, Le Cercle du Livre.

Küchler, W. (1919), *Romain Rolland, Henry Barbusse, Fritz von Unruh*, Würzburg, Verlagsdruckerei.

Kvapil, J. (1971), *Romain Rolland et les Amis d'Europe*, Prague, Statni Pedagogicke Nakladatelstvi.

Lefebure, A. (1993), *Les Conversations secrètes des Français sous l'Occupation*, Plon.

Leuwers, D. (1981), 'Pierre Jean Jouve et Romain Rolland', in *Bousquet, Jouve, Reverdy. Colloque de Cérisy la Salle*, pp.198–211.

Levy, A. (1946), *L'Idéalisme de Romain Rolland*, Nizet.

Lyons, E. (1937), *Assignment in Utopia*, London, Harrap.

March, H. (1971), *Romain Rolland*, New York, Twayne.

Marshall, B. (1992), *Victor Serge: The Uses of Dissent*, Oxford/New York, Berg Publishers.

Massis, H. (1915), *Romain Rolland contre la France*, H.Floury.

Maugendre, L-A. (1977), *Alphonse de Châteaubriant*, André Bonne.

McClain, W.H. (1954), 'Soviet Russia through the eyes of Zweig and Rolland', *Modern Language Notes*, 69, pp.11–17.

McClain, W.H. & Zahn, H., 'Zweig and Rolland: the literary and personal relationship', *Germanic Review*, 28, pp.262–81.

Melet, B. (1976), *L'Eros d'une héroïne. Trois études sur l'Ame enchantée*, La Pensée universelle.

—— (1989), 'Romain Rolland l'enchanteur', *Cahiers du Cerf XX*, pp. 115–18.

Mentel, M. (1966), *Romain Rolland und die bildende Kunst*, Salzburg, Friedens-Verlag.

Motyleva, T. (1972), 'Romain Rolland au tournant décisif', *La Pensée*, 163, pp.99–114.

—— (1976), *Romain Rolland*, Moscow, Editions du Progrès.

—— (1983), 'Romain Rolland et le problème de l'action (*L'Ame enchantée*)', in *La Guerre et la paix dans les lettres françaises (1925–1939)*, Presses universitaires de Reims.

Nadeau, M. (1967), 'Romain Rolland', *Journal of Contemporary History*, 2, pp.209–20.

Naliwajek, Z. (1990), *Romain Rolland en Pologne (1910–1939)*, *Les Cahiers de Varsovie*, 17.

Nedeljkovic, D. (1958), 'Réponse caractéristique de Romain Rolland à une autocritique de Maxime Gorki', *Bulletin de la Faculté des Lettres de Strasbourg*, 36, pp.365–75.

—— (1970), *Romain Rolland et Stefan Zweig*, Klincksieck.

Noeckler, H-W. (1983), 'Romain Rolland, *Robespierre*. Engagement social et expression littéraire', in *La Guerre et la paix dans les lettres françaises (1925–1939)*, Presses universitaires de Reims.

Pérus, J. (1968), *Romain Rolland – Maxime Gorki*, Editeurs Francais Réunis.

Pichler, R. (1962), *Romain Rolland*, Leipzig, Verlag Encyclopädie.

Pierruges, M. (1955–6), 'Romain Rolland à la recherche de lui-même', *Revue des Deux Mondes*, 15, pp.624–36, & 16, pp.60–71.

Plaud, R. (1952), 'La longue amitié de Gorki et de Romain Rolland', *Europe*, 76, pp.44–58.

Prochasson, C. (1993), *Les intellectuels, le socialisme et la guerre*, Seuil.

Racine-Furlaud, N. (1985), 'L'amitié de Romain Rolland et de Marcel Martinet, de la première à la seconde Guerre mondiale', in *Le Pacifisme dans les lettres françaises de la Belle Epoque aux années Trente*, Orléans, Centre Charles Péguy.

Rakic, Z.M. (1964), *Romain Rolland et Beethoven*, thesis, University of Paris.

Ricard, F. (1976), 'Péguy vu par Romain Rolland', in *Péguy mis à jour. Colloque international tenu à l'Université de McGill, mars 1973*, Quebec, Presses Universitaires de Laval.

Robichez, J. (1961), *Romain Rolland*, Hatier.

Rogister, M. (1991), 'Romain Rolland, one German view', *Modern Language Review*, 86, pp.349–60.

Roos, J. (1957a), 'Romain Rolland et Goethe', *Bulletin de la Faculté des Lettres de Strasbourg*, 35, pp.383–91.

—— (1957b), 'Romain Rolland et Spinoza', *Revue de Littérature Comparée*, 31, pp.48–56.

—— (1961), 'Romain Rolland et l'Italie', in *Venezia nelle Letterature Moderne*, Venice/Rome, Istituto por la Collaborazione Culturale, pp. 300–12.

—— (1962), 'Romain Rolland et Tolstoy', *Revue de Littérature Comparée*, 36, pp.5–31.

—— (1979), *Etudes de littérature générale et comparée*, Ophrys.

Scales, D.P. (1972), 'Feeling for nature in Romain Rolland', *Australian Journal for French Studies*, 9, pp.40–54.

Schrade, L. (1942), *Beethoven in France*, Yale University Press.

Seippel, P. (1913), *Romain Rolland. L'homme et l'œuvre*, Ollendorff.

Sénéchal, C. (1933), *Romain Rolland*, Editions de la Caravelle.

Sices, D. (1968), *Music and the Musician in Jean-Christophe*, Yale University Press.

Sipriot, P. (1968), *Romain Rolland*, Bruges, Desclée de Brouwer.

—— (1994), 'Le pacifiste. Il y a cinquante ans, le 30 décembre 1944, mourut Romain Rolland', *Revue des deux Mondes*, 12, pp.129–34.

Smith, J.C. (1987), *Freedom and liberation in Jean-Christophe. A study in the imagination of Romain Rolland*, thesis, University of Oxford.

Sorella, *Histoire d'une amitié: Romain Rolland et Alphonse de Châteaubriant*, Perrin.

Starr, W.T. (1956a), *Romain Rolland and a World at War*, Evanston, Ill., Northwestern University Press.

—— (1956b), 'Romain Rolland and Thomas Hardy', *Modern Language Quarterly*, 17, pp.99–103.

—— (1957), 'Romain Rolland and H.G.Wells', *French Review*, 30, pp.195–200.

—— (1971), *Romain Rolland: One against All. A Biography*, The Hague, Mouton.

—— (1972), 'Water symbols in the novels of Romain Rolland', *Neophilologus*, 56, pp.146–61.

Stegmann, R. (1959), 'Von den Wandlungen Romain Rollands', *Die Neueren Sprachen*, 8, pp.164–70.

Stelling-Michaud, S. (1966), 'Romain Rolland et Paul Seippel, quelques lettres', *Etudes de Lettres*, 9, pp.221–9.

—— (1967), 'Le choix de Romain Rolland en 1914', *Pensée*, 132, pp. 23–30.

—— (1970), 'Romain Rolland, Edmond Rossier et la *Bibliothèque Universelle*', *Cahiers Vilfredo Pareto*, 22–3, pp.109–21.

Tison-Braun, M. (1958), *La Crise de l'humanisme: Le conflit de l'individu et de la société dans la littérature française moderne*, Nizet, 2 vols.

Tosi, G. (1963), *D'Annunzio visto da Romain Rolland*, Florence, La Nuova Italia.

Vermorel, H. & M. (1993), *Sigmund Freud et Romain Rolland. Correspondance 1923–1936*, PUF.

Viard, J. (1986), 'Proust, Bernard Lazare, Péguy et Romain Rolland', *Bulletin de la Société des Amis de Marcel Proust*, 36 pp.566–74.

Watson, G.D. (1965), 'Socialism and revolution in *Jean-Christophe*', *Essays in French Literature*, 2, pp.30–42.

White, R. (1966), *Les Débuts dramatiques de Romain Rolland (1890–1897)*, thesis, University of Paris.

—— (1973), 'Ibsen in France. Romain Rolland and Norwegian drama', *AUMLA*, 40, pp.260–70.

Willis, W.S. (1951), *Romain Rolland musicien*, thesis, University of Paris.

Willocq, L. (1976), 'Romain Rolland et la Révolution russe (1917–1918), *Revue d'Histoire Littéraire de la France*, 76, pp.922–35.

Wilson, R.A. (1939), *The Pre-War Biographies of Romain Rolland and their place in his work and the period*, Oxford University Press.

Zweig, S. (1920), *Romain Rolland. Der Mann und das Werk*, Frankfurt, Rütten und Loenig.

Index

164, 254, 257–8
illusion, 12, 119, 175–6, 178, 182–4,
   186–8, 191, 193, 196, 200, 208–9, 227,
   256
Impressionism, 92
independence, 90, 93, 95, 102, 109–11,
   145, 150–2, 231, 240
India, 106, 112, 132–8, 141, 149, 151,
   163, 166, 188–90, 193, 200–1, 206,
   209, 211–3, 254
individualism, 24, 53, 76, 87–8, 95, 97,
   123, 125, 129, 131, 135–6, 138, 148,
   150, 154, 164–6, 181, 186–8, 191, 193,
   196–7, 202, 205, 239, 245, 258
Indo-China, 141
internationalism, 20, 60, 85, 90, 92, 102,
   124, 128, 134, 207, 239, 256
International Women's League for Peace
   and Liberty, 129, 141
irony, 12, 28, 52, 70, 81, 115, 119, 206
Isaiah, 58
Istrati, Panait, 147–8
Italy, 31–2, 35, 55, 81–2, 91, 97, 107,
   126, 135, 137, 140, 141–2, 189–90
   192

Jacobins, 45, 114, 172–3
James, William, 175, 195, 248
Janiculum, éclair du, 21–2, 42, 64, 75,
   103, 116, 204–5, 250, 253
Japan, 112
Jaurès, Jean, 43–5, 50, 105, 240–1, 248
Jerusalem, 245
Jews, 10, 30, 34, 41, 43, 72–4, 78, 85–6,
   150, 201, 228, 231, 244
Johannot, René, 90
Joliot-Curie, Jean-Frédéric, 250
Jourdan, Francis, 249
Journal de Genève, 101, 106
Jouve, Pierre-Jean, 109–10, 116, 118,
   122, 127, 139n5
joy, 57–60, 67, 81, 116, 138, 179, 183,
   189, 217
Joyce, James, 185, 236
Judas, 245–6

Kâlî, 208–10, 212
Kant, Immanuel, 248
Kay, Helena van Brugh de, 91, 99, 107,

126, 146–7, 174–7, 179, 188
Kirov, Serge, 151–3
Kogan, Piotr, 144–5
Kölnische Zeitung, 150
Koudachev, Serge, 145, 153, 158, 193,
   232, 249, 256
Koudacheva, Maria, *see* Rolland, Marie
   Romain
Kruchkov, Piotr, 154, 156

Lao-Tse, 211
Laparcerie, Cora, 39, 72
Larréguy, Marc de, 116
Lavisse, Ernest, 90, 93, 107, 189, 240
Lavoisier, Antoine, 166
Leconte de Lisle, Charles, 15
Lemaître, Jules, 35, 226
Lenin, Vladimir Ilich, 113, 136–7, 141–2,
   164, 188, 248
Leningrad, 142
Leo XIII, 248
Lettres françaises, Les, 247
Libertaire, 142
liberty, 12–13, 49, 51, 86, 99–100, 105,
   113, 116, 119, 124, 130–1, 141–2, 154,
   165, 169, 177, 183, 186, 188, 192, 202,
   206, 210, 225, 237, 239, 241, 246, 253,
   255–6
Lichtervelde, Olga de, 91
Liebknecht, Karl, 115
Litvinov, Maxim, 159
London, 105, 129, 136
Louis IX, 29, 43
Louis XIV, 50
Louis XV, 168
Louis XVI, 168
Louvain, 101
Louvet de Couvray, Jean-Baptiste, 167
Loyson, Paul-Hyacinthe, 92, 104–5, 109
Lubac, Henri de, 233
Lugano, 147
Lugné-Poë, Aurélien-François, 39, 42, 44,
   77
Lully, Jean-Baptiste, 31, 58
Lunacharsky, Anatoly, 110, 113, 142
Luther, Martin, 37
Luxemburg, Rosa, 115
Lycée Louis-le-Grand, 6, 10
Lyons, Eugene, 147